Infant Motor Development

Jan P. Piek, PhD

Curtin University of Technology
Perth, Australia

HUMAN KINETICS

Library of Congress Cataloging-in-Publication Data

Piek, Jan P.
    Infant motor development / Jan P. Piek.
        p. ; cm.

    Includes bibliographical references and index.
    ISBN 0-7360-0226-X (hardcover)
    1. Motor ability in children.   2. Infants--Physiology.   I. Title.
    [DNLM: 1. Motor Skills--Infant.   2. Child Development.   3. Motor
Skills Disorders--Infant.   WE 103 P613i 2006]
    RJ133.P545 2006
    152.3'083--dc22

2005021671

ISBN-10: 0-7360-0226-X
ISBN-13: 978-0-7360-0226-4

Acquisitions Editor: Judy Patterson Wright, PhD; **Developmental Editor:** Renee Thomas Pyrtel; **Assistant Editors:** Ann M. Augspurger, Kim Thoren, Kevin Matz, and Carla Zych; **Copyeditor:** Joyce Sexton; **Proofreader:** Julie Marx Goodreau; **Indexer:** Dan Connolly; **Permission Manager:** Dalene Reeder; **Graphic Designer:** Nancy Rasmus; **Graphic Artist:** Yvonne Griffith; **Photo Manager:** Sarah Ritz; **Cover Designer:** Keith Blomberg; **Photographer (cover):** Jupiter Images/Comstock; **Photographer (interior):** Jan P. Piek and Mona Francis; **Art Manager:** Kelly Hendren; **Illustrator:** Andrew Tietz; **Printer:** Sheridan Books

Printed in the United States of America   10 9 8 7 6 5 4 3 2 1

Human Kinetics
Web site: www.HumanKinetics.com

United States: Human Kinetics
P.O. Box 5076
Champaign, IL 61825-5076
800-747-4457
e-mail: humank@hkusa.com

Canada: Human Kinetics
475 Devonshire Road Unit 100
Windsor, ON N8Y 2L5
800-465-7301 (in Canada only)
e-mail: orders@hkcanada.com

Europe: Human Kinetics
107 Bradford Road
Stanningley
Leeds LS28 6AT, United Kingdom
+44 (0) 113 255 5665
e-mail: hk@hkeurope.com

Australia: Human Kinetics
57A Price Avenue
Lower Mitcham, South Australia 5062
08 8277 1555
e-mail: liaw@hkaustralia.com

New Zealand: Human Kinetics
Division of Sports Distributors NZ Ltd.
P.O. Box 300 226 Albany
North Shore City
Auckland
0064 9 448 1207
e-mail: info@humankinetics.co.nz

This book is dedicated to my parents, Alice Louisa and Peter James Livesey, in appreciation of their enduring support, encouragement, and love.

contents ■■■

part IV   Motor Control and Developmental Disorders   205

preface

The period of infancy is generally acknowledged as the time when movement control undergoes its most rapid development. The newborn infant demonstrates little voluntary control and has difficulty coping with environmental factors such as gravity. However, by 12 months of age, a baby can maintain posture, reach, grasp, and manipulate objects and may even achieve independent walking. This is a period of substantial change in the infant's ability to move. Nevertheless, there are very few texts dedicated specifically to this important stage of motor development. In 1993, two edited volumes were published in this particular area, one by Geert Savelsbergh and another by Alex Kalverboer, Brian Hopkins, and Reint Geuze, although only the first of these was dedicated exclusively to infant motor development. Esther Thelen and Linda Smith also published two books (1993 and 1994) that included infant motor development. These volumes were important contributions as they described the changes that occurred in this field of research in the 1980s and early 1990s. The aim of this book, *Infant Motor Development*, is to examine the progress that has been made in this area in the decade following those publications. Examining the contribution of recent research to assessment and intervention practices is another purpose of this volume.

This volume is unique in relation to most books on motor development as it focuses on infant development. The literal definition of "infancy" is the period of no speech. Hence, although there is no distinct cutoff point from infancy to the next stage of early childhood, the period of infancy is usually considered to be from birth to around 18 to 24 months. Van Sant (1994) provided a more movement-oriented definition by describing infancy as "the period from birth until the child is able to stand and walk" (p. 6), usually around 12 months of age. Although this book describes motor development up to around two years of age, the main focus is on the first year, the stage in which the greatest qualitative changes occur in relation to the entire life span. Why dedicate a whole book to the study of such a small part of one's life? In this volume, I describe how the first year of one's life, and also the nine months preceding this year (the gestational period), are the most crucial periods in determining a human's subsequent motor ability.

In the foreword to the book by Kalverboer, Hopkins, and Geuze (1993) titled *Motor Development in Early and Later Childhood: Longitudinal Approaches,* David Magnusson (chairman of the European Science Foundation Network on Longitudinal Studies on Individual Development Coordination Committee) noted that "motor control per se is a fundamental aspect of individual adaptive behaviour in the course of ontogeny" (p. xiii). However, despite this, Magnusson argues that, for the subfield of motor development, there is a "conspicuous lack of systematic empirical studies and the sound knowledge that ensues from this" (p. xiii). This situation has changed somewhat since 1993, and the present book elucidates the theoretical and empirical progress that has been made, primarily over the last decade, in terms of our understanding of both normal and abnormal infant motor development. This volume also investigates how motor control can be assessed throughout infancy and examines how recent research has influenced the way in which practitioners and therapists approach intervention. Clues to how this research will affect future intervention strategies are also provided.

This book is intended as both a textbook, primarily for graduate students, and a reference book for health professionals and researchers. However, it is not merely a review of the literature; it aims to combine theory with application to provide the most recent account of infant motor ability and disability.

Motor development is of interest to many disciplines, including psychology, physical therapy, neuroscience, occupational therapy, nursing, pediatrics, human movement studies, and kinesiology. Some disciplines, such as psychology and human movement studies, have focused on understanding the theoretical nature of infant motor development. Others, such as physical and occupational therapy, as well as nursing, have been more concerned with issues relating to assessment and intervention. This book integrates the literature from these different disciplines as it is only by examining all of the findings that a complete picture emerges. Hence this volume introduces readers to the theories, principles, and strategies of disciplines other than their own. However, it should not be difficult for readers to follow the literature from disciplines other than their own as new terms and notions are carefully described and a glossary is provided. The book is designed to challenge the reader to view issues in a different light; and indeed, one of the aims of this book is to encourage the reader to take on a broader perspective by understanding the techniques and priorities of other disciplines.

Features to Assist the Reader

The following features have been included to assist in understanding the material within this text.

- Chapter objectives. Chapter objectives have been provided at the beginning of each chapter. These reflect the main issues and concepts presented within the given chapter.
- Key points. Key points are highlighted within text boxes throughout.
- Research–therapy relationship. An important characteristic of this volume is the linking of research, in particular current research,

and intervention practices. At the end of each chapter, a special element titled "How Does This Research Inform Therapeutic Practice?" is included that discusses the importance of the literature and research reviewed in relation to current and future intervention and therapy approaches.

- Summary. Each chapter concludes with a synthesis of the material presented, with a particular emphasis again on practical applications.

- Glossary. Given that this text is multidisciplinary, many terms commonly used in one discipline may be unfamiliar in another discipline. Hence a comprehensive glossary is provided at the end of the text. Terms found in the glossary are distinguished within the text using **bold.** Other important terms that are described within the text but not presented in the glossary are in *italics.*

Organization

The book is divided into four parts, roughly representing theory, research, assessment, and intervention. The first part includes a chapter describing the types of movements found in infancy. It is followed by a chapter on traditional and current theoretical approaches to motor control and the ways in which these have influenced our understanding of infant motor development. The final chapter in part I investigates neural development and its relationship to motor control.

In order to understand the processes disrupted in abnormal motor development, we must first understand the processes of normal development. This has become a key research issue over recent years and is the focus of part II of the text. The three chapters in this section examine recent research on postural control, reaching and grasping, and locomotion, with a chapter dedicated to each of these topics.

In order to treat abnormal motor development, it must first be identified. This can be problematic in infancy. Part III addresses this issue by discussing the difficulties of appropriate identification of disability in infancy and the most popular assessment tools used to examine infant motor ability. The first chapter in this part of the book discusses important issues related to the use of appropriate assessment tools for infants. Two additional chapters further examine instruments that assess infant motor ability, with one chapter dedicated to neonates and the other to older infants.

The final part of the book is dedicated to understanding abnormal motor control and the interventions that have been applied to improve motor functioning of infants with particular problems. The first chapter in this section discusses the unique difficulties faced by preterm infants. The final two chapters examine two specific disabilities. Cerebral palsy is a devastating motor disability that warrants particular attention. Down syndrome has been included as it is a disorder identifiable at birth with both mental and motor consequences.

acknowledgments

This text has been evolving for over 5 years, and I have many people to thank for their input throughout this period. Firstly, I would like to thank Natalie Gasson, Thelma Pitcher, Mona Francis, Rosemary Skinner, Fiona Geddes, and Carol Rolston for their assistance with the literature searches and reference hunting. They have spent many hours scouring libraries and databases on my behalf. A special thanks to Mona Francis for taking most of the photographs which appear in this volume and assisting with the preparation of the final figures and tables. She has been invaluable in helping me to make my deadlines. I would like to extend my appreciation to all those who appeared in the photos. Many of the infants pictured have been involved in the infant motor development research program at Curtin University of Technology, and I am very grateful for their families' support over the years.

Several of my family members, friends, and colleagues graciously agreed to read and comment on various chapters of this book. My sincere thanks to Peter Livesey, Carol Rolston, Annie Mullan, Natalie Gasson, Nick Barrett, Bill Piek, and Rosie Rooney. Thanks also to Daniela Corbetta and Nida Roncesvalles for their insightful comments. The contents of this volume have also been influenced by discussions with colleagues, fellow researchers, and research students. I am grateful for their valuable input. Thanks to Jillian Pearsall-Jones from the Cerebral Palsy Association of WA and Arlette Coenen from King Edward Memorial Hospital for their assistance. I acknowledge the support of my university and department, and I would like to particularly thank Leigh Smith, Head of the School of Psychology, for his support.

Throughout this long process, Judy Patterson Wright and Renee Thomas Pyrtel have been there to provide assistance. My sincere thanks to them, and all the staff at Human Kinetics, for their support. Finally, I am indebted to my husband, Bill, and children, Ben, Jessica, and Sean, for their patience, encouragement, and sacrifice.

credits ■■■

Tables

Table 1.1 Adapted from Rosenblith, J.F., 1992, *In the beginning: Development from conception to age two.* Thousand Oaks, CA: Sage.

Table 1.2 Adapted from *Early Human Development,* Vol 7, J.I.P. de Vries, G.H.A. Visser, and H.F.R. Prechtl, The emergence of fetal behaviour. I. Qualitative Aspects, p. 311, Copyright (1982), with permission from Elsevier.

Table 6.1 Reprinted, by permission, from K. Haywood and N. Getchell, 2005, *Life Span Motor Development,* 4th ed. (Champaign, IL: Human Kinetics), 76.

Table 7.1 Adapted, by permission, from D. Livesey, 1997, *Use of the Movement Assessment Battery for Children with young Australian children: Identifying 3- and 4-year old children at risk of motor impairment,* 4th Biennial Motor Control and Human Skill Research Workshop, Perth, Western Australia.

Table 7.2 Reprinted from *Brain Research,* Vol 76, H.F.R. Prechtl, *The behavioural states of the newborn infant* (a review), p. 187, Copyright (1974), with permission from Elsevier.

Table 7.3 J.F. Rosenblith, *In the beginning,* 2nd edition, pg. 207, Copyright © 1995 by Sage Publication, Inc. Reprinted by permission of Sage Publications, Inc.

Table 7.4 Data from Thoman, E.B., 2001, Sleep-wake states as context for assessment, as components of assessment, and as assessment. In L.T. Singer & P.S. Zeskind (Eds.), *Biobehavioral assessment of the infant* (pp. 125-148). New York: Guilford Press.

Table 8.2 Adapted from A. Majnemer and Mazer, B., 1998, Neurologic evaluation of the newborn infant: Definition and psychometric properties. *Developmental Medicine and Child Neurology, 40,* 708-715.

Table 8.3 Reprinted, by permission, from T.B. Brazelton & J.K. Nugent, 1995, *Neonatal behavioral assessment scale.* (London: MacKeith Press), 9.

Table 8.4 Adapted from A. Majnemer and Mazer, B., 1998, Neurologic evaluation of the newborn infant: Definition and psychometric properties. *Developmental Medicine and Child Neurology, 40,* 708-715.

Table 8.5 Adapted, by permission, from B.M. Lester & E.Z. Tronick (2001), Behavioral assessment scales. In *Biobehavioral assessment of the infant,* edited by L.T. Singer & P.S. Zeskind (New York: Guilford Publications, Inc.), 371 & 372.

Table 9.1 Adapted from A.W. Burton and D.E. Miller, 1998, *Movement skill assessment* (Champaign, IL: Human Kinetics).

Table 9.2 Adapted from A.W. Burton and D.E. Miller, 1998, *Movement skill assessment* (Champaign, IL: Human Kinetics).

Table 10.1 Data from Moore, 2003, Preterm labor and birth: What have we learned in the past two decades. *Journal of Obstetric, Gynecologic, and Neonatal Nursing, 32,* 638-649.

Table 11.1 Adapted with permission from K.B. Nelson and J.H. Ellenberg. "Antecedents of cerebral palsy: Multivariate analysis of risk," *New England Journal of Medicine,* 315(2), Copyright © 1986 Massachusetts Medical Society. All rights reserved.

Table 11.2 Reprinted, by permission, from R. Boehme, 1990, *Approach to treatment of the baby,* (Regi Boehme), p. 4.

Table 12.1 *Current approaches to Down Syndrome,* S.E. Henderson. Copyright 1985 by Greenwood Publishing Group. Reproduced with permission of Greenwood Publishing Group, Inc., Westport, CT.

Figures

Figure 1.1 Reprinted from *Before we are born: Essentials of embryology and birth defects* (4th ed.), K.L. Moore, and T.V.N Persaud, Human birth defects and their causes, p. 130, Copyright (1993), with permission from Elsevier.

Figure 1.3 Reprinted, by permission, from B. Abernethy et al., 2005, *The biophysical foundations of human movement,* 2nd edition (Champaign, IL: Human Kinetics), 211.

Figure 1.7a-c Adapted from Gallahue and Ozmun, 1998, *Understanding motor development: Infants, children, adolescents, adults.* Boston: McGraw Hill.

Figure 1.8 Adapted from Gallahue and Ozmun 1998, *Understanding motor development: Infants, children, adolescents, adults.* Boston: McGraw Hill.

Figure 2.1 Page 9 from DEVELOPMENTAL DIAGNOSIS: NORMAL AND ABNORMAL DEVELOPMENT by ARNOLD A. GESELL and CATHERINE S. AMATRUDA. Copyright 1941, 1947 Arnold Gesell, copyright renewed © 1975 by Gerhard A. Gesell and Katherine Gesell Walden. Reprinted by permission of Harper Collins Publishers Inc.

Figure 2.2 Figure 74 from THE EMBRYOLOGY OF BEHAVIOR by ARNOLD GESELL. Copyright 1945 by Arnold Gesell, copyright renewed © 1973 by Gerhard A. Gesell and Katherine Gesell Walden. Reprinted by permission of Harper Collins Publishers Inc.

Figure 2.3 Adapted, by permission, from R.H. Largo et al., 1985, "Early development of locomotion: Significance of prematurity, cerebral palsy, and sex," *Developmental Medicine & Child Neurology* 27, 187.

Figure 2.5 Adapted from D.J. Glencross, 1958, Control of skilled movements. *Psychological Bulletin, 84,* 14-29.

Figure 2.6 Adapted from C.M. Jackson, 1928, Some aspects of form and growth. In *Growth,* edited by W.J. Robins et al. (New Haven: Yale University Press), 118.

Figure 2.9 Adapted from *Motor control and sensory motor integration: Issues and directions,* B. Abernathy et al., Temporal coordination of human gait, pg. 995, Copyright 1995, with permission from Elsevier.

Figure 2.10a-c Reprinted, by permission, from E. Thelen and L.B. Smith, 1994, *A dynamic systems approach to the development of cognition and action,* (London: MIT Press), 60.

Figure 2.11 Adapted, by permission, from J.A.S. Kelso, 1995, *Dynamic patterns: The self-organization of brain and behaviour,* (London: MIT Press), 47.

Figure 2.12 *The epigenetic landscape revisited: A dynamic interpretation,* M. Muchisky, et al., 1996. Copyright © 1993 by Ablex Publishing Corporation. Reproduced with permission of Greenwood Publishing Group, Inc., Westport, CT.

Figure 2.13a-b Reprinted from K. Haywood and N. Getchell, 2005, *Life span motor development,* 4th ed. (Champaign, IL: Human Kinetics), 21. Adapted, by permission, from E. Thelen, B.D. Ulrich, and J.L. Jensen, 1989, The developmental origins of locomotion. In *Development of posture and gait across the life span,* edited by M.H. Woolacott and A. Shumway-Cook (Columbia, SC: University of South Carolinia), 28.

Figure 3.1 Reprinted, by permission, from J.H. Wilmore and D.L. Costill, 2004, *Physiology of sport and exercise,* 3rd ed. (Champaign, IL: Human Kinetics), 77.

Figure 3.2 Reprinted, by permission, from J.H. Wilmore and D.L. Costill, 1999, *Physiology of sport and exercise.* 2nd ed. (Champaign, IL: Human Kinetics), 65.

Figure 3.3 Adapted from Greer 1984.

Figure 3.4 From C. Sherrington 1906. *The integrative action of the nervous system* (Ann Arbor, MI: University Microfilms International).

Figure 3.5 Reprinted, by permission, from B. Abernethy et al., 2004, *The biophysical foundations of human movement,* 2nd edition (Champaign, IL: Human Kinetics), 219.

Figure 3.6 Adapted, by permission, from M.L. Latash, 1998, *Neurophysiological basis of movement* (Champaign, IL: Human Kinetics), 130.

Figure 3.8 Reprinted, by permission, from B. Abernethy et al., 2005, *The biophysical foundations of human movement,* 2nd edition (Champaign, IL: Human Kinetics), 214.

Figure 6.11 a-f Adapted from *Biomechanics and motor control of human gait*, Vol 32. E. Thelen, G. Bradshaw, and J.A. Ward, Spontaneous kicking in month-old infants: Manifestation of a human central locomotor program, pg. 47. Copyright 1981, with permission from Elsevier.

Figure 6.12 a-b Reprinted, by permission, from D.A. Winter, 1987, *Biomechanics and motor control of human gait,* (Waterloo, Canada: University of Waterloo Press), 22.

Figure 6.14 Reprinted, by permission, from J.E. Clark, T.L. Truly and S.J. Phillips, 1993, On the development of walking as a limit-cycle system. In *A dynamic systems approach to development* (London: MIT PRESS PUBLISHERS), 83.

Figure 7.1 Reprinted from *The development of coordination in infancy,* R.H. Largo, p. 431, Copyright (1993), with permission from Elsevier.

Figure 8.1 Adapted, by permission, from C. Vogler and K.E. Bove, 1985, "Morphology of skeletal muscle in children," *Archives of Pathology and Laboratory Medicine,* 109: 238-242.

Figure 8.2 Reprinted, by permission, from H. Prechtl, 1977, *Clinics in developmental medicine 63: The neurological examination of the full term newborn infant,* 2nd ed. (London: MacKeith Press), 40.

Figure 10.2 Reprinted from Infant Mental Health Journal, 3, A. Heidelise, *Towards a synactive theory of development: Promise for the assessment of infant individuality,* p. 234, Copyright (1982), with permission from The Michigan Association for Infant Mental Health.

Figure 11.1 Reprinted, by permission, from G. Surman, H. Newdick, and A. Johnson, 2003, "Cerebral palsy rates among low-birthweight infants fell in the 1990s," *Developmental Medicine and Child Neurology* 45: 458.

Figure 11.3 Reprinted, by permission, from J. Aicardi and M. Bax, 1998, Cerebral Palsy, In *Diseases of the nervous system in childhood,* 2nd ed, edited by J. Aicardi (London: MacKeith Press), 218.

part I ■■■

Foundations of Infant Motor Development

Movement control is an essential facet of life. It is required for the basic survival of all animals. In humans it provides a means to communicate with others orally, through gestures and expressions, or through written expression. As Wyke (1975) pointed out, movements establish us as social organisms, and muscles are the instruments for communicating thoughts and feelings, that is, what is on our mind.

An infant begins his or her life with little motor control. In the first chapter, these early movement capabilities of the newborn are examined. What types of movement are present, and why are they important? The next chapter then explores traditional and current theories on how movement is controlled. Some of these theories date back to the early 1900s, whereas others have gained popularity only in the last few decades. Chapter 2 also explores the impact of these theories on current views of motor control and intervention strategies.

An important component of any discussion on motor control and coordination is the role of the central nervous system. Chapter 3 discusses this role, including a description of how brain function fits into the theoretical perspectives outlined in the previous chapter.

one ▪▪▪

Early Movement Capabilities

chapter objectives

This chapter will do the following:

- Examine development in the prenatal period
- Examine the sensory capabilities of the newborn
- Describe infant reflexes
- Discuss early spontaneous movements found in infancy

The human infant is one of the most immature newborns in the animal kingdom. Unlike many other mammals, such as the ungulates that are capable of running within a few hours of birth, the human infant requires on average a full year before being capable of independent walking. Even then, the infant requires several months of practice in order to become an accomplished walker—before tackling other more complex forms of locomotion such as running, skipping, and jumping.

Given their immature beginnings, what movement capabilities do infants have? This chapter investigates the types of movements found in early infancy prior to the development of complex motor skills. Perhaps the best-known movements of the newborn, or **neonate,** are **reflexes,** originally thought of as the "building blocks" of voluntary motor control. In recent years, however, this notion has been challenged. Theorists now believe that the relationship between reflexes and the development of voluntary motor control is one of parallel processes rather than one in which the latter is dependent on the former (McDonnell & Corkum, 1991).

More recently, another set of early infant movements has attracted considerable research interest. These **spontaneous movements** have been identified as important in the development of motor control. They are present within 8 to 10 weeks of conception and are readily observed in normally developing infants up to one year of age.

It is now recognized that infants produce rudimentary forms of intentional or controlled movements virtually from birth (e.g., von Hofsten, 1982). A description of these is provided in part II of this volume. First, it is important to consider development prior to birth, as motor development begins many months before the infant is born. Thus, this chapter addresses development in utero, followed by a description of the types of movements found in early infancy. As perception and action are closely linked, a brief description of the young infant's sensory capabilities is also provided.

Prenatal Period

The normal gestational period in humans is 40 weeks. This is taken from the first day of the mother's last menstrual cycle to when the infant is born.

By the time an infant is born, a considerable movement repertoire has been acquired. This has developed in an environment unique from the one that will be experienced following birth. However, there is growing evidence that this early movement experience is essential for normal motor development.

Examination of the literature on prenatal development reveals various ways of describing prenatal age. It is essential to understand the differences in terminology to avoid inappropriate comparisons between studies that have defined prenatal age differently. Perhaps the most common term is **gestational age,** which is taken from the first day of the mother's last menstrual cycle. This is also called **postmenstrual age** (Prechtl et al., 1997). Normally, this gestational period lasts for 40 weeks. An alternative approach is to describe prenatal age in terms of **conceptional age.** In this case, prenatal age is from the time that fertilization occurs, usually around two weeks after the beginning of the last menstrual period. The normal conceptional age of a newborn is 38 weeks.

Prenatal Development Stages

The **prenatal** period begins with fertilization, the union of the *ovum* (female egg) with the *spermatozoon* (male sperm). On penetration of the egg, the tail of the sperm detaches from the head. The head contains the 23 **chromosomes** from the father, which combine with the 23 chromosomes located in the nucleus of the egg to produce a new cell with 46 chromosomes. Following this, there are three primary stages of development: the germinal stage, the embryonic stage, and the fetal stage.

Germinal Period

The first stage of development, the germinal period, lasts around two weeks and is characterized by the migration of the fertilized ovum, now called the **zygote,** along the fallopian tube and into the uterus. Throughout this stage there is a rapid increase in the number of cells present as a result of cell division, a process called *cleavage.* Within three to four days of fertilization, the zygote has reached the uterus. It now has around 12 to 16 identical cells called *blastomeres.* By the fourth day, the zygote consists of 16 to 64 cells that now begin to change shape and position, producing two separate layers. The outer layer, or *trophoblast,* is a large group of flattened cells that forms the placenta, **amnion,** and amnionic sac. The cell mass is now termed a *blastocyst,* and by 9 to 12 days from fertilization it has eroded the wall of the uterus, embedding itself into the thick lining called the *endometrium.* (An *ectopic pregnancy* occurs when the zygote does not reach the uterus but embeds within the wall of the fallopian tube or elsewhere within the pelvic cavity. This can result in the rupturing of the tube and the mother's death from internal bleeding if it is not surgically removed.) Implantation of the blastocyst into the uterus wall signals the end of the germinal period and beginning of the next stage, the embryonic period.

Embryonic Period

The second stage, the embryonic period, lasts around six weeks. It begins with zygote implantation and ends at eight weeks (or day 56) after conception. During this period, the cells that make up specific body organs and systems are defined in a process called **organogenesis.** This process begins even as the zygote is being embedded within the uterus, with the inner cell mass dividing into two separate layers, an internal, or *endodermal* layer and an outer, or *ectodermal* layer, that further differentiates to produce a middle, or *mesodermal* layer. These three different types of cells produce different parts of the body.

The endoderm produces most of the internal structures such as the digestive and respiratory systems; the mesoderm produces the surrounding organs such as the muscles, skeleton, circulatory system, reproductive system, and the *dermis* (inner skin layer); the ectoderm develops into the central and peripheral nervous system including the sensory systems such as the ears and eyes, pituitary and mammary glands, and the outer skin layers.

The time frame for the emergence of some of the organs can be seen in figure 1.1. One of the first organs to emerge is the central nervous system, which initially develops as the neural tube in the third week. This is followed by the heart at around 24 days. The organism's first muscular activity occurs when the heart begins to beat, at around four weeks conceptional age (Hooker, 1969). At this stage the embryo is only about 6 mm, or one-quarter of an inch in length, and weighs around 28 g, or 1 oz (Gallahue & Ozmun, 1998). The striated muscle has now differentiated adequately to react to direct stimulation (Wyke, 1975). By the end of the embryonic period, around eight weeks conceptional age, striated muscles are innervated with the alpha motoneurons, resulting in **myogenic movements.** These are movements that occur through local stimulation of individual muscles without nervous or other external stimulation.

The first eight weeks is a time of rapid cell growth, making it a particularly sensitive period of development. It can be seen from figure 1.1 that different organs are developing at different times throughout the embryonic period. This means that the *critical period* of development will be different, but at times overlapping, for different organs. It is during these critical periods that the embryo is particularly susceptible to potentially harmful substances or events, called **teratogens,** that may result in **congenital malformations** at this age.

A distinction should be made here between genetic and environmental causes of congenital disorders. Genetic abnormalities are often caused by chromosomal defects that may occur as a result of heredity in conjunction with environmental factors such as certain drugs, irradiation, or the long-term effect of aging on the stored eggs (Rosenblith, 1992). For example, *Down syndrome,* a chromosomal abnormality that is described more fully in chapter 12, is linked with the age of the mother, with the risk of a Down syndrome infant in an older mother being significantly higher than in a younger mother. In contrast, **phenylketonuria,** a metabolic disorder, is the result of an abnormal recessive autosomal gene located on chromosome 12. Many genetic disorders can now be diagnosed prior to birth using techniques such as *amniocentesis,* in which a sample of amnionic fluid is taken for analysis, or *ultrasound,* which uses high-frequency sound waves to image the fetus and its organs. If the diagnosis is early enough, it may leave the parents with the difficult decision of whether or not to terminate the pregnancy.

There are many environmental causes of embryonic or fetal damage. Oxygen deprivation is one such cause that is discussed further in chapter 10 in relation to preterm infants. Congenital abnormalities can be

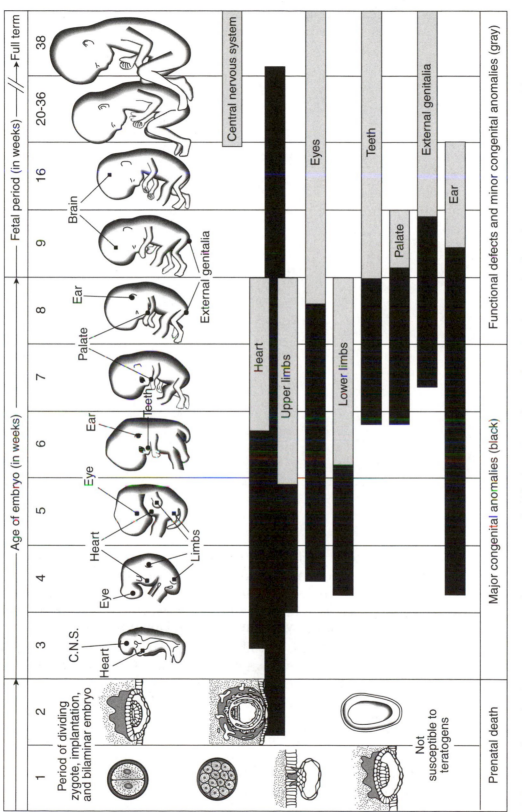

Figure 1.1 Time frame for the emergence of key organs. The black sections denote the critical periods when the organ is most susceptible to teratogens that can result in major defects.

Reprinted from *Moore and Persaud*, 1993.

Table 1.1 Teratogens That Affect the Embryo and Fetus

Categories of teratogens	Examples
Infectious maternal diseases	Rubella Syphilis Human immunodeficiency virus (HIV) AIDS
Chronic maternal conditions	Hypothyroidism Hyperthyroidism Diabetes
Nonpsychotropic drugs	Thalidomide Steroid hormones Aspirin Excess vitamins (especially A and D) Antiepileptic drugs Folic acid antagonists Inhalant anesthetics
Psychotropic drugs	Alcohol Cigarettes Caffeine Opiates (heroin and methadone) Marijuana Cocaine LSD PCP (angel dust) Crystal methamphetamine (ice)
Other factors	Radiation Malnutrition Maternal stress (physical or psychological)

Adapted from text of Rosenblith, 1992.

caused by factors such as drugs, radiation, and infectious diseases. Some of these factors are listed in table 1.1 (also see Rosenblith, 1992 for a comprehensive description of each of these). The outcome of these agents can vary considerably, with some infants being unaffected and others having minor abnormalities; at the extreme, the result can be spontaneous abortion or stillbirth. The outcome depends on many factors; it may be affected by genetic factors, for example. The dosage of drug or severity of the disease will have an effect. Also, the time period when the teratogen was introduced to the embryo will influence the outcome. This means that the mechanisms associated with the development of abnormalities are complex and difficult to study. However, *teratology*, "the study of the causes of congenital malformations" (Rosenblith, 1992, p. 132), is an important field and one that strongly influences health policy and practices.

Fetal Period

The final stage of prenatal development, the fetal stage, covers the period from eight weeks postconception, when organ differentiation is complete, to birth. It is during this period that the fetus grows to the appropriate size and dimensions of the newborn infant. It is during this stage that **neurogenic movements** appear. In contrast to myogenic movements, neurogenic movements are generated by the central nervous system through the appropriate motoneuron pool, and appear around 20 weeks conceptional age.

Neurogenic movements are dependent upon the process of myelination, which begins at approximately 16 weeks. **Myelin** is a protective lamella or coating around some nerve fibers and is made of nonneuronal glial cells. Myelination is designed to increase conduction velocity. Breaks in the myelin sheath called *nodes of Ranvier* produce action potentials that jump from one node to another in a process called *saltatory conduction* (Garrett, 2003). The graded potentials produced by this saltatory conduction are faster than when a series of action potentials are produced by the unmyelinated membrane. The insulating effect of the myelin sheath further improves the speed of conduction. The process of myelination is not complete at birth but continues into early infancy. It exerts an influence on the process of neural conduction in the early stages of the infant's development and therefore affects the infant's motor capabilities. This is described further in the section on plasticity in chapter 3.

Prenatal Sensory Development

Are sensory systems developed prior to birth? Determining the capacity of the sensory systems at birth is challenging and has resulted in the development of many novel investigative techniques and paradigms. Examining sensory systems before birth is even more challenging. However, some researchers have provided information on this issue.

The tactile or skin senses appear first during fetal development, with evidence that the mouth is the most sensitive area initially. Evidence also suggests that there is an aversive reaction to clinical interventions such as the touch of the needle during amniocentesis procedures or fetal scalp sampling (Lecanuet & Schaal, 1996). This has been noted in the third trimester of pregnancy (Birnholz, 1988). The vestibular system also appears to be functioning by the end of gestation, with changes in heart rate noted in response to rocking and swaying by the mother (Lecanuet & Schaal).

Perhaps the most widely researched sensory system in the fetus has been audition, as sound waves can penetrate the uterus wall. It was known as early as 1924 that the fetus reacts to different sounds with startle responses and other changes in movement (Rosenblith,

1992). These findings have been confirmed more recently with the use of ultrasound that has identified startle responses to sudden sounds (Birnholz & Benaceraff, 1983). Birnholz and Benaceraff used high-resolution ultrasound imaging to examine the eye-blink startle in response to sudden sounds. The startle reactions were first identified in fetuses with gestational ages between 24 and 25 weeks. By 28 weeks, all fetuses were found to produce these reactions to sudden sounds. Recent reviews suggest that fetuses react to acoustic stimulation from about 23 weeks gestational age (e.g., Kisilevsky & Low, 1998).

Taste and smell are extremely difficult to assess in utero. However, there is evidence that these senses are highly developed at birth. Other evidence suggesting that these senses are present in the fetus comes from research on preterm infants indicating that they have the ability to differentiate various tastes and smells when born preterm (Rosenblith, 1992). Also, there is evidence to suggest that infusing sweet-tasting solutions into the amniotic fluids may result in an increase in fetal swallowing (DeSnoo, 1937, cited in Birnholz, 1988). However, Lecanuet and Schaal (1996) caution that this finding may be suspect due to spontaneous fluctuations in the volume of amniotic fluid. Although there is no direct evidence of olfaction in the human fetus, animal studies have identified it in sheep and rat fetuses (Lecanuet & Schaal).

There is very little opportunity for visual stimulation in utero. Further, although the eyelids open at around 20 weeks gestational age, photoreceptors needed for vision are not completely developed until a few months after birth (Lecanuet & Schaal, 1996). Again, there is some evidence of visual stimulation in the sheep fetus, but there has been very little research in the human fetus. The introduction of new techniques such as magnetoencephalography appears promising in allowing visual evoked potentials to be recorded in the human fetus (Eswaran et al., in press).

Prenatal Motor Development

Prenatal movements have been documented for over a century. This work is multidisciplinary, including studies by anatomists, embryologists, neurologists, physiologists, and psychologists. Two main approaches were adopted in these early studies to investigate fetal movement. One approach involved examining movements through the body wall of the mother. In a second procedure, observations were made on aborted human fetuses or those of other animal species that were operatively removed.

Much of the early fetal research involved studies using the latter technique, in which aborted animal fetuses were immediately transferred to an isotonic bath at body temperature. As a result of this procedure, the fetuses generally survived a few minutes. This enabled the researcher to observe the movement patterns either with or without mechanical stimulation. Most of these early investigators believed that reflexes were the basic units of behavior, and their research was designed to describe reflexive movements or to elucidate the neural connections that underlie them (see Bekoff, 1981 for a review). In his book *The Prenatal Origin of Behavior,* Hooker (1969) concluded that "there is a tendency for voluntary acts, where and when they appear, to develop in a sequence based upon the earlier reflexogenic sequence of prenatal life" (p. 120). However, these earlier studies were carried out in artificial conditions in which the fetus investigated was dying. Given that the studies involved the nervous system under anoxic conditions, the behaviors witnessed may have been latent functional capacities (Prechtl, 1993). One needs to remember, though, that there were few methodological alternatives at the time.

Preyer carefully examined movements in the human fetus. He relied on observations of pregnant women, or listened with a stethoscope for palpitations of the fetal movements through the abdominal cavity. His findings were documented in his book *Die spezielle Physiologie des Embryo* in 1885 (cited in Prechtl, 1993). Preyer reported fetal movements as early as 12 to 15 weeks gestational age, that is, before they can be felt by the expectant mother. He also noted that the newborn's movements appear to be a continuation of the intrauterine movements, an observation supported by more recent studies by Prechtl and colleagues (e.g., Prechtl, 1984; Prechtl & Hopkins, 1986). Provine (1993) acknowledged the enormous contribution made by Preyer, describing him as "the founder of child psychology" (p. 53).

Preyer also examined animal fetuses that were operatively removed. In one such study, he removed developing trout from the egg sac at successive stages following fertilization. He observed stronger and more regular movements with increasing development, which confirmed his observations of the human fetus through the abdominal wall (Prechtl, 1993). Preyer attributed this spontaneous motor activity to central origins rather than any peripheral influences; but this notion of centrally controlled movements at such an early age disappeared in the early 20th century when views on reflexive control and behaviorism became popular. Indeed, Preyer's description of early fetal activity as *spontaneous* activity appeared forgotten until later in the century. Many researchers have noted that this emphasis on reflexes retarded early investigations of the development of the brain and, in particular, coordination (e.g., Bekoff, 1981; Prechtl, 1993). Although many of these early views based on reflexive control have now been refuted, they still influence many current theories and therapies.

Another early approach to the study of fetal motor development was a procedure implemented by Hamburger and Oppenheim (1967). One can examine chick embryos by making a small hole or "window" in the eggshell that can be resealed with tape or paraffin. Provided that the conditions remain sterile, the embryo will continue to develop normally, allowing the development to be followed through to hatching. This approach has been extended recently to include **kinematic** and electromyographic recordings of fetal motility in the chick embryo (e.g., Bekoff, 1995; Watson & Bekoff, 1990). Watson and

■■■ Highly coordinated flexion and extension of the limbs have been found in animal fetal movements and spontaneous movements in preterm human infants.

Bekoff (1990) found that what appeared to be jerky, uncoordinated movements when observed through standard behavioral analyses, such as those used by Hamburger and Oppenheim (1967), were in fact highly coordinated **flexion** and **extension** movements. All limb joints of the right leg were found to flex and extend in synchrony. Although this type of analysis has not been carried out on the human fetus, these strong synchronous joint relationships have been found in preterm infants by Heriza (1991) using kinematic analysis. Heriza demonstrated strong synchronous flexion and extension of the leg joints in preterm infants at 34 weeks gestational age, which was still evident at 40 weeks gestational age.

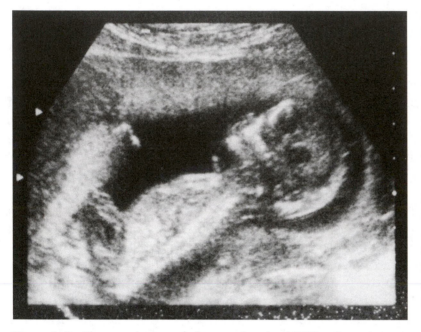

Figure 1.2   The introduction of ultrasound in the 1970s allowed movements to be examined in the fetus. Note that the body and limb positions of this 12-week-old fetus can be clearly identified.

In the 1970s, the development of the ultrasound (see figure 1.2) provided an opportunity to examine human fetal movements more extensively than was previously possible. This new technique allowed researchers to investigate fetal movement in real time and over extended periods of observation. The later introduction of video analysis into the technique meant that the observations could be examined more extensively off-line (Prechtl, 1993).

A series of papers were published by deVries and colleagues (1982, 1985, 1988) describing a comprehensive longitudinal analysis of fetal movement using ultrasound. The authors observed 12 fetuses from seven weeks gestational age to birth. A 1 hr session of videotaped ultrasound was recorded each week until 20 weeks of age. From 20 weeks of age until birth, sessions took place every four weeks. Table 1.2 identifies the times at which each of the different types of movements emerged in these studies. The first movements, which were slow neck extensions, were identified at seven to seven and one-half weeks, followed by startle and general movements at eight weeks gestational age. Startles involve the rapid, synchronous contraction of all limb muscles. General movements are described as forceful complex movements involving the neck, trunk, and limbs that vary in speed and intensity. The investigators noted how surprising it was to find such patterned movement at this age, when there is very little differentiated neural structure.

Table 1.2 Age of Onset of Early Fetal Movement Patterns Found by deVries and Colleagues (1982)

Gestational age (in weeks)	Movement pattern
7	Slow neck extensions
8	Startle General movements Hiccup Isolated arm movements Isolated leg movements
9	Head retroflexion Head rotation
10	Hand–face contact Breathing movements Stretch Jaw opening Head anteflexion
11	Yawn
12	Sucking-swallowing

Adapted from de Vries, Visser, and Prechtl, 1982.

The Importance of Prenatal Motility

Do fetal movements have functional significance? According to Provine (1993), these early movements are an important part of the developing neuromuscular system, not simply a "meaningless epiphenomenon." Prechtl (1984) provides several possible functions for these early fetal movements. Firstly, they are important for the infant's survival within the uterus, as they ensure there are no adhesions or local stasis of circulation in the fetal skin. The position within the uterus can be altered when the fetus rotates along the longitudinal axis and also when alternating leg movements are produced.

Secondly, patterns such as general movements, startles, stretches, yawns, eye movements, and breathing movements may anticipate post-natal functions. Poor development of lung tissue has been detected in cases in which fetal breathing movements were absent (Prechtl, 1993). Movements such as rhythmical sucking and swallowing are thought to be important in the regulation of amniotic fluid, with the fetus taking in nearly a liter of fluid every 24 hours toward the end of gestation (Prechtl). An excessive amount of amniotic fluid (polyhydramnios) has been found in cases in which the fetal digestive tract has been blocked.

Fetal motility may also have an important role in the shaping of the skeletal system by producing mechanical influences on the bones and joints (Prechtl, 1984). Evidence for this has been provided by several animal experiments. Drachman and Sokoloff (1966) suggested that early movements in the chick embryo were essential for normal development. They used several methods to induce paralysis, including neuromuscular blocking agents (decamethonium and botulinum toxin) and spinal cord extirpation. All were found to produce muscle atrophy and permanent joint malformations, even when the drugs were used for as little as 24 to 28 hr. The findings also suggested that constant movement of the joint during its formation was essential for the appropriate fit of the ball and socket joints (Provine, 1993).

These findings have important implications in terms of current medical procedures and the impact of such procedures on motor development. If early fetal activity is important for appropriate **morphogenesis,** then any conditions that may impede these prenatal movements need to be determined to ensure that infants are not at risk of developmental disorders. Such conditions may include any drugs or therapeutic interventions during pregnancy (Provine, 1993). Provine advised against using any medical treatment that may significantly inhibit fetal movement.

Not only are fetal movements important in the development of postnatal behavior; they are also thought to shape central nervous system structure. That is, the experience of the fetus influences the development of the appropriate neural pathways, with early neural activity aiding development of the neural networks or pathways. This is discussed more fully in chapter 3.

Sensory Capabilities in the Newborn

Early infant development has been extensively studied. Topics such as physical growth and sensory development have been widely covered in developmental textbooks. In particular, the capabilities and limitations of the young infant's sensory abilities have been the subject of a great deal of research. At one stage, it was thought that the only way an infant could obtain information was via perception through the sensory systems. This was the **empiricists'** viewpoint. This purely environmentalist view argued that the child's mind is void of information at birth; that is, it is an unmarked page or "tabula rasa" (Thomas, 1996). In order to refute this view, it was necessary for the **nativists** to demonstrate that the newborn was not a "blank slate."

The issue of how much influence the environment has on the developing infant, and how much is genetically programmed, has been a contentious one since the philosophers of the 18th century. A *nature* perspective holds that human development is genetically governed or predetermined, whereas a purely *nurture* view argues that experience is the primary determinant of development. Alternative terminologies include the following:

Nativism versus cultural relativism

Genetics versus social controls

Maturation versus learning

Innate traits versus acquired characteristics

All ask the same question: "How do inborn factors compare with environmental factors in contributing to a child's development?" (Thomas, 1996, p. 31). Present-day views generally hold that an interactionist approach is the most appropriate, according to which both genetics (nature) and the environment (nurture) have their own roles and should not be considered on the same continuum. Here it is important to note that as a result of these conflicting views, the area of infant perception flourished. There is now strong evidence to support the view that infants' early sensory capacities are well developed. The previous section on prenatal sensory development clearly shows that these sensory capabilities are present before birth and that many are highly developed.

Sensory information is taken in via specialized receptors located in the sense organs. There are three main types of sensory receptors:

- *Interoceptors* or *enteroceptors* sense stimuli from within the body organs (e.g., provide information about blood pressure, stomach fullness, thirst).
- *Exteroceptors* provide sensory information from the environment, such as light waves and sound vibrations.
- *Proprioceptors* detect information about body motion and position as a result of tension in muscles and tendons.

It is the latter two that are most relevant to motor development, and a very brief description of these early sensory abilities follows. For further elaboration, there are some excellent reviews available on early sensory abilities (e.g., Aslin, 1987; Crook, 1987; Rosenblith, 1992).

Vision

Vision is generally considered the most important sense in adults, yet it is the last of the senses to develop in infancy (Mercer, 1998). The fovea and ocular muscles are not completely developed at birth, resulting in poor fixation, focusing, and coordination of eye movements. Despite this, infants achieve visual pursuit movements by one to two weeks of age.

Although the findings differ according to the techniques used, adult-like visual acuity, which is the ability to discriminate fine detail, appears to be achieved by six or seven months of age. Color vision appears to be present at birth, with the newborn gazing longer at blue and green and less at yellow. It appears that infants as young as two or three months are capable of perceiving depth.

Hearing

Infants have acute hearing even before birth, as described earlier. Newborns can discriminate a wide range of sounds at birth and are good at localizing sounds. That is, as evidenced by their head and eye movements, they can accurately detect where the sound is coming from. Myelination is well developed at birth for the auditory nerve and

■■■ The nature versus nurture controversy stimulated research on the sensory capabilities of the newborn infant.

lower brainstem. However, it takes several years for complete myelination to occur within the auditory cortex, suggesting that some aspects of hearing are not fully developed at this early stage.

Smell and Taste

The chemical senses of smell, called **olfaction,** and taste, or **gustation,** are also well developed in the neonate. Newborns can discriminate between a variety of smells, such as aniseed, acetic acid, and phenylethyl alcohol. They also appear able to discriminate the four taste sensations of sweet, sour, bitter, and salty and can respond differentially within these taste dimensions, depending on stimulus intensity. Sweet appears positive and can also calm a distressed infant, whereas the other three produce negative reactions as measured through observation of distinctive tongue and facial reflexes (Crook, 1987).

Proprioception

Proprioception is often defined as including tactile, vestibular, and kinesthetic information (Abernethy et al., 1996). The term **somatosensory** is also often used to describe the kinesthetic and tactile sensors (Haywood & Getchell, 2001).

Touch is often divided into light touch and pressure, as these rely on different skin receptors for their perception. It also includes the sensations of pain and temperature. Touch is considered to be highly developed in the newborn. Although they may not have reached the level of complexity found in adults, all these specialized receptors are present in the newborn. The perception of pain has generally been identified by the reaction that occurs in both preterm and full-term infants to medical procedures such as heel lancing, used to collect blood samples, and circumcision. These often result in crying and increased heart rate and blood pressure. Although infants have difficulty in thermoregulation in the first five days, they are responsive to both hot and cold applied locally.

The **vestibular** system is responsible for balance and motion perception. Like touch, it is almost completely mature at birth and is necessary for fundamental processes such as maintaining equilibrium, controlling eye movement, and sensing motion. It is considered to be one of the most highly developed senses at birth and was identified by Minkowski in 1922 to be well developed in early human fetuses (Carmichael, 1946). Like the visual system, the vestibular system is located in the head, specifically in the vestibule of the inner ear (see figure 1.3). It comprises three semicircular canals, the superior, horizontal, and posterior canals, which provide information on the angular acceleration of the head in the horizontal, lateral, and vertical planes. Linear acceleration in all directions is picked up by the utricle and saccule. These latter organs play a very important role in postural control as they monitor absolute head position in space (Latash, 1998a).

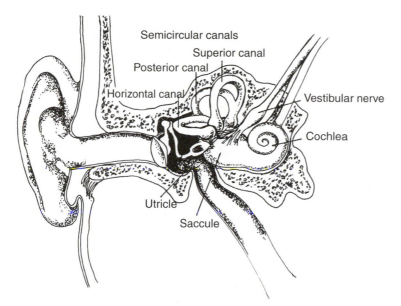

Figure 1.3 Diagrammatic representation of the anatomy of the vestibular system located within the inner ear.

Reprinted from Abernethy et al., 2005.

Kinesthesis and **proprioception** are terms that are often used interchangeably in the literature. However, kinesthesis does not generally include the vestibular and touch sensations, but is specifically concerned with information on where the body parts are and how they are moving (e.g., distance and velocity). Kinesthesia literally means "sensation of movement in the muscles, joints, and tendons" (Barnhart & Barnhart, 1982, p.1156). Very little is known about this sense in infancy as it is very difficult to measure, even in children and adults. However, von Hofsten and Lindhagen (1979) found that infants as young as four months of age could make contact with a moving object at speeds of up to 30 cm/sec (12 in./sec). To do this, "The infant not only has to correctly perceive the spatial parameters of the surrounding space and the motion characteristics of the moving object, but must correctly judge his own capacities when acting in this situation" (p. 170).

Motor Development in Infancy

Unlike the sensory system, the newborn motor system is very immature. The first problem the newborn infant faces is the impact of gravity. Prior to birth, the infant is cushioned in a liquid environment. Despite this environmental change, Prechtl (1993) noted that one of the most surprising findings of his 10-year systematic study on fetal motility was that no "fetus-specific" patterns were observed (de Vries et al., 1982). That is, all the movements observed in the fetus were also present in the newborn infant. However, the newborn infant has a much larger repertoire of movements than the fetus. In particular, many of the so-called **primitive reflexes**, which appear soon after birth, are not present in the fetal stage.

Reflexes

Reflexes are defined as involuntary movements that are generally elicited by some external stimulus specific to that particular reflex or response. There is usually a short latency between the stimulus presentation and the response. Reflexes are not learned responses, and they cannot fatigue or habituate. That is, they continue to occur at the same strength despite numerous presentations of the stimulus.

Reflexes have been categorized in a number of ways. Gallahue and Ozmun (1998) describe two types of reflexes. Primitive survival reflexes, such as the sucking reflex, are described as critical for an infant's survival. Primitive **postural reflexes**, such as reflexive walking, occur later in infancy and are defined as "the precursors of voluntary movements" (p. 140). This is a controversial issue and will be covered more extensively in chapter 6, where the development of voluntary control is described.

Infant reflexes have more often been categorized as either primitive, postural, or locomotor (e.g., Haywood & Getchell, 2001). Table 1.3 provides a list of common reflexes found in infancy that are based on this categorization. The approximate age at which these are found in infants is also given. These age ranges vary from text to text, but note that all the infant reflexes mentioned are elicited within the first 12 months, most within the first 6 months. Persistence of reflexes longer than normally seen is often considered a warning sign of a neurological problem. Such a warning sign would be the continuation of the rooting reflex past 12 months (Haywood & Getchell).

Table 1.3 Some Common Reflexes Found in Young Infants

Type of reflex	Reflex	Age range of presentation
Primitive reflexes	Moro	Prenatal to 6 months
	Startle	7 to 12 months
	Rooting/search	Birth to 12 months
	Sucking	Birth to 3 months
	Doll-eye	Prenatal to 2 weeks
	Palmar grasp	Prenatal to 4 months
	Palmar mandibular	Birth to 3 months
	Plantar grasp	4 to 12 months
	Babinski	Birth to 4 months
	Asymmetric tonic neck	Prenatal to 6 months
	Symmetric tonic neck	6 to 7 months
Postural reactions	Labyrinthine righting	2 to 12 months
	Optical righting	6 to 12 months
	Pull-up	3 to 12 months
	Parachute	4 to 12 months
	Propping	4 to 12 months
	Neck righting	Birth to 6 months
	Body righting	6 to 12 months
Locomotor reflexes	Crawling	Birth to 4 months
	Stepping/walking	Birth to 5 months
	Swimming	Birth to 5 months

Primitive Reflexes

Table 1.3 lists only a few of the primitive reflexes found in infancy, as up to 70 have been described in the newborn. These have been well documented in many earlier volumes, such as Heinz Prechtl's (1977) *The Neurological Examination of the Full Term Newborn Infant.* Many of these reflexes are thought to be prenatal in origin and can be found in the fetus and in preterm infants.

Touwen (1984) questioned the use of the term *primitive reflex,* arguing that this term was based on the notion that the infant's brain was primitive at birth and functioned only at a reflexive level. We now know that this is not the case. Despite this, Touwen acknowledges that the category of primitive reflexes is useful in the neurological examination to assist in understanding the infant's developmental course. With this in mind, the remainder of this section describes what are commonly termed "primitive reflexes."

The young infant is particularly vulnerable from the period when he or she is no longer nourished within the mother's uterus to the time when essential voluntary actions are acquired. It is during this period that many of the initial reflexes are necessary to sustain life processes. For example, two reflexes are considered essential for appropriate feeding responses in the newborn infant. If the area around the baby's mouth is touched, the head turns toward the side of the mouth that is touched. This *rooting reflex,* also termed *search reflex,* is aimed at facilitating the search for the nipple. Bly (1994) states that head turning while the baby is in a **prone** position is also lifesaving, as it could prevent suffocation. The rooting reflex is generally followed by the *sucking reflex,* which is activated when the nipple touches the back of the palate, resulting in jaw movements needed to express milk. These two reflexes have obvious functional significance and are found in all mammalian species (Prechtl, 1993).

Another primitive reflex that has adaptive function is the *withdrawal reflex,* shown in figure 1.4. If the sole of an infant's foot is gently scratched with a fingernail or pin, this results in a simultaneous flexion of the hip, knee, and foot, which is often followed by a similar response in the unstimulated leg (Prechtl, 1977). The function of this reflex is the avoidance of injury. For infants who have had a breech birth, this reflex can be weak or even absent.

There are two main types of *grasp reflex.* The first, the *palmar grasp,* shown in figure 1.5*a,* occurs when the palm of the hand is gently pressed, resulting in grasping of the fingers around the object. The infant can grasp so strongly that she or he can be lifted while holding on to the object. This reflex has been found to occur in **preterm** infants as early as 28 weeks gestational age (Bly, 1994). The *plantar grasp* occurs when pressure is applied to the sole of the foot, resulting in the toes curling around (see figure 1.5*b*). This reflex occurs around the fourth month and may persist throughout the first year. Prior to the fourth month, stimulation of the sole of the foot often results in

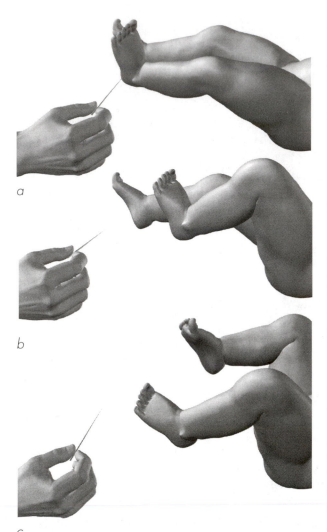

extension of the toes, called the *Babinski reflex*. The stimulation applied in this case needs to be a scratch on the sole of the foot on the **lateral** side rather than application of pressure, which can result in plantar flexion (Prechtl, 1977). There is considerable disagreement, however, as to when and how the Babinski and plantar reflexes are elicited (Zafeiriou, 2004).

The grasp reflexes are common to all primate infants. They increase in strength during sucking, and this has been associated with their original function of clinging to the mother's fur. As Prechtl (1993) pointed out, "In humans they have outlived their function with the loss of maternal fur during the evolution of the hominids and must now be considered as phylogenetically vestigial" (p. 46).

Other reflexes common to all primates are the *Moro* and *startle* reflexes. The Moro reflex results from the infant's sensing a loss of support, producing an initial **abduction** of the arms at the shoulders, with open hands and extended fingers. This is followed immediately by **adduction** of the arms and flexion of the fingers. This reflex, which occurs in the first few months, can be elicited by dropping the head a few centimeters while supporting the infant's back and buttocks. The Moro response is considered to be an important reflex to assess. If it is weak or absent, this is considered an indicator of serious

Figure 1.4   The withdrawal reflex. *(a)* It is stimulated by gentle scratching of the sole of the infant's foot with a sharp object. *(b)* This produces a simultaneous flexion of the hip, knee, and foot and *(c)* is often followed by a similar response in the unstimulated leg.

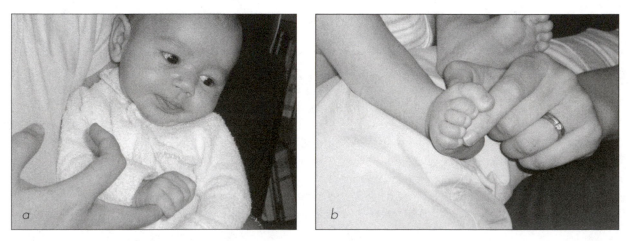

Figure 1.5   *(a)* The palmar grasp and *(b)* the plantar grasp.

neurological problems (Prechtl, 1977). The startle reflex, which involves the flexion of the arms and legs as a result of a tapping of the infant's abdomen when in a **supine** position, occurs around 7 to 12 months of age. Self-induced startles can also be elicited when the infant coughs or sneezes, or can result from a loud noise. At times, this can lead to the infant's becoming distressed and crying.

The *asymmetric tonic neck reflex* (ATNR) is considered to be the most widely researched of the primitive reflexes (Gallahue & Ozmun, 1998). It is elicited as a result of neck rotation. If the head is turned to the right in the supine position, the right arm and leg extend and the left arm and leg flex. This is often termed the "fencing position" (see figure 1.6a) and is reversed if the infant's head is facing to the left. Although the ATNR can appear at any time during the first three months, it is most common in the infant's second month, with the highest frequency of occurrence usually around six to eight weeks of age (Jouen & Lepecq, 1990). The developmental course differs for the arms and the legs. Whereas the leg response appears to be strong throughout the neonatal period, there is little evidence of arm responses at this stage. These increase to a peak level between four and eight weeks, whereas the leg responses decline throughout this period (Coryell et al., 1982). This is evident in figure 1.6b, in which the arms respond strongly to the turn of the head, but the leg response is no longer evident. The ATNR has been implicated in the development of asymmetries and is discussed more fully in chapter 5.

Less well known is the *symmetric tonic neck reflex*, which is elicited when the infant is supported in a sitting position. Simultaneous arm extension and leg flexion occur as a result of extending the head and neck. Flexion of the head and neck results in the inverse, namely arm flexion and leg extension (Jouen & Lepecq, 1990). This reflex is found in less than 30% of "normal" infants, and then occurs only fleetingly,

> ▆▆▆ Primitive reflexes that occur in the infant's first 12 months are essential for life processes such as feeding and avoidance of injury.

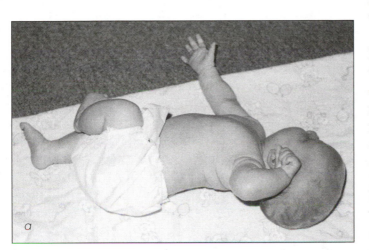

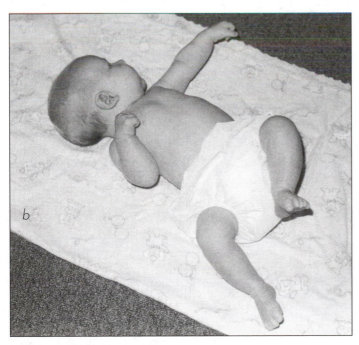

Figure 1.6 (a) The asymmetric tonic neck reflex in a seven-week-old infant, elicited by a turn of the head to the right side. Right arm and leg are extended, and left arm and leg are flexed. (b) The partial asymmetric tonic neck reflex elicited by a turn of the head to the left side. The reflex persists in the arms but is no longer evident in the legs.

usually between four and six months of age. A more pronounced presence of this reflex has been linked to motor-impaired children (Capute et al., 1984).

Postural Reflexes

The reflexes needed to maintain the infant's posture in a changing environment develop postnatally. These are also termed postural responses, postural reactions, or gravity reflexes. They can be divided into righting reflexes and equilibrium reflexes.

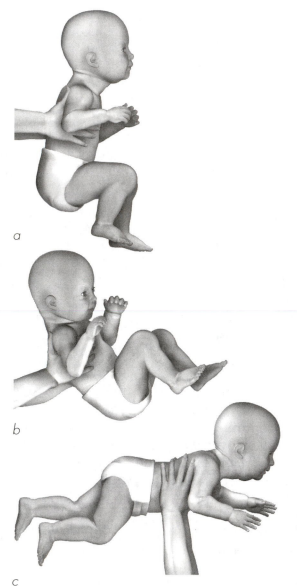

Figure 1.7 The labyrinthine righting reflex from (a) upright, (b) tilted backward, and (c) prone positions.

Adapted from Gallahue and Ozmun, 1998.

Righting reflexes maintain the body in a constant orientation to gravity and were first described by Magnus in the 1920s (cited in Styer-Acevedo, 1994). The *labyrinthine righting reflex* maintains the face in a vertical position and the mouth horizontal. It can be elicited if one holds the baby in an upright position, then tilts the infant forward, backward, or to the side (see figure 1.7). It is so named as it is thought to occur as a result of stimulation of the labyrinths or vestibular system, resulting in contraction or extension of the neck muscles that maintain the head in the appropriate orientation (Bly, 1994). Gravity is the controlling factor.

The *neck righting reflex* orients the body in relation to the head. Extension of the head through dorsiflexion results in extension of the vertebral column, whereas ventroflexion of the head causes flexion or rounding of the vertebral column. If the head is inclined laterally toward one of the shoulders, this produces lateral curvature of the spine with the concavity directed toward the same shoulder. Neck rotation results in the thorax's being brought into symmetry with the head.

Another righting reflex is the *body righting reflex*, which orients the head in relation to the ground. This emerges at around six months of age and is important for voluntary rolling. This reflex can be elicited in infants up to 18 months of age.

The *pull-up reflex* appears around three to four months and occurs when the infant is in an upright sitting position. When held by either one or both arms, the infant will attempt to remain upright using a reflexive pull-up reaction of the arms (see figure 1.8).

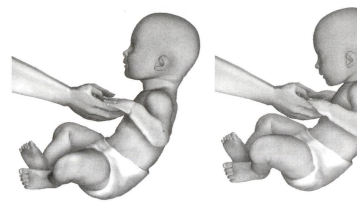

Figure 1.8   The pull-up reflex.
Adapted from Gallahue and Ozmun, 1998.

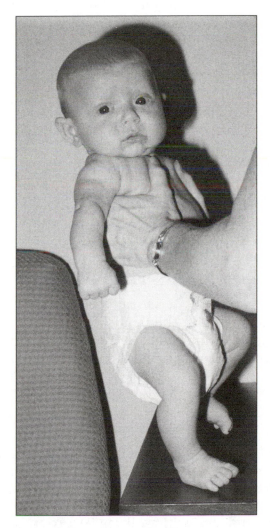

Figure 1.9   The stepping reflex.

Equilibrium reactions require a response by the entire body and are needed to restore balance after disruption of the center of gravity. They are generally present in all postures (except standing) by 12 months of age and require rotation and activation of both extensor and flexor muscles (Styer-Acevedo, 1994).

Locomotor Reflexes

Locomotor reflexes relate to the voluntary movements they resemble. For example, the *crawling reflex* is usually present at birth and disappears around the third or fourth month. It can be elicited in the prone position through application of pressure to the sole of the foot, which results in a crawling response from all four limbs. If an infant is placed in or over water in the prone position, the *swimming reflex* is elicited. This is a well-organized response of flexion and extension of the arms and legs. It is generally present in the first two weeks of life and disappears around the fourth to fifth month.

Perhaps the best-known and most widely researched locomotor reflex is the *stepping reflex* (see figure 1.9). This is normally present in the first six weeks and disappears by five months of age. It is elicited when one places the baby's feet on a flat surface with its body weight forward. The baby will "walk" forward.

The Role of Reflexes

As a result of the extensive research carried out in the first half of the 20th century, "Reflexes were thought to be the basis for the young infant's brain functioning, implying that the infant is a reflex organism" (Touwen, 1984, p. 117). This view remained popular into the second half of the 20th century. For example, Wyke (1975) stated that "the neurological mechanisms that produce and control bodily movement throughout the first year of each individual's existence *are entirely reflex*" (p. 27). Wyke was referring to the development of the infant from conception to around three months of age. However, there is growing evidence that neonates are capable of intentional movements (e.g., see the von Hofsten study described in chapter 5), suggesting that reflexive control is not as dominant in the neonatal period as early evidence suggested. Reflexes have also been described by Gallahue and Ozmun (1998), as the "first forms of human movement" (p. 140). Again, this can be disputed given the previous discussion of fetal spontaneous motility, which suggests that early spontaneous activity precedes reflexes. Indeed, Bekoff (1981) noted that evidence for spontaneous movements occurring before reflexogenic movements dates back to Preyer in 1885.

Although it is clear that postural reflexes are essential for appropriate motor control, there appears to be little support for the idea that primitive reflexes are the basis for later movement abilities. McDonnell and colleagues (1989) suggested that primitive reflexes are causally independent of emerging voluntary control, with these two processes being both neurologically and developmentally distinct. Rather than being causally linked, they run in parallel with each other. This has been termed the "motor-genre" theory (McDonnell et al.). Hence there is concurrent development of reflexive behaviors and voluntary behaviors, although primitive reflexes would be declining while voluntary behaviors are increasing. Cortico-maturational processes such as synaptic development and myelination progress favor cortical control rather than primitive reflexes.

However, there is no doubt that reflexes are an essential aspect of the infant's early movement repertoire and that they have been influential in our understanding of early, and also later, motor development for most of this century.

Spontaneous Movements

Over the last few decades, considerable research has focused on infant spontaneous movements, also referred to as rhythmical stereotypies (Thelen, 1979). These are movements that are often rhythmical in nature and are prevalent in infancy, virtually disappearing in normal infants once they have achieved independent walking at around 12 months of age.

Spontaneous motor activity demonstrates *cyclic fluctuations*, which emerge at a gestational age of around 12 weeks (de Vries et al., 1982).

These rhythmical fluctuations continue once the infant is born, but have been found to be persistent and irregular in the first few months. These irregularities have been attributed to an intrinsic neuromotor mechanism (Robertson et al., 2001).

The initial interest in rhythmical motor patterns related to their existence in infants and children with disabilities such as Down syndrome, Tourette's syndrome, psychomotor retardation, blindness, deafness, and schizophrenia. Wolff (1967, 1968) termed these types of movements *stereotypic mannerisms*. The rhythmicity of these types of movements was of particular interest to Wolff, who suggested that they were important in the development of complex temporal sequences as a result of phase-locking or interaction of several patterns. Rhythmical movements were found to persist in children with such disabilities (Kravitz & Boehm, 1971; Wolff, 1968), and it was thought that they could be of value in the earlier diagnosis of such conditions. The value of examining movement in early infancy for the diagnosis of autism remains a current research interest (e.g., Teitelbaum et al., 1998).

Although it was suggested over half a century ago that these early rhythmical behaviors are an important precursor to motor skill development (Lourie, 1949), only recently have researchers taken an interest in understanding the nature of this spontaneous activity in normal infants. Many investigators now acknowledge that these movements are important for appropriate motor development (Parker, 1992; Piek, 1995, 1998; Prechtl & Hopkins, 1986; Thelen et al., 1991; Turvey & Fitzpatrick, 1993).

Early research has provided extensive descriptions of spontaneous movements through observational analysis. For example, Cioni and Prechtl (1988) demonstrated a natural progression of spontaneous movements from the fetus to the newborn. The work of Prechtl and his colleagues focused on the spontaneous motility of the neonate and infant up to around 18 weeks of age. The authors described several types of spontaneous activity in the young infant, but they focused on the types of movements they called general movements. Normal *general movements* are defined as

> gross movements, involving the whole body. They may last from a few seconds to several minutes or longer. What is particular about them is the variable sequence of arm, leg, neck, and trunk movements. They wax and wane in intensity, force, and speed, and their onset and end are gradual. The majority of extension and flexion of arms and legs is complex, with superimposed rotations and often slight changes in direction of the movement. These additional components make the movements fluent and elegant and create the impression of complexity and variability (Prechtl, 1990, pp. 152-153).

The quality of these movements appears to remain the same from their emergence in the fetus at nine weeks gestational age until the infant is two to three months of age (Prechtl, 1993). Initially, the movements tend to vary in speed, intensity, and force in what has been described as a *slow writhing quality* (Prechtl, 1984). At around two to three months, there appears to be a significant change in the characteristics of the general movements (Prechtl, 1993; Takaya et al., 2003). They become small, rounded, elegant movements involving primarily the limbs and head, described as having a *fidgety quality*. These movements can be seen from four to six weeks. Prechtl (1993) suggested that these types of movements indicate the emergence of the first transitional stage in postnatal neurological development. It is a time when many of the signs of "incompetence" in the infant's movement abilities disappear. Postural control improves, and muscle power increases at around this age. Also, the infant's head becomes centered in the midline when lying in the supine position. All of these factors contribute to an increased interaction with the environment, which includes social interaction with the parents, siblings, and so on.

In her seminal paper, Thelen (1979) described a longitudinal study in which 47 patterned movements termed "rhythmical stereotypies" were classified in 20 infants up to 12 months of age. Thelen's (1979) criterion for classification of these movements was that the movement must be repeated at least three times in succession to be recorded. When the movements were categorized into separate body parts or postures and compared across age, developmental profiles emerged suggesting that characteristic rhythmical patterns were the precursors to particular stages of motor development. For example, hands-and-knees rocking preceded hands-and-knees creeping in infants, a pattern noticed as early as 1940 by Gesell and Ames.

Piek and Carman (1994) also found that posture was closely linked to the frequency of various spontaneous movements. Thelen's (1979) work was extended in this study through use of a cross-sectional analysis including video analysis to record the spontaneous movements of 50 infants from 2 to 50 weeks of age. In all, 53 different types of spontaneous movements were observed and classified. Some of the more common spontaneous movements found in both studies are pictured in figure 1.10.

Thirty-three of Thelen's original spontaneous movements were identified, and 20 others not described by Thelen were defined by Piek and Carman (1994). A less rigid definition of spontaneous movements was employed in the more recent study, as the repetition of a movement at least three times in succession was not required. The work of Prechtl and colleagues (1979) indicated that many of the spontaneous movements produced by young infants are single, isolated movements; consequently, these were deemed important for inclusion in the study. This methodological difference resulted in a much higher percentage of movements recorded for the young infants under 20 weeks of age.

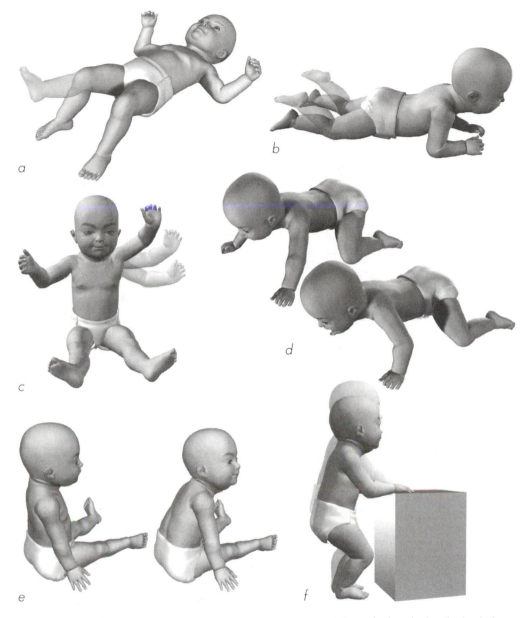

Figure 1.10 Some common spontaneous movements: (a) single leg kick, (b) both legs together kick, (c) arm wave, (d) hands-and-knees rock, (e) sit rock, (f) stand bounce.

As depicted in figure 1.11, the most common types of movements in the first 10 weeks are single leg kicks, followed by both legs kicking synchronously.

Posture has a significant influence not only on the type of spontaneous movement, but also on the frequency of movements. Piek and Carman (1994) found that most spontaneous movements were produced in the supine position. As infants moved to prone, sitting, and then upright

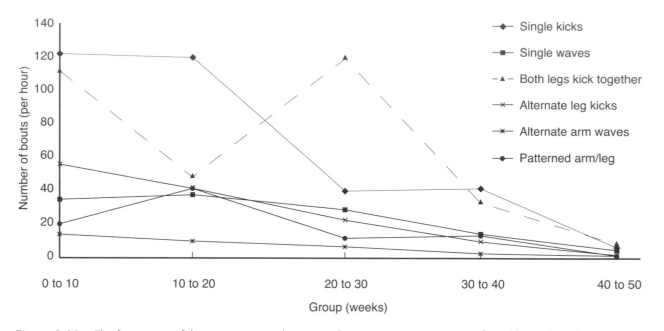

Figure 1.11 The frequency of the most commonly reported spontaneous movements found by Piek and Carman (1994). In the first 10 weeks, the most common types of movements found were single kicks and both legs kicking together.

postures, the frequency of spontaneous movements diminished. Using hierarchical regression analysis, the authors found that once posture was taken into account, age did not significantly add to the variance accounted for in the frequency of spontaneous movements. That is, posture, not age, determined the frequency of spontaneous movements produced. The supine posture is therefore important for promoting spontaneous activity in the young infant.

Spontaneous activity is also influenced by context (Thelen, 1981). The frequency and type of spontaneous activity are related to such factors as interactions with caregivers, feeding situations, and objects of interest, although all these are a function of age. Thelen indicated that spontaneous activity may be functional in nature, particularly with respect to caregiver interactions; she suggested that "these patterned movements communicate some message" (p. 10).

In a study by Kawai and colleagues (1999), spontaneous arm movements of full-term infants tested in the first week of life were influenced by environmental factors. The researchers investigated the frequency of arm movements both in and out of water, either upright with the body fully immersed (water total) or immersed up to the waist (water semi), and in the vertical versus the supine position. Significantly more arm movements occurred in the vertical position than in any other condition. Kawai and colleagues also found that more movements occurred out of the water than in it. This was unexpected, as previous studies by Thelen and colleagues (Thelen et al., 1984) showed an increase in infant stepping when the legs were immersed in water. As the water reduces the constraint caused by gravity, it was predicted that the infants in water would produce more arm movements. Despite these contradictory findings, the authors pointed out the importance of finding two behavioral modes, one in water and one out of water. They described the infant as a "complex open system" in which "the system has the ability to acquire new spatial, temporal or functional structure by itself" (p. 25).

The infant's ability to modify his or her own spontaneous actions has been demonstrated for several decades. In a classic study by Rovee and Rovee (1969), infants between the ages of one and six months were placed supine in a crib. One end of a ribbon was attached to the infant's foot and the other end to a mobile overhead that the infant could see. When the infant kicked, the mobile moved. The infants soon learned the relationship between kicking and the mobile, and the frequency of kicking increased. This is a case of adapting the infant's kicking rate using the process of **operant conditioning,** in which the reward for the infant is seeing the mobile moving. Using a similar procedure, Thelen (1994) demonstrated that three-month-old infants could learn a novel pattern of kicking, namely in-phase kicking (i.e., kicking the legs together). More recent research has extended this study (e.g., Angulo-Kinzler, 2001; Angulo-Kinzler & Horn, 2001; Angulo-Kinzler et al., 2002; Chen et al., 2002). These studies have demonstrated that the types of movements produced using this procedure can be influenced by the task demands. That is, particular movement outcomes can result if the appropriate task constraints are incorporated into the environment. There is considerable potential for the use of this procedure in early intervention therapies. This will be discussed more fully in chapter 10.

■■■ How Does This Research Inform Therapeutic Practice?

This chapter outlines the importance of early fetal spontaneous activity in later motor development. The importance of these movements once the infant is born has also been recognized. Several issues arise from these findings. Firstly, if early fetal activity plays a significant role in later motor development, how does this affect very preterm or high-risk infants who are not able to produce normal fetal activity in utero? This issue is addressed in chapter 10. Also, if intervention could increase the amount of prenatal motility, would this lead to an improvement in developmental outcome?

The ability to change spontaneous activity in infants by altering such factors as context and arousal, or through operant conditioning, has also been discussed in this chapter. These research findings suggest that where the rate and quality of spontaneous activity in infants may be adversely affected, there may be techniques that can be implemented to modify the spontaneous movements produced. Such techniques are discussed more fully for particular types of problems in the final section of this text.

Summary

This chapter described the infant's early sensory and motor capabilities. Although sensory capabilities are well developed at birth, movement ability is limited. Motor development begins very early in the infant's history, even prior to birth. A description of the types of spontaneous motor activity found in utero was provided, and the functions that these movements may have were outlined. Reflexes are perhaps the best known of the infant's early motor capabilities. They can be divided into three types—primitive, postural, and locomotor. Examples of the most common types of reflexes in each of these categories were provided, and the possible functions of reflexes briefly discussed. It is now well recognized that the newborn infant is not just a "reflexive" organism but has a wide range of other movements prior to birth. A brief description was provided of the types of spontaneous movements found throughout the first year of life. In the following chapter, the importance of these movements for later motor development is discussed in the context of theories of motor development.

two ■ ■ ■

Theoretical Approaches to Motor Development

chapter objectives

This chapter will do the following:

- Provide an overview of the important historical periods in infant motor development theory
- Describe three different approaches to understanding motor development: maturational, cognitive, and dynamic systems
- Discuss the limitations associated with these approaches in accounting for motor development

In the previous chapter, the limited movement capabilities of the newborn infant were discussed. However, in the first year of life, the infant's movement capabilities change dramatically. How does this occur? This chapter addresses this issue by providing a description of the theories developed over the last century that have contributed to our understanding of developmental and motor processes. Researchers such as Shirley, Preyer, and Gesell were interested in early infant development. Others such as Piaget and the Gibsons (James and Eleanor) were interested in development through to adulthood, but their theories have had considerable impact on our understanding of early motor development. Some researchers discussed in this chapter have not necessarily been concerned with either development or infancy. These include Bernstein, Kelso, Keele, and Turvey. However, their views on motor control in general have made significant contributions to the understanding of early motor development. Researchers such as Thelen, Newell, Forssberg, Ulrich, and Prechtl have made use of the various theoretical approaches to explain how they view the development of movement in the infant's early months and years of life.

Three different theoretical perspectives are outlined in the following sections. One of the earliest approaches, originating from an interest in fetal motility in the late 19th and early 20th centuries, is the **maturational approach.** Around the 1960s to '70s, the cognitive approach became increasingly popular, and it remains a dominant perspective in the field of motor control. Over the last 20 years, the dynamic systems approach has emerged and has gained considerable popularity in the field of motor control and development. Each approach has made a significant contribution to our understanding of early motor development.

Historical Overview of Theoretical Approaches

The history of infant motor development is important to understand as it has significantly influenced many theoretical and therapeutic approaches that remain to this day. The primary theoretical approaches that have influenced research in infant motor development are the prescriptive approaches (e.g., maturational and cognitive) and the ecological approaches (e.g., dynamic systems). These approaches have their roots in one of the most important theoretical debates shaping developmental psychology, namely the nature–nurture issue. This issue was outlined briefly in the previous chapter.

An investigation of the history of motor development and its various theoretical perspectives requires a search of many disciplines. Indeed, different theoretical approaches have evolved as a result of research within different disciplines. Clark and Whitall (1989) suggest that two disciplines, psychology and biology, were responsible for the emergence of motor development as a field of study. However, since then, researchers in many other disciplines have investigated this topic.

Four different periods in the history of motor development have been identified by Clark and Whitall (1989):

1. Precursor period (1787-1928)
2. Maturational period (1928-1946)
3. Normative/descriptive period (1946-1970)
4. Process-oriented period (1970-present)

Some of the significant research carried out during the precursor period was outlined briefly in chapter 1 in the section on fetal motility. This research resulted in a predominantly reflexive view of infant motor development. The period described by Clark and Whitall (1989) as the normative/descriptive period involved research undertaken primarily by physical educationists, who were not interested in infant research. The focus of this research was on describing motor development in terms of such factors as physical growth and strength. Perhaps the greatest criticism of this era of research is that it had very little theoretical grounding and was primarily descriptive. The purpose of such research was to establish a sound understanding of the developmental changes that occur throughout childhood in order to develop better approaches to teaching motor skills and motor control. One important contribution of this era, however, was the use of cinematographic techniques for investigating movement. This was the precursor for recent motion analysis techniques that are now used extensively in infant research on motor control. Given its limited contribution to the understanding of infant motor development, the normative/descriptive period does not require further discussion.

Two periods in the history of motor development are discussed at length here as they have provided many significant contributions. These are the maturational period, arguably the most influential of the periods for infant development, and the current process-oriented period. It is only in this current period that an understanding of the processes and mechanisms underlying developmental changes has become a significant component of infant research (Clark & Whitall, 1989).

Maturational Perspective

The maturational perspective argues for the importance of "nature" over the environment. Its popularity was based on experiments using exteriorized fetuses. For example, Carmichael (1926, 1927, cited in Provine, 1993) reared amphibian embryos in a paralyzing Chloretone solution prior to movement onset. Despite this, once removed from the solution and placed in water, the embryos swam in a manner similar to what would be expected from normally reared embryos. This implied that the environmental change did not affect movement development, supporting a maturational perspective. Coghill (1929, cited in Bekoff, 1981) also made a significant contribution in terms of understanding motor development based on a maturational perspective. Coghill's works, published between 1902 and 1941, examined the embryonic movements of the salamander. "Coghill's most important contribution was his demonstration that steps in the development of behavior could be correlated with specific anatomical changes in the nervous system" (Bekoff, 1981, p. 135). As a result of these views, theorists such as Gesell and McGraw developed their theories on early infant development.

A strict maturational view explains motor development purely in terms of the biological or physiological changes that occur in the infant, without regard to environmental or cognitive influences. For example, the developing neural structures of the infant have been described as the cause of emerging behaviors (e.g., McGraw, 1940). The newborn infant is developmentally immature at birth, with around one-quarter of its brain mass present at birth (Purves, 1994). Therefore, new behaviors may emerge as the infant's nervous system matures. According to the maturational perspective, these new behaviors are a direct result of the biological changes occurring in the infant.

The maturational perspective dominated the field of motor development in the early half of the 20th century. Although many researchers utilized this theoretical framework in their analysis of early motor development, two researchers stand out as perhaps the most influential, namely Arnold Gesell and Myrtle McGraw.

Gesell's Theory of Behavioral Development

Arnold Gesell investigated development of both movement and **cognition,** dividing them into the functional categories of motor, adaptive, language, and personal-social behavior (Gesell, 1946, 1952; Gesell & Amatruda, 1945). According to Gesell, development could be described in terms of rule-based progressions, as outlined in the following quote:

> The morphogenesis of human behavior, therefore, is subject to lawful sequences which normally are never circumvented. The motor control of the eyes precedes that of the fingers; head balance precedes body balance; palmar prehension precedes digital prehension; voluntary grasp precedes voluntary release. . . . These are but a few simple examples of the sequential order inherent in the structuralization of human behavior, from its lowest to its highest manifestations (Gesell & Amatruda, 1945, p. 162).

Gesell's interpretation of the trends and sequences of early development is shown in figure 2.1. He saw the fetal period as an important part of the developmental cycle, particularly for motor development. All four behavioral fields are closely coordinated in their development.

In their 1945 book *The Embryology of Behavior,* Gesell and Amatruda described seven principles of behavioral development (see table 2.1). The importance that they placed on **endogenous** control is exemplified in several of these principles. For example, in describing the first principle, Gesell and Amatruda argued that although the environment influenced the appearance of the developmental changes that occurred, it had no

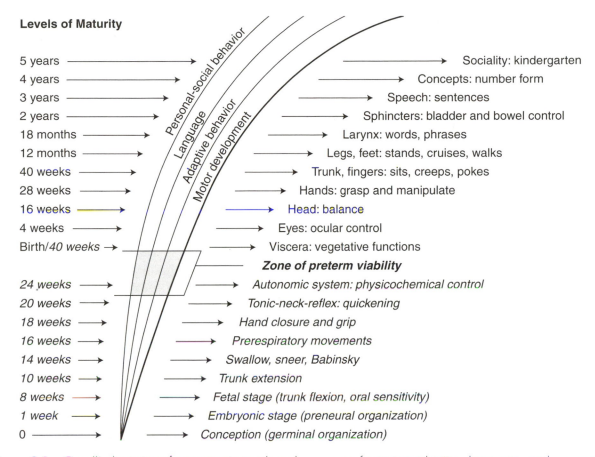

Figure 2.1 Gesell's depiction of ontogenetic trends and sequences for motor, adaptive, language, and personal-social behavior.

Reprinted from Gesell and Walden, 1975.

input in producing the actual progressional changes in that development. They further argued that the first and last principles reflect the importance of maturational processes defined through genetic traits.

Gesell and Amatruda (1945) acknowledged the importance of the environment in other developmental processes. They pointed out the importance of culture, for example, on personality when they argued that development was sensitive to cultural influences, and that through the influence of others, personality begins to take shape from the moment of birth by the process of acculturation.

The second principle outlined in table 2.1 is that of developmental direction. This principle has had a profound influence on developmental research. Gesell and Ames (1940) argued for a **cephalocaudal** direction (i.e., from the head to feet) of **ontogenetic** organization. For example, in the first week, infants can lift their head, whereas at the end of the first year, they can stand independently. Figure 2.1 reflects this view of developmental direction. The authors also argued for a *proximal* to *distal* progression for the body segments, that is, from the points close to the body center to the body's periphery. Hence, the upper arm and upper leg will develop before the forearm, foreleg, hand, and foot. The

Table 2.1   Gesell's Seven Principles Based on the Description Provided by Gesell & Amatruda

Number	The principle of . . .	Description
1	individuating fore-reference	Action or movement develops through intrinsic morphogenetic processes uninfluenced by experience.
2	developmental direction	Maturation occurs in a cephalocaudal direction, and transversely from proximal to distal segments.
3	spiral reincorporation*	Exceptions to principle 2 occur as a result of successive head-to-foot sweeps of development resulting in a spiral trend to growth.
4	reciprocal interweaving	Ontogenetic organization is not linear but has periodic fluctuations in counterbalanced functions such as right and left extremities. There is a progressive interweaving evidenced by successive shifts in the dominance of one aspect over the other.
5	functional asymmetry	Asymmetries develop as a result of the process of reciprocal interweaving. They include preferences in handedness, eyedness, footedness, etc.
6	self-regulatory fluctuation	The growing system moves from unstable states to stable states, with stability and variability mutually coexisting. This self-regulating process results in developmental fluctuations.
7	optimal tendency	Behavioral growth always aims for maximum realization. Even when compromised, mechanisms of regeneration, substitution, and compensation take over to promote maximum potential.

*Arnold Gesell, in his 1952 book *Infant Development*, incorporated principle 3 into principle 2, hence describing only six principles.
From Gesell, 1945.

foot is described as "both a caudal and distal terminus; the final fulcrum for locomotion" (p. 262).

Although the principle has been widely accepted, even in more recent developmental literature (e.g., Bly, 1994; Payne & Isaacs, 1995), it has been challenged. For example, as described in chapter 1, the fetus develops a large repertoire of movements from seven weeks onward. A surprising finding in these investigations was simultaneous onset of arm and leg movements at eight weeks (see table 1.2, p. 13), suggesting that the principle of cephalocaudal development is not adhered to in the development of fetal motility (de Vries et al., 1982). Also, there is evidence to suggest that proximal and distal muscle control develop simultaneously as the skill of reaching develops (Fetters et al., 1989). Recently, Galloway and Thelen (2004) have also found evidence that a strict cephalocaudal progression does not apply, as they observed that infants can interact with toys using their feet before they can reach with their hands.

Newell and van Emmerik (1990) suggested that this principle may be task specific. For example, examination of the principle using a broader manipulation of task constraints may demonstrate many exceptions to the rule. These authors argue that the early maturationists used a particular set of task constraints that were implicitly or explicitly designed by the observer to investigate motor development. If the particular task constraints are not suitable for eliciting a certain movement pattern at the chronological age under investigation, then it will not be obvious that the infant can produce that movement. This does not mean that the infant cannot do the task, simply that the infant cannot do the task with those specific constraints. For example, an object may be too small or too big to pick up, but given a different size the infant may achieve the milestone of grasping (Newell & van Emmerik, 1990).

Gesell (1952) used the metaphor of the loom to describe his principle of reciprocal interweaving. He considered growth as an "intricate braiding process, in which multitudinous strands are interwoven into patterns which are manifested in co-ordinating patterns of behavior" (p. 67). For example, Gesell described 23 distinct stages of prone behavior that an infant must go through to achieve upright posture and walking. Every one of these sequential stages was considered essential to achieve walking "because of the numerous motor relationships which must be coordinated, that is, reciprocally interwoven" (Gesell, 1946, p. 305). However, research has now shown that there are many different variations of movement sequences that can be "braided" together to produce walking, not just the sequence described by Gesell.

This principle of reciprocal interweaving does recognize the nonlinear nature of development, as does the principle of spiral reincorporation, according to which apparent regressions in development are necessary for the organism to move to a higher level of functioning (Hopkins et al., 1993). Also, Gesell's principle of self-regulatory fluctuation acknowledges development as shifting patterns in which the organism moves from states of instability to stability, with stability and variability mutually coexisting. "The maturing organism oscillates between self-limiting poles as it advances. The forward thrusts are comparable to gropings which seek a pathway. The flowing stream of development thus finds its channels" (Gesell, 1952, p. 69). In Gesell and Amatruda's 1945 volume, the chapter titled "The Dynamic Morphology of Behavior" includes a "dynamic map" (see figure 2.2) that depicts the nonlinear evolution of a behavior through the interaction of different morphological events as the infant matures, hence a dynamic morphology of behavior. As Hopkins and colleagues (1993) pointed out, Gesell's views on the nonlinear nature of development as described in several of

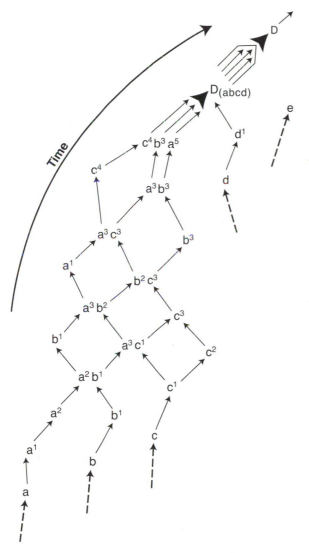

Figure 2.2 A time–space diagram of the morphogenetic processes that underlie the patterning of behavior according to Gesell and Amatruda (1945). *a, b, c, d* = behavior traits or components; *D* = a developed complex of these components; broken lines indicate *latency*.

Reprinted from Gesell and Walden, 1973.

his principles are only now being recognized for their true value. The recently popular dynamic systems perspective incorporates several of the elements laid down originally by Gesell (Newell et al., 2003).

Despite recent findings demonstrating that some of his principles may not necessarily be accurate, the contribution of Gesell and his colleagues to our understanding of developmental processes has been enormous and remains influential.

McGraw's Neural Maturational Approach

Myrtle McGraw was another influential researcher of the early 20th century. As maturationists, both McGraw and Gesell attempted to link the developmental changes they observed with the biological development of the infant (Haywood, 1993). However, the ways in which they viewed the maturational process were quite different. Whereas Gesell saw development in relation to morphological maturation, McGraw explained developmental changes through neural maturation.

McGraw's maturational approach is reflected in her statement that "delineation of changes in overt behavior provides a basis for interpreting gross reorganization of the central nervous system" (McGraw, 1940, p. 747). Hence, she attributed the development of walking and other milestones to the development of control by the cerebral cortex over muscular function. Her cortical inhibition hypothesis argued that early reflex-based movement patterns were inhibited through a process of **neurogenesis,** resulting in increasing cortical control.

Primitive reflexes were thought to interfere with emerging voluntary behaviors. Inhibition of these primitive reflexes was thought to occur around three to four months of age, when the cortical centers develop control of the lower brain and spinal cord. Milani-Comparetti and Gidoni (1967) adopted McGraw's approach when they proposed that these "primitive motor automotisms" must be dissolved or extinguished before voluntary motor control becomes possible. This implies an inherent antagonism between reflexes and voluntary motor actions. For example, the continuation of the asymmetrical tonic neck reflex beyond two to three months can prevent the infant from rolling over, resulting in a delay in motor development. Milani-Comparetti and Gidoni, too, proposed that primitive reflexes were actively inhibited by the cortex. However, this view is no longer widely supported, as there is little evidence for cortical inhibition of infantile reflexes (Prechtl, 1981). Although this view has been refuted on the basis of neurological evidence (e.g., Touwen, 1984) and by experimental research with infants (e.g., Thelen & Smith, 1994), it remains a dominant principle in many intervention strategies for young infants and children with motor disabilities.

A Maturational Perspective on Intervention

One of the outcomes of the early maturationist research on motor development was the notion that a difference in the sequence of motor milestones may be an indicator of abnormal development. Any variation in the timing or the order of motor milestones was associated with possible impaired brain function (Touwen, 1978). Hence, it was considered that if part of the sequence was omitted, for example, if the infant did not go through the stage of creeping, he or she would have missed out on an essential aspect of development.

This view was extended by researchers in the 1950s and '60s into a controversial therapy called the Doman-Delacato patterning method (Delacato, 1963, 1966), more commonly termed psychomotor patterning (Shaw, 2002). In order for children to achieve their full developmental potential, it was argued that there must be no variation in the sequential pattern of development or any incomplete development. Although the sequences that needed to be maintained related largely to motor development, the resultant deficits were argued to include mental retardation, learning disabilities, and behavioral problems. A therapy program was developed to correct the "CNS [central nervous system] disorganization." This program included passive movements, sensory stimulation, rebreathing of expired air, and various dietary restrictions. For example, the older child might be placed in a prone position, and various passive ipsilateral and contralateral patterns of head turning and arm and leg movements produced by the therapist. The child was taken through graded developmental stages of crawling, creeping, and walking.

Despite the severe demands on both parent and child, this program became quite popular. In 1968, the American Academy of Pediatrics Committee on the Handicapped Child critically reviewed the approach, providing a policy statement that questioned the principles underlying this therapy. It was again dismissed as completely ineffective by the American Academy of Pediatrics in 1982 and 1999. It is now known that infants who have quite variable patterns of early motor milestones still develop normal motor and cognitive abilities (Bottos et al., 1989; Largo et al., 1993). In summing up the potential of the Doman-Delacato patterning method, Scherzer and Tscharnuter (1990) stated that "positive results are considered by many to be questionable; harmful effects likely to be common and extensive" (p. 73). For example, it has been suggested that because of the high demands and expectations placed on the family, there may be a considerable financial burden. The time demands may also impact the relationship between the parents and siblings of the child (American Academy of Pediatrics, 1999).

Assessing Maturational Approaches

The importance of sequential phases of development such as creeping and crawling in the appropriate development of movement has been a contentious issue for many decades. Newell and van Emmerik (1990) point out that there is intuitive face validity in the notion that motor sequences are endogenously generated through maturational processes when one considers how similar these sequences are both within and across cultures.

Considerable emphasis has been placed on the invariant sequencing of early movement patterns. However, there has been little consideration of the exceptions to these. A major criticism of the maturational perspective is that there is a tendency to investigate the "norm," with little interest taken in exceptions to the norm, in terms of both intraindividual and interindividual differences (Hopkins et al., 1993; Newell & van Emmerik, 1990; von Hofsten, 1993). If children who are exceptions to the norm continue to develop normally, then it is clear that maintaining the appropriate sequence is not a prerequisite of appropriate development. It is these exceptions that demonstrate the inadequacy of the maturationist explanation of motor development (Newell & van Emmerick).

There have been an increasing number of studies emphasizing the considerable variability in development in children who ultimately achieve normal motor control (e.g., Bottos et al., 1989; Cioni et al., 1993; Darrah, Redfern et al., 1998; Largo et al., 1993). Largo and colleagues found huge variations in the development of early locomotion (see figure 2.3). Clinicians need to be aware that unusual behaviors can still lead to normal development, and differences in the sequence of motor development should not necessarily be labeled as pathological. Furthermore, Largo and colleagues found that children with mild

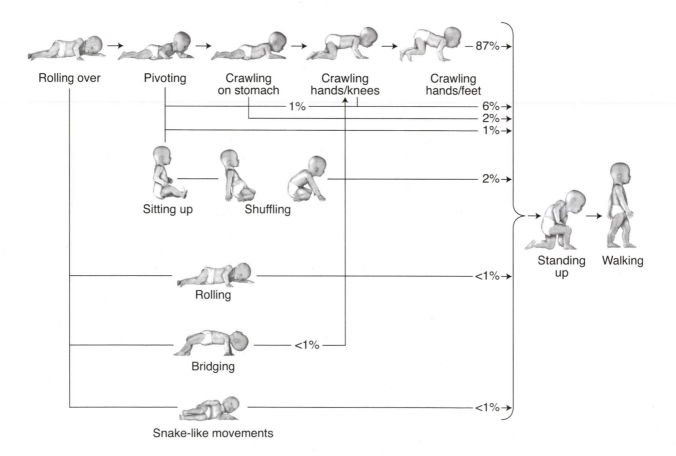

Figure 2.3 The different pathways to walking identified by Largo (1985).

to moderate cerebral palsy were still well within the normal age range for taking their first steps. That is, even though children may achieve motor milestones such as creeping and walking within the normal range, this does not mean they have no neurological damage. "Only severe neurological impairment leads to a delay in motor development such that all affected children are beyond the normal range" (p. 257). Children with mild neurological impairment may produce deviant pathways of locomotion rather than retarded development, and this would be evident by a presence of awkward rather than delayed motor performance (Largo et al., 1993).

Despite the controversies surrounding the maturationist perspective, the research efforts of the early theorists such as Gesell and McGraw have provided comprehensive descriptive classifications of early infant development. These led to other influential studies emerging throughout the period. Notable examples include the chronological account of early development by Mary Shirley (1931), a detailed account of prehensile movements by H.M. Halverson (1931), and the creation of normative scales for both motor and cognitive development in infants and young children by Nancy Bayley (1933, 1936). These have formed the basis for many test instruments used for measuring early motor and cognitive development and are still used extensively today, as described in detail in chapter 9.

Cognitive Approaches

The topic of infant motor development did not generate a great deal of interest around the middle of the 20th century. Connolly (1970) suggested two reasons for this. Firstly, he suggested that the earlier researchers such as Gesell and McGraw provided the answers to the questions posed at that time, and using the techniques available at the time (largely observational). Hence there appeared little need for further investigation. A second explanation related to the influence of the experimental psychologists of the time, who largely regarded infant behavior as having little meaning or purpose. As a result, interest in infant motor development essentially remained dormant until the 1980s, when new techniques were devised to investigate movement in infancy.

Although infant research was largely ignored around this period, the 1970s were significant for motor control research in general. It was in this decade that the cognitive approach became popular, with psychologists having a considerable impact on our understanding of motor behavior. The cognitive approach emerged in the field of motor development, primarily as a result of an interdisciplinary meeting held in London in 1968. The proceedings of this meeting were published by Kevin Connolly (1970) in a book called *Mechanisms of Motor Skill Development,* which examined the status of motor development research at that time.

According to a cognitive perspective, in order to solve a particular problem or perform a particular skill, a number of mental operations need to be performed (Stelmach, 1982). One of the first theorists to discuss early development in relation to mental operations was Jean Piaget (Piaget, 1953). He is best known for his theory of cognitive development, in which he argued that all knowledge is imparted to us initially through our early motor actions. Given the importance Piaget placed on early motor development, this theoretical approach warrants some discussion.

Piaget's Cognitive Schemas

Jean Piaget has often been described as the most influential developmental psychologist to date. He highlighted the importance of reflexes in early development (Piaget, 1953), not only in relation to motor development, but also in relation to cognitive development. According to Piaget, knowledge is acquired through action, either physical or mental. He described the development of cognition as a progression through four distinct stages, with each involving quite discrete processes. It is the first of these stages, the sensorimotor stage occurring from birth to two years of age, that is particularly relevant to understanding early infant development.

Throughout the sensorimotor stage, physical action is the primary source of new information. Piaget argued that infants are not born with any reasoning or representational capacity, but that these cognitive abilities emerge as a result of sensorimotor experiences. He placed considerable importance on these early movements as he argued that newborn infants must actively explore their environment in order to interpret their world and self.

Piaget's sensorimotor stage of cognitive development consists of six different substages as outlined in table 2.2. These substages were derived primarily from observations of his own children, Jacqueline, Lucianne, and Laurent (Piaget & Inhelder, 1969).

In the first few months (substages I and II), the young infant acquires knowledge through **schemas,** with schema defined as "a concept or framework that organizes and interprets information" (Myers, 2001, p. 127). Schemas are the way in which each individual acts on the environment, and can be biological or mental in nature. Schemas available to a young infant are biological and very limited, and they initially consist primarily of reflexes. For example, one schema that allows the infant to acquire knowledge is the sucking reflex. There are two processes involving existing schemas that can be used to take in information from the environment. The first, *assimilation,* occurs when the environment is altered to fit an existing schema. The sucking reflex is designed to draw milk from the mother's nipple. However, through assimilation, the infant can use the same sucking reflex to acquire information about other objects that are sucked on, such as the infant's thumb. When the schema needs to be changed to fit with the environment, the second process of *accommodation* occurs. For example, if the infant tries to suck on her fist, she needs to change the shape of her mouth

■■■ Jean Piaget argued that sensorimotor experience is the source of new information, with the precedence of action over perception.

Table 2.2 Piaget's Sensorimotor Stage of Cognitive Development

Substage	Age range	Characteristics
I	Birth–1 month	Dominated by reflexes Functional and generalized assimilation Behaviors repeated over and over again without being changed
II	1–4 months	Primary circular reactions First acquired adaptations occur through the processes of assimilation and accommodation Behaviors are not just reflexes but involve only the infant's body Infant unable to distinguish the means from the goal
III	4–8 months	Secondary circular reactions Differentiation of means and goal Repetitive movements involve objects and other people, not just own body Beginnings of intention although not goal directed at this stage
IV	8–12 months	This period marks the beginning of true intelligence Behaviors become purposeful and deliberate Can adapt old behaviors to new situations Object permanence develops
V	12–18 months	Tertiary circular reactions Trial and error used to solve new problems Variations in behaviors are intentionally introduced
VI	18–24 months	A transitional period Mental combinations occur Planning in advance Symbolic representation has developed

to accommodate the larger size of the fist. Hence the original schema is changed to accommodate the fist.

Knowledge is therefore gained by the repetition of interesting or pleasing events that were originally experienced by chance. This repetitious process is called a *circular reaction* (see figure 2.4). Initially these are basic repetitions of the same action, termed a *primary* circular reaction (figure 2.4*a*). Primary circular reactions occur in substage II. These reactions appear to lack an external goal but are repeated simply because the infant gains pleasure from them. At the same time, infants are learning about their own bodies. At around four months of age, *secondary* circular reactions become evident (figure 2.4*b*) and mark the beginning of substage III. Objects and events that are external to the infant are incorporated into these responses. An example of a secondary circular reaction produced by Piaget's son, Laurent, occurred when he continually kicked or shook the crib to produce sound and movement.

Substage IV occurs at around 8 to 12 months of age. The infant now combines a series of secondary schemas to form new behaviors. This is thought to mark the beginning of "true intelligence" (Piaget & Inhelder, 1969).

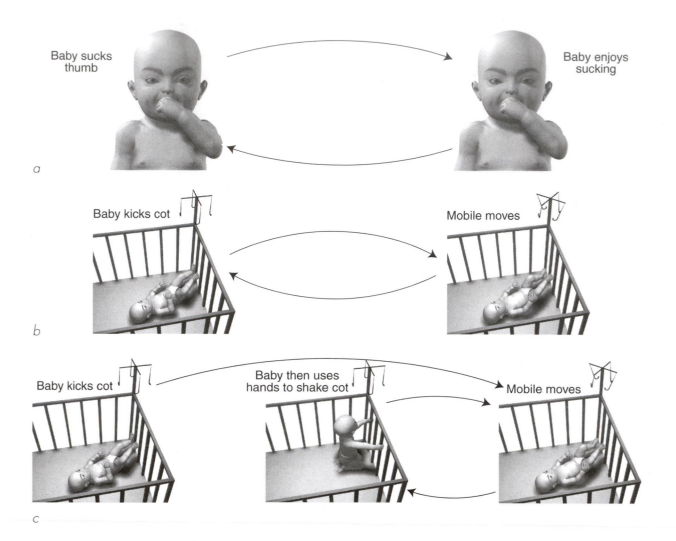

Figure 2.4   Circular reactions: *(a)* primary circular reaction, *(b)* secondary circular reaction, *(c)* tertiary circular reaction.

Whereas both primary and secondary circular reactions involve repetition of the same movement, *tertiary* circular reactions involve adaptation of those movements to produce a different outcome (figure 2.4c). This begins at around 12 months of age and inaugurates the period of experimentation, substage V. The sixth and final substage depicts the final transition from a purely sensory and motor level of functioning to symbolic or mental representation. This is a bridging stage in which infants start to make use of more advanced thinking skills that involve symbols, images, and language.

Piaget's theory shifted motor development to a different level. From a naturist's perspective, perception had generally been viewed as the source of new knowledge. Piaget argued that all knowledge was a result of action. Hence, early motor development took on a new importance.

Piaget's theory has been very influential in research on early development. Some of this research has now demonstrated inaccuracies in his approach, which tends to underestimate a young infant's cognitive abilities. For example, Meltzoff and Borton (1979) found that newborn infants could match visual and tactile stimuli, demonstrating some form of mental representation at this early age. Research by von Hofsten (1982) on eye–hand coordination, and by Butterworth and Hopkins (1988) on hand–mouth coordination in neonates, for example, has demonstrated some form of nonreflexive "intent" from birth. These studies are discussed further in chapter 5, when the development of reaching and grasping in infants is examined more closely.

Information-Processing Approach

The information-processing approach describes motor behavior as a hierarchical process with the central nervous system acting as a central controlling unit. The approach uses the analogy of a computer, with the human seen as an "active" information processor (Stelmach, 1982). This top-down approach describes motor control in terms of distinct processes that can be categorized as input, central, output, and feedback processes. Each process can be analyzed separately as it is broken down into distinct steps or stages. This approach has been particularly useful over the last few decades to analyze developmental disorders such as developmental coordination disorder (e.g., Laszlo & Bairstow, 1985; Wilson & McKenzie, 1998) and attention deficit hyperactivity disorder (e.g., Sergeant, 2000), as it enables researchers to investigate which stages or steps have been affected by the disorder.

A typical information-processing model is shown in figure 2.5. The first stage involves the input of information from the body and environment in response to stimuli. The sensory information available to the young infant was discussed in the previous chapter. Sensory information feeds into the central component of the model and is involved in the first stage of perception, which includes both the detection of the stimulus and its recognition. Memory is considered important for encoding, storage, and retrieval of information (Stelmach, 1982). It is an important component for both the recognition phase and the next stage of selection, the decision-making process in which the appropriate response is determined. Appropriate schemas, representations, or

▰▰▰ An information-processing approach enables the researcher to analyze distinct processes that are considered part of motor control.

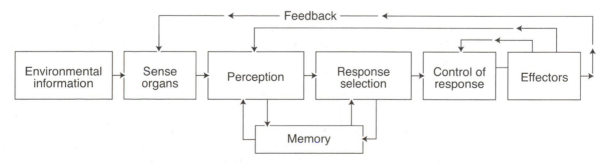

Figure 2.5   An information-processing model of motor control.
Adapted from Glencross, 1977.

motor programs (Glencross, 1977; Schmidt, 1975) are stored as part of the decision-making process. The motor program was initially defined as "a set of muscle commands that are structured before a movement sequence begins, and that allows the entire sequence to be carried out uninfluenced by peripheral feedback" (Keele, 1968, p. 387). Schmidt (1988) has since developed the notion of the generalized motor program in which a basic framework provides the invariant features of the general motor plan, and situation-specific parameters are mapped in later in the planning sequence. Once the motor plan is initiated, the final output stage occurs, evident by the execution of the response.

Two main types of processing models have been identified. The *closed-loop* or *cybernetic* models have been the more dominant of the two, and provide "pre-established set-points which serve as reference values for the signals controlling movements" (Hopkins et al., 1993, p. 348). The *open-loop* or *algorithmic* models contain stored execution instructions but have no feedback mechanisms that can detect any errors or changes in the system as a result of the response. Figure 2.5 is a closed-loop system because it contains peripheral feedback mechanisms crucial for monitoring the performance and providing the external information. A further feedback mechanism is that of efference copy, which provides a copy of the motor commands that are sent out.

The information-processing approach investigates such concepts as memory, feedback, and perception. With the increase in popularity of this approach came a proliferation of research on infant development in the areas of perception and cognition (Cohen, 1998). However, the approach did not have a similar effect on infant motor development. Most research on motor development based on the information-processing approach focused on older children rather than infants. Such studies were primarily concerned with understanding the learning processes of a limited range of motor skills, with explanations based on symbolic knowledge structures (Hopkins et al., 1993). As a result, while the information-processing approach dominated the field of motor control in the 1970s and into the 1980s, little research was carried out on infant motor development.

Assessing Prescriptive Approaches

Approaches such as the maturational and cognitive perspectives involve top-down processes relying on central control mechanisms. Whereas motor development from a maturational perspective involves developmental advances through the maturation of the appropriate morphology and neural pathways, the cognitive approach explains development in terms of the development of more complex schema, representations, or motor programs (Hopkins et al., 1993).

Several underlying difficulties have been associated with the prescriptive approaches. One such difficulty is the problem described by early philosophers as *infinite regress* (see Kelso, 1995). Basically, if central processes control behavior, who controls the controller? This has also been termed the *homunculus dilemma* (e.g., Hopkins et al., 1993), in which decision making regresses back to some form of "little person" within the brain who has all the necessary instructions or programs to produce movement.

Many other fundamental difficulties are encountered in any attempt to explain how movement control is accomplished based on a prescriptive perspective. Most of these issues relate to the problem of storage. With the potential for an infinite number of solutions to the production of movements, what is the potential of the CNS to store the exact specifications of all of these solutions (Hopkins et al., 1993)? Bernstein (1984), whose work had a substantial influence on the later development of the ecological or dynamic systems approach, was the first to elucidate some of these problems.

The Influence of Nikolai Bernstein

Nikolai Alexandrowitsch Bernstein has been described as "one of the premier minds of our century" (Latash, 1998b, p. v). Over the last two decades, the work of Bernstein has been acclaimed in several volumes dedicated to him and his work (e.g., Latash, 1998b; Whiting, 1984). The volume by Latash was based on the proceedings of an international conference, "Bernstein's Traditions in Motor Control," held in 1996 at the Pennsylvania State University.

Perhaps the best known work of Bernstein is his volume titled *The Coordination and Regulation of Movements*, which was published in Russian in 1947. It was another 20 years before this significant text was published as an English translation (Bernstein, 1967). It was in this volume that Bernstein developed the notion of motor control. Bernstein was not interested in the issues of when, how, or what we move, which had been examined up to that point. He was interested in understanding why we move—that is, what are the underlying control mechanisms that produce voluntary coordinated movements? He recognized that movement control could not be described in terms of muscular force alone, but must also incorporate inertia and reactive forces (Turvey, 1982). He identified four fundamental problems associated with understanding how we control our movement (Bernstein, 1984). These were the *degrees of freedom* problem, and the problems of *redundancy*, *contextual variations*, and *change*. Each of these is outlined next.

Degrees of Freedom

Turvey and colleagues (1982) define *degrees of freedom* as "the least number of independent coordinates needed to identify the positions of the elements in the system without violating any geometrical constraints" (p. 244). Bernstein argued that the many joints and linkages, with an even greater number of muscles, are too numerous to be able to provide a prescriptive solution to each movement problem. As the brain has a finite processing capacity, each fiber and joint could not be controlled directly by the motor cortex (Hopkins et al., 1993). This problem, termed the degrees of freedom problem, points to the question of how the CNS can regulate this multitude of variables. The importance of this process was demonstrated by Bernstein's definition of the coordination of a movement, namely "the process of mastering redundant degrees of freedom of the moving organ" (Bernstein, 1984, p. 355).

Bernstein suggested that this problem can be overcome through the formation of linkages between the different subsystems, hence reducing the multiple degrees of freedom present in the motor system. These linkages have been termed *coordinative structures*, defined by Tuller and colleagues (1982) as "a group of muscles often spanning several joints that is constrained to act as a single functional unit" (p. 253).

Redundancy

A second problem described by Bernstein is the notion of *redundancy*. When one considers the complexity of the neural system, comprising approximately 10^{10} neurons with each having up to 10^4 connections (Kelso, 1995), there are innumerably more executable solutions for any movement than there are learned examples. Again, to store all possible combinations would require huge storage capacity. It would also be a grossly inefficient method of control given that any particular combination may not necessarily be repeated.

Contextual Variations

Movements are not always produced in the same context. Even a highly learned skill such as walking involves huge *contextual variations* in many instances. For example, according to an open-loop account of movement control, every change in the terrain in which one is walking would require a new program to overcome bumps, gullies, objects, and so on. A small variation in context calls for a variation in motor commands. How could the CNS store the exact specifications of all movements when a change in the immediate conditions would result in a change in the commands needed to execute the appropriate movement? Hence, contextual changes cannot be accounted for by the notion that movements are stored as a set of specific neural commands. This was another issue that needed to be addressed in efforts to explain motor control.

Change

The final issue is particularly relevant to motor development. Consider figure 2.6. It can be seen that the bodily proportions of the fetus are considerably different from those of the newborn, which are immensely different from those of the adult. Biomechanical and morphological characteristics of the organism continue to change with age. Therefore,

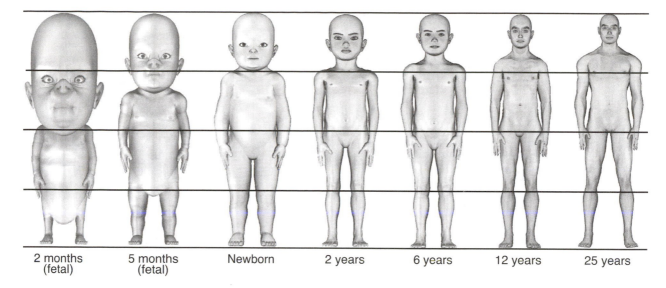

| 2 months (fetal) | 5 months (fetal) | Newborn | 2 years | 6 years | 12 years | 25 years |

Figure 2.6 Changes in form and proportion of the human body during fetal and postnatal life.
Adapted from Jackson, 1928.

movements made at the fetal stage would produce completely different outcomes from those for a 12-month-old infant. This is further evidence against programmed movement output. If a motor program is considered in the strict sense of a stored set of muscle commands that is innately specified (e.g., Keele, 1968), then a different set of commands would need to be stored for each change in body structure. Motor development processes must account for this change.

Addressing Bernstein's Issues From a Cognitive Perspective

Bernstein's views stimulated theorists to question the paradigm popular at the time, namely the information-processing approach. This led cognitive theorists to reexamine their approach and suggest ways in which their approach could overcome the problems described by Bernstein.

Such an attempt was made by Schmidt (1975), who developed the notion of a *generalized motor program.* Schmidt argued that only invariant features of the movement are stored as a motor program or schema. As a result, this reduced the amount of storage required for motor programs. In order to allow for variations in the movement due to such factors as context, or physical change such as growth, situation-specific parameters like force, time, and muscle selection are mapped onto the generalized program prior to response execution rather than being stored as a specific program.

For example, if handwriting is considered, the style of each letter appears to be an invariant feature. In figure 2.7, the line "The quick brown fox" is written using various parts of the body. Although features such as the size and steadiness of the letters differ, the letter

■■■■ Bernstein made a significant contribution to motor control theory by pointing out the fundamental problems of degrees of freedom, redundancy, contextual variation, and change. These issues must be taken into account when one considers how movements are controlled.

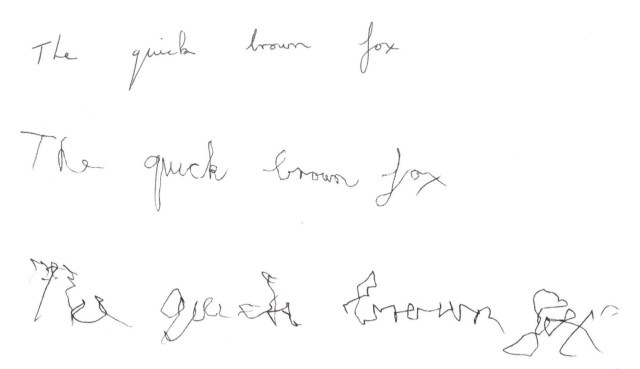

Figure 2.7   This figure shows the invariant nature of handwriting for each individual. The first line was written with the right hand by a right-handed person. The second line was written with the left hand, and the third line was written with the right foot. Despite differences in the quality and size of the letters, the style appears invariant.

styles for an individual appear very similar. Hence, the letter style would be considered an invariant feature of the stored motor program, whereas the speed of movement and the limb used would be movement parameters (Schmidt, 1988). Other invariant characteristics that could be stored as a generalized motor program may include order, such as the muscular pattern, temporal phasing, and relative force.

Bruner (1970) was one of the earliest researchers in motor development to acknowledge the substantial contribution made by Bernstein. Although Bernstein's work has been primarily linked to the more recent dynamic systems approach, Bruner utilized Bernstein's notion of mastering degrees of freedom to explain development from an information-processing perspective. Mastery, or the achievement of control, of a new task was described through a process of *modularization,* which produces an action that is more automatic, is less variable, and has a predictable spatiotemporal pattern (Bruner). This modularized act can then be incorporated into new, more complex serial patterns. As Newell (1986) pointed out, this was a computational solution to Bernstein's degrees of freedom problem. The solution is quite different when considered from an ecological or dynamic systems perspective. This approach was adopted by other theorists who looked for an alternative to the prescriptive approaches.

Ecological/Natural Systems Approach

In the late 1970s, a theoretical paradigm emerged that argued against the prescriptive approaches to motor control. Instead, this new ecological approach, also termed the natural-physical approach, suggests that movements emerge from the intrinsic properties of the whole system rather than through hierarchically organized central control. The principle of this approach is that behavior occurs as a result of the interaction of many subsystems, where the emergence of new behaviors (such as movements) can be described in terms of natural laws rather than a prescribed pattern inherent in the system (Thelen & Smith, 1994). Rather than taking a central controlling role, the CNS is considered to be one of many systems responsible for the movement outcome.

Thanks to the critical mind of Bernstein (1967), a whole new chapter of motor control research was inspired with the development of this new approach. The work of James and Eleanor Gibson was also instrumental in shaping this new approach to understanding motor control and development.

Gibson's Ecological Theory

In his description of how we perceive the world, James Gibson (1979) emphasized the importance of a dynamic relationship between perception and action, in which "organisms do not simply perceive the physical properties of their environment" but "perceive the physical properties of their environments *in relation to* their action capabilities" (Lockman, 1990, p. 88). In the "active" theory of perception provided by Eleanor and James Gibson, "the sea of stimulus energy in which an observer is immersed is always an array and always a flow" (Gibson & Gibson, 1991, p. 506). This contrasts markedly with the cognitive-based explanations of perception given by such renowned psychologists as Richard Gregory, in which stimuli need to be interpreted indirectly by the brain in order to be meaningful (i.e., indirect perception). Rather, the Gibsons argue that there is information within stimuli that does not need to be translated or interpreted by a higher center (i.e., direct perception).

This information is not automatically picked up from the environment, but it must be actively perceived. Hence the close interaction between action and perception as they mutually guide each other in a process that detects *invariants*. The notion of invariants is the key to the ecological approach. Invariants are described as higher-order relationships in the flow of stimulation that specify the properties of events, objects, and places. These properties specify the world through the detection of constancies within the environment. However, they should not be considered as either pictures of objects or coded signals, but rather "mathematical relations in a flowing array, nothing less" (Gibson & Gibson, 1991, p. 506).

By actively seeking out and detecting invariants, an organism perceives events, objects, places, and their *affordances* (Gibson, 1977). Affordances are what the perception can offer the perceiver, that is, what it provides, either good or bad, for the animal (Gibson, 1979). Consequently, affordances emphasize the utility of some aspect of the environment for an animal. For example, rain affords getting wet, whereas a cave affords keeping dry. Of particular relevance to the ecological approach is that affordances do not require any stored patterns, as they are directly perceived.

In contrast to more traditional views such as those of Piaget (1953), Gibson argued that many of the mechanisms that are required to detect affordances are present at birth, although immature. Eleanor Gibson and Richard Walk (Gibson & Walk, 1960) devised the *visual cliff* to investigate the affordance of a "surface of support" in young infants (see figure 2.8*a*). An infant or animal perceives information about two different surfaces, one that provides support and one that does not. The latter gives the perception of depth despite a glass or Perspex cover that prevents the infant or animal from falling. Many newborn animals were found to perceive the differences in support— evidence that this "affordance" of support is present at birth. Young infants are able to differentiate the two surfaces by the time they are crawling (Gibson, 1982). Furthermore, research by Campos and colleagues (Campos et al., 1978) demonstrated a change in heart rate in infants under five months of age when they were presented with the different support cues. Interestingly, there was a drop in heart rate associated with increased attention on the part of the infants, rather than the predicted increase in heart rate that would be linked to fear. This did not emerge until infants were over nine months of age. Recent research at Deakin University in Australia has addressed the different reactions to a dry (figure 2.8*a*) versus wet surface (figure 2.8*b*) in order to investigate why infants may approach wet surfaces such as swimming pools. Epidemiological data indicate that a leading cause of death in infants and toddlers in Australia is drowning, most commonly in domestic swimming pools.

Unlike Piaget, who argued that the actions determining knowledge are accidental, the Gibsons argued that early exploratory activities are directed toward the searching out of information. As the new perceptual and motor abilities mature, or become modified with experience, the sensitivity to invariants increases. However, as Summers (1998) pointed out, there has been a great deal of ambiguity in the definition of the term *affordance*, which can be compared with the concept of *schema* in cognitive psychology with respect to its "definitional imprecision" (p. 388). As a result, empirical analysis of Gibson's approach has been limited.

The mutual importance of the organism and environment in development is emphasized in the ecological approach of Gibson (1979). This has led to the establishment of the dynamic systems approach as one of the leading theoretical perspectives in motor control research over

James and Eleanor Gibson described the process of direct perception, in which the organism actively detects invariants and their affordances.

a   b

Figure 2.8 Experimental data collected over 40 years show that visual "falling-off places" elicit *avoidance* behavior in infants and toddlers on a visual cliff designed by Gibson and Walk (1960). Recent research by Hooley and Crassini (2003) utilized the visual cliff to determine whether (a) dry edges produced *avoidance* behavior and (b) wet edges produced *approach* behavior, which can have catastrophic consequences in situations in which infants are exposed to possible drowning.

the last few decades. Indeed, the proliferation of research on infant motor development over recent years has been directly attributed to the recent popularity of this approach (Savelsbergh, 1993).

Dynamic/Dynamical Systems Approach

There has been some confusion with respect to the term "dynamic" in relation to the *dynamic* (e.g., Kelso, 1995) or *dynamical* (e.g., van der Maas & Hopkins, 1998) systems approach. From a biomechanical perspective, dynamics refers to "the world of forces and moments, the causes of motion, in a manner synonymous with kinetics" (Wimmers et al., 1998, p. 60). However, in terms of the dynamic systems approach, dynamics refers to how a system or particular variable evolves over time (Wimmers et al.). This definition does not emphasize mechanical properties like mass, length, and stiffness, but it is based on the notion that complex systems are open systems influenced by flows of energy and information from the environment (Schmidt & O'Brien, 1998).

Several key concepts define the dynamic systems approach, and specific terminology has evolved to describe the important characteristics of this theoretical paradigm.

Nonlinear Systems

Dynamic systems can be *linear* or *nonlinear*, where linearity is defined by simple proportionality. In a **linear system,** there is a one-to-one relationship between the input (y) and the output (x), where, for example, if x is proportional to y, then x is a linear function of y (van der Maas & Hopkins, 1998). Dynamic systems theorists (e.g., Kelso, 1995; Thelen, 1995; Turvey, 1990) argue that linear dynamics are often unable to describe the complexities of human behavior, in particular motor behavior, as "they often require not one solution but a system of equations through which data is fed back into the system as a process of iteration" (van der Maas & Hopkins, p. 2). Dynamic systems are more appropriately defined as nonlinear systems, as they may have periods of stability that can change rapidly as a result of changes in the control parameter, resulting in qualitatively different types of behavior (Hopkins et al., 1993). Van Geert (1994) describes *iteration* as the primary principle behind his interpretation of the dynamic systems approach. An iterative process uses the output as its input, producing new output. This continues *ad infinitum.* In mathematical terms it is described as

$$x_{i+1} = f(x_i)$$

Order and Control Parameters

Schmidt and O'Brien (1998) describe the system's *collective variable* or *order parameter* as "the foundation concept" of this approach. This measurable variable summarizes how the system is organized. It is created as a result of the cooperation of the individual parts of the system (Kelso, 1995). The order parameter is not a controlling entity but is a description of the current state of the system. An example of an order parameter in behavior is the phase relations between the limbs during walking. Even though the rate of walking may vary, the order parameter does not differ. In Gibson's (1979) terminology, this would be described as an invariant feature of this particular behavior.

The state of the system is influenced by external properties described as *control parameters.* Hermann Haken introduced the distinction between the order parameter and the control parameter in his theory of *synergetics* that describes the phenomenon of dynamic pattern formation (Kelso, 1995). Such pattern formation can be seen in chemical reactions and fluid dynamics as well as motor development and control. For example, a well-known phase transition resulting in new pattern formation is the changing of water molecules into the three states of solid, liquid, and gas. This is shown in figure 2.9a. These three states are the phases, and the state of the molecules is the order parameter. In the case of water molecules, the control parameter is temperature. In this example, a continuous, or linear, change in the control parameter will produce a discontinuous, or nonlinear, shift in the order parameter. That is, the control parameter acts as a catalyst for an organizational change.

Two other examples related to motor control are provided in figure 2.9, *b* and *c*. Note that for human gait, the control parameter can be defined by the speed of the gait. However, the order parameter, that is, the invariant characteristic that defines the different states of walking and running, is unclear. Abernethy and colleagues (1995) discuss the features needed to define such an order parameter. It needs to be continuously measurable and needs to show a sudden jump in value with the change from walking to running, but still remain stable throughout each of the separate behaviors of walking and running. Hoyt and Taylor (1981) noted that the different gaits found in horses, namely walking, trotting, and running, entail the smallest possible energy expenditure, and they suggested that minimal energy expenditure may be an important factor in determining the transition to different gait patterns. When a change in velocity affects the level of energy efficiency, a shift in the gait pattern occurs. However, this does not appear to be as simple for human gait, and causal mechanisms remain unclear (Usherwood & Bertram, 2001).

Bifurcations

Bifurcations result from a shift from one stable state or *attractor* to another. For example, if there is a shift from walking to running as shown in figure 2.9b, then the order parameter changes, resulting in what is termed a *phase transition* or *bifurcation*. This occurs as a result of a change in the *control parameter*. Figure 2.10 illustrates the notion of a bifurcation. The ball can be seen in different states of stability. When on top of the slope or hill (2.10b), the ball is in an unstable state and requires little energy to roll to either side into one of the troughs. These troughs represent stable states or attractors, and a large amount of energy would be required to shift the ball to a different state.

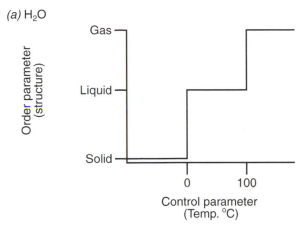

(a) H$_2$O

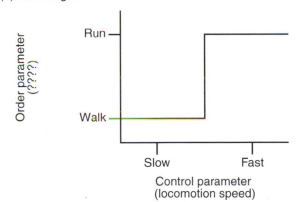

(b) Human gait

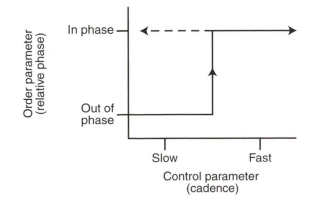

(c) Finger movements

Figure 2.9 Examples of dynamic pattern formation.
Adapted from Abernethy et al., 1995.

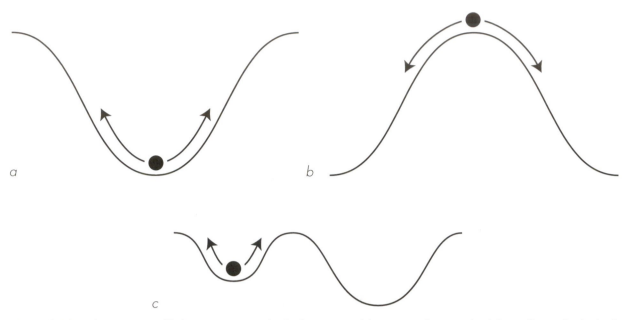

Figure 2.10 The process of bifurcation. In *(a)* the ball is in a stable state in the trough of the gully. In *(b)* the ball is in an unstable state. In *(c)* there is a series of possible states determined by the depth of the gullies.
Reprinted from Thelen and Smith, 1994.

One of the seminal experiments demonstrating a phase transition in relation to motor control is the bifurcation study by Kelso (1984). In this study, Kelso explored the oscillation of the two index fingers in either antiphase or in-phase mode, as shown in figure 2.11. The order parameter was the relative phase of the fingers (see figure 2.9*c*)—that is, either antiphase, with homologous muscle groups contracting in an alternating fashion, or in-phase, involving simultaneous contraction of homologous muscle groups. The control parameter was the oscillation frequency of the fingers. When this was systematically increased, there was a spontaneous shift in the order parameter from antiphase to in-phase. The reverse, however, did not occur. That is, if the subjects started with in-phase, there was not a shift to antiphase. Therefore, in-phase appears to be the preferred movement pattern at high frequencies. These findings have been verified in many studies that have examined a variety of muscle groups, including hands, arms, and ankles.

How resistant a behavior is to a **perturbation** is one measure of stability. For example, a young infant who has just taken his or her first steps has very little resistance to perturbation. Any change in the walking surface will quite likely result in the infant's falling over and returning to a more stable form of locomotion such as creeping. Another measure of stability is variability.

Variability

The early information-processing theorists viewed variability as a deviation from the ideal performance. It was usually measured by determining the variance or standard deviation from the mean. From

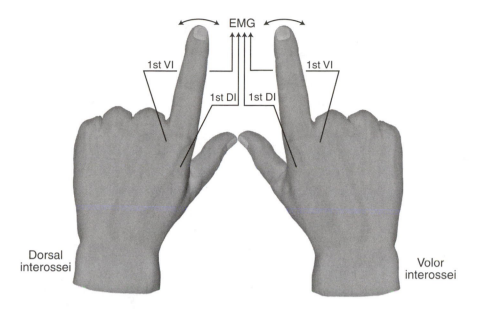

Figure 2.11 The bimanual phase transition paradigm developed by Kelso (1984). Adapted from Kelso, 1995.

a maturational perspective, variability was considered an indicator of abnormal development. For example, any variability in the time taken to achieve motor milestones, or any deviation from the normal sequence, was thought to be an indicator of impaired brain function (Touwen, 1978).

It is now well recognized that variability is an important component of the healthy infant (e.g., Piek, 2002; Touwen, 1978). A large range of spontaneous movements early in life allows infants to explore their own intrinsic dynamics (Turvey & Fitzpatrick, 1993), and a lack of variability in the newborn is considered an indicator of abnormal development (e.g., Piek, 2002; Prechtl, 1990). This issue is taken up further in chapter 10 when research examining variability in high-risk infants is discussed. However, it is important to recognize that variability has different meanings for different subdomains of motor control (Newell & Slifkin, 1998). Whereas large variability is important for the young infant who is exploring his or her body and environment, athletes aim to reduce variability in order to produce the best and most cost-effective performance in terms of energy required.

The introduction of the dynamic systems approach has raised the status of movement variability from its traditional interpretation as simply *noise* in the system to a defining feature of a behavior (Newell & Slifkin, 1998). From a dynamic systems perspective, variability is a measure of the strength and stability of a particular motor pattern or behavior. During a **phase shift**, the variability would be expected to increase until a stable state is reached. Therefore, understanding the structure as well as the degree of variability provides insight into the processes that lead to transitions to new behaviors (Thelen & Smith, 1994).

A Dynamic Systems Perspective of Infant Motor Development

Thelen and Smith (1994) provide an excellent representation of early motor development based on a dynamic systems perspective using an ontogenetic landscape (see figure 2.12). This depicts the changing stability and instability of movement from prenatal development to the development of walking. Different behaviors are depicted by separate troughs. The steepness of the walls indicates the level of stability of each of these behaviors. This can be related back to the earlier discussion on bifurcations, suggesting that shallow troughs represent less stable behaviors and as a result are more prone to bifurcation. In this landscape, the relative width of the troughs indicates movement variability. As preferred states emerge throughout development, the hills and troughs change shape depending on the relative stability of a given behavior at a given stage of development. Landscape models have become a popular way of representing motor development (see also Newell et al., 2003).

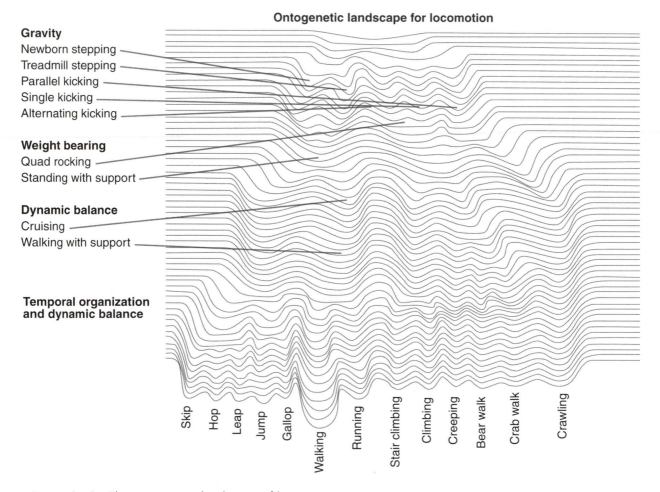

Figure 2.12   The ontogenetic landscape of locomotion.
Reprinted from Muchisky et al., 1996.

According to Ulrich and Ulrich (1993), the description of motor development from a dynamic systems perspective requires several basic tenets. Firstly, the organism must be a self-organizing system, with new behaviors occurring spontaneously as a result of the interaction of many different subsystems. That is, there is no single central controlling process. Subsystems can include nervous, musculoskeletal, perceptual, and affective, to name but a few. Furthermore, these subsystems mature at different times and rates, resulting in nonlinear development. Nonlinear development was recognized as early as 1945 by Gesell and Amatruda, who argued that "ontogenetic organization does not advance on an even front" (p. 164), in the principle of reciprocal interweaving. This view was revisited by Esther Thelen in 1986 in her depiction of locomotor development in infancy as a multilayered system, and by Thelen and Ulrich (1991) in their depiction of the development of alternating treadmill steps.

Figure 2.13 is a diagrammatic representation, redrawn from the original figures of Thelen (1986) and Thelen and Ulrich (1991), showing how the different developing systems produce new behavior in a nonlinear fashion. In this case there are four different subsystems. Assume, for example, that the behavior is creeping. Hypothetically, System 1 may refer to appropriate vestibular development needed for balance. This is at the level required for creeping right from birth. System 2 could refer to the motivation needed by the infant to crawl. The infant must want to crawl. System 3 may refer to limb strength, and finally, System 4 may be postural control. Only when all subsystems have reached a particular level does the new behavior emerge. As each system matures at a different rate, there is nonlinear development of the behavior depicted on the right side of the figure. In a real situation, there are of course many subsystems involved.

Recent studies (Corbetta & Bojczyk, 2002; Corbetta & Thelen, 2002) provide support for this dynamic systems multilayered view of development. For example, Corbetta and Bojczyk noted that when infants

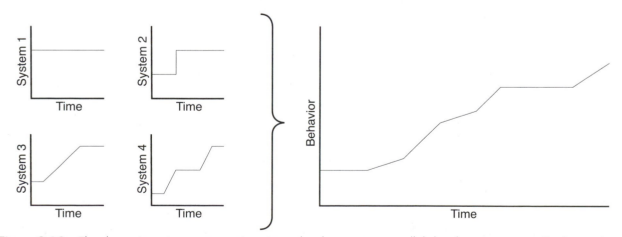

Figure 2.13   The dynamic systems perspective views development as parallel developing systems. Each system acts as a rate controller. The horizontal line is time; the vertical is some quantity of a system or behavior.
Reprinted from Haywood and Getchell, 2005.

began to walk, their reaching pattern shifted from competent unimanual reaching to an increase in two-handed reaching. The authors argue that this is a direct result of the new movement pattern, that of walking, a skill that appears unrelated to reaching behavior. As infants gained balance control, the unimanual pattern reemerged. Hence, the infant's reaching pattern self-organizes in response to the emergence of a new and seemingly unrelated movement pattern (walking). A similar argument was presented by Corbetta and Thelen to account for the fluctuating asymmetries in infant reaching that have been observed.

Each new behavior can be described or constrained by one or more collective variables. Collective variables provide a simple definition of a highly complex behavior (Ulrich & Ulrich, 1993). Furthermore, the infant has preferred states, acting as dynamic attractors. If these states become unstable, then new behavior may emerge. It is worth noting from a historical perspective that the notion of the *emergence* of behavior has been described by developmental psychologists for nearly a century. For example, the paper by Lovejoy (1926, cited in Carmichael, 1946) titled "The Meanings of 'Emergence' and Its Mode" provides a critique of what is meant by emergence. Carmichael defined emergence as "a relationship between events antecedent in time and a new and different event which is itself also described" (p. 45). This remains an appropriate definition for the present-day dynamic systems approach.

The example in figure 2.13 includes four subsystems related to biological (sensory, cognitive, and neuromuscular) aspects of the individual. However, according to Newell (1986), factors that influence development can come from three sources—the organism, the environment, and the task. Newell termed these factors *constraints*, as they are features or boundaries that restrict movement. According to Newell, "The patterns of coordination that emerge during infancy and early childhood are due to the changing constraints imposed on action" (p. 345). Hence, in order to understand how movements emerge it is necessary to understand the role of these constraints.

Newell's (1986) model of constraints is depicted in figure 2.14. The circular arrows reflect the continuous interaction among all three types of constraints. The *organismic constraints* were divided by Newell into two categories. Factors such as body height and weight change slowly with development and as such are relatively time independent. These are termed *structural constraints*. Relatively time-dependent factors such as the development of synaptic connections or the infant's attention are termed *functional constraints*. Constraints that are considered external to the organism have been termed *environmental constraints*, and include variables such as gravity, ambient temperature, and friction. An important environmental constraint discussed in the first chapter is the prenatal versus the postnatal environment. This has a considerable impact on the infant's motor coordination.

The most distinctive aspect of Newell's model is the introduction of *task constraints*. These are considered to be **phylogenetic** as opposed

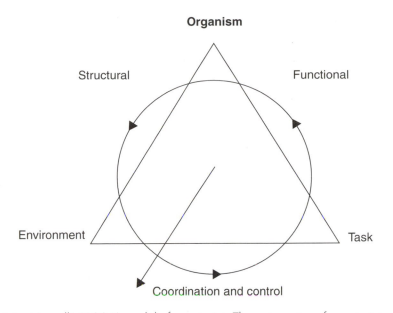

Figure 2.14 Newell's (1986) model of constraint. The categories of constraints specify the optimal pattern of control and coordination.

to ontogenetic factors (Newell, 1989). Three categories of task constraints are outlined by Newell (1986). Firstly, there is the task goal, which specifies the outcome of the particular action. For example, an infant shakes a rattle in order to hear the sound it makes. Next, the response dynamics are often specified or constrained by rules. An important characteristic of competitive sport is to optimize performance within the constraints that are imposed by the rules. Also, different performers' interpretations of these rules or constraints can lead to quite different coordination patterns. Similarly, the response dynamics are often constrained by the implements or machines used for a particular action. Such factors as the size and weight of an object to be manipulated will affect performance and the ability to do a particular task. Object size is an issue that has been studied extensively in relation to the development of grasping in infancy and is discussed more fully in chapter 5.

Recently, the issue of phase transitions throughout development has elicited considerable interest among developmentalists (Hopkins et al., 1993). This interest was highlighted in an article by van der Mass and Hopkins (1998) titled *Developmental Transitions,* which appeared in a special edition of the journal *British Journal of Developmental Psychology.* The publication focused on development in general and includes several papers discussing the identification and modeling of developmental transitions based on a dynamic systems perspective. Developmentalists have been discussing developmental transitions for the last century, although the terminology has been quite different. Maturationists and cognitive theorists have used the term *stages of development,* as opposed to *developmental transitions.* However, as van der Maas and Hopkins point out, earlier research focused on describing these transitions with little attempt to understand the processes that resulted in such transitions.

There is another important consideration in research examining developmental transitions. This is the issue of individual differences. Averaging out development tends to lead to a smoothing of the developmental "bumps," or, in other words, eliminating the noise or variability. In order to examine phase transitions it is important to look closely at these individual "bumps" or changes to obtain a true understanding of the nonlinear changes in development. Von Hofsten (1993) provided an excellent illustration of this issue relating to the emergence of stereopsis, or binocular space perception, in human infants. Group data indicated a relatively linear increase in the achievement of stereopsis in infants from the age of two months to around six or seven months. However, this says very little of the actual time frame for this achievement for individuals. When individual data were examined, infants were found to achieve stereopsis at different ages, and the transition to stereopsis was quite sudden and dramatic, occurring over the space of a few weeks. The individual data provide a more accurate interpretation of the processes occurring during this developmental transition than is apparent from examination of the group data.

■■■ How Does This Research Inform Therapeutic Practice?

The emergence of the dynamic systems approach provides a new theoretical framework in which to investigate developmental transitions. This will provide a greater understanding of how new behaviors emerge. Also, it may provide clues as to why some infants produce abnormal or inappropriate behaviors compared with the mainstream. If it is possible to identify the systems that are important in determining a particular transition, researchers may be able to locate which system or systems are slower or different in development. These systems may be considered as the *rate limiters* or *rate controllers* (von Hofsten, 1993). The implications are evident in terms of early identification and intervention strategies.

Summary

This chapter provided a historical perspective of the theoretical approaches utilized in understanding infant motor development since the beginning of the 20th century. The maturational approach of the early 20th century saw the emergence and dominance of researchers such as Arnold Gesell and Myrtle McGraw, whose views are still widely utilized to the present day. This approach, which emphasized stages of development and age-related changes, led to the creation of many of the current tests of infant motor development that are reviewed later in part III of this text.

The cognitive approaches emerged around the middle of the 20th century. Jean Piaget heightened the status of early motor development with his view that early actions were important, not only for later motor development but also for cognitive development. Nevertheless, cognitive theorists did not show a great deal of interest in infant motor development, and as a result, little new research occurred in this area in the middle of the last century.

It was not until the 1980s, when the ecological approach emerged, that a new interest in motor development arose. The introduction of the dynamic systems approach has led to a huge resurgence in research on motor development in infancy. Not only has this provided a greater understanding of the processes that lead to motor coordination in infancy, but this theoretical perspective also has potential for the development of new approaches to therapy and intervention.

three ■■■

Motor Control and the Brain
Motor Development and Neural Plasticity

chapter objectives

This chapter will do the following:

- Describe the main central nervous system structures involved in motor control

- Discuss environmental influences on brain structure and function and their implications for intervention

- Discuss how different theorists have incorporated central nervous system involvement into theories of motor development

The central nervous system (CNS) is clearly an important component of motor control, but how does it function in the early development of motor coordination? In the previous chapter, the role of the CNS was seen to vary depending on which theoretical perspective was adopted. For example, for proponents of a purely maturational viewpoint, development is determined solely by the maturation of the CNS. As new brain structures mature, new movement patterns or behaviors emerge. This implies that investigating such processes may lead to information on how motor coordination emerges in the infant. However, it is now clear that the story of development is not this straightforward. While new behaviors are dependent on the maturation of appropriate neural structures and connections, they are also dependent on many other factors—biological, environmental, and even task related (Newell, 1986).

Research into the brain structure and function involved in motor coordination has become increasingly popular. While a comprehensive review of such research is beyond the scope of this book, this chapter aims to provide a brief description of the major neural structures involved in motor coordination, with specific attention given to the environmental influences on brain structure and function. It concludes with a discussion of the types of models developed to explain CNS involvement in early motor development. These views include maturational, selectionist, and constructionist approaches.

Neurophysiology of Movement

The major brain structures involved in motor control—cerebral cortex, cerebellum, basal ganglia, brainstem, and spinal cord—are outlined in figure 3.1. These are described separately in the following subsections. For more extensive descriptions of the brain's role in motor control, there are several volumes available (e.g., Abernethy et al., 1996; Banich, 1997; Latash, 1998a; Porter & Lemon, 1993).

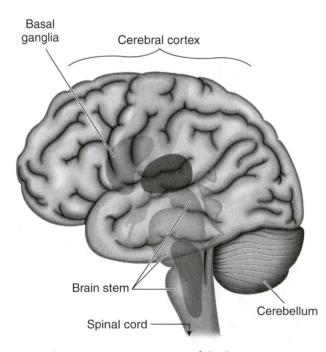

Figure 3.1 Major motor areas of the brain.
Reprinted from Wilmore and Costill, 2004.

Cerebral Cortex

The *cerebral cortex* is part of the largest brain structure, the *cerebrum* (also termed *telencephalon*), which consists of two separate hemispheres connected by a mass of neural fibers called the *corpus callosum*. The surface of the cerebrum, the *cerebral cortex*, is between 2 and 5 mm deep and can be divided into four pairs of lobes, frontal, parietal, temporal, and occipital, with each represented in each hemisphere. They are delineated by deep fissures (see figure 3.2).

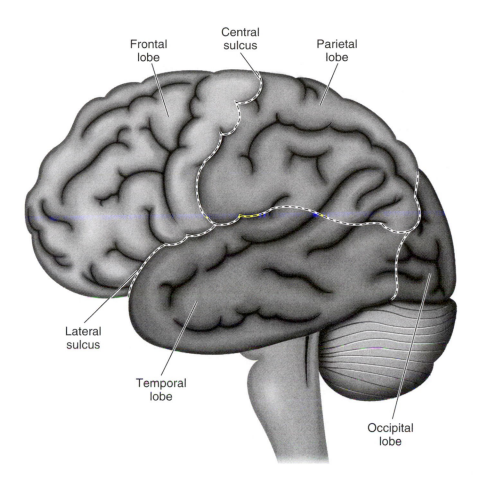

Figure 3.2   The lobes of the cerebral cortex.
Reprinted from Wilmore and Costill, 1999.

Within the frontal lobe are structures of major importance for the control of voluntary movement. These include the *primary motor area* (or *motor cortex*), which is directly in front of the *central sulcus* (see figure 3.2); the *premotor area*, which is anterior to the motor cortex and contains the *premotor cortex* (on the lateral surface); and the *supplementary motor area* (in the superior and **medial** areas).

The frontal cortical regions of the brain are considered the most significant evolutionary development of our species. These areas are slow to develop, with a long postnatal maturation period. As a result, they are extremely vulnerable to neurodevelopmental disorders (Bradshaw, 2003). This aspect is discussed further in the last section of this book dealing with abnormal motor development.

While distinct regions of the brain are given separate names, a major feature of these various structures is their vast array of complex interconnections, making for a continuous interplay among them. Figure 3.3 illustrates the complexity of the interconnections between the motor areas and other parts of the CNS. The motor areas receive input from other areas of the cerebral cortex (i.e., *cortico-cortical* inputs), particularly the parietal cortex, which receives kinesthetic information essential

■■■ The frontal lobe of the cerebral cortex contains the primary motor cortex, the premotor cortex, and the supplementary motor area, which are essential for motor control.

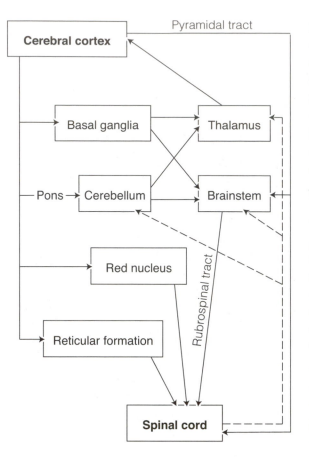

Figure 3.3 Schematic representation of the major motor pathways.

Adapted from Greer, 1984.

for appropriate motor control. The motor areas also receive input from structures outside the cerebrum, in particular, *thalamocortical* projections from the ventrobasal nuclei of the thalamus. The *thalamus*, considered to play a key role in sensorimotor integration, receives information from the other main CNS regions essential for motor control, namely, the spinal cord, basal ganglia, and cerebellum (Latash, 1998a).

Output pathways are equally complex, with projections to areas such as the basal ganglia, cerebellum, the red nucleus, and the reticular formation, but particularly to the spinal cord. Projections from the motor areas of the cortex can go directly to the muscles via the spinal cord. The direct pathway is the *corticospinal* or *pyramidal tract*. The indirect pathway, via the other main structures involved in motor control, is the *extrapyramidal tract*. Approximately half the spinal cord's 1 million efferent axons are projected directly from the primary motor cortex, and a large proportion of the remaining fibers are from the supplementary motor area (Latash, 1998a). There are two corticospinal tracts, one for each hemisphere. These cross over at the upper end of the spinal cord so that the left hemisphere controls the voluntary musculature of the right side, and the right hemisphere controls the left.

Is there a relationship between areas of the motor cortex and different muscles of the body? This question was investigated at the beginning of the 20th century by Charles Sherrington (1906) using chimpanzees and gorillas. Sherrington applied electrical stimulation to the brain surface while recording the responding motor output and discovered that stimulation of particular localized areas of the cerebral cortex resulted in responses from particular parts of the body. This can be seen in figure 3.4, which shows Sherrington's *topographical map* of the motor cortex in the brain of a chimpanzee, indicating which areas of the cortex were linked with which part of the body. Sherrington did point out, however, that there was a great deal of overlap between these different areas.

Among those who worked with Sherrington in Oxford was Wilder Penfield, who was the first to publish topographical mappings in humans. Penfield used patients who were undergoing surgery for the removal of cerebral tumors. These patients were under local anesthesia and therefore were conscious. Direct observations of responses were recorded during stimulation of the human brain with weak electrical shocks. In a procedure similar to that used by Sherrington (1906),

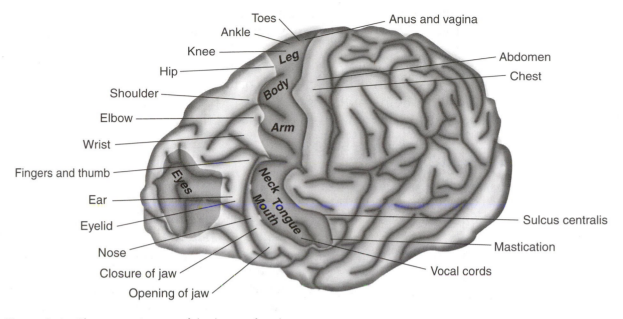

Figure 3.4 Sherrington's map of the brain of a chimpanzee.
Adapted from Grünbaum and Sherrington, 1906.

Penfield and Rasmussen (1952) produced a topographical map of the human motor cortex, shown in figure 3.5, by applying weak electrical pulses to distinct areas of the motor cortex and observing the resultant muscle contractions.

A significant finding was that all muscles are not represented proportionally in the motor cortex on the basis of size, but rather on the basis of precision. For example, it can be seen that the hand and mouth represent around two-thirds of the total area of the motor cortex. Another important discovery was that the **distal** musculature (i.e., of the extremities) was entirely **contralateral,** that is, on opposite sides of the body from the controlling side of the motor cortex. For example, the left motor cortex controls the right hand, and the right motor cortex the left hand. **Proximal** muscles (those close to the trunk of the body) were represented in the motor cortex of the cerebral hemisphere on both the **ipsilateral** (i.e., same), and the contralateral sides of the body. As stimulation was

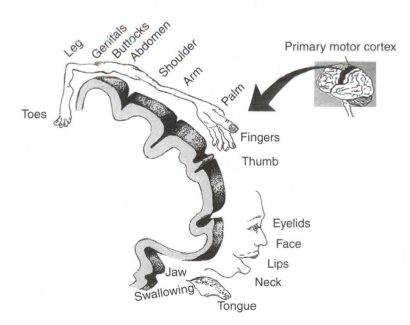

Figure 3.5 The representation as a homunculus of movements of the human body as depicted by Penfield and Rasmussen (1952). These resulted from stimulation of the contralateral cerebral cortex.
Reprinted from B. Abernethy et al., 2004.

moved forward into the premotor cortex, gross movements of muscle groups, rather than fine movements of discrete muscle groups, were observed.

These findings imply a neatly organized representation of the various body parts within the cerebral cortex. However, recent research has indicated the incredible **plasticity** of these so-called representations. These studies are discussed in the section on plasticity.

Cerebellum

The second largest brain structure, the *cerebellum,* is also crucial for motor control and is considered part of the extrapyramidal system. It is located below the occipital lobe of the cerebral cortex, behind the brainstem. Like the cerebrum, the cerebellum contains two hemispheres separated by a midline ridge called the *vermis.* There are three lobes, the anterior, posterior, and flocculonodular lobes. These are separated by the primary and posterior-lateral fissures. The cerebellum also includes three pairs of nuclei, the fastigial, the interposed, and the dentate nuclei, that are symmetrically arranged in the midline (see figure 3.6).

Like the cortical areas, the cerebellum has many interconnections with other parts of the CNS, although **afferent,** or incoming, fibers are far more prevalent than **efferent,** or outgoing, fibers (Latash, 1998a). Afferent fibers are of two types— the climbing fibers, which originate in the medulla (located in the brainstem), and the mossy fibers, originating primarily from the brainstem and spinal cord. Like the motor cortex, the spinocerebellar tract forms a topographical map of somatosensory information on the cerebellar surface. Efferent fibers are of only one type, called Purkinje cells, which project mainly to the thalamus and the brainstem. These inhibitory cells are the largest neurons in the brain (Latash).

The cerebellum has been termed *the seat of motor coordination* (Abernethy et al., 1996), as it has been associated with functions essential to smooth, coordinated motor control such as timing, motor learning, and regulation of muscle tone. Evidence from neuroimaging and patients with cerebellar lesions has suggested that an internal timing mechanism is located within the cerebellum (Ivry, 2003; Ivry & Spencer, 2004). Poor cerebellar function has been linked to problems associated with children who have motor coordination problems in disorders such as developmental coordination disorder (e.g., Lundy-Ekman et al., 1991; Piek & Skinner, 1999; Williams et al., 1992) and attention

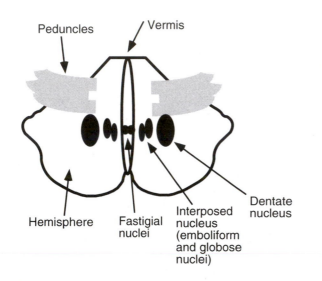

Figure 3.6 Dorsal representation of the cerebellum showing the hemispheres, vermis, and nuclei buried deep in the white matter. Three pairs of peduncles connect the cerebellum to other neural structures.

Reprinted from Latash, 1998.

The cerebellum is important for the appropriate timing of movements.

deficit hyperactivity disorder (e.g., Bradshaw, 2003). However, another set of brain structures, the basal ganglia, has also been implicated in these disorders.

Basal Ganglia

The *basal ganglia* are located deep within the inner layers of the cerebral hemispheres near the thalamus. They consist of five interconnected nuclei that, like the cerebellum, are part of the extrapyramidal system. Two nuclei, the *caudate nucleus* and the *putamen* (see figure 3.7), form the *striatum,* which is primarily involved in input from the cerebral cortex and the thalamus. The major output nuclei are the *internal globus pallidus* and the *substantia nigra,* which project to the ventral thalamus. The globus pallidus, which is phylogenetically the oldest nucleus, has both internal and external parts, each of which appears to have quite different connections and functions. Both the external globus pallidus and the remaining nucleus, the subthalamic nucleus, are interconnected with other nuclei of the basal ganglia with no direct pathways to other parts of the brain.

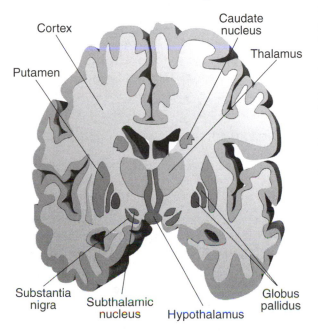

Cortex

Putamen

Caudate nucleus

Thalamus

Substantia nigra

Subthalamic nucleus

Hypothalamus

Globus pallidus

Figure 3.7 The location of the basal ganglia.

The basal ganglia play an important role in the mediation between the higher and lower brain structures. Their functions have been investigated in humans, primarily through examination of diseases that result from dysfunctional basal ganglia activity such as Parkinson's disease and Huntington's disease. Parkinson's disease is known to be linked with a loss of production of dopamine, a neurotransmitter essential for the nigrostriatal pathway. Around 80% of the total dopamine found in the brain is contained within the basal ganglia (Latash, 1998a). It is thought that Parkinson's disease is a result of a loss of neurons in the substantia nigra, which produces dopamine. It is this drop in dopamine secretion that is thought to produce the **hypokinesia**, or **bradykinesia** (slowing of the movements), and **akinesia** (difficulty in movement initiation) found in patients with Parkinson's disease. In contrast, **hyperkinesia**, or excessive movements, are found in Huntington's disease, where there appears to be a loss of projections between the striatum and external globus pallidus. The motor excesses found in children with attention deficit hyperactivity disorder have also been linked to the basal ganglia (Swanson et al., 1998). There is some evidence that the basal ganglia may influence variability in force production, which is also disrupted in disorders such as developmental coordination disorder (e.g., Lundy-Ekman et al., 1991; Pitcher et al., 2002).

Brainstem

The *brainstem*, located in front of the cerebellum, links the spinal cord with the cerebrum (see figure 3.1) and contains three major areas of significance to motor control, the *medulla*, the *pons*, and the *reticular formation*. The medulla, located directly above the spinal cord, is important for autonomic functions such as respiration, cardiovascular function, and digestion. The pons, a bulbous structure above the medulla, is also involved in respiratory control. Both the medulla and pons are important for the integration of information from the cerebral cortex, cerebellum, and basal ganglia as well as afferent sensory information. They are important for the control of involuntary movements, in particular those linked to muscle tone and posture.

The reticular formation is a network of neural cells and fibers extending through the brainstem that are important in the regulation of the cerebral cortex. Descending fibers that project directly into the spinal cord are considered important for supraspinal reflex function.

Spinal Cord

The *spinal cord* is located within the vertebral column and consists of pairs of spinal nerves responsible for relaying afferent information to the higher centers and efferent information from the brain to the muscles. Figure 3.8 is a cross section of the spinal cord showing the posterior, or **dorsal**, root involved in transporting the afferent information, as well as the anterior, or **ventral**, root, which contains primarily alpha motor neurons and is involved in transporting efferent information to the muscles.

Another primary role of the spinal cord is in the production of "nonconscious" spinal reflexes, defined by Latash (1998a) as muscle contractions that occur as a result of an external stimulus that cannot be influenced by an intentional or conscious act. The reflexes found in early infancy were discussed in detail in chapter 1, although there is considerable debate over whether many of these early responses are in fact reflexes (e.g., Touwen, 1984).

Reflexes vary in complexity, from the simplest, *monosynaptic reflex* involving two neurons, and hence only one synapse, to *polysynaptic reflexes* involving

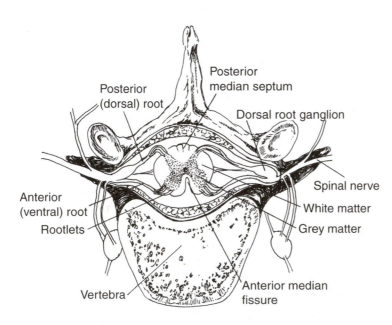

Figure 3.8   A cross section of the spinal cord.

Reprinted from Abernethy et al., 2004.

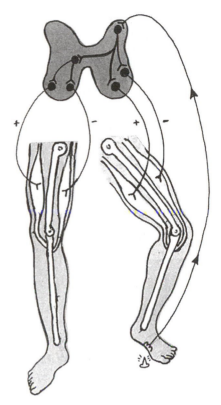

Figure 3.9 A representation of the flexion withdrawal reflex and the crossed extensor reflex.

Reprinted from Abernethy et al., 2004.

many synapses. One of the best-known monosynaptic reflexes is the knee jerk that occurs as a result of a tap on the patella tendon of the knee. This is an example of the *stretch* or *myotatic* reflex, an important reflex as it is a reaction to excessive stretch of the muscles. These reflexes are important in the prevention of damage to the muscles through overstretching. When the muscle spindles detect excessive stretch, an impulse is sent to the dorsal root where the afferent neuron synapses directly with the alpha motor neuron. An impulse is then sent back to the extrafusal muscle fibers, resulting in their contraction, which relieves the excessive stretch.

The flexion reflex is an example of a polysynaptic reflex. A good example in the infant is the withdrawal reflex (shown in figure 1.4 in chapter 1), an important reflex for the protection of the infant against stimuli that may cause damage. The pathway for the flexion reflex is shown in figure 3.9. Notice also the crossed extensor reflex, which maintains stability of the opposite limb to prevent the individual from falling over. In the case of the withdrawal reflex in the infant, both limbs often demonstrate the flexion reflex as the infant pulls both limbs away from the noxious stimulus. The crossed extensor reflex is not needed for an infant lying supine. This demonstrates unique aspects of the early reflexes found in infants.

Brain Development and Neural Plasticity

The newborn infant's brain is only 25% of the size of an adult brain, and the thickness of the motor cortex does not reach adult proportion until around two and a half years of age. Why is the human infant born so immature? What are the advantages and disadvantages of this phenomenon? The generally accepted explanation is that as a result of evolution, the infant's brain size has developed to such a degree that if it were fully developed at birth, the head would be too large for the pelvic structure of the mother. Hence, the infant needs to be born before the brain is fully developed.

There have been other explanations to account for this immaturity. For example, Prechtl (1993) argued that the newborn's body weight must also be considered. A comparison of maternal body weight and newborn body weight in different primates demonstrates that the human infant is considerably heavier than it should be for the mother's body capabilities. "For a body weight of Western mothers of about 60kg, a newborn infant should weigh not more than 2200g, but actually weighs about 3400g. African pygmy mothers of about 40kg have babies of 2200g" (Prechtl, 1993, p. 47). Again, evolution can account for this increase in body weight for the neonate. Around 3% of the body weight in the monkey consists of fat, whereas humans have around 16% body fat. Approximately 80% of human body fat is subcutaneously localized to act as thermal insulation to compensate for the loss of fur that provides the necessary insulation in other primates.

Gesell and Amatruda (1945) suggested that this "lengthened stretch of developmental immaturity is one of the most impressive end products of evolution" (p. 160), reflecting the limitations of the newborn infant, but also a huge potential in terms of plasticity. One of the most significant effects of such an immature infant is the potential for considerable variability in the developing newborn. This has both advantages and disadvantages, namely the potential for problems to occur with inappropriate conditions but also the potential for remediation with appropriate conditions.

Several different processes are involved in the development and maturation of the brain and nervous system. The process of myelination was described in chapter 1. It begins at around 16 weeks following conception and results in improved neural conduction. At birth, myelination of the nerve cells is not complete, with different parts of the brain being myelinated at different times. For example, myelination of the connections between the cerebellum and cortex begins only after the infant is born and is not completed until around four years of age. These connections are important for motor coordination. It can be seen that this is a case in which appropriate maturation of the nervous system would affect the child's motor ability.

An important process in brain development is **synaptogenesis,** which results in an increase in neuronal connections. Like myelination, this begins very early in development (five weeks gestational age according to Herschkowitz, 1988) and continues after birth with rapid growth and differentiation in the first few years of life. The development of these connections is associated with both genetic and environmental/experiential factors (Greenough et al., 1987; Herschkowitz).

It was long considered that the neural growth that occurred once the infant was born was not due to any increase in the number of nerve cells. Rather, the increasing mass was attributed to the factors described earlier, such as growth of the neurons, particularly in terms of their connecting branches, and myelination of axons, as well as generation of glial cells and new vascular and connective tissue (Purves, 1994). This view was tested by Rakic in rhesus macaque monkeys, and the findings were published in *Science* in 1985 (Rakic, 1985). Rakic supported this earlier view by providing evidence that all neurons in the cerebral cortex had been produced in prenatal and very early postnatal life. The finding in the rhesus monkey was then generalized to humans.

Recent research has now provided evidence that this may not be correct. Evidence that new cortical neuron generation occurs in humans has been provided by Shankle and colleagues (1998, 1999). They reanalyzed a database developed by Conel from 1939 to 1967 that contained neuroanatomical measurements of the cerebral cortex of infants and children aged 0, 1, 3, 6, 15, 24, 48, and 72 months. Their findings demonstrated that from the ages of 24 to 72 months there was a 60% to 78% increase in the total number of cortical neurons compared with the number at birth. At 72 months, the total number of cortical neurons found (1.156×10^{10}) was within the range found by other researchers in adult populations (1.0-2.50×10^{10}).

Shankle and colleagues (1999) also noted there were both rises and falls in the total number of cortical neurons over the age range examined. This may be linked to the process of **apoptosis,** or programmed cell death. In the embryonic period, there appears to be an overproduction of nerve cells. These are subsequently eliminated in postnatal life through apoptosis, which appears to be important for greater specificity of function. Hamburger and Oppenheim (1982) found that cell death may not necessarily be "programmed," as it can be influenced by changes in the target that is innervated. Generally, between 49% and 60% of motor neurons die in the first trimester of incubation in the chick embryo. However, if the size of the skeletal muscle mass that is innervated is altered (by removal of a limb bud or addition of an extra bud), there is a corresponding change in the cell death of the motor neurons innervating this area. That is, cell death appears to be dependent upon the activity of appropriate pathways (Changeux & Danchin, 1976; Sporns & Edelman, 1993). This is consistent with the suggestion of Gould and colleagues (1999) that new cortical cells must be "used" in order for them to survive. Gould and colleagues provided evidence that rhesus monkeys continue to produce cortical neurons throughout adulthood. Furthermore, these cells appear to last only one to two weeks unless they are involved in new learning.

It appears, then, that the brain has the capacity to change the number of nerve cells throughout the person's life span, although these changes appear to be more dramatic in the early years. This is an example of plasticity, whereby the CNS is modified through development and environmental influences. Greenough and colleagues (1987) suggested that there may be two different types of plasticity used in the storage of information resulting from experience. "Experience-expectant" plasticity may be dependent on a critical period in which information that is common to all members of the species (e.g., elements of pattern perception) is stored. This may develop as a result of selection and pruning of overproduced nerve cells as described earlier. Information that is unique to the individual is thought to be stored through an "experience-dependent" process that relies on the active formation of new connections. This emphasizes the view that sensorimotor experience is an important component of neuroanatomical change.

Normal

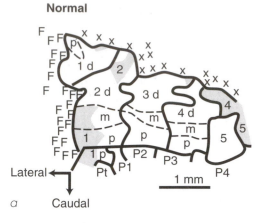

a   Caudal

62 days after digit 3 amputation

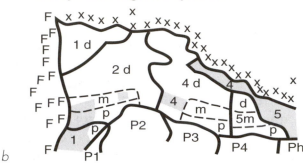

b

Figure 3.10 Changes in the topographical mapping in the somatosensory cortical region *(a)* before and *(b)* 62 days after amputation of digit 3. Note that following amputation the area occupied previously by digit 3 has been taken over by the adjacent digits 2 and 4.

Reprinted from Merzenich et al., 1990.

■■■ Topographical maps found in the motor cortex are not "hard-wired" but are influenced by the level of activity of the body part that maps onto the given area of the cortex.

Another example of plasticity can be seen when the effects of the environment on the topographical maps of the cerebral cortex are investigated. It appears that these topographical areas can be modified through experience. This has been demonstrated by several ingenious studies by Merzenich and colleagues (Jenkins et al., 1990; Merzenich et al., 1990), who investigated the primary somatosensory cortex in New World monkeys. Merzenich and colleagues (1990) initially mapped the fingers and found that these were represented in accurate topographical order in the cortex. However, when one or two of the fingers were amputated, the space that was originally occupied by these fingers in the cortex was eventually "taken over" by the palm of the hand and the adjacent digits (see figure 3.10). In another study, fingers were sutured together. In this case, after several months, the cortical areas representing these two digits merged together and overlapped. The boundaries between these areas appeared again once the fingers were separated. Training could also affect the cortical mapping. When monkeys were trained to pick up their food reward with only the tips of one or two fingers, it was found that the area represented by these particular fingers became greatly enlarged.

These studies demonstrate that function is not inherent in the structure. That is, there is no "hard-wiring" of structure with function. Kelso (1995) suggested that the mechanism for these changes is not a migrational growth of neurons. Rather, changes occur as a result of the amount of time that the neurons are activated, producing a spatial shift in the collective activity of the appropriate neurons. This is also one of the basic tenets of Gerald Edelman's neuronal selectionist theory of behavior, which is discussed later in this chapter.

Function of Central Nervous System in Motor Development

In the previous chapter, several theoretical perspectives were discussed to account for motor control in general. The role of the CNS is considered to be quite different for these different approaches. The remainder of this chapter addresses how this role varies for a maturational approach compared with a dynamic systems approach.

Central Pattern Generators—a Maturational Perspective

Motor activity is often rhythmical and cyclical in nature, such as the early spontaneous activity that is found even before the infant is born (e.g., Robertson, 1990). It has been suggested that the rhythmical patterned nature of locomotion is generated by lower centers in the CNS, namely neural circuits found in the spinal cord (van Heijst et al., 1999) that have often been termed central pattern generators, or CPGs (Forssberg, 1985; Hadders-Algra, 2002). A CPG "explicitly generates a rhythmic neural activity that is later transformed into a rhythmic muscle activity leading to a rhythmic behavior, such as locomotion" (Latash, 1998a, p. 172).

The notion of the CPG emerged as a result of studies on other animal species, particularly the early work of Hamburger and colleagues around the middle of the 20th century (Hamburger & Oppenheim, 1967). In contrast to the notion that early motor activity was purely reflexive, this early research on chick embryos demonstrated that motor behavior could be generated by the CNS without any sensory input and thus was not reflexive (Bekoff, 1981). Basic patterns of leg movements that were identified in chick embryos would reappear once chicks had hatched if sensory input was removed through deafferentation. Bekoff (1995) suggested that these neural circuits found in the embryo were retained rather than replaced throughout development, and that "This circuitry is normally modulated by sensory input to produce the more complex patterns characteristic of later behaviors" (p. 198). That is, CPGs identified in the embryo are retained and incorporated into more complex networks with development.

The CPG has been used to describe locomotor control in other species (e.g., Grillner, 1975) and also used to account for the regularity of early spontaneous movements through excitatory and inhibitory connections in the brain and spinal cord (Sprague & Newell, 1996). Latash (1998a) describes the connections of a CPG, as shown in figure 3.11, indicating that they can be driven either by a "higher center" or by afferent information.

Evidence for CPGs in the spinal cord of mammals has been provided by experiments involving the complete transection of the spinal cord in the cat while maintaining intact sensory input. Although cats were able to produce a walking pattern in the hindlimbs that closely resembled the pattern found in intact cats (i.e., providing evidence for CPGs), there was no control of postural equilibrium and muscle tone, and no anticipation of obstacles obstructing the hindlimb. Parameters such as movement intensity, muscle tone, and adaptation are thought to be controlled by supraspinal mechanisms.

In another review, Vilensky and O'Connor (1997) examined whether there was evidence of CPGs in humans. They took a phylogenetic

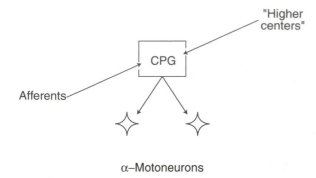

Figure 3.11 Representation of a central pattern generator (CPG), driven by both descending efferent and ascending afferent information.
Reprinted from Latash, 1998a.

perspective, investigating evidence found in mammals such as cats, dogs, and primates. Although it has been shown that cats and dogs can regain their ability to support weight and generate stepping movements following complete transection of the spinal cord, complete transection in the monkey has provided mixed results. It has been shown that extensive transections of around 75% result in monkeys regaining their locomotor abilities. In contrast, in humans, there has been little evidence of improvement in stepping movements or weight-bearing ability even with incomplete transections. However, Villensky and O'Connor (1997) suggest that the techniques used to produce stepping in nonprimates are inappropriate for primates. They were able to elicit stepping movements in squirrel monkeys with completely transected spinal cords by using different forms of stimulation, and they argued that CPGs in primates require "greater and/or different forms of stimulation than that required for nonprimate mammals" (p. 289).

Evidence to suggest that CPGs are found in humans comes primarily from isolated cases. Observations of humans with spinal damage have provided some evidence that involuntary stepping movements are present, suggesting the presence of CPGs primarily in the lower thoracic and upper lumbar areas (Latash, 1998a). However, some investigators (e.g., Thelen & Spencer, 1998) are far from convinced that these play a major role in motor coordination, suggesting that the dynamic systems approach provides a better interpretation of how early motor patterns emerge.

Neuronal Selection—A Dynamic Systems Perspective

In attempting to explain brain function as a dynamic system, Kelso (1995) described the brain as "like a river, whose eddies, vortices, and turbulent structures do not exist independent of the flow itself" (p. 1). The dynamic activity of the brain is what is responsible for mental processes and cannot be considered at a single or static point in time. Kelso (1995) argued for a move away from a *reductionist* perspective, in which the complexities of behavior are investigated via efforts to explain macroscopic states through microscopic analysis. For example, how does activation of individual parts of the brain provide information on brain function, when there is such interconnectedness between different brain regions?

Kelso (1995) suggested that the same self-organizing processes that describe motor behavior can also describe brain function at several levels of organization. Not only can motor control be accounted for by the dynamic self-organizing principles described in chapter 2, but other behaviors such as perception, learning, and memory can also be described by "meta-stable spatiotemporal patterns of brain activity that are themselves produced by cooperative interactions among neural clusters" (p. 257). One theory on brain function that incorporates the view of self-organization is the neuronal selection approach put forward by Gerald Edelman and colleagues (Edelman, 1987, 2001; Edelman & Mountcastle, 1978).

Edelman (1987) supported Gibson's views on perception–action coupling (see chapter 2) and developed a theory that attempts to account for direct perception at the neural level. An important aspect of his approach is the variable nature of brain connections. Not only do these differ between individuals (i.e., there are no two identical brains), but the connections within the brain also vary from moment to moment (Edelman, 2001). The considerable plasticity of brain connections was discussed earlier. The neuronal selection theory is dependent on this variable nature of brain connections.

Individual variability is determined through experience and development. From a developmental perspective, it is proposed that successive selection of neural connections will produce a stable repertoire of movements. This repertoire can be modified according to the changing demands of the growing infant and the environment (Sporns & Edelman, 1993). Changeux and Dehaene (1989) originally suggested that this "stable repertoire" emerged through a progressive regression of synapses as the infant develops. That is, part of the learning process appears to be the regression of the multi-innervations present at birth to the selection of a single motor pathway, which would consequently reduce the likelihood of subsequent variation. Apoptosis, described earlier, is an important principle of neuroembryology, whereby selective pruning is believed to result in greater specificity.

According to Sporns and Edelman (1993), the selection process is dependent upon activity of the appropriate pathways. That is, the eventual neural pathway is dependent upon the spontaneous or evoked activity that occurs prior to selection. Sensory input that is generated from every movement produces local network maps that overlap with the motor system. As a result of repeated perception–action cycles, stable actions become consolidated, whereas less functional actions disappear. These *somatic selective processes* (Sporns & Edelman) produce diverse output as a result of the dynamic variability of local collectives of interconnected neurons called "neuronal groups."

Sporns and Edelman (1993) outline the basic steps for the development of sensorimotor coordination based on this selectionist perspective. First, during development, a basic repertoire of movements is produced as a result of the *spontaneous generation* of a variety of movements. That is, this self-generated activity in infancy allows the infant to explore all possible movement patterns. This notion of self-generated activity was described by Ulrich and Ulrich (1993) as one of the main principles of the dynamic systems approach with respect to development. Neural selection occurs through the process of *adaptive value,* whereby the organism has the ability to sense the outcome of different movements on the environment. That is, there appear to be information-seeking perceptual systems, referred to as value systems, available at birth that provide the constraints when the movements for various global mappings are selected. Based on this notion of adaptive value, movements that prove more effective in accomplishing a task result in the strengthening of the appropriate synaptic connections. Turvey and Fitzpatrick (1993) referred to this as "chaos with feedback," where the "chaos" is the initial generation of random patterns of movement and the "feedback" is provided by the adaptive value system that allows the individual to determine the most effective patterns. The selection of the neural connections most useful to the organism has been linked to the Darwinian notion of natural selection and is often referred to as *neural Darwinism* (Purves, 1994).

As argued by Sporns and Edelman (1993), this global theory of brain function can provide a satisfactory understanding of early human development that cannot be provided by either the current prescriptive or the dynamic systems approach. The prescriptive approach has the degrees of freedom and contextual difficulties addressed in chapter 2, whereas the dynamic systems approach failed to take into account the specific neural mechanisms that are responsible for motor control. Although this theory appears to fit in well with the dynamic systems perspective, it is still in its early stages, with the notion of *adaptive value,* like Gibson's notion of *affordances,* requiring further definition and verification.

The selectionist viewpoint is still subject to considerable debate (e.g., Purves et al., 1996). A contrasting view is the *constructionist* perspective that argues for growth rather than selection. That is, with development, dendritic and axonal processes are extended with an increase in the complexity of connectivity and neuronal morphology (Purves, 1994). These two theories are debated among Sporns, Changeux, and Purves et al. in a 1997 volume of *Trends in Neuroscience.* Although quite distinct mechanisms account for brain development, the two views agree that neural changes as a result of experience are of "overwhelming importance" to understanding development (Purves, 1994).

How Does This Research Inform Therapeutic Practice?

What are the implications of these views of neural plasticity on infant development and intervention approaches? Latash (1998a) suggests that plasticity is an important component of motor learning and is also essential for the adaptation of the individual to any brain trauma that may occur. Maturationists have argued that environment has very little influence on development and hence that very little would be accomplished through changing an infant's environment. However, evidence now shows that both genetic makeup and environment play an important role in development. The malleable neural substrate described in this chapter would therefore be of considerable benefit to infants who have been brain injured. If the environment can influence brain structure as has been demonstrated, then it follows that, given the large amount of change that can occur in the infant's neural structure, infants are ideal candidates for appropriate intervention when they have been subject to neural trauma. Hence, researchers need to focus on appropriate approaches for intervention at this early stage when the young infant's brain has the greatest plasticity. Some of this recent research relating to early intervention is discussed more fully in the last section of this book.

Summary

Understanding the structure and function of the CNS is clearly an important part of understanding motor development. In this chapter, the main structures of the brain responsible for motor control have been outlined. Yet throughout this chapter it has been emphasized that the brain is made up of a multitude of interconnections and that in order to understand brain function, we must take into account the brain as a whole.

The other important feature identified in this chapter is brain plasticity. That is, motor development does not involve the hard-wiring of neural connections that produce particular motor responses. Rather these connections vary over time as a result of development (e.g., synaptogenesis, neurogenesis, and apoptosis) and experience. This is especially important when we consider the development of infants in general, and in particular those with brain damage, as it means that with appropriate experience there is the potential to improve the outcome for all infants.

part II ■■■

The Development of Voluntary Movement Control

One of the earliest investigations to be published on infant development dates back to 1787, when Tiedemann detailed his son's behavior from birth to 2 1/2 years (cited in Clark & Whitall, 1989). Because behavior is expressed through motor control, this work documented many of the developmental changes in movement during these early years. As described by Clark and Whitall, Tiedemann's approach of *descriptive observation* led to similar *baby biographies* by Darwin ("Biographical Sketch of an Infant," 1877) and Preyer (*The Mind of the Child,* 1909).

Arguably, the most widely documented behavioral changes in infants are the *motor milestones*. Many of these are well known to new mothers who watch and encourage their young infant in anticipation of each new accomplishment. The achievement of each milestone is a landmark in the infant's development and provides an essential base for the development of future skills. These motor milestones, or voluntary movements, can be categorized into three different types, namely postural control or stability, prehension (which is also termed reaching and grasping) or manipulation, and locomotion.

These chapters cover the issue of *how* infants develop motor control. It is *not* the aim of this volume to provide a descriptive account of the changing movement patterns in the infant. Many excellent books are available that provide such information. For example, Alexander, Boehme, and Cupps (1993) and Bly (1994) provide thorough descriptions of motor skills from birth to 12 months in normal, full-term infants, with many illustrations and photos. Bly points out that her book is not designed to determine whether the well- documented developmental milestones are appropriate but rather to describe in detail how these milestones are performed and their subsequent transformation into skills. Both of these volumes point out how essential it is for therapists to have a sound understanding of normal motor development in order to successfully identify abnormal responses. However, one must always be mindful that abnormal responses do not necessarily mean abnormal development.

How do infants change from a helpless individual dominated by gravity and poor muscle control to a coordinated, independently mobile individual? How do they produce these coordinated movements? Part II reviews recent empirical research that has investigated the processes associated with these huge developmental changes.

four ■■■

Postural Control
Development of Stability, Balance, and Orientation

chapter objectives

This chapter will do the following:

- Define and describe the terms postural stability, balance, and orientation
- Discuss the postural milestones of head control, sitting, and standing
- Describe the factors that influence postural development

One of the basic functional components of motor development is postural control (Reed, 1989). In order for an infant to acquire the many motor skills accomplished in the first year of life, a prerequisite is appropriate postural control.

Despite its importance, this aspect of motor development has been largely neglected in the literature until quite recently. Part of the problem was that individuals are often unaware of many of the postural responses that are made. As a result, posture has been regarded as having lower "status" or less importance than other voluntary movements. Regardless of the status accorded to this aspect of motor development, there is also a fundamental difficulty in researching posture. That is, it is very difficult to examine postural responses in isolation.

In this chapter, the primary postural achievements made in infancy are reviewed in the context of recent research evidence. The most commonly cited postural achievements include the development of head control, sitting, and the ability to stand erect prior to walking. The main variables affecting early postural development are examined in relation to the various theoretical approaches outlined in chapter 2. As much of the postural research has also been carried out in relation to particular motor skills such as reaching and locomotion, chapters 5 and 6, which outline these developments in detail, also contain relevant literature on postural control.

Definition and Description of Postural Control

The term **posture** simply means the positions adopted by the body or parts of the body (Jouen & Lepecq, 1990). Appropriate postural control is necessary for *stability, balance,* and *orientation.* Stability is achieved through maintaining the center of body mass low and within the object's or individual's base of support (Shumway-Cook & Woollacott, 1993). The center of body mass, or **center of gravity,** refers to the point of concentration of the earth's gravitational pull on an object or individual. It is a balance point where "all the particles of the object are evenly distributed" (Enoka, 1994, p. 43). When one considers the changes in body dimensions with age depicted in figure 2.6, it is clear that there are considerable changes in the center of gravity throughout infancy that would influence stability. The lower the center of gravity, the more stable the object or individual. As the head takes up a larger proportion of the body mass in young infants as compared to older children and adults, the center of gravity is higher. It becomes lower with increasing age.

When an individual maintains equilibrium, this is termed *balance.* This term is often used interchangeably with "stability" (e.g., Shumway-Cook & Woollacott, 1993). However, balance can be achieved even in an unstable situation (Haywood & Getchell, 2001). For example, a ballerina can balance on her toes on one leg even though this is a very unstable posture.

As an infant grows, the body's center of gravity becomes lower, thereby increasing stability with age.

Postural control also provides *orientation*. Appropriate orientation ensures that the alignment or configuration of the body segments is maintained in the appropriate order with respect to one another for the movement or task required (Shumway-Cook & Woollacott, 1993). In the case of walking, for example, a vertical posture or alignment is required.

Developmental Transitions in Balance Control

Newborns appear to have little postural control, although they can balance their head very briefly (a few seconds) when held or placed in a sitting position (Prechtl, 1977). Within a few months they have developed head control, followed by trunk control, which allows the infant to sit, initially with support but eventually without any support. By around 12 months of age, infants achieve independent vertical posture involving support on two legs. This eventually leads to locomotor activities such as walking, running, and skipping.

It appears from this description that postural control develops in a cephalocaudal direction as originally described by Gesell and Amatruda (1945) in their principle of developmental direction. The early maturationists such as Gesell argued that these "stages" of development are determined through internal or genetic mechanisms. However, it is now evident that many factors, internal and external, guide the developmental process. Hence, the term *developmental transition* is used rather than *stage.*

The Development of Head Control

The ability to raise the head in the prone position is seen as one of the first major motor achievements of the newborn. Given the dimensions of the head in relation to the body at birth, it is no mean feat to raise the head, as the head has a large proportion of weight and body length at birth. Even at seven weeks of age the young infant in figure 4.1 is struggling to raise his head. Indeed, although 90% of neonates at two weeks of age can lift their head from a horizontal surface, it is not until they are three months of age that they can fully extend their neck while lying in a prone position (Frankenburg et al., 1992). Following this achievement, the infant soon develops the ability to raise the head and chest, eventually pushing up on extended arms. This has been achieved by the infant pictured in figure 4.2.

At three months of age, the infant can usually maintain the head erect and upright while being held in a sitting or standing position. A more difficult task is raising the head while supine, a feat that is generally achieved by five months of age.

As the head contains two sensory systems essential for balance control, namely the vestibular system and the visual system, head control

■■■ Head control is particularly important for balance, as the head contains the visual and vestibular sensory receptors.

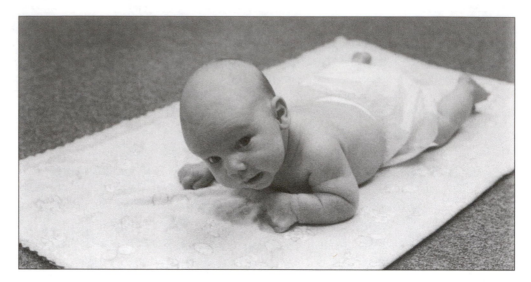

Figure 4.1   A 7-week-old infant struggles to overcome gravity in order to raise his head.

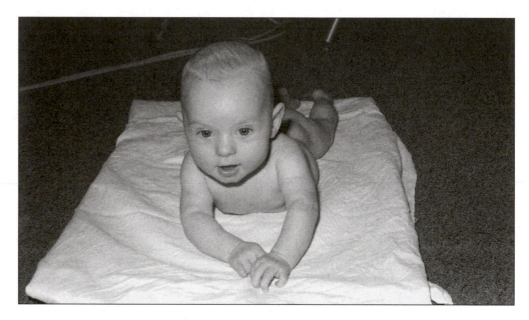

Figure 4.2   At 12 weeks, this infant has developed good head control.

is "especially important" in the development of postural control (Bertenthal, 2001). One issue that has received considerable attention is the ability of young infants to track targets with their eyes and the role that head movements play in this. The infant in figure 4.1 would have considerable difficulty tracking objects by turning the head. Although neonates can track objects at birth, they tend to use eye movements initially and turn their head only after their eye movements have reached the periphery (Bloch & Carchon, 1992). By one month of age, head movements play a significant role in object tracking (Bertenthal & von Hofsten, 1998).

The Development of Sitting

In order to sit unsupported, the infant must achieve appropriate trunk and head control. By five months of age, most infants can sit unsupported but cannot sit upright. The trunk is supported over, or aligned with, the pelvis and legs, which form a relatively stable base of support. However, an infant at this stage (figure 4.3; the infant in this figure is 22 weeks of age) shows an exaggerated forward lean necessary to support the head.

Around six to eight months of age, the upper half of the body has gained adequate control to enable the infant to sit upright unsupported. This is an important achievement as it allows the infant to free her arms and hands for exploration, as can be seen in figure 4.4. The complex interrelationship between postural control and reaching is discussed more fully in the next chapter.

Developing the Upright Posture for Walking

One of the prerequisites for independent walking is the ability to maintain postural stability on two legs. Maintaining balance in the upright position requires that the center of gravity be kept over the supporting surface. Latash (1998a) described the ability of humans to maintain the vertical posture as "a miracle," as the area of support in humans is relatively small.

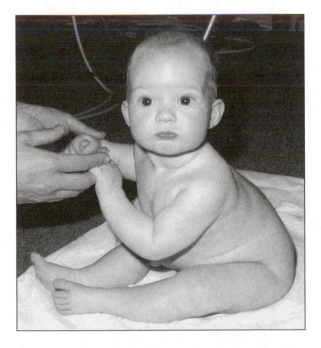

Figure 4.3 Although infants can sit unsupported at five months of age, they show an exaggerated forward lean required to support the head.

Figure 4.4 Once an infant has achieved adequate postural stability while sitting, she is able to more easily manipulate objects.

Infants are usually able to pull themselves into the upright position by around eight months of age. However, when infants first achieve this upright posture, they make use of the surrounding environment for support. The infant shown in figure 4.5 makes use of a toy box to support herself in the upright posture. It is not generally until around 11 months of age that infants can stand unsupported (Capute et al., 1985).

It is even more difficult for an infant to acquire the ability to maintain balance when producing forward propulsion such as in walking or running. Again, this is first achieved by the use of supporting objects, a behavior called *cruising*, as shown in figure 4.6. Cruising involves the use of all four limbs. In the initial stages of cruising, the infant usually moves only one limb at a time as he struggles to maintain the upright position. However, with practice, the infant is soon able to involve multiple limbs as balance becomes more stable (Haehl et al., 2000).

Eventually, the infant makes his or her first unsupported steps, which require that the weight of the whole body be supported on one leg at a time as the other leg swings forward. However, once infants achieve these first steps they rapidly become competent walkers. The following sections explore how infants develop the appropriate postural control for these difficult and complex motor tasks.

Figure 4.5 The environment is utilized for support when the infant first achieves the vertical posture.

Figure 4.6 An infant cruising, using both arms for support

Influences on the Development of Postural Control

Assiante (1998) suggests two main functional principles that describe the types of strategies adopted in maintaining appropriate postural control. The first principle, relating to appropriate balance, involves choosing a frame of reference, which can be either the gravitational vector or the type of surface that the individual is standing on. In the first case, balance control is considered to occur temporally from the head down to the feet (i.e., in a cephalocaudal direction), whereas in the latter it is from the feet to the head. Assiante considers that in the first six months infants are guided primarily by gravitational forces and thus develop balance in a cephalocaudal direction. Once infants acquire the upright stance, their frame of reference shifts to the type of surface they are standing on, and balance control is then initiated in the feet and moves up to the head.

The second principle, based on Bernstein's notion of degrees of freedom (see chapter 2), involves mastering the degrees of freedom that need to be simultaneously controlled during postural control. This is relevant to maintaining the appropriate orientation, as "postural orientation requires an understanding of how the many degrees of freedom represented by the body's muscles and joints are to work together in a coordinated fashion" (Metcalfe & Clark, 2000, p. 392). Assiante and Amblard (1995) note that the head-trunk unit and the degrees of freedom of the neck are of particular importance. As the head contains both the visual and vestibular sensors essential for appropriate postural control, it is important to minimize head movements. This reduces degrees of freedom, thus producing a reference point for further movements.

Developmentalists have recently become interested in understanding the processes that lead to developmental transitions. In particular, they have investigated the rate-limiting variables that may be responsible for behavioral shifts. Appropriate postural control is considered a rate-limiting variable as it is an essential requirement for the development of motor skills (Shumway-Cook & Woollacott, 1993). However, the development of appropriate postural control is also dependent on a number of variables, and recent research has identified several variables that influence postural development (Woollacott, 1993). One such variable is the development of the appropriate sensory systems, in particular, the somatosensory, vestibular, and visual systems. Other variables that have been investigated include neuromuscular development, muscle strength, body mass, and the changing center of gravity through changes in body morphology.

The Importance of Sensory Input in Postural Control

Although individuals are generally unaware of it, the body is continually making changes to posture in response to the information that is received from our sensory systems. Such a relationship is termed a closed-loop system by information-processing theorists. On the other hand, from an ecological or dynamic systems perspective, this is a perfect example of perception–action coupling as outlined by Gibson (1979). Regardless of the theoretical distinction, the systems that are considered of key importance for postural control are visual, vestibular, and somatosensory. One of the key questions asked in postural research is whether one sensory system is dominant over another and if so, whether this priority changes with development.

The Visual System

In the adult, *exteroceptive* information from the visual system (and to a lesser degree, the auditory system) plays an important role in postural control. This is best illustrated by standing with the eyes closed, which usually results in increased body sway. It was also clearly demonstrated by David Lee and colleagues (Lee & Thomson, 1982), who designed a room where the walls moved but the floor did not. This is illustrated in figure 4.7. The individual placed within the room does not move. As a result there are no changes in the information provided by *proprioceptors* (vestibular, kinesthetic, or tactile). Despite this, the misleading visual information provided by the moving walls results in the individual's overbalancing, thus demonstrating the dominance of the visual information over the proprioceptive information.

Does vision play as significant a role in postural control for the young infant? The visual system is considered the most poorly developed of the senses in the newborn infant (see chapter 1), suggesting that it may

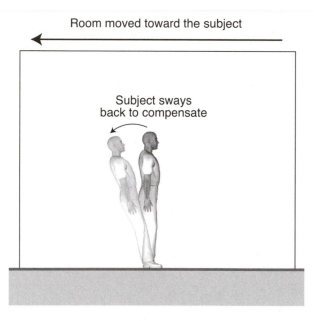
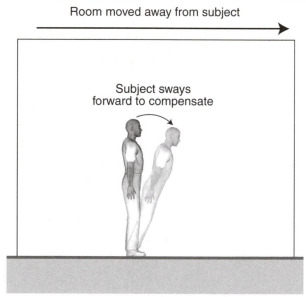

Room moved toward the subject

Subject sways back to compensate

Room moved away from subject

Subject sways forward to compensate

a   b

Figure 4.7 David Lee's "moving room" setup. This experimental paradigm has been used to demonstrate visual dominance in balance control.

play a less significant role. Despite this, there is evidence to suggest that neonates utilize vision to achieve postural control. Jouen (1988) placed infants as young as three days of age in an infant seat that could measure the infant's forward and backward head movements. When a light stimulus was moved toward and away from the infants, 83% of the newborns reacted, although they did not consistently respond in the appropriate direction. This implied that although the infants could perceive the moving stimulus and make postural adjustments, they did not have the correct reference value to respond appropriately.

The "moving room" just described for adults has also been used in a doctoral study to test the dominance of vision in infants and children. Pope (1984, cited in Woollacott & Jensen, 1996) observed that two-month-old infants sitting on a stationary platform reacted similarly to adults, responding to the visual information and ignoring the vestibular and kinesthetic information. Barela and colleagues (2000) also used the "moving room" paradigm with sitting infants aged six, seven, eight, and nine months. These authors also found the relationship between the visual information and the body sway to be similar to that in adults. There was no evidence of any developmental differences between the four age groups, despite the greater proficiency of the older groups in sitting. This is consistent with the findings of Bertenthal and colleagues (2000), who argued that although infants develop faster reactions to movement perturbations and their coordination increases with age, their "postural control system is not fundamentally different than the adult's system" (p. 313).

It has been suggested that infants may rely even more on visual information than other types of information when shifting from one level of postural control to another (Jouen & Lepecq, 1990). From a dynamic systems perspective, these would be periods in which there is a phase transition from one behavior to another and therefore a period of instability. However, once stability is achieved, there is a shift in dependence from exteroceptive input from the visual system to the proprioceptive and vestibular systems. Woollacott (1993) considers the adaptive mechanisms that implement this modality shift a further limiting variable.

Vestibular and Somatosensory Systems

In order to maintain a stable posture, the segments within the body must maintain appropriate muscle tone. This is thought to occur through the use of sensory information from kinesthetic and vestibular receptors, which initiate the appropriate postural reactions. The vestibular system is highly developed at birth, and it is assumed that the kinesthetic system must also be highly developed, although very little research has been undertaken in this regard.

In one of the few studies that have addressed the contribution of somatosensory information on postural control in infants, Barela and colleagues (1999) investigated the importance of sensory information from surface contact when infants were in the upright position. They

■■■ As in the adult system, visual information appears to override proprioceptive information in the maintenance of postural control in infants.

examined the relationship between body sway and the force applied by the infant's hand to a supporting surface during four different stages of development, namely, pull to stand, standing alone, the onset of independent walking, and experienced walking (around 1 1/2 years). The authors identified a shift in the function of the somatosensory information provided by the supporting surface. In the first three stages, they argued that the infant's hand provided mechanical support, as the forces applied appeared in phase with body sway. However, in the last stage, in which the infants had become accomplished walkers, the somatosensory information from the hand appeared to take on more of an informational rather than supporting role, evidenced by a shift in the time lag between the forces applied and body sway. The applied force, which also decreased to a *light touch* in the last stage, led the body sway by around 140 msec, which is similar to the value observed in adults. Barela and colleagues argued that this was evidence for a feed-forward mechanism that enabled the infant to control body sway and suggested that these feed-forward relationships are an important part of the development of appropriate postural control.

Musculoskeletal Components

The ability to support the body is dependent on appropriate muscular strength. This is an obvious variable, yet it has not been adequately researched, especially in relation to postural control. Muscular strength is also closely related to body mass, as an infant who is "chubbier" than another would be required to lift or move a greater mass. Hence the muscles would need to be stronger, or development may be delayed. This issue is discussed by Thelen (1983) in relation to the ability to perform the stepping response and by Kawai and colleagues (1999), who examined spontaneous arm movements in the first week of life (as described in chapter 1). Both studies manipulated body mass by immersing the infants in water. Thelen also added weights to the infants' legs. Movements were found to be influenced by the changes in body mass produced by the different conditions that were imposed.

As described earlier, the body proportions change dramatically in the first year of life. The young infant is grossly restricted at birth because a large proportion of the body mass is composed of the head. Consequently, this is one of the variables limiting early performance. The rapid growth of the infant redistributes these proportions, giving the infant increasing control of the head. Following this, neck and trunk development allows the infant to roll over, sit up, and eventually become mobile through creeping, for example. Finally, as the infant's center of gravity is lowered, the infant can gain the appropriate postural control and balance for standing and walking.

It can be seen that muscular strength, body mass, and the notion of gravity are closely interrelated. Brenière (1996) describes a *natural body frequency* (NBF) in adults, a parameter incorporating gravity, body parameters of mass, body center of mass, height, and body moment of inertia. Despite variations in anthropometric data, no changes in the NBF were evident from one adult to another. The author suggested that this may be a kinetic invariant that is specific to posture and gait. The NBF "integrates gravity and the body's material structure and establishes a correspondence between the programming of locomotor parameters and their postural consequences" (Brenière, 1999, p. 197). Natural body frequency does, however, change with growth. Brenière (1999) examined how the NBF altered on a sample of children from the onset of independent walking to seven years after the onset of independent walking. As gravity has a greater effect on younger children compared to those who are older, the NBF decreases with age.

The concept of gravity as one of the constraining variables was also examined by Jensen and colleagues (1997). They investigated the impact of physical growth on the relative change in joint moments produced by gravity. Their results showed that as the infant became older, there was a decrease in the slope of the gravitational moment, suggesting that changes in the gravitational moments during infancy may be a variable influencing phase shifts in motor patterns during development.

Neuromuscular Development

A further variable is the development of the appropriate neuromuscular pathways necessary for maintaining balance. Several different theoretical approaches view the development of the relationship between nervous system and muscle quite differently. One is based on a maturational approach proposing that postural responses are controlled by innate central pattern generators (CPGs; see chapter 3), which are neural networks that generate the rhythmic motor patterns found in locomotion (e.g., Hadders-Algra et al., 1996). Unlike the *muscle synergies* or *coordinative structures* described from a dynamic systems perspective, these neuronal connections are thought to be predetermined through endogenous maturation. That is, their maturation is not dependent upon experience. Forssberg and Hirschfeld (1994) suggested two levels of control based on CPGs. At the first level is selection of the appropriate CPG. At the second level, the CPG is fine-tuned through sensory feedback from visual, vestibular, and kinesthetic systems. It is only this fine-tuning that is influenced by experience.

The notion of postural control developing only as a result of the maturation of specific CPGs is considered no longer appropriate given more recent research findings (Thelen & Spencer, 1998). For example, the high variability in postural development would not be expected if the appropriate responses are "prewired." Evidence of such variability was provided by Harbourne and colleagues (1987, cited in Woollacott, 1993), who examined the transition to sitting in infants at two to three months and then at four to five months of age. The infants were held around the trunk for support and then were released. Electromyographic (EMG) recordings from the back and hip muscles were taken to determine the patterns of muscular activity present at each of the two stages. In the earlier stage, there was greater variability in the order in which each muscle was activated; but by four to five months, the infants developed their own particular pattern of muscular activation. Although some patterns were more common than others, the emergence of several solutions to the problem of maintaining balance while sitting demonstrated that the solution did not exist as an innate pattern. Rather, it was proposed that these synergies emerged as a result of the infants' past experiences.

From a dynamic systems perspective, muscle synergies can be considered in terms of Bernstein's notion of degrees of freedom (Whiting, 1984). Rather than the appropriate postural responses being innate CPGs, there are many possible solutions, and synergies are assembled "online" when needed. Through trial and error, the infant discovers the most appropriate response. Several recent studies have utilized Bernstein's notion of degrees of freedom to investigate muscle synergies in the development of postural control. For example, Harbourne and Stergiou (2003) investigated sitting posture, and Haehl and colleagues (2000) have examined cruising. Cruising has been identified as an important stage of development and has been investigated using techniques such as motion analysis (see figure 4.8). Cruising appears to be responsible for the development of the appropriate postural control for the transition to independent walking (Haehl et al.).

Harbourne and Stergiou (2003) examined three different stages of sitting, namely sitting with support when infants could hold up their head and upper trunk, independent sitting for only a brief period, and controlled independent sitting. These three stages of development demonstrated very different levels of postural control. The authors' measure of postural stability or sway was used to determine the changes in the center of pressure while the infant sat on a force platform. In order to determine the number of degrees of freedom in each of these levels of control, they measured dimensionality (Newell, 1997), described as "a way to characterize the geometry of the attractor organization and the number of independent degrees of freedom in system control" (p. 73). Using a method called correlation dimension, Harbourne and Stergiou found that the dimensionality diminished from stages 1 to 2. This supports the notion that degrees of freedom are reduced or "frozen" as a new skill is being learned (Vereijken et al., 1992). There was then an increase in dimensionality from the second stage to the third, in which independent sitting had been mastered. Again, this supports Bernstein's notion of degrees of freedom, suggesting that once a skill is accomplished there is a

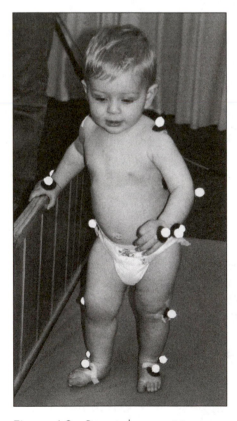

Figure 4.8 Research on cruising uses markers to track the movement dynamics. This infant is cruising using only one hand for support.

freeing of the degrees of freedom, "providing the infant with increased adaptability or flexibility in maintaining postural support over the base of support in sitting" (Harbourne & Stergiou, 2003, p. 375).

Haehl and colleagues (2000) also considered the transition from cruising to independent walking in terms of Bernstein's notion of reducing the degrees of freedom (Bernstein, 1967). They provided a graphical representation of this as shown in figure 4.9. Phase I represents Bernstein's notion that initially the degrees of freedom are "frozen" through tight coupling in order to minimize the initial complexity of the task. Haehl and colleagues suggested that this stage was important for cruising to provide a stable base for an infant to experiment with moving more than one limb at a time. As development progresses, these tight couplings are loosened so that the individual can explore more complex patterns (phase IIa). With practice, preferred patterns are identified, usually described as synergies or coordinative structures, and the degrees of freedom are again reduced as this preferred solution is implemented. This final solution emerges as a result of a combination of biological, environmental, and task variables, although Haehl and colleagues suggested that postural control is the primary component that is improving throughout the infant's cruising to allow the shift to independent walking.

This model was investigated by Haehl and colleagues (2000) through examination of changes in the coordination of the thorax and pelvis using motion analysis techniques. They identified an initial "wobble"

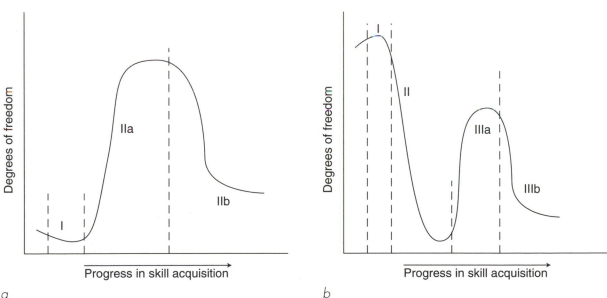

a   b

Figure 4.9   Haehl and colleagues (2000) used (a) Bernstein's phases of skill acquisition, namely (I) freezing degrees of freedom, (IIa) release of degrees of freedom, and (IIb) selecting the most efficient or economical movement patterns to hypothesize (b) the phases of skill acquisition during cruising in infants, namely (I) poor control and wobbly, (II) freezing the degrees of freedom, (IIIa) releasing the degrees of freedom, and (IIIb) selecting the most efficient or economical movement patterns.

stage that they attributed to the infants' limited experience in the upright position. "Cruising presents a unique challenge to infants; they must coordinate multiple segments of the body while locomoting in a new posture" (p. 709). However, the findings failed to support Bernstein's sequence of change in respect to the degrees of freedom. Rather, the authors found a gradual reduction in the degrees of freedom leading to a plateau a few weeks before the onset of independent walking. They suggested that "the task of cruising itself may simply not require infants to tightly constrain the movements of the trunk" (p. 710), as there were many solutions that could be adopted.

Prior Motor Experience

Another rate-limiting variable that one needs to consider when investigating the development of motor abilities is prior motor experience, which is often determined by the opportunity the infant has for action. Throughout, this volume refers to the importance of early movements to later development. As discussed in chapter 1, there is evidence to suggest that a reduction of early fetal movements may have implications for later development. Differences in child-rearing practices also indicate that movement opportunity may affect development. The importance of opportunity was highlighted by Bower (1977) when he commented that "it seems clear that the environment-initiated opportunities for practice in fact have a great deal to do with both the rate and direction of motor development" (p. 91).

Early spontaneous activity has been linked to later motor development (Piek & Carman, 1994; Thelen, 1979) and appears to influence postural development. For example, Haas and Diener (1988) argued that the early bouncing, rocking, and rhythmical swaying that young infants produce once they pull themselves to the upright stance is an important precursor to postural control as it provides valuable information in feedback mechanisms. That is, the rocking on the hands and knees shown in figure 1.10 is an important precursor to creeping. Haas and Diener (1988) found that less active infants with delayed motor development had difficulty in adjusting to postural perturbations. Prior activity is also clearly important for the development of muscle strength, again emphasizing how different variables or subsystems interact to produce the appropriate conditions for a developmental transition.

The impact of prior motor experience on postural development was examined in a series of longitudinal studies by Sveistrup and Woollacott (1996, 1997). They examined the automatic postural response from pull to stand to late independent walking in infants. They were interested in how these postural synergies, defined as "multiple muscles that are constrained to act together as a functional unit, with fixed temporal and spatial parameters" (Sveistrup & Woollacott, 1996, p. 58), developed in infancy. These synergies are highly consistent in adults during a perturbation while standing. On the basis of EMG recordings, Sveistrup and Woollacott found evidence to suggest that these postural synergies developed in the infant in a generative process as a result of experience. A rudimentary form of the automatic postural response was found in infants prior to independent walking. It appears that muscles are activated individually initially and then gradually integrated one at a time into the "motor map" producing the functional synergies.

The investigators pointed out that these changes could also have resulted from an "unfolding of a preprogrammed genetic code" (p. 68), that is, through maturation rather than experience. However, a further study (Sveistrup & Woollacott, 1997) addressed the effect of different early experience on the onset of the postural response by varying the number of perturbations experienced on the movable platform. Extensive training was found to produce a larger proportion of trials with functionally appropriate muscle activity for postural control compared with no perturbation training. Although experience clearly had an effect on postural muscle development, Sveistrup and Woollacott pointed out that maturational effects are also important to consider, as muscle onset latency was not affected by practice. Factors such as myelination or the maturation of appropriate neural connections may be an important rate limiter for this aspect of postural control.

Early experience has not received as much attention as other variables in the search for rate-limiting variables, perhaps because it requires quite intensive longitudinal research. Also, for ethical reasons, there are situations in which we cannot manipulate experience in research on human infants—another reason why this factor has not received a great deal of attention (von Hofsten, 1993). Longitudinal studies are essential in the investigation of developmental transitions, as cross-sectional analyses will give only the present state of the group investigated, saying nothing about how this level was achieved.

▮▮▮▮ How Does This Research Inform Therapeutic Practice?

This chapter has emphasized the importance of appropriate postural control for the development of later motor milestones. This has been recognized by researchers and therapists for many years, and posture has been an integral part of many traditional and recent therapy techniques. Many of these therapies aim to provide the appropriate posture to allow the infant to explore new movements. The research presented in this chapter indicates that many factors lead to the development of appropriate posture. In order to train the infant to initiate appropriate postures, it is important to gain an understanding of how these different variables interact. For example, what techniques can be used to promote a variable that may not have developed to a suitable level?

Summary

Infants have several major postural accomplishments in their first year, namely the development of head control, trunk control, and the ability to maintain upright posture that is necessary for walking. In this chapter, several variables that influence the development of postural control were discussed. The essential relationship between sensory systems and the motor mechanisms required for postural control was highlighted as a major component of appropriate postural control. In particular, visual, vestibular, and somatosensory information are of primary importance. Neuromuscular and musculoskeletal variables were also discussed, both from a maturational and from a dynamic systems perspective. The developing infant undergoes major neurological and morphological changes, and one needs to consider these when examining the processes that influence postural development. Of particular importance to balance is the change in the infant's center of gravity during growth. The final variable described was the influence of experience, a factor that has been largely neglected in the literature on postural control. It is important to note that these factors are all interrelated. Balance, like any other behavior, develops as a result of the changes that occur in the organism, the task required, and the surrounding environment (Newell, 1986).

An integral part of all motor tasks is appropriate postural control. This is essential for the maintenance of balance during movement and also ensures the appropriate body orientation for the specific task required. Postural control is considered a rate-limiting variable in the achievement of motor tasks and is discussed more fully in relation to manual and locomotor skills in the following two chapters.

five ■■■

Manual Control
Development of Reaching and Grasping

chapter objectives

This chapter will do the following:

- Outline the main milestones achieved in reaching and grasping in the infant's first year
- Discuss rate-limiting variables that affect the development of reaching and grasping
- Describe early tool use
- Discuss manual asymmetries found in the first year and look at their relationship to later hand preference

Although walking is often considered the primary motor milestone in an infant's development, the ability to grasp and manipulate objects is of great significance in everyday life, as these skills are needed in order to function on a daily basis. For example, using a knife and fork, spoon, or chopsticks for eating requires manual dexterity that is often not developed until well into childhood. The foundation for these complex manipulative skills is established in the first year of life.

The infant appears to have few reaching and grasping skills at birth, and it is nearly six months before he or she can competently reach and grasp an object. In this chapter, the processes that lead to the development of prehension are described, along with a discussion of manual asymmetries and whether these are linked to the later development of handedness.

Definitions and Descriptions of Prehension

Prehension, or manual control, can be divided into *reaching* and *grasping.* Reaching is concerned with moving the hand from its initial location to the target location, whereas grasping requires the shaping of the hand around the object. These two types of motor behavior are thought to be very different. For example, in his *visuomotor channels hypothesis,* Jeannerod (1981, 1984, 1996) described two distinct or parallel phases of prehension. The first phase is considered the transport phase, in which the hand is transported to the target area, and requires the greatest amount of time (70-80% of the total movement time). The second, or grasp, phase of the movement occurs when the hand is shaped and placed in the appropriate orientation to facilitate the gripping of the object. Jeannerod's model has been very influential in shaping research on reaching and grasping.

The reaching and grasping components of prehension are thought to be controlled by separate neuromotor mechanisms (e.g., Jeannerod, 1988; Sugden & Keogh, 1990; von Hofsten, 1986). Jeannerod (1996) argued that there must be different structures and modes of action for the gross motor reaching action compared with the fine motor manipulation phase. Whereas reaching is a more primitive behavior utilizing proximal arm joints, grasping requires distal joints for the precise finger and hand movements that have evolved in primates and humans. Jeannerod provides neurophysiological evidence that these two action components can be dissociated through lesioning of the motor and parietal cortex.

Although they are parallel processes, the two components of prehension share a common time course. That is, although the molding of the hand in preparation for the grip is part of the manipulation component, this occurs during the reaching or transportation phase. Therefore, as the two components are functionally interrelated, it is artificial to isolate them (Jeannerod, 1996). Despite this, for ease of presentation, most texts on reaching and grasping have separated these two components, as does this one. This separation is particularly useful when

Research evidence suggests that reaching and grasping are distinct parallel processes that are controlled by separate neuromotor mechanisms.

one is investigating prehension in infancy, as reaching and grasping emerge at different times in the infant's first year.

Reaching in the First Few Months

Early reaching movements occur prior to what is usually termed *successful reaching*, that is, when the infant can reach and grasp an object of interest. This early reaching behavior in newborn infants is often termed **prereaching** (Trevarthen, 1982).

Researchers have been interested in studying reaching in the newborn for several reasons. One is to understand the developmental profile of reaching behavior. This type of research was popular in the first half of the 20th century when the maturational theorists mapped the stages of motor development. Another issue that has been of considerable interest to researchers is whether these reaching movements are spontaneous or coincidental or whether they can be classed as "intentional." This issue can be linked back to early theorists such as Piaget (1953), who argued that infants had no intent (and no intelligence) in the first few months and therefore that any movements that appeared intentional were simply coincidental. This has been investigated in the newborn infant with two main types of studies, those on hand-to-mouth actions and those on newborns' reaching responses to an object.

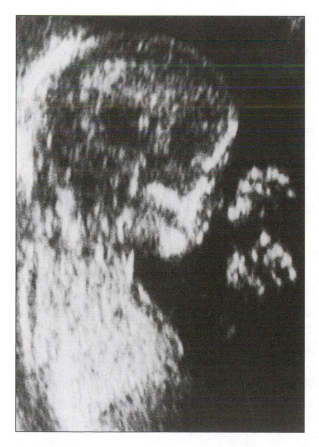

Figure 5.1 The hands can be clearly seen in relation to the mouth in this ultrasound of a 12-week-old fetus.

Hand-to-Mouth Movements

Reaching movements are present prenatally, as movements of the hand to the mouth have been identified in the fetus as early as 10 weeks gestational age (de Vries et al., 1982). De Vries and colleagues used ultrasound to investigate these types of movements. This procedure allowed the researchers to investigate the infants' hands in relation to their mouth. As shown in figure 5.1, the hands are well formed by 12 weeks gestational age, and their position can be easily tracked. Given the level of brain development at this early stage, it is clear that these first movements would not be intentional but would be considered spontaneous movements.

Hand-to-mouth movements continue after birth (Rochat, 1993), and according to a purely reflexive perspective (e.g., Piaget,

1953; Wyke, 1975), these reaching movements are unintentional and uncoordinated. That is, infants do not develop intent, in particular, eye–hand coordination, until several months later. However, there is now considerable evidence suggesting that this may not be the case. For example, Butterworth and Hopkins (1988) used frame-by-frame video analysis to demonstrate that newborn infants have some form of hand-to-mouth coordination. They observed instances in which newborn infants opened their mouths as the hand approached the face, suggesting that newborn reaching movements may have intent.

To understand the function of this early hand–mouth coordination, Rochat and colleagues (1988) examined the relationship of this response to sucrose delivery to the mouth. They found significant increases in the number and duration of hand-to-mouth contacts, compared to baseline recordings, with the delivery of a sucrose solution to the mouth. Duration of hand-to-mouth contact almost doubled with the introduction of the sucrose solution into the mouth. This was evidence that this relationship can be an active, coordinated response in the newborn, and not just a chance occurrence. Rochat and colleagues suggested that the introduction of the sucrose solution initiated the suckling mechanism and that the hand may provide something for the infant to suck on once this sucking or feeding system is engaged.

In the following few months, the functional role of hand–mouth coordination changes considerably. At around two months of age, once infants can grasp an object placed in their hand, they attempt to bring the object to the mouth for oral/haptic exploration. By four to five months, infants tend to bring the object within their field of vision to look at it before drawing it to the mouth (Rochat, 1993). Oral exploration, as shown in figure 5.2, continues to play an important role in the infant's discovery of his or her environment during the first year.

Figure 5.2   Infants enjoy oral exploration of objects.

Reaching to an Object

Early researchers such as Trevarthan (1974, cited in von Hofsten, 1986) and Bower and colleagues (1970) found evidence for a coordinated reaching movement in the newborn. Bower and colleagues' evidence was based on video analysis of neonates (less than a month old) reaching for objects. The authors investigated both orientation of the arm toward the object and intent. Their findings provided evidence that, given the appropriate postural support, newborn infants can produce surprisingly efficient prereaching movements.

One of the "landmark" studies of reaching in infants was carried out by Claes von Hofsten (1982) using a two-camera system to plot the course of hand movements in young infants (see figure 5.3). He investigated the arm movements of 14 newborn infants aged between five and nine days. The infants were strapped into a chair that provided the appropriate postural control, and both arm and eye movements were observed as a brightly colored ball of yarn was moved along a horizontal path in front of them.

Von Hofsten (1982) argued that many earlier studies failed to find evidence for voluntary reaching because they did not take into account the **orienting response.** That is, when a new or interesting object or event is presented, there is a reduction in motor activity as the infant attends to this novel stimulus. By recording eye movements as well as hand movements, von Hofsten could determine the number of reaching movements produced when the infant fixated on the object, in contrast to movements that occurred when the infant was not looking at the object. As predicted, there were significantly more movements when the object was absent rather than present, supporting the hypothesis relating to the orienting response. However, there were also significantly more forward-extended movements when the infants were fixating on the object than when they were not, implying some intentional relationship between the infant and the

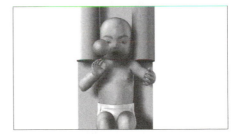

Figure 5.3   The experimental setup used by von Hofsten (1982), showing the two cameras and the view of the infant from each camera.

Adapted from von Hofsten, 1982.

object. A second experiment demonstrated that when the infant was fixating on the object, the arm movements were aimed more toward the object compared with when there was no fixation. These results provided compelling evidence to suggest that the newborn has some form of *prefunctional* eye–hand coordination at birth. Von Hofsten suggested that this may serve as an attentional mechanism rather than manipulative behavior at this early age.

Newborn reaching is considered to be similar to the first transport phase found in adults (von Hofsten, 1993). The arm movement appears to be monitored by proprioception and involves the extension of the arm with the fingers extending. There is, however, no flexion of the hand or zooming in on the target; because of a synergistic coupling of the arm and hand, the newborn infant cannot grasp objects. Furthermore, there appears to be a considerable amount of muscle coactivity in these early arm movements (Hadders-Algra et al., 1992). Using electromyography (EMG) to monitor the muscle activity, Hadders-Algra and colleagues found that this coactivation appeared to continue up to around three months of age, with coactivation of the antagonists initially present more than 70% of the time. However, there were substantial changes in the nature of the EMG activity after three months of age. The phasic muscle activity became shorter, the amplitude was attenuated, and there was a reduction in the tonic background activity. These changes were thought to be due to a decrease in the co-contraction of antagonist muscle groups with a corresponding increase in reciprocal activation (Hadders-Algra et al., 1992). It was suggested that as a result of spinal and supraspinal reorganization, there was a reduction in the motor unit sensitivity that would account for the observed changes in EMG activity.

Spencer and Thelen (2000) investigated this further by examining the changes in muscle activity that occurred during the transition from early prereaching movements to successful reaching. They measured the muscle activity in the biceps, triceps, anterior deltoid, and trapezius muscles in four infants presented with a toy at their midline. Video analysis was used to determine where the infants moved their arms in relation to their body and the toy. Although the authors found no evidence of the co-contraction between the muscle groups that was observed by Hadders-Algra and colleagues (1992), they found that different muscle groups were involved in prereaching as opposed to reaching. Movements prior to successful reaching involved primarily either the biceps or the triceps muscle. The investigators suggested that these simple movements, which flex the elbow and shoulder joints, are useful in guiding the hand to and away from the mouth. As described earlier, these are common reaching movements found in the first few months. Once successful reaching was achieved, however, the deltoid and trapezius muscles demonstrated increased activity. These muscles are important for guiding the arm to objects in the midline.

■■■■ Newborn infants produce prefunctional reaches that indicate some early form of eye–hand coordination at birth.

Development of Successful Reaching

Successful reaching, that is, successfully transporting the hand so that it makes contact with an object, usually occurs around three to four months of age (von Hofsten & Lindhagen, 1979). Unlike the smooth, controlled reaches of an adult, these first successful movements appear jerky, with multipeaked speed–time trajectories (Fetters & Todd, 1987) and poor control of the hand. These early movements are composed of a series of accelerations and decelerations described by von Hofsten and Lindhagen as multiple *movement units.* As the infant becomes older and more proficient at reaching, the number of movement units made in each reaching movement declines.

The Role of Sensory Information

Mathew and Cook (1990) carried out an extensive kinematic analysis of reaching movements on three groups of infants with mean ages of 4.5, 6, and 7.5 months. With increasing age, the infants became more successful with their reaches, although the youngest group was already successful in making contact with the object 71% of the time. There were also improvements in the time taken to achieve the reach, as well as a simplification of the movement pattern indicated by a smoothing of the speed profile, with a more direct path of the hand to the target. Mathew and Cook's detailed analysis of the movement curves provided evidence to suggest that there was continuous correction of the movement as a result of sensory feedback, although they did not investigate what type of feedback was being used to correct the hand trajectory.

In adults, both vision and proprioception are essential for accurate reaching (Jeannerod, 1996). Proprioception provides positional information on the relative joint angles, whereas vision is required to provide information on the position of the limb in relation to the target. An essential part of this mechanism appears to be the vision of the limb prior to the movement. However, the findings from several studies have suggested that vision of the hand is not essential for successful reaching in infants. For example, Clifton and colleagues (1994) developed a testing procedure in which a toy was presented to the infants in darkness so they could not see their arm or hand. The infants could identify the toy's location either through the use of glow-in-the-dark paint or through sound (from a noisy toy), or both. In all these conditions, the reach was unaffected by the loss of vision of the hand. This suggests that proprioception may play a more significant role in reaching by infants compared with adults.

The Role of Posture

Woollacott (1993) argued that before prehension can be established, a preparatory or postural stage of development is necessary to provide

■■■ Postural control is considered an important rate-limiting variable for successful reaching.

a stabilizing framework for the appropriate manipulative skills. It has consistently been demonstrated that if young infants are placed in the appropriate posture or given appropriate support, they are capable of reaching and grasping at a much earlier age than generally acknowledged. The study by von Hofsten (1982) presented earlier is a good example. Another example is provided by a study conducted by Savelsbergh and van der Kamp (1994). They found that infants aged between 12 and 19 weeks produced more reaching movements in the vertical position compared to the supine position. The authors attributed this difference to a greater difficulty in producing the appropriate force to compensate for the gravitational torque generated in the supine position as opposed to the vertical position. That is, frequency of occurrence not only is dependent on the infant's own physical constraints but is also related to external environmental influences.

Good head control is considered a necessary precursor for the development of reaching. In a longitudinal study examining the development of reaching in four infants, Thelen and Spencer (1998) noted that successful reaching was achieved in all infants several weeks after they had produced good head control. Rochat (1992) pointed out the importance of postural control in understanding unimanual and bimanual reaching. He allocated 32 infants aged five to eight months into two groups, those who either had or had not achieved independent sitting. Infant reaching was videotaped while the infant was in one of four different postures, namely sitting, sitting reclined, supported upright slightly prone, and supine, as illustrated in figure 5.4. Rochat provided evidence for a trend from symmetrical and synergistic bimanual reaching to asymmetrical, unimanual reaching. However, there were distinct differences in the reach structure and hand preparation for the two groups of infants. When the infants had stable postural control while sitting (i.e., the group that could sit independently), they were more likely to reach with one hand in all four postures. This result was interpreted according to Bernstein's principle of degrees of freedom. When infants have not mastered postural control, they tend to reduce the degrees of freedom by forming synergies between the two arms. Once stability is mastered, these synergies are no longer needed and unimanual arm movements become more prevalent.

An important milestone in the development of reaching skills is the ability to sit

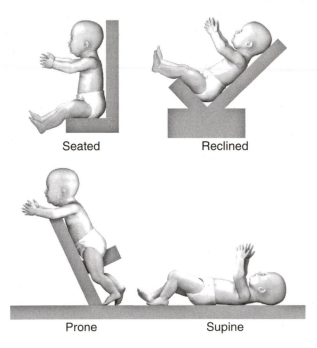

Seated   Reclined

Prone   Supine

Figure 5.4   An illustration of the four different postural conditions used by Rochat (1992) to examine the influence of posture on reaching control.
Reprinted from Rochat, 1992.

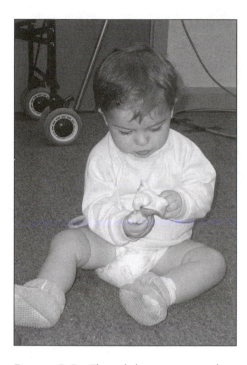

Figure 5.5 The ability to manipulate an object is enhanced by a stable sitting posture.

independently, which occurs at around six months of age. As shown in figure 5.5, once the infant has achieved a stable sitting posture, she is capable of using both hands to manipulate a toy.

The Role of Previous Experience

Another important factor is the infant's previous experience. Thelen and colleagues (1993) argued that when young infants attempt to reach for an object they desire, they need to adapt their "current ongoing spontaneous and intentional movements to the specific, new task of reaching and grasping" (p. 1059). This emphasizes the importance of the individual's early experience, not just with reaching movements but also with spontaneous movements. Considering that arm movements are evident in the 10-week-old fetus, infants already have a long history of arm movements before they achieve successful reaching. Recent research has demonstrated that early experience can affect the emergence and facilitation of early infant reaching (e.g., Lobo et al., 2004; Thelen & Spencer, 1998).

Thelen and colleagues (1993) examined rate-limiting variables in the development of reaching in a longitudinal study involving four infants. Reaching movements were examined at several different stages, namely, two weeks before the infants achieved successful reaching, the week they achieved this, and then the following two weeks. Infants were presented with a toy while supported in an infant chair. It was noted that the speed of early spontaneous movements may be a factor in determining when and how infants will achieve successful reaching. Investigation of the four infants' reaching patterns demonstrated that the two infants who had the fast and energetic movements achieved reaching at 15 and 12 weeks of age, whereas the two slower and quieter infants both achieved reaching at 20 weeks.

Another finding relating to speed was that in the early reaching attempts, as the speed of the reach increased, the trajectory path decreased in straightness with an increase in the number of movement units. Thelen and Spencer (1998) suggested that this may be due to a tight coupling of timing and load levels at this early stage of development. The larger forces produced by the faster movements may disrupt stability of the surrounding segments, leading to unstable reaching trajectories. These relationships disappeared once the infants produced competent or stable reaches, which took between 10 and 18 weeks.

This study, one of the few that has investigated early reaching longitudinally, demonstrates the importance of understanding the early history of the infant prior to reaching. As stated by Thelen and colleagues (1996), "Reaching as a new pattern is not imposed on the system but evolves as a product of the infants' current movement preferences and abilities, the histories of those preferred patterns, and from the everyday activities that allow them to discover new patterns" (p. 1071). Each infant demonstrated a unique solution to the problem of mastering successful reaching. The infants achieved this milestone at different ages and levels of activity and with different preferred patterns of movement. For example, the infants who initially produced fast and forceful spontaneous movements needed to slow down to achieve successful reaches, whereas the slower infants needed to generate greater muscular forces. This is consistent with the views of the dynamic systems perspective, which argues that the movement solution is not endogenous. Rather, it "must be discovered by each infant in relation to his or her given muscles, energy levels and the tasks at hand" (Thelen, 1998, p. 275).

Development of Grasping

As with other motor milestones, the development of grasping has been described in terms of invariant sequences. H.M. Halverson systematically examined reaching and grasping in infants in the early 20th century. In his classic study in 1931, Halverson detailed the progression of infant prehension through the use of cinematography, a very innovative approach for that period. He outlined 10 developmental phases of grasping (outlined in figure 5.6) by observing infants aged between 16 and 52 weeks as they reached for a 1-in. (2.54-cm) cube. Around five months of age, the infants were able to touch and squeeze the object and eventually to support the object between the palm of the hand and the undersurface of the fingers in types of grips termed *power grips*. Although the infants could grasp the object by six months of age, they did not utilize what is termed a *precision grip* until around one year of age. The precision grip involves the use of one or more fingers and the thumb to grasp the object without its being supported by the palm of the hand.

In 1937, Halverson produced a series of three papers (Halverson, 1937a, b, c) that extensively examined grasping in early infancy. This research was based on the maturational perspective. As described in chapter 2, many of the principles guiding this approach are now considered inappropriate. Even so, the work of Halverson is recognized as a major contribution to our understanding of the development of the grasp.

More recently, many researchers investigating the development of grasping have adopted a dynamic systems perspective. Of particular relevance is the notion of movement *constraints* depicted in figure 2.14. Newell (1986) argued that motor coordination is influenced by three main sources of constraint to action, namely, environmental, organis-

■■■ H.M. Halverson pioneered the research on grasping in infants, describing the shift from the power grasp to precision grasp in the infant's first year.

Type of grasp	Weeks of age	
No contact	16	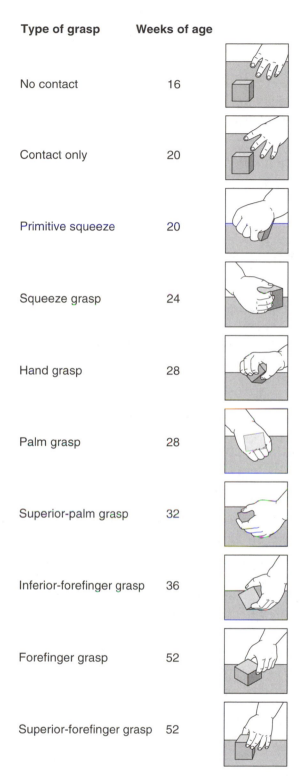
Contact only	20	
Primitive squeeze	20	
Squeeze grasp	24	
Hand grasp	28	
Palm grasp	28	
Superior-palm grasp	32	
Inferior-forefinger grasp	36	
Forefinger grasp	52	
Superior-forefinger grasp	52	

Figure 5.6 Halverson's (1931) 10 phases of grasping, determined through a comprehensive cinematographic study.

Reprinted from Halverson, 1931.

mic, and task constraints. Several particular constraints have been associated with the development of grasping.

The Role of Neural Development

Initially, young infants appear to have neurological constraints that limit their ability to grasp an object in their first few months. According to Newell's (1986) model, these would fall into the category of organismic constraints. When the palmar grasp reflex is initiated (see figure 1.5a), the newborn infant appears to grasp objects. However, when the infant's arm is extended, the newborn cannot grasp objects, as there appears to be a synergistic coupling of the arm and hand that results in an extension of the hand as the arm is extended. Likewise, as the arm is flexed the hand tends to close (von Hofsten, 1990). This response can be demonstrated through several of the newborn reflexes described in chapter 1, such as the Moro reflex, and appears to be related to the development of the appropriate cortico-motoneuronal connections. Also, the asymmetric tonic neck reflex (figure 1.6) produces a synergistic relationship with the head and arm, limiting the ability to perform successful prehension. Although most of these synergies appear to diminish at around two months of age, the infant then produces a fisted response during arm extension (von Hofsten, 1989). Once the infant begins fixating on the object to be grasped, at around three months of age, then the appropriate hand movements become evident.

Later in development, independent finger control is needed to produce the pincer grip. Again, this may partly be determined by neural development, as von Hofsten (1993) suggests that one of the many factors that determine the development of grasping is the appropriate maturation of the pyramidal pathway. Evidence for this has been provided by Kuypers (1962), who found that the pyramidal pathway was linked to independent finger control in the rhesus monkey at around seven months of age. Wallace and Whishaw (2003) have found that infants ranging from one to five months of age produce spontaneous hand and digit patterns that resemble precision grips such as the pincer grip. However, they emphasize that these patterns are not functional grips, as infants this young cannot use them to grip objects. Like others, Wallace and Whishaw suggest that these movements may be mediated by the developing pyramidal tract.

The Role of Task Constraints

Task constraints are also an important factor in understanding the development of grasping. The early maturationists often used a particular set of task constraints when investigating motor development. For example, Halverson (1931) used a 1-in. (2.54-cm) cube to describe the stages of grasping. As a result, Newell, Scully, McDonald, and Baillargeon (1989) have argued that the stages of prehension depicted by the early maturationists may be a result of the task imposed rather than the capabilities of the infant or child. Consequently development may be underestimated, and abilities may appear less adaptive or flexible.

> ■■■ Task constraints are an important variable in determining success and the type of grasp that an infant will produce.

Newell, Scully, McDonald, and Baillargeon (1989) investigated this issue in young infants aged between four and eight months by varying the task constraints required in gripping an object. They presented four objects of varying size and shape, namely a 2.54-cm (1-in.) cube (as used by Halverson, 1931) and three toy cups with diameters of 1.25, 2.5, and 8.5 cm (0.5, 1, and 3.3 in.), to over 100 infants. The cups were presented to the infants both facing up and facing down, therefore requiring different grasping techniques. Several key findings emerged. Firstly, the number of digits (fingers and thumb) used to grasp the objects was not related to age, but to the size and orientation of the object, although the younger infants (four months) were more variable in the pattern of digit use. These younger infants were also less likely to successfully grasp the object, although they were still successful 71% of the time. This contrasts with the milestones described earlier by Halverson (1931), who found that infants started grasping only at around five months of age. Newell, Scully, McDonald, and Baillargeon suggested that their findings may be a result of the postural support provided for the infants in their study. As described earlier, newborn infants were capable of early reaching behavior once they were provided with appropriate postural support (von Hofsten, 1982).

The Role of Sensory Information

Newell, Scully, McDonald, and Baillargeon (1989) identified one aspect of grasping that was influenced by age. This was the type of information used to differentiate the different grip configurations. In order to be efficient at grasping, the infant needs to anticipate the shape of the object to prepare the shape of the hand. Studies investigating adult grip configuration (e.g., Cesari & Newell, 2000) have noted that adults utilize visual information to facilitate prospective control of grasping. Hence, another variable influencing the development of grasping is the appropriate use of visual information to guide the hand to the object.

The findings of Newell, Scully, McDonald, and Baillargeon (1989) contradicted the progression of grasping outlined by the early maturationists. Newell and colleagues provided evidence that even infants four months of age could produce a precision grip (thumb-index finger configuration), primarily with the small upright cup. Prior to this study, it had long been acknowledged that infants were not capable of precision grip until they were nearly one year of age, primarily due to neural constraints such as those outlined in the previous section. Thus Newell and colleagues argued that "the traditional estimates of the so-called milestones of the development of coordination are too conservative and inflexible" (p. 828).

Newell, Scully, McDonald, and Baillargeon (1989) noted that at four months of age, the infants relied primarily on haptic information to shape the hand around the object. With increasing age, dependence on haptic information decreased and that on vision increased, with vision used to anticipate the shape of the hand required for the particular object. A similar conclusion was reached by von Hofsten and Rönnqvist (1988), who noted that although younger infants opened their hand in anticipation of the object, it was only when the infants were around 13 months of age that their hand began to close in anticipation of the object.

Other studies (e.g., Corbetta et al., 2000; Fagard, 2000), however, have failed to support the finding of Newell, Scully, McDonald, and Baillargeon (1989). Corbetta and colleagues also found that infants produce distinctive reaching and grip configurations for different types of objects, but this did not occur until the infants were around eight months of age. In their study, Corbetta and colleagues utilized objects with two different textures, one hard and one soft (soft pom-poms). In contrast with Newell and colleagues, they did not find any evidence suggesting that younger infants can adjust grip configuration through the use of haptic information. Rather, they emphasize the need to consider both sensory *and* motor constraints when examining the infant's ability to grasp an object. In the case of the younger infants, the motor constraints, such as those described earlier, appear to be the rate-limiting variable in the ability to adjust grip configurations. Once these motor constraints disappear at around eight months of age, "Infants are able to use and integrate visual and haptic information to scale their actions to objects" (p. 351).

Bimanual Reaching and Grasping

Although there have been extensive investigations of one-handed reaching in infants, bimanual reaching has received less interest, even though it appears to play an important role in the infant's development of reaching (Corbetta & Thelen, 1994).

One- and two-handed prereaching was examined by von Hofsten and Rönnqvist (1993). They used three-dimensional motion analysis to examine the organization and structure of neonatal spontaneous arm movements in three- to five-day-old infants who were fully supported in an infant chair. They noted that the two arms were closely coupled, moving together in 3-D space. This is surprising given that in the fetus, unimanual hand-to-head contacts have been noted at all ages (12 to 38 weeks gestational age) except 36 weeks. At 38 weeks, unimanual contacts remained dominant (de Vries et al., 2001). Infants in these two studies would have very different postural demands, and this may be a factor in determining one- and two-handed reaching.

In a review of hand–mouth coordination, Rochat (1993) examined whether one- or two-handed transport of an object to the mouth occurred in infants aged between two and five months. He noted that 7 of the 10 three-month-old infants preferred bimanual transport, whereas one-handed transport was noted in the majority of the two-month-old (7 out of 10), four-month-old (6 out of 10), and five-month-old (8 out of 10) infants. Although the number of infants studied was quite small, these results demonstrate shifting patterns of one- and two-handed transport in infants. Overall, however, it appears that for infants under six months of age, bimanual synergisms are more common in reaching than the use of one arm only.

■■■ Infants fluctuate between unimanual and bimanual reaching and grasping in their first year, and this appears to be largely influenced by factors such as posture and the characteristics of the object to be grasped.

The properties of the object to be grasped also influence whether there will be unimanual or bimanual reaching (Fagard, 2000; Newell, Scully, McDonald, and Baillargeon, 1989; Rochat, 1992). In their study on task constraints in grip patterns, Newell and colleagues noted that the object properties of shape and size were the primary determinants of whether the infant used one or two hands to manipulate an object. That is, the task constraints determined unimanual versus bimanual reaching and grasping. However, it should be noted that in this study, in which the infants were between four and eight months of age, only 5% of the trials were performed with two hands, despite other studies suggesting that infants between five and six months tend to reach and grasp more often with both hands (Fagard, 2000; Rochat, 1992). Fagard, for example, found that 60% of all reaches by her group of five- to six-month-olds were bimanual when infants were reaching for small, medium, and large objects. However, even the small objects in Fagard's study (mean diameter × height was 3.7 cm × 8.1 cm [1.5 × 3 in.]) were larger than most of the objects used by Newell and colleagues in their study. Furthermore, when Fagard examined groups of children aged 7 to 8, 9 to 10, and 11 to 12 months, object size was the primary determinant of whether the infant used unimanual or bimanual reaching in the 11- to 12-month-old infants (see figure 5.7).

The ability of an infant to reach across the body's midline to an object that is positioned laterally to the infant is considered another in the multitude of infant accomplishments. This initially occurs when the infant is around 4.5 to 7 months of age (van Hof et al., 2002), although it is a task that is difficult to master. Van Hof and colleagues provided evidence to suggest that the ability to cross the midline emerges

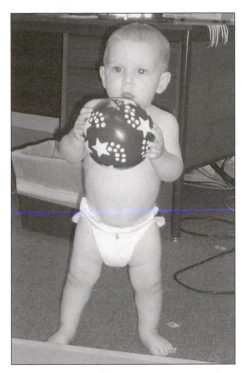

Figure 5.7 Holding an object of this size clearly requires two hands.

at around the same time as bimanual reaching. Although the emergence of contralateral reaches appears to be dependent upon the maturation of the corpus callosum (Bishop, 1990), object size again appears to be an important variable in determining whether an infant uses *ipsilateral* or *contralateral* reaching (van Hof et al.). It is only when children are around 10 years of age (and sometimes older) that they appear to master this difficult task requiring a limb to cross over the body's midline (Haywood & Getchell, 2001).

Tool Use

A more functional aspect of grasping that has received some attention in the literature is tool use. *Tools* have been defined as "extensions of the limbs" that "enhance the efficiency with which skilled actions are performed" (Connolly & Dalgleish, 1993, p. 174). The use of pens and pencils, in particular, has been of interest to developmental researchers. However, at the stage of infancy, implements for eating and drinking are usually the first tools to be explored; and, as can be seen in figure 5.8, this initially proves a difficult task for the young infant (figure 5.8*a*) and continues to be a challenge for the older child (figure 5.8*b*).

a   b

Figure 5.8 Infants' early attempts at feeding with a spoon. *(a)* At 14 months; the transverse palmar grip is used to hold the spoon. *(b)* At 2 1/2 years of age; this child is using the adult clenched grip, although clearly he has a way to go before he becomes proficient at its use.

The spoon is often the first implement that the young infant is introduced to, usually in the second half of the first year. One of the earliest descriptions of the development of spoon use by young infants can be found in a book by Gesell and Ilg (1937), titled *Feeding Behavior in Infants* (cited in Connolly & Dalgleish, 1989). More recently, Connolly and Dalgleish described spoon use in a longitudinal study of infants from 12 to 24 months of age. The individual findings for four of these infants from age 12 to 18 months were examined further by Connolly and Dalgleish in a 1993 publication. These papers provided an extensive description of the changes that occur as the infant learns to become a proficient spoon user. Overall, 11 different grip patterns were identified in the infants, although no infant displayed all of these. The infants displayed between three and eight of these patterns in the first six months of the second year, but by around 18 months, all four infants had established a preferred grasp pattern. The transverse palmar-radial grip pattern was the most commonly used by the infants, and this is the pattern used by the 14-month-old infant pictured in figure 5.8*a*. The other most popular grip pattern was the clenched digital-radial. The position for holding the spoon was also established by 18 months.

Manual Asymmetries in Infancy

Estimates of right-handedness in the human population range from 70% to 95% depending on cultural background, with estimates in Western culture at around 85% to 95% (Hopkins & Rönnqvist, 1998). Why this asymmetry, and why is the preference generally for the right hand? The answers to these questions still elude us; but, as with most developmental trends, the right-hand preference appears to be related to biological, social, and cultural influences (Bishop, 1990). That is, like many other aspects of motor development, handedness may be guided by organismic, environmental, and task constraints (Newell, 1986).

At issue in this section is whether manual asymmetries present in the young infant provide any clue to later hand preferences. This is an important issue when one considers the evidence that handedness, specifically non-right-handedness, has been linked to neurological impairment. For example, Saigal and colleagues (1992) identified a larger proportion of non-right-handed children (31%) in a cohort of infants born with birth weights less than 1,000 g (2.2 lb). These children were more likely to have neurological deficits such as cerebral palsy and mental retardation than the right-handed children.

Although manual asymmetries are present in infancy, it is now recognized that these preferences may fluctuate considerably in the first year of life. It is only when the child is around three years of age that hand preference is thought to remain stable (McManus et al., 1988).

Few studies have addressed handedness in the newborn infant. However, several studies of newborn reaching have provided information on handedness. For example, Rochat and colleagues (1988) found that when they introduced sucrose solution into the mouths of newborn infants (between 7 and 57 hr old), right and left hands were used equally for hand-to-mouth responses, and there was no significant interaction between hand and condition (sucrose and no sucrose). In contrast, von Hofsten (1982) found a right-hand preference in the reaching responses of newborn infants between five and nine days old in the reaching study described earlier in this chapter.

Early studies by Gesell and Ames (1947) and Seth (1973) provided evidence to suggest a left- rather than a right-hand preference in infants at around 16 to 20 weeks of age. This, of course, conflicts with the fact that the majority of adults are right-handed and implies that infants have an initial left-hand preference before developing right-handedness at a later stage. McDonnell and colleagues (1983) examined arm movements in 15 full-term infants tested longitudinally from three to eight weeks of age and found that 14 of them demonstrated left-hand dominance. The authors suggested that at this young age "the right hemisphere is more responsive to visuospatial stimulation than the left" (p. 297). A model put forward by Best (1988) suggests that the right hemisphere may develop earlier than the left, implying functional asymmetries, although Iaccino (1993) warns that morphological asymmetries do not necessarily reflect any functional differences between the hemispheres.

In contrast, Young and colleagues (1983) described 17 studies of infants under five months of age that examined directed arm movements toward a target. Thirteen of these studies provided evidence of right-hand preference (although several discussed nonsignificant trends), and only four demonstrated a left-hand preference. Only three studies showed significant right-hand preference. As a result, the authors suggested that it was misleading to argue for an absolute differentiation of hand behavior in early infancy. Rather, it appears that in the first four months, the right hand shows preference for "more directed target-related activity" (p. 27), whereas the left hand appears to play more of a role in nondirected activity. These findings could be described in terms of the task constraints. That is, hand preference was related not to any specific biological preference, but rather to the task required of the infant. Newell and colleagues (1989), in the study described earlier in this chapter, found no evidence of hand dominance when infants were required to grasp objects of different sizes and shapes. Although the experimenter always moved the object to the midline of the infant from the infant's right side, the right and left hands were each used around 50% of the time for one-hand grasps.

According to Annett (1981, 1998), many factors influence hand use, including neural factors, tool design, physical power, social factors, imitation, and specific instructions. Despite this, Annett argues that right-handed bias in humans fits a simple genetic model in which the presence of a single **allele** in an individual will favor right-handedness. Individual variability in handedness will emerge when the allele is absent. Annett's *right-shift theory* of handedness suggests that a gene for left hemisphere speech produces a *by-product* of right-handedness. If this gene is not present, then there is no right- or left-hand bias. Clearly, in the latter case, other factors, or constraints, would come into play in determining whether the individual will be right- or left-handed.

Michel and colleagues (Michel, 1983, 1998; Michel & Harkins, 1986; Michel et al., 2002) suggest that handedness may relate to early lateral asymmetries present in the neonate and that early experience in infancy is responsible for the emergence of later handedness. This is a modified version of the progressive lateralization theory proposed by Lenneberg in 1967. The original theory argues that lateral asymmetries continue to develop through to puberty and are controlled by maturational processes (Hinojosa et al., 2003). This explanation, of course, would have to account for why the majority of infants become right-handed. The right-shift theory of Annett (1998) has recently been incorporated into this explanation (Michel et al., 2002).

As argued by Michel and colleagues, evidence exists to show that in young infants under three months of age, the right hand and arm are more active than the left. This preference appears to be due to the tendency of most infants to turn their head to their right more often, resulting in the right hand's being fisted more often than the left. As a result of this early postural preference, the infant observes the right hand more often. The asymmetric tonic neck reflex (see figure 1.6) has also been implicated in the development of hand preference. This reflex results in greater exposure of the visual regard of one hand versus the other. Again, given the preference of turning the head to the right in young infants, the right hand would be observed more than the left. This view is further supported by the finding that there appears to be little lateralized preference in the fetus prior to birth (de Vries et al., 2001).

Although this preference declines after the second month, Michel (1983) argued that this early experience is still important in determining hand preference. He suggested that "proprioceptive and tactile-kinesthetic feedback from the asymmetrical activity of the hands could facilitate the formation of cortically lateralized sensorimotor programs involved in hand use preferences" (p. 39). In support of this, Michel and Harkins (1986) demonstrated that between the ages of 3 and 18 months, infants maintained a consistent hand-use preference for reaching. If there was a head orientation preference for the left side in the first two months, then left-hand preference was found throughout the 3- to 18-month period. Similarly, right-hand preference was noted for rightward head orientation. Further evidence for this theory was noted recently by Michel et al. (2002) and Hinojosa et al. (2003). Hinojosa and colleagues found that infants maintained their hand-use preference from ages 7 to 11 months with little indication of fluctuations in preference. The hand-use preference for early prehensile grasping continued into unimanual manipulation at age 11 months.

In contrast to the findings of Michel and colleagues, Ramsay (1984), and Gesell and Ames (1947) observed systematic fluctuations in hand-use preferences when examining object manipulation. Corbetta and Thelen (1999) suggest that the fluctuations in hand asymmetries that have been identified in young infants may be a result of poor motor control. As a result of inefficient reaching and grasping skills, these types of movements may not be useful in attempts to identify preferred lateral bias in infants. Rather, the authors suggest that it would be more appropriate to investigate early spontaneous activity for evidence of handedness, as these movements are not susceptible to the task demands required of intentional movements.

Evidence of lateral asymmetries in spontaneous arm movements has been found in our research on the development of coordination in early infancy (Piek et al., 2002). Rather than investigate frequency of movement, this study addressed the relationship between limb joints in order to determine how this joint coordination changes with age. For infants aged from 6 to 18 weeks, the elbow and shoulder joints of the left arm were found to be more synchronous (they had significantly shorter lag time for angular displacement when producing spontaneous movements) than the right side. Given past research arguing that an important part of early development of coordination is a loosening of this synchrony (e.g., Piek & Gasson, 1999; Thelen, 1985), this appears to provide evidence that the right arm may be more developed than the left. Other lateral asymmetries were also identified that were linked to the gender of the infant. This may be associated with ontogenetic sex differences in maturation of the right and left hemispheres (Schucard & Schucard, 1990). However, at this stage, no link has been made between these early movement asymmetries and the development of later handedness.

Corbetta and Thelen (1999) investigated whether there was a relationship between arm asymmetries in spontaneous movements and later reaching movements in four infants (three boys and one girl) from age 3 weeks to 52 weeks. A relationship between these two types of arm movements was identified, particularly toward the end of the first year, when the infants became quite proficient at reaching. Furthermore, although there were many shifts in laterality, there was a tendency for more right-sided responses of longer duration, in contrast to short or sporadic left-sided responses. These findings were then compared with the children's hand preference when they reached three years of age. All four children were right-handed. However, given the proportion of right- versus left-handedness in the population, this finding is not surprising. It would be of interest to find children displaying a dominant left-sided pattern in their first year in order to determine whether the dominance is expressed as left-handedness in childhood.

Research on spoon use has also identified a hand preference in older infants aged 17 to 23 months. In their investigation of 16 infants, Connolly and Dalgleish (1989) found that all had a hand preference, based on the definition of preference for at least 80% of the spoon use during the recorded feeding times. Thirteen infants were right-handed and three were left-handed, which is consistent with estimates of adult handedness. However, whether these same hand preferences remained later in life was not investigated.

■■■ How Does This Research Inform Therapeutic Practice?

An infant's early years are an important time for the development of the basic skills needed for manual dexterity. Yet most intervention programs at present focus on gross motor skills with the aim of improving locomotor ability. This chapter again highlighted the influence of early experience on the development of reaching behavior. Spontaneous movements may be important for this development. Posture is another variable that affects reaching and grasping skills. Can research identify the key variables that could influence the development of appropriate reaching and grasping? How then could these be used for intervention in infants? This area is still very new, but very significant, given the importance of manual skills such as handwriting, computer use, and appropriate grooming in many aspects of an individual's life (e.g., motor, cognitive, and social).

Summary

Infants require manual skills to explore their environment. They appear to want to explore the environment virtually from birth, as their early reaching movements have been identified as intentional. However, it is not until they are around three or four months of age that they can successfully reach out and touch or grasp an object. Many factors determine when an infant can successfully reach and grasp, but one major factor is postural control.

Once infants can grasp an object, they may use a variety of grasp patterns that are largely determined by the shape and size of the object. Task constraints such as object size and shape are also important in determining whether the object will be manipulated with one or two hands.

Handedness is an area that has received a great deal of attention for many decades. However, the research on manual asymmetries in infants demonstrates many conflicting results, making it difficult to determine whether these early asymmetries indicate later handedness. This is a dilemma that needs considerably more investigation. In particular, longitudinal studies are required that follow the hand preferences of infants and children from birth through to three years of age, when hand preference is established.

six

Locomotion
The Development of Creeping and Walking

chapter objectives

This chapter will do the following:

- Outline the major locomotor milestones in the infant's first year
- Describe the processes that lead to the development of hands-and-knees creeping
- Discuss ways in which the different theoretical approaches account for how walking is achieved
- Discuss leg asymmetries and their link with later limb preferences

ndependent walking is often considered the pinnacle of achievement in infant motor development and was the topic of considerable research for most of the last century. Although a large proportion of earlier research focused on describing the qualitative changes that occur in locomotion with age, there has been a focus more recently on understanding how and why these changes occur.

In chapter 1, the early movement capabilities of infants were outlined. In the first few months, the motor output of an infant consists primarily of reflexes and spontaneous movements. Both have been implicated in the development of locomotion. This chapter examines the role of these early movements in the development of locomotion based on the various theoretical perspectives outlined in chapter 2. First, however, the major locomotor milestones achieved in infancy will be outlined.

Locomotor Milestones

Mary Shirley outlined the locomotor milestones in 1933 (Shirley, 1963). The sequence of motor activity that she mapped is shown in figure 6.1. The sequence also includes postural milestones such as sitting supported and unsupported, as well as prehension milestones such as reaching and grasping objects. As with most maturationists of the time, this sequence was assumed to be invariant in nature and

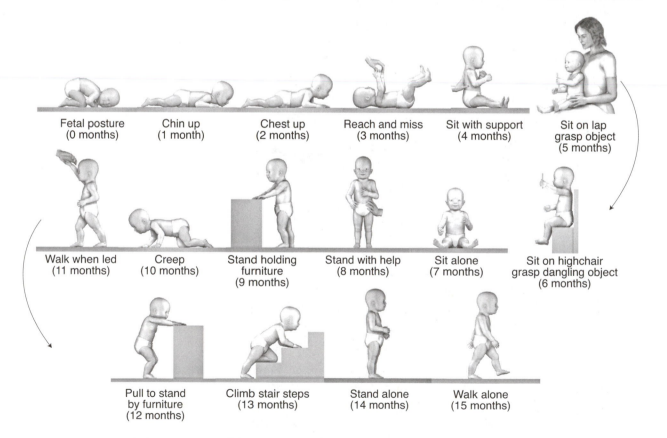

Figure 6.1 Mary Shirley's account of the sequence of motor milestones.
Reprinted from Shirley, 1963.

was consistent across all cultures. Even though we now know that there can be substantial variability in the patterning of early motor responses, the basic order and age of occurrence for these milestones are still relevant today.

It is interesting to note, however, that when one compares the ages of onset for Shirley's motor milestones described in 1933 (Shirley, 1963) and the Bayley scales devised in 1969, one can see a progressive shift in the age at which infants can achieve these locomotor milestones. For example, it can be seen from table 6.1 that Shirley's sequence lists walking alone as occurring around 15 months, yet Bayley gives a mean age of 11.7 months. This trend has continued, and present-day infants appear to be achieving these skills earlier than infants 70 years ago (Gallahue & Ozmun, 1998). Capute and colleagues (1985) observed this shift when they carried out a longitudinal examination of the onset of 12 common gross motor milestones in 381 children born full term. They found that motor milestones were achieved at earlier ages than reported by Gesell in the early half of the century. Different child-rearing techniques may have affected this shift. For example, research over the last 15 years into the causes of sudden infant death syndrome has resulted in the recommendation that young infants be placed in the supine rather than prone position while sleeping (Ponsonby et al., 1993). Does this increase the spontaneous activity generated, and will this result in earlier motor milestones? Such questions will only be resolved with further research.

The study by Capute and colleagues (1985) also showed that race, socioeconomic status, and sex influenced the onset of milestones. Race was recorded as black or white, and longitudinal results demonstrated that black infants achieved motor milestones at an earlier age than white infants. Although there were some inconsistencies between the cross-sectional and longitudinal results, the longitudinal findings suggested that males achieved gross motor milestones earlier than females. Cultural and gender issues will be discussed more fully in chapter 7 in terms of their potential impact on assessment of motor ability.

The first form of locomotion in young infants is generally rolling, which occurs once adequate control of head and trunk muscles is achieved. There are considerable differences in the literature in relation to when infants roll, and also on whether they roll from supine to prone first or from prone to supine. According to Piper and Darrah (1994), infants roll from supine to prone first at around 5 1/2 to 6 1/2 months of age. Prone-to-supine rolling occurs a little later, at around 6 to 7 months of age. In contrast, Bly (1994) suggests that rolling from supine to prone is more difficult for the infant, requiring greater coordination and control. She suggests that rolling from prone to supine usually occurs at five months of age, with supine-to-prone rolling occurring at the sixth month. These developmental transitions are often quite brief, with the main forms of infant locomotion, creeping and walking, occurring soon after. As a result, most of the research on locomotion has been carried out on these two milestones, and these are the focus of the current chapter.

■■■ Infants appear to be achieving motor milestones at an earlier age compared with half a century ago.

Table 6.1 A Comparison of the Onset of Motor Milestones Identified by Shirley (1933, cited in Shirley, 1963) and Bayley (1969)

Average age (mo)	Age range (mo)	Milestone (Bayley Scales of Infant Development)	Milestone (Shirley Sequence)
0.1		Lifts head when held at shoulder	
0.1		Lateral head movements	
0.8	0.3–3.0	Retains red ring	
0.8	0.3–2.0	Arm thrusts in play	
0.8	0.3–2.0	Leg thrusts in play	Chin up
1.6	0.7–4.0	Head erect and steady	
1.8	0.7–5.0	Turns from side to back	
2.0			Chest up
2.3	1.0–5.0	Sits with slight support	
4.0			Sits with support
4.4	2.0–7.0	Turns from back to side	
4.9	4.0–8.0	Partial thumb opposition	
5.0			Sits on lap
			Grasps object
5.3	4.0–8.0	Sits alone momentarily	
5.4	4.0–8.0	Unilateral reaching	
5.7	4.0–8.0	Rotates wrist	
6.0			Sits in chair
			Grasps dangling object
6.4	4.0–10.0	Rolls from back to front	
6.6	5.0–9.0	Sits alone steadily	
6.9	5.0–9.0	Complete thumb opposition	
7.0			Sits alone
7.1	5.0–11.0	Prewalking progression	
7.4	6.0–10.0	Partial finger prehension	
8.0			Stands with help
8.1	5.0–12.0	Pulls to standing	
8.6	6.0–12.0	Stands up by furniture	
8.8	6.0–12.0	Stepping movements	
9.0			Stands holding furniture
9.6	7.0–12.0	Walks with help	
10.0			Creeps
11.0	9.0–16.0	Stands alone	Walks when led
11.7	9.0–17.0	Walks alone	
12.0			Pulls to stand
14.0			Stands alone
14.6	11.0–20.0	Walks backward	
15.0			Walks alone
16.1	12.0–23.0	Walks up stairs with help	
16.4	13.0–23.0	Walks down stairs with help	
23.4	17.0–30.0+	Jumps off floor, both feet	
24.8	19.0–30.0+	Jumps from bottom step	

Reprinted from Haywood and Getchell, 2005.

Crawling and Creeping

Gesell and Ames (1940) were among the first researchers to document the pattern of development for infants in prone position. Their 1940 paper expands on an earlier paper by Ames (1937, cited in Gesell & Ames) on the sequential patterning of prone progression. Gesell and Ames describe 23 distinctive movement patterns that they identified in the prone infant, beginning at one week of age with the *passive kneel* and ending at stage 23 and age 60 weeks with *walking*. Included in this progression are different forms of *crawling* and *creeping*. It is important to carefully define these terms, as modern authors do not necessarily agree on the types of movement patterns denoted by this terminology.

Gesell and Ames (1940) define *crawling* as a movement pattern in which the infant pulls the trunk forward by extending and simultaneously flexing the forearms. The legs extend symmetrically and are dragged forward passively. According to the authors, this occurs at around 34 weeks of age. However, the pattern changes within a few weeks so that the forearms still pull the weight forward by extending, but flex alternately. In both cases the head is lifted 90° or more, and the stomach or abdomen remains on the floor. This is depicted in figure 6.2*a* and is often termed *belly crawling* or, more commonly by parents, the *commando* or *combat crawl*. Recent textbooks cite this as occurring at around six or seven months of age.

Creeping is defined by Gesell and Ames (1940) as follows: "Both arms *extend downward* from shoulder, then *extend* forward, alternately. Legs *flex* forward *alternately*. Arm and leg on opposite sides of body move simultaneously" (p. 251). Abdomen and chest are off the supporting surface as seen in figure 6.2*b*. Gesell and Ames, and Shirley (1933) as well, noted that creeping occurs around 10 months of age (see figure 6.1).

a   *b*

Figure 6.2 *(a)* Belly crawling, also termed combat or commando crawling, and *(b)* creeping.

■■■ Although the stages of prone locomotion identify belly crawling followed by hands-and-knees creeping as two key movement patterns, many infants will not perform belly crawling, and a small proportion will not creep at all. However, this is not necessarily an indication of abnormal development.

Some more recent literature has used the term *crawling* rather than *creeping* for the final stage of hands-and-knees forward progression (e.g., Adolph et al., 1998; Freedland & Bertenthal, 1994; Goldfield, 1989; Mondschein et al., 2000). It may be that this term is used because the movement is commonly called crawling by parents. However, the current volume follows the definitions given by Gesell and Ames (1940).

There are two types of prone progression patterns, *homolateral* and *contralateral.* If the limbs on the same side move forward or backward simultaneously, this is referred to as a *homolateral* pattern. It is usually seen initially with belly crawling. Hands-and-knees creeping generally displays a *contralateral* pattern in which the limbs on each side are opposing each other. This is the most proficient form of creeping.

Crawling initially involves little leg movement, but instead, a sliding forward movement. Generally, this crawling pattern develops into the contralateral creeping pattern, although it is quite common for infants to initiate creeping on the hands and knees without having gone through the earlier belly crawling stage. Furthermore, some infants do not crawl at all, or they perform a modification of the typical hands-and-knees creeping. Largo and colleagues (1993) categorized the different types of locomotion that first enable infants to achieve independent locomotion (see figure 2.3). Around 87% of their sample of children followed the "classical" pathway of locomotion, namely, crawling on stomach, followed by creeping on hands and knees, then on hands and feet prior to standing. The stages of creeping were also variable in the study by Adolph and colleagues (1998). Nearly half of their sample (13 of the 28 infants) progressed directly to hands-and-knees creeping without any indication of belly crawling. There were some consistencies, however. All belly crawlers progressed to hands-and-knees creeping, and all 28 infants produced hands-and-knees creeping.

In a recent study examining longitudinal development of locomotion, we have also investigated the relationship between initiation of early and later creeping. Locomotor patterns are shown in figure 6.3. As just described, not all infants belly crawled before they started contralateral creeping. In agreement with the findings of Adolph and colleagues (1998), nearly half of the sample (9 of the 20) progressed directly to hands-and-knees creeping, with the remainder of the infants producing different crawling patterns prior to hands-and-knees creeping. The length of time infants spent creeping before independent walking was achieved varied considerably.

Walking

The ultimate achievement for the young infant is the progression to independent walking. Infants usually start to cruise, or walk with support (see figure 4.6), between 7 and 12 months of age. When cruising, infants often step sideways rather than forward so that both the arms and legs can provide support (Haehl et al., 2000). Cruising aids in the development of appropriate balance (see chapter 4) necessary for

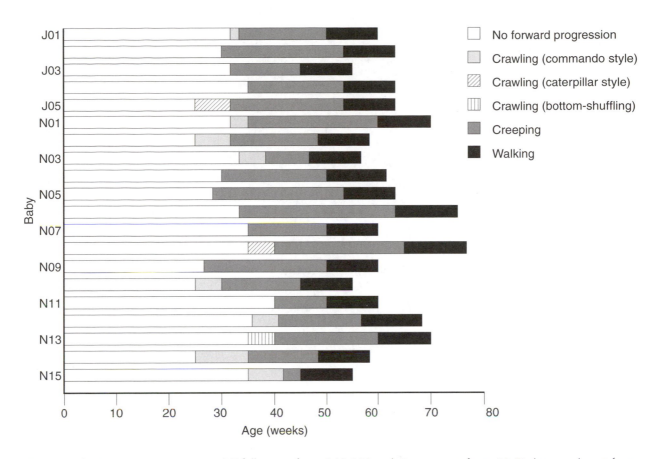

Figure 6.3 Locomotor patterns in 15 full-term infants (N1-15) and 5 preterm infants (J1-5) shown when infants initiated different crawling and creeping patterns leading to independent walking (note: preterm ages are corrected for gestational age).

Figure 6.4 Initial steps are awkward and flat-footed with the arms raised.

the infant to walk without support, which occurs anywhere between the 10th and 15th month in most infants.

It takes several months for infants to achieve competent walking once they have taken their first unsupported steps. Initial steps are awkward and hesitant, with each step flat-footed and generally independent of the other. Initially, balance is of primary importance, and therefore the infant has a wide stance as shown in figure 6.4. As the infant becomes more proficient, stride width diminishes, decreasing the base of support and increasing the degree of mobility by allowing for greater stride length (Adolph et al., 2003), and range of speed increases substantially (Bril & Breniere, 1989). The flat-footed steps disappear, to be replaced by the standard heel-to-toe pattern characteristic of the **plantigrade gait** found in adults (figure 6.5). Adult gait is distinguished by a marked heel strike in front of the body with the toes in the air, followed by the toe contact, with the heel lifting

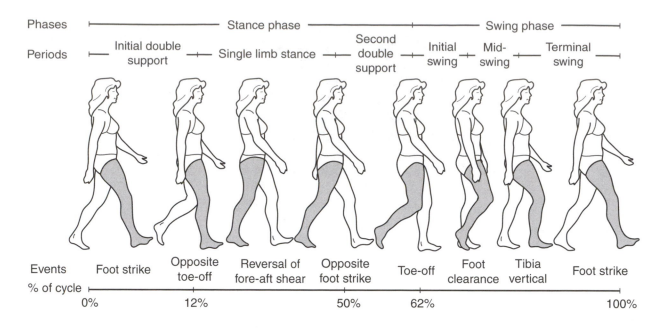

Figure 6.5 Typical heel-toe stride plantigrade gait in adult walking.
Reprinted from Abernethy et al., 2005.

 Competent walking involves both the legs and the arms, as the arms counterbalance trunk rotation caused by the leg gait.

during the maintained toe contact. Each leg spends around 60% of the time in stance (i.e., contact with the ground) and 40% in swing (Woollacott & Jensen, 1996).

Arm swing is considered an essential part of the adult gait pattern as it counterbalances trunk rotation around the vertical axis. When the infant first walks, the arms are generally raised in what is termed the "high guard" position (see figure 6.6). Ledebt (2000) examined arm posture in the early stages of walking and noted that the arms stayed in a fixed posture for an average of 10 weeks. This fixed arm posture was considered important to stabilize posture and also to minimize the degrees of freedom as the infant learns this difficult skill. Initial reduction of degrees of freedom is considered an important part of learning a new skill (e.g., Vereijken et al., 1992). Over this initial 10-week period, there is a shift from the high, to middle, to low guard position, until eventually the infant incorporates the arms into the walking pattern. As with other aspects of development, there is considerable variability, and not all infants undergo all of these stages.

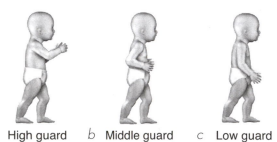

a High guard   b Middle guard   c Low guard

d Flexed arm   e Reciprocal swing

Figure 6.6 Stages of arm swing as outlined by Ledebt (2000), showing (a) high guard, (b) middle guard, (c) low guard, (d) flexed movement, and (e) reciprocal arm swing.
Adapted from Ledebt, 2000.

Prescriptive Views
of Locomotor Development

Traditional views such as the maturational and cognitive approaches argue that behaviors are "single-causal," generally attributing responsibility for the emergence of new behavior patterns to the central nervous system (CNS) (Thelen & Smith, 1994). Many of these authors saw reflexes as a key to understanding how voluntary movements develop, although they viewed the role of reflexes quite differently. Whereas some saw the need to inhibit reflexes in order for locomotion to develop (e.g., McGraw, 1940; Milani-Comparetti & Gidoni, 1967), others argued that locomotor skills developed from the basic infant reflexes (e.g., Sherrington, 1906; Zelazo, 1983). Some of these approaches are described next.

A Maturational Perspective

The development of walking was a topic of immense interest for developmentalists throughout the 20th century. Myrtle McGraw (1940) was one such investigator. In her 1940 paper, McGraw examined the sequential changes that occur in the infant's progression to independent walking. She argued that independent walking is dependent on two skills: the ability to maintain balance in the upright position and the ability to propel the body forward using alternate leg movements.

McGraw (1940) analyzed a total of 3,387 observations from 82 infants and children supported in the upright position. As a result, she identified seven distinct phases that an infant produces during the progression from the newborn state to acquisition of independent walking. These are outlined in figure 6.7. McGraw examined the onset and offset times of each phase for all children and related these to the development of appropriate neural centers and pathways. As outlined in chapter 2, McGraw believed that the reflexes interfered with the development of locomotion and therefore needed to be inhibited. For example, she argued that the loss of the stepping reflex in phase 2 is a result of the onset of cortical inhibition of the subcortical or nuclear areas, as this stage could be linked to the maturation of cortical centers that control the lower brain and spinal cord. However, little evidence has been found to support the notion of cortical inhibition of infant reflexes.

Central Pattern Generators

Forssberg (1985) argued that a hierarchical system controls human locomotion. He suggested that the complex patterns of muscular contractions required for walking are produced by *central pattern generators* (CPGs) located in the spinal cord (see chapter 3 for a description of these). When Forssberg (1985) compared infant stepping patterns and adult plantigrade locomotion, he identified striking differences,

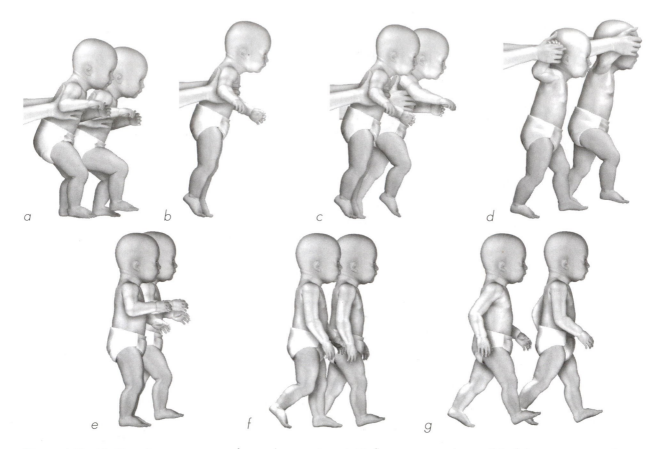

Figure 6.7 McGraw's seven stages of erect locomotion. *(a)* Reflex stepping phase; *(b)* inhibitory or static phase; *(c)* transition phase, which includes activities such as stomping of foot or stand bouncing and the reappearance of stepping movements; *(d)* deliberate stepping phase with erect posture; *(e)* independent stepping phase marking the start of independent walking; *(f)* heel-toe progression; *(g)* adult pattern of walking with synchronous swinging of the arms with the opposite lower extremity.

Reprinted from Mcgraw, 1940.

which he argued were a result of maturational changes occurring within the CNS. Rather than the adult heel-toe gait, infant stepping is more like a **digitigrade** pattern found in quadrupeds and bipedal monkeys and apes, where there is no knee-ankle coordination. As a result, Forssberg argued that at birth, infants have an innate CPG that is programmed for the digitigrade pattern rather than the adult-like plantigrade gait. When the stepping pattern becomes inactive at around six to eight months of age, he suggested that this may be due to the developing CNS, in particular to the efferent locomotor system. It is only when the infant starts to walk without support that there is a "gradual transformation towards a human plantigrade pattern" (p. 490), as a system unique to humans transforms the CPG from a digitigrade to a plantigrade gait.

As described in chapter 3, although some evidence suggests that CPGs are present and play some role in locomotion, there is doubt as to whether they control the sequencing and timing of locomotion, particularly given the influence of sensory input on the patterning of the movements (Thelen & Spencer, 1998; Woollacott & Jensen, 1996).

A "Behavioral-Cognitive" Approach

In contrast to the reflex inhibition notion of McGraw (1940), other developmentalists believed that reflexes were the "building blocks" for later motor control. This notion was described by McDonnell and Corkum (1991) as the *motor-continuity* theory of reflexes. This view was utilized by Zelazo (1983), who described a *behavioral-cognitive* approach to understanding motor development. Zelazo (1983) argued that, rather than disappearing, newborn reflexes are integrated into controlled behavior through a process of instrumental conditioning. That is, the newborn reflexes become modified to produce voluntary movements.

Zelazo (1983) investigated this proposal using the stepping reflex in young infants (see figure 1.9). Normally this disappears at around five months of age. However, Zelazo argued that this disappearance was due to child-rearing practices rather than through inhibition of the response, as argued by developmentalists such as McGraw. In support of this idea, Zelazo cited examples from Desert San infants from the Kalahari Desert in Botswana who appear to maintain the stepping reflex throughout the first year. This appeared to be the result of parents playing games with the infants that promoted the stepping reflex. Furthermore, these infants appear to be advanced in their early motor milestones, including independent walking (Konner, 1973, 1977, cited in Zelazo, 1983). Further evidence of cultural differences in motor development is provided in chapter 7.

Zelazo (1983) suggested that early and persistent practice of the primary stepping reflex affects the onset of voluntary walking behavior. He argued that the stepping reflex was the behavioral ancestor, or building block, of normal walking, and provided evidence that the reflex can be conditioned into the instrumental activity of walking through regular exercise. For example, Zelazo and colleagues (1972) administered daily exercise over a seven-week period to a group of six male infants and found that the stepping progressed from a reflexive to an instrumental response (see figure 6.8). Instrumental conditioning requires a reward for the response that is being conditioned. The authors argued that the task was intrinsically rewarding, that is, that the reward was the stepping itself, which was demonstrated by the infant's smiling and laughing throughout the training. The specific intrinsic properties that were rewarding were vertical orientation and varied visual stimulation.

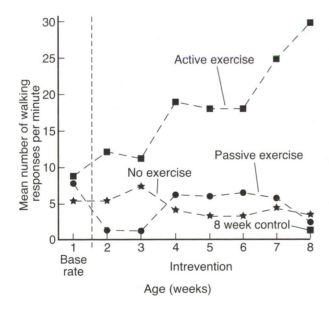

Figure 6.8 Zelazo and colleagues' (1972) results showing the increase in the mean number of stepping responses that result from active exercise. There was no effect of passive exercise or of no exercise.

Reprinted from Zelazo et al., 1972.

There is an alternative explanation for Zelazo's findings. Thelen and Fisher (1982) suggested that the stepping response disappeared once the infants' body fat, or mass, increased to a level at which they were no longer able to lift their legs against gravity. Zelazo's training of the infants may have resulted in stronger muscles, allowing the infant to maintain the reflex for a longer period. In order to test this, Thelen et al. (1984) manipulated the mass of the infants' legs in several ways to determine whether this influenced the rate of stepping behavior (see figure 6.9). They found that when weights were added to the infants' legs (figure 6.9a), the stepping reflex decreased in frequency. Furthermore, submerging the infants' legs in water, as demonstrated in figure 6.9b, led to an increase in the stepping reflex.

Although the stepping response was maintained over the period during which it is expected to dissipate, infants were still unable to produce independent walking much earlier than nine months. Zelazo (1983) argued that other constraints are present that limit the onset of independent walking, in particular a cognitive constraint based on information-processing ability. He argued that "improved access to memory may permit the necessary integrative capacity for balance and coordination to occur, thereby permitting unaided walking to develop" (p. 99). Again, Thelen (1983) pointed out that locomotion is, phylogenetically, an old behavior. Given that locomotion is a characteristic of all but the most primitive animals, there appears to be no need for a cognitive change to produce independent walking. Instead, Thelen has suggested a dynamic systems approach to understanding how locomotion develops (Thelen, 1983, 1995).

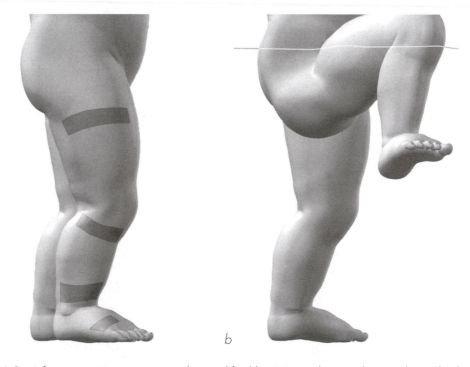

a   b

Figure 6.9   Infant stepping patterns can be modified by (a) weights, resulting in diminished stepping, and (b) water, which increases the stepping responses.

Locomotor Development
From a Dynamic Systems Perspective

As a result of the emergence of the ecological and dynamic systems approaches in the 1980s, there has been a resurgence of interest in investigating motor development and, in particular, how infants acquire locomotion. Thelen (1995) argued that new behaviors such as walking result not from maturational processes such as reflex inhibition, CPGs, or cognitive constraints, but rather as a result of the processes of self-organization. Development is described as a series of changes in relative stability and instability, as shown in the ontogenetic map depicted in figure 2.12. The map depicts the dynamic and self-organizing nature of development as well as the relatively invariant nature of early development portrayed by researchers such as Gesell and McGraw. At the same time, it demonstrates the ability of the infant to digress from this sequential pattern, given that the pathways have different degrees of variability and stability. The next sections outline some of the recent research carried out using a dynamic systems perspective to investigate the two primary locomotor achievements in infancy, namely, the development of creeping and walking.

How Infants Learn to Creep

Early motor development has been a topic of renewed interest to researchers over the last quarter-century. Despite this, very little additional research has been carried out on the development of creeping in infancy since the middle of the 20th century. This is surprising given that it often represents the infant's first opportunity for independent mobility. Goldfield (1989) noted that this was also a trend throughout the 20th century. Carmichael's *Manual of Child Psychology* included many sections on creeping in the 1946 and 1954 editions. However, as Goldfield points out, in the 1970 and 1983 editions, crawling did not even appear in the subject index. Why are so few recent studies examining creeping? In part the reason may be that the creeping behavior of infants is considerably more variable than walking and is generally transient, lasting only a few months if produced at all. It is thus more difficult to observe and measure.

Despite these problems, several researchers have investigated the emergence of creeping, notably Eugene Goldfield (1989), Robert Freedland and Bennett Bertenthal (1994), and, more recently, Karen Adolph and colleagues (Adolph et al., 1998; Mondschein et al., 2000).

From a dynamic systems perspective, it is argued that many factors contribute to the development of a particular behavior. Goldfield (1989) examined a number of these factors in the development of creeping. He was particularly interested in the influence of head orientation, hand use, and kicking and utilized Gesell and Ames's (1940) stages of forward progression as a basis for investigating the development of creeping (note that Goldfield's definition of crawling is in fact Gesell and

Ames's definition of creeping). Fifteen infants were videotaped at weekly intervals to examine their locomotor and reaching patterns. The results suggested that orienting, reaching, and kicking all contribute to the development of creeping. Orienting involves the eye–head coordination leading to a motivation to reach a particular object or person. Evidence that this was an important factor was obtained when a relationship between head orientation and arm extension and flexion was found in the early stages of pivot (trunk pivoting on the abdomen) and low creep (chest and abdomen making contact with the supporting surface). Reaching involves the steering of the body, and Goldfield found that hand preference could be linked to different stages of forward progression. Furthermore, when infants dropped from a sitting to a prone position, they used their nonpreferred hand for support, leaving their preferred hand to initiate the first reach leading to creeping (for the target). Finally, kicking can be linked to forward propulsion; and again, a relationship was found between the stage of creeping, leg activity, and head orientation.

Adolph and colleagues (1998) examined 28 full-term infants in a longitudinal study that tracked the infants from the initiation of prone progression through to independent walking. They were interested in examining the effect of experience on the development of proficient hands-and-knees creeping patterns. Their findings demonstrated a large range in the age of onset for the different stages of movement, which they attributed in part to the body dimensions of the infants. "Slimmer, smaller infants tended to crawl earlier than chubbier, more top-heavy babies, suggesting that crawling may depend in part on how much weight infants must support and propel forward" (p. 1309).

Our recent research (Piek et al., 2005) has addressed the development of infant creeping using motion analysis. Unlike previous researchers (e.g., Freedland & Bertenthal, 1994), we investigated the coordination between different joints rather than single measurements or markers for each limb (see figure 6.10). Like Freedland and Bertenthal, we have found a great deal of variability in the initial creeping. This initial variability is expected, as there are many solutions that are equally appropriate rather than one highly stable solution in these early stages (Adolph et al., 1998).

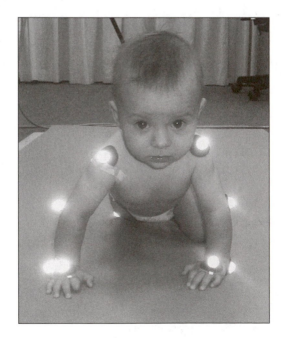

Figure 6.10   Investigating crawling using 3-D motion analysis.

How Infants Learn to Walk

In order to understand how walking develops from a dynamic systems perspective, it is important to first examine the early motor activities of the infant. However, unlike the maturationists who believed that reflexes played a major role in the development of walking, dynamic systems theorists such as Esther Thelen saw the early spontaneous movements playing a key role in the development of later motor ability. Thelen was one of the first researchers to investigate the relationship between early spontaneous motor activity and the development of walking in human infants. Her earlier work mapped out the type of spontaneous activity, or rhythmical stereotypy, that occurred prior to the onset of particular motor milestones (Thelen, 1979, 1981). These movements were described more fully in chapter 1. Of particular interest over the past few decades have been early infant kicking and stepping and the relevance of these movements to later walking.

Infant Kicking

In the early to mid-1980s, Thelen and colleagues (e.g., Thelen, 1985; Thelen & Fisher, 1983b; Thelen et al., 1983) used electromyography (EMG) and motion analysis to examine the organization of leg movements in young infants. Markers were placed on the hip, knee, and ankle joints of the infant's leg, and frame-by-frame video analysis was used to determine temporal and spatial characteristics of infant supine kicking. The infant kicking pattern involves a flexion phase and an extension phase as outlined in figure 6.11. The primary aim of these earlier studies was to investigate any coalitional organization between the leg joints.

When the ankle, knee, and hip joints were compared in two- and four-week-old infants, it was found that the joints produced a coordinated pattern, suggesting a synergistic relationship between these leg joints (Thelen & Fisher, 1983b). Analysis of the EMG patterns of these early kicking movements demonstrated co-contractions of the agonist and antagonist muscle groups during leg flexion, followed by no contraction during the extension phase. That is, the legs appeared to extend as a result of such factors as gravitational forces, the elastic properties of the leg, and the inertia of the preceding flexion response. These patterns of movements were described as "more simple and more primitive than control of such phasic movements in adults" (Thelen, 1985, p. 5).

The flexion and extension components of infant kicking have also been examined in our laboratory in a study of full-term infants aged from 2 to 26 weeks (Piek & Carman, 1994). Using frame-by-frame video analysis to measure the timing of the flexion and extension of leg kicks, we found a significant negative correlation between age and the mean time taken for both leg flexion and leg extension. The extension phase was significantly longer than the flexion phase, and there was a significant difference in the variability of the leg flexion and extension. Overall, the extension or return phases of the movements were slower than the flexion or lift phases, particularly for the younger infants. In the very young infants, in many cases the limb appeared to rely on passive forces such as gravity to return to its original position. This was consistent with the EMG findings of Thelen and Fisher (1983b) and would account for the greater variance found in the extension or return phases of the movement, as these movements are dependent to

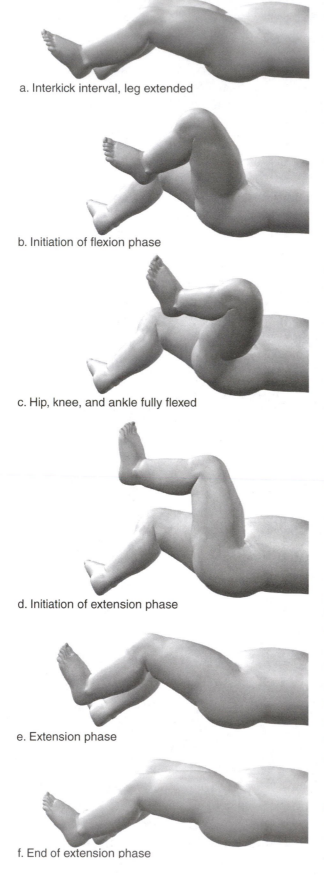

a. Interkick interval, leg extended

b. Initiation of flexion phase

c. Hip, knee, and ankle fully flexed

d. Initiation of extension phase

e. Extension phase

f. End of extension phase

a greater degree on external forces acting upon them. As the internal active forces develop, the movements become faster and less variable.

A relative invariance of the timing of flexion and extension in infant kicking has also been noted. Although changes in the frequency and vigor of kicking have been associated with changes in the level of arousal and context of the kicking, the timing of neither the leg flexion nor the leg extension appears to differ when the context is varied. For example, no differences were found for these measures when infants were in an active, moving state compared to a state of crying (Thelen et al., 1981), nor was the timing affected when infant kicking was reinforced by attaching the leg to a mobile (Thelen & Fisher, 1983a).

The upright stepping response has been examined in a manner similar to that for supine kicking (Thelen & Fisher, 1982). When infants are held in an upright position and produce the stepping response, the joint patterns that emerge appear the same as those for supine kicking. Thelen (1985) cited this as evidence to suggest that this stepping is not a reflex, but rather "an expression of the same tonic arousal that tunes up the kicking response" (p. 7). Furthermore, there appear to be close links between the early kicking and stepping patterns and the kinematic parameters found in adult gait (Thelen et al., 1989). It appears that during the swing phase of mature walking (i.e., when the leg is in the air and it first flexes and then extends out before touching the ground), the hip, knee, and ankle joints act in a similar way to the flexion, pause between the flexion and extension phases (see figure 6.11) of infant kicking and stepping. Hence, even

Figure 6.11 Flexion and extension of spontaneous kicking in infants, showing the different phases in the kicking pattern.
Adapted from Thelen et al., 1981.

at this very early age, infants are producing movement patterns that may be integrated into later motor functions.

Kinematic analysis was utilized in these studies to describe the kicking pattern of infants in different postures. Kinetic variables have also been used to describe the forces that produce these different kicking patterns. Most of these studies rely on determining net torque through inverse dynamics (Kamm et al., 1990). Studies by Schneider and colleagues (1990) and Jensen and colleagues (1994), for example, have provided evidence that the kicks of three-month-old infants follow a simple mass-spring model. As suggested from the kinematic data, flexor muscle torque is responsible for the initial driving force of the kick. However, gravity and inertial forces appear responsible for the extension phase. Using similar techniques, Jensen and colleagues (1995) compared vertical kicking in infants aged two weeks, three months, and seven months. Whereas in younger infants the flexion phase is vigorous and is followed by a passive extension phase, seven-month-old infants produce a vigorous extension phase that the authors argue represents the infant's learning to "tune his or her own springs" (p. 373), evidence of emerging limb control at this age. They further suggest that the kinematic patterns that emerge are a result of, or secondary to, kinetic control.

From Stepping to Walking

In order for an infant to adopt an adult gait, there must be a transition from the primitive patterns found in early infancy to the more complex movement patterns found in walking. These different patterns can be seen in figure 6.12. During infant kicking, hip, knee, and ankle joints are synchronous, with little delay or lag between the displacement curves (figure 6.12*a*). In contrast, the hip, knee, and ankle joints are in phase, but not synchronous, for walking (see figure 6.12*b*).

This change in pattern has been described by Forssberg (1985) and others as occurring due to a shift to a plantigrade CPG once the infant has achieved independent walking. Dynamic systems theorists such as Esther Thelen have a different explanation, arguing that these changes emerge not only as a result of neural maturation but also as a result of changing environmental and other biological conditions. Indeed, there has been substantial evidence to indicate that infants can utilize the plantigrade pattern of gait well before it is assumed to mature, according to Forssberg. The strongest evidence comes from studies using the treadmill to investigate the mechanisms of pattern generation in walking. Not only do young prewalking infants produce an adult walking pattern on the treadmill, but it has been shown that they can even adjust this pattern in response to perturbations. For example, Thelen and colleagues (1987) examined treadmill walking in eight infants who were seven months old. Infants stepped on two separate belts, with one belt moving at twice the rate of the other belt. Despite this perturbation, infants still maintained a regular alternating walking pattern by adjusting the stepping rate of the leg that was

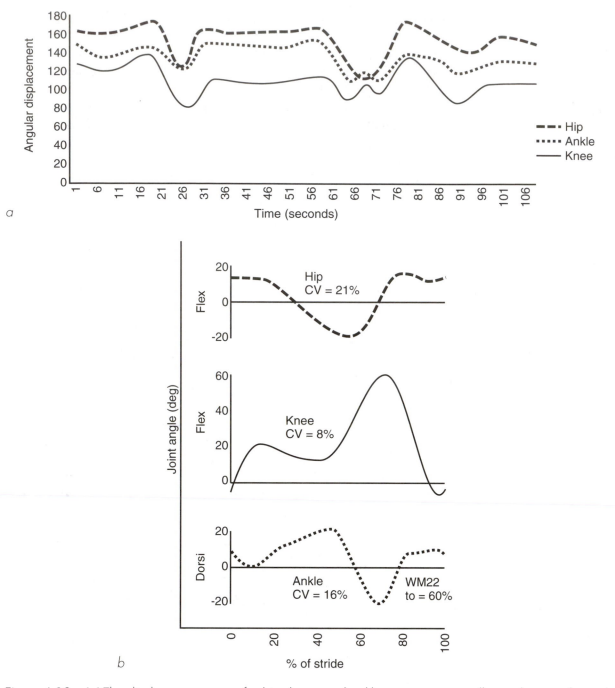

Figure 6.12 *(a)* The displacement curves for hip, knee, and ankle joints are generally synchronous for early spontaneous kicking. *(b)* The hip, knee, and ankle joints continue to be coordinated during adult walking but are no longer synchronous.

Reprinted from Winter, 1987.

on the slower belt so it caught up with the other leg. The authors also suggested that the neural mechanisms involved in this were probably spinal, relating to findings in similar treadmill studies carried out on cats with spinal cord transections.

How, then, do the strong synchronous joint couplings in early infancy relate to the later joint couplings found in the walking gait? Thelen

(1985) plotted the cross-correlations between the joint pairs for supine kicking for four infants over a period from age two weeks to 10 months. Throughout this period there were changes in joint synchrony, that is, a shifting relationship between the hip, knee, and ankle joints. For example, prior to four months, the joints were tightly coupled as shown in figure 6.12a. This was followed by what Thelen described as a process of joint "individualization" at around four to five months of age, in which the joints are more independent of one another, particularly for the hip and ankle joint, where the correlation between the two was not significant at five months of age. By eight months of age, the joints were again tightly coupled.

The relevance of these developmental shifts in joint synchrony to later motor development can be described from a dynamic systems perspective using Bernstein's notion of changing degrees of freedom (see chapter 2). Infant kicking can be considered another situation in which "freezing" of the degrees of freedom occurs (Vereijken et al., 1992) through production of rigid or fixed joint angles. This plays an important role in development, as it provides a means for the infant to explore the intrinsic dynamics of the limbs (Turvey & Fitzpatrick, 1993) without being overloaded with information. However, in order for more complex patterns to emerge, these tight synchronies cannot continue—hence the shifting pattern of joint synchrony found by Thelen (1985) and more recently by others who have investigated both full-term and preterm infants (e.g., Piek & Gasson, 1999; Piek et al., 2002; Vaal, 2001).

The relationship between the joints of one limb, the **intralimb** coordination, is one aspect of the development of walking. However, another equally important aspect is **interlimb** coordination. In order to walk, an infant needs to develop appropriate phasic relationships, not only between the joints of the same limb, but also between the two limbs. As demonstrated in figure 6.5, adult walking requires a regular and coordinated relationship between the two legs. How do the two limbs learn to function as one unit in the skill of walking? Although this question has received a great deal of attention in adult populations (e.g., Swinnen et al., 1994), very few studies have considered interlimb coordination in early motor development.

There is evidence to suggest that some level of coordination exists between the two legs in the newborn infant. Hayes and colleagues (1994) examined the discrete movement patterns in the first few weeks after birth in eight low-risk infants born with conceptional ages of less than 35 weeks. The average testing time was at 29.5 weeks gestational age. The results suggested that organized bilateral leg movements were present in the preterm infant at this age, and that "individual and bilateral leg movements tend to occur in temporally segregated movement clusters" (p. 277). In other words, isolated leg movements were quite distinct from bilateral-coordinated leg movements.

Thelen (1985) also described early interlimb coordination in the young infant. As with intralimb coordination, Thelen (1985) argued that interlimb coordination moved from periods of stability to instability in which unilateral kicking again dominated. Alternating kicking was found in the two-week-old infant for both supine and erect postures, suggesting a synergism between the legs at this early age. However, between the ages of one and five months, unilateral kicking appeared to dominate, followed by synchronous kicking from the ages of four to six months. Piek and Carman (1994) also identified simultaneous kicking of the right and left leg as the most frequent type of spontaneous movement in infants between 20 and 30 weeks of age.

More recently, we have investigated interlimb coordination in young infants in their first six months. By means of motion analysis, all four limbs were recorded simultaneously while infants lay in the supine position (see figure 6.13). A reduction in the lag between contralateral joints (e.g., left and right knee) was identified in the first few months (Piek et al., 2002), particularly with the knee joint (Piek & Gasson, 1999). There was also a tightening of the synchrony between the right and left limbs, and both arms and legs appear to have this relationship. It appears that the infant is learning to synchronize the limbs. Is this part of the developmental process for the establishment of coordination between the limbs? This process may be facilitated by the reduction of degrees of freedom through strong interjoint synchrony within each limb as described earlier. As pointed out by Whitall and Clark (1994), animal studies have generally argued for a sequential development in which interlimb coordination follows the development of intralimb coordination (Bekoff, 1981). This also appears to be the pattern for infants.

The arms play an important role in walking, and recent studies have identified stable patterns of coordination between the arms and legs during walking (e.g., Donker et al., 2001). Therefore, coordination of the arms and legs is also necessary, not just for walking but also for earlier locomotor activities such as creeping. Even to roll over, there needs to be cooperation between all four limbs. As with intralimb and interlimb coordination, there is evidence for changes in the relationship between joints of the arms and legs. In particular, correlations

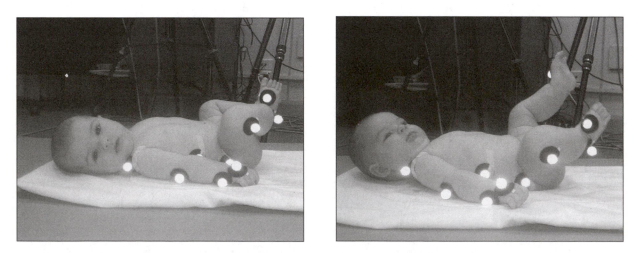

Figure 6.13   Motion analysis has been used extensively to investigate infant kicking.

become stronger between joints of the arm and leg on the same side (i.e., ipsilateral) in the first few months. Hence, "the experience generated from these early spontaneous movements may be important, not only for the emergence of cooperative behavior between the two legs, or for bimanual coordination, but also for the emergence of movement patterns involving both arms and legs" (Piek et al., 2002, p. 635).

What Determines When an Infant Will Walk Independently?

What factors are important in the shift to independent walking? According to Thelen and colleagues (Thelen et al., 1989), there are two primary rate limiters that determine when an infant will make the transition to upright locomotion. One is the appropriate postural control, which was covered quite extensively in chapter 4. The infant must learn to balance as he or she shifts weight from one leg to another. Appropriate balance needs to be maintained as the infant manages the complexities of forward propulsion, gravitational forces, inertia, and rotational components of the different body segments (Thelen et al.).

■■■ Although many rate-limiting variables determine when an infant will walk, two of the most important are muscle strength and postural control.

The other key variable is muscle strength, particularly for the trunk and leg extensor muscles. Considerable strength is required given the small base of support that occurs in the upright position. This variable may partially account for the large individual differences found in the age at which infants can walk, as body size and dimensions are quite variable in young infants and are influenced by other factors such as diet, amount of exercise, and so on.

Many other important factors produce a shift to independent locomotion. The appropriate coordination of the limbs was discussed in the previous section. Also, the infant must have the motivation to walk. If infants are locomoting well using other means, such as creeping or in wheeled walkers, they may not feel motivated to explore other forms of locomotion.

Once Independent Walking Is Achieved

A dynamic systems approach describes walking as a cyclic behavior. Clark and colleagues (Clark & Phillips, 1993; Clark et al., 1993) describe the behavior of the two legs during walking as "consistent with the behavior of coupled nonlinear limit-cycle oscillators" (Clark et al., 1993, p. 74). The legs are coupled, as they do not act independently but rather are synchronized through entrainment. Not only are the two legs entrained (interlimb), but the segments within each leg are also coupled (i.e., intralimb or intersegmental coordination). Walking is described as nonlinear because "an injection of energy results in a brief alteration in the oscillation that is followed rather quickly by a return to the original oscillatory behavior" (p. 75) as opposed to a linear system in which an injection of energy changes the oscillatory behavior. Finally, walking can be described as a limit cycle, as it exhibits stable periodic behavior despite small perturbations. Figure 6.14 displays phase portraits that demonstrate the cyclical, periodic nature of walking throughout different stages of

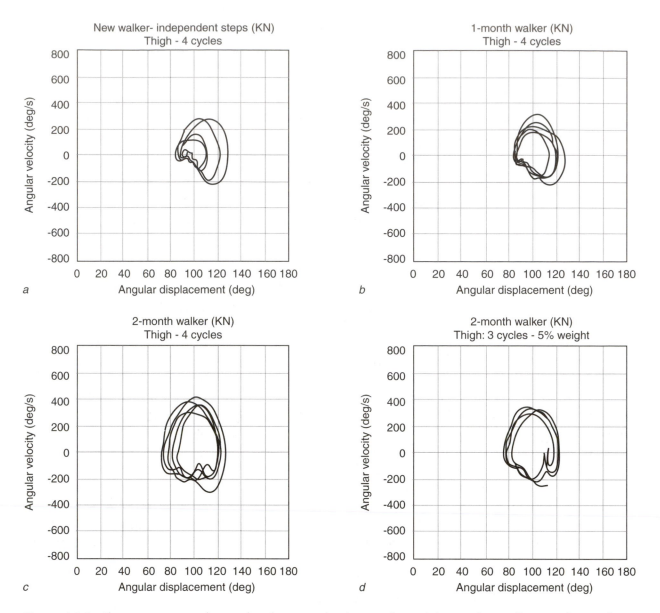

Figure 6.14 Phase portraits can be used to determine the degree of variability in infant walking: (a) four walking cycles of a newly walking infant; (b) the same infant after one month; (c) after 2 months of independent walking; (d) when the stable pattern at 2 months is perturbed by adding 5% of body weight to the ankle.

Reprinted from Clark et al., 1993.

development (6.14a, b, c) and when there is a change in conditions by adding weights to the leg (6.14d). Clark and colleagues describe it as follows:

> "...phase plane orbits are closed and attracted to particular regions of the state space; and if they are perturbed (such as when they start up) or if the inertial conditions are altered (as in the asymmetric ankle weighting), they return quickly to the original orbit. This property of limit cycles is referred to as their *structural stability*" (Clark et al., 1993, p. 77).

When an infant first starts to walk independently, the phase portrait shown in figure 6.14*a* demonstrates instability with less consistency in the region of state space visited with each cycle. However, despite this instability, there is still the closed orbit behavior of a limit-cycle oscillator. With practice (figure 6.14*b* and *c*), the phase portraits reveal more stable trajectories, and after around three months of walking experience the infant has a stable coordinative relationship between segments similar to that found in adult walkers (Clark & Phillips, 1993; Clark et al., 1988). The differences in size and shape of the phase portraits are a result of differences in the control parameters such as level of postural control, muscle strength, and the utilization of sensory information. Provided these control parameters do not exceed a critical magnitude, they would not create a new, qualitatively different pattern.

Once an infant initiates her first steps, practice appears to be the most significant predictor of improved walking (Adolph et al., 2003). Practice aids in the improvement of factors such as muscle strength and balance.

■■■ Walking has been described from a dynamic systems perspective as a *coupled nonlinear limit-cycle oscillator.*

Leg Asymmetries in Infancy

In chapter 5, manual asymmetries in infancy were discussed in relation to their link to later handedness. But what about leg asymmetries? Footedness is also a characteristic of humans; that is, they generally have a preferred leg.

Despite the considerable attention given to handedness and asymmetries in arm reaching, very few studies have investigated leg asymmetries in infants. Part of the difficulty in investigating leg preference is in identifying what defines a "preferred leg." Manual asymmetries can be easily determined, based on such skills as writing, pointing, and tasks like bead threading and picking up small objects. But how do we define footedness? Peters (1988) suggests that the preferred foot is the one that can be used to manipulate objects or may be the one that leads out in movements such as jumping. In contrast, the nonpreferred foot may be used to support these activities, that is, provide stability. A good example of a suitable skill to test for footedness is kicking a ball; there is a population preference for right-footed kicking. Furthermore, right-footed preference is usually associated with right-handed preference, although left-handers do not necessarily show a preference for left-footedness. This contrasts with the observation of von Bonin (1962, cited in Peters, 1988) that we tend to be right-handed and left-footed. This observation, however, was based on anatomical differences found between the right and left arms and legs using X-ray studies, rather than behavioral evidence.

These ways of determining footedness in children and adults, however, are difficult to apply to infants, as skills such as kicking a ball have not been achieved. The main variables used to investigate leg asymmetries in infants have been the leading leg during the stepping reflex (e.g., Kamptner et al., 1985; Melekian, 1981; Peters and Petrie, 1979) and frequency of kicking (e.g., Droit et al., 1996). Like results for early arm asymmetries, those for leg asymmetries have been conflicting. For example, whereas Peters & Petrie (1979) and Melekian (1981) found a strong right-foot bias for the newborn stepping reflex, no such bias was found by other investigators (e.g., Kamptner et al., 1985; Thelen et al., 1993).

In the 1980s and 1990s, infant kicking was investigated using kinematic analysis. Many researchers using this technique have recorded only one limb, usually the right limb (e.g., Geerdink et al., 1996; Thelen & Fisher, 1983a), or have alternated the testing of right and left leg between infants (e.g., Heriza, 1988a, b; Thelen et al., 1981), making it impossible to examine any asymmetries. In their study on four- to six-week-old full-term infants, Thelen and colleagues (1981) noted that all infants had a favored leg, but they did not observe any consistent laterality in the eight infants investigated.

More recently, Piek and Gasson (1999) studied leg asymmetries in spontaneous kicking by examining whether the level of joint synchrony differed between the two legs. They found evidence of asymmetries for all three joint couplings, namely the hip/knee, ankle/knee, and ankle/hip joints. In particular, stronger coupling was demonstrated in the right leg for the ankle/hip and ankle/knee couplings. However, this does not necessarily mean that the right leg is the preferred leg. It has been argued that in order to produce adaptive movement patterns, a loosening of this strong coupling is required, suggesting that the right leg may in fact be more delayed in development compared with the left. It is therefore necessary to explore the functional significance of these early leg asymmetries in order to determine whether they are indicative of later foot preference. For example, Piek and Gasson found that there were no age effects for the hip/knee correlations in the left leg, but by 24 weeks the right leg was not as tightly coupled. If the right leg is to take on a more functional role, as suggested by Peters (1988), it may need a looser coupling of the hip and knee joints than the left leg, which may take on a postural role.

■■■ How Does This Research Inform Therapeutic Practice?

Many of the variables needed for independent locomotion such as walking are available to the infant early in the first year. One example is the plantigrade stepping pattern, which can be initiated in infants supported on a treadmill. The main variables that prevent the infant from walking appear to be muscle strength and postural control. An important component of appropriate intervention for infants with developmental delay may be in identifying which of these rate-limiting variables may be responsible for the delay. Studies examining cultural differences have suggested that training may improve muscle strength. This type of training may be utilized as an appropriate intervention strategy. Such a strategy is outlined in chapter 12 for infants with Down syndrome.

Summary

The motor milestones of creeping and walking are two of the most important in the infant's motor development. Once infants become mobile, they are more able to explore their environment. Hence these skills are important not only as a base for the development of other functional skills such as running, hopping, and climbing but also for social and cognitive development. The relationship between motor and cognitive development is discussed more fully in the next chapter.

Many different theories have been proposed to explain how locomotor skills develop in the first year of life. Earlier views were based on prescriptive approaches that argued for single causal factors (such as neural development) for the development of new locomotor behaviors. Recently, the dynamic systems approach has suggested that many factors are responsible for the emergence of these milestones. For walking, the factors that are particularly significant are postural control and muscle strength. Individual differences in the development of these skills may be accounted for by the different ages at which these rate-limiting variables achieve the appropriate levels.

part III ■■■

Assessment of Motor Ability in Infants

The first sections of this book dealt with understanding the normal development of motor coordination in the infant. It is essential to have a good understanding of normal motor development in order to investigate abnormal development. The study of normal development provides clues on the normal processes that lead to appropriate development. In addition, such knowledge can be utilized to determine whether an infant is performing appropriately in certain conditions and at particular ages. Hence, the information that has been gathered over the 20th century has been used to develop assessment tools to identify abnormal or delayed movement ability.

Many of the assessment tools used today are based on the early maturationists' observational analysis that mapped the stages of development. Indeed, Goodman (1990) referred to Arnold Gesell as the "grandfather" of infant testing. However, infant assessment tools are renowned for their inability to predict later outcome (Goodman, 1990). In particular, early identification of movement disabilities such as cerebral palsy is difficult. The first chapter in this section addresses the important characteristics of a good assessment tool. It also describes the unique characteristics of infant assessment.

Infant assessment tests can be broadly divided in two stages. Those designed specifically for the neonatal period are discussed in chapter 8. Chapter 9 reviews tests with a much wider assessment age. These can include the neonatal period but also extend into the later months of infancy, and often into later childhood.

seven ■■■

Motor Assessment Tests

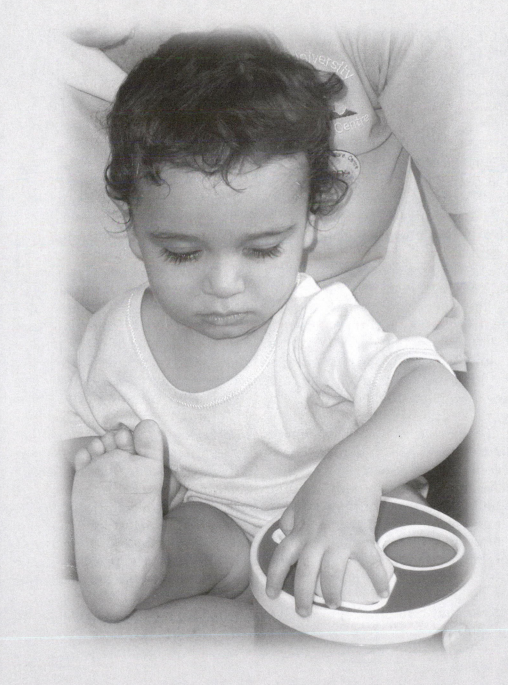

chapter objectives

This chapter will do the following:

- Investigate why it is important to assess infant motor development

- Examine why reliability, validity, and standardization are important components of any assessment instrument

- Investigate the unique aspects of assessment that one must consider when examining infants

"Assessment is a way of gaining some understanding of the child in order to make informed decisions" (Sattler, 2001, p. 3). Can we accurately assess motor development in infancy, and how useful is this? There is a huge array of assessment instruments that examine infant motor development, but how do we know that these tests are appropriate? Many statistical techniques provide information on how good an assessment instrument is. In choosing a test, it is essential to understand what the statistical information is telling us about the suitability of the test for a given individual. Also, infants are a unique population, and when one is assessing them, there are many important issues to consider. These unique characteristics are outlined in this chapter.

Importance of Motor Assessment

Both clinicians and researchers rely on assessment tools for a variety of reasons. Firstly, assessment is used to identify movement problems and to categorize individuals into levels of skill (Burton & Miller, 1998). If an individual has a level of skill that is considered a disability, then assessment is essential to determine the appropriate service delivery.

Assessment for identification can be carried out at many different levels (Sattler, 2001). One way to provide a quick assessment of a large number of infants is through *screening instruments.* These have been developed to identify infants *at risk* of a disorder or disability. If at-risk children are shown to be at a level indicative of abnormal development, the screening should be followed by *diagnostic* assessment. Diagnostic assessment requires a detailed analysis of the infant's ability, and a multitude of such tests have been developed recently to assess infant motor ability. These are usually quite lengthy to administer and are generally used only when the infant is considered at risk of developmental delay or disability.

Assessment also provides information about what types of problems the infant or child is having with movement. Most assessment tools measure different aspects of motor development. For example, in infancy, most assessments include an evaluation of reflexes, muscle tone, and the achievement of various motor milestones. This information allows intervention to be targeted to the relevant areas. "Focused," or "problem-solving," assessment (Sattler, 1990) involves the evaluation of a particular function rather than an overall ability.

Especially important for infant assessment is the ability to evaluate change over time, a further use of assessment tools. Many infant tests require multiple testing over time in order to determine ongoing development. This approach is also important to evaluate the progress of infants as they proceed through intervention. The infant is assessed on a regular basis to determine any change in performance. These assessments may be administered on a daily, weekly, monthly, or even a yearly basis.

Another use of assessment is in prediction. Assessment may be used to determine a child's potential for successful treatment and recovery and the ability to carry on with daily activities. These instruments are termed *counseling* and *rehabilitation* assessments (Sattler, 2001). Predicting an infant's later developmental status is essential if early intervention strategies are to be implemented. Despite its importance, it is this latter use of assessments that has had limited success in early infancy.

Criterion- and Norm-Referenced Assessments

An individual score on a test is meaningless unless it can be related to some predetermined level of performance. When the individual's performance is compared to some predetermined performance criterion, the test is referred to as a **criterion-referenced test.** These tests determine whether an infant has achieved some preestablished standard of performance. They provide information on the infant or child's capabilities in specific tasks (Burton & Miller, 1998) and are particularly useful to assess performance over time. The infant may have regular assessments, and comparison of the infant's own performance can indicate how he or she is progressing. Criterion-referenced tests can also be used to determine whether the infant or child has achieved a particular milestone or mastered a particular skill. Many of the neonatal tests are criterion referenced, such as Prechtl's Neurological Examination of the Full Term Newborn Infant (Prechtl, 1977), as they indicate whether the appropriate muscle tone or reflexes are present or absent in the infant.

When a test compares the performance of the individual to a normative group, it is referred to as a **norm-referenced test.** Test norms reflect the test performance of a large representative sample of infants, termed the **standardization sample.** This normative group is considered to be a representative sample containing individuals who are similar to those being tested. Many of the tests that measure movement ability in older infants are norm referenced, such as the Bayley Scales of Infant Development (BSID; Bayley, 1993) and the Peabody Developmental Motor Scales (PDMS; Folio & Fewell, 1983). However, norm-referenced and criterion-referenced tests are not mutually exclusive (Burton & Miller, 1998), and many norm-referenced tests can also be used as criterion-referenced assessments. That is, in addition to providing information on performance in relation to a representative sample of infants, they can provide information on specific tasks.

Despite their popularity and common use, norm-referenced tests have been criticized for several reasons. When motor development is considered from a dynamic systems perspective (see chapter 2), it has been argued that age norms disregard the considerable variability in development (e.g., Newell & van Emmerik, 1990; von Hofsten, 1993), in terms of both rate of development and sequence of development. A further criticism is based on the fact that norms are dependent on the group used for the standardization, and it is important that the group be a suitable reflection of the individuals who will be tested. This is an important consideration in the choice of a suitable test to administer and is discussed more fully in the next section.

Components of Good Assessment Tools

For a test to be useful, it is important that the test can be repeatedly administered with consistent results. This is the test's *reliability*. It is also important to know whether a test is really measuring what it purports to measure. This is termed the test's *validity*. Finally, appropriate standardization procedures must be developed, including the testing of a sample that is representative of the population being tested. That is, there needs to be an appropriate *standardization sample.*

Reliability

Part of the test standardization is ensuring that the test is administered in exactly the same way to all infants. In order to ensure uniformity of testing, infant tests describe the most suitable testing environment and appropriate scoring conditions. Many of the neonatal, and some of the infant, tests require rigorous training in test administration to ensure uniform testing and scoring procedures. These procedures are important to ensure that the test is reliable. Even when these conditions are adhered to, no test is perfectly reliable, as other factors influence the test score.

Given these uniform procedures, how consistent is a test? That is, when the test is repeatedly administered, how stable or "reliable" is the score that is determined? Anastasi (1968) states that test reliability "indicates the extent to which individual differences in test scores are attributable to 'true' differences in the characteristics under consideration and the extent to which they are attributable to chance errors" (p. 71). A reliable test means that there is minimal *measurement error,* that is, minimal error that occurs as a result of variability in the administration and interpretation of the test. There are several avenues through which variability can occur that will lead to reduced reliability.

The stability of test administration is measured through *test-retest reliability,* which determines how reliable a test is when the same examiner tests the same performance at different times. The time interval between the testing sessions needs to be stated. One problem with test-retest reliability in infant testing is the rapid rate of development at this period of life. If the interval between testing is too great, low reliability scores may reflect true changes in the infant's ability rather than measurement error. Despite this criticism, test-retest is commonly used to determine reliability in infant assessments. Other types of reliability such as *split-half* and *alternate-form* reliability are seldom seen in infant tests.

Reliability also needs to be established for the test administrator or *rater*. This is particularly important in infant tests, as many of the items are determined through observation of the infant's performance, and reliability can be influenced by aspects of the test items such as how objective they are for scoring. The more objective the scoring criteria, the higher the reliability. *Intrarater* reliability determines how consistent an individual is when repeatedly administering the test. It is generally established by videotaping the test administrator and determining the consistency of performance across test administrations. The test also needs to be suitable for administration by many different testers. *Interrater* reliability is the consistency of two different testers on the same test performance. Common factors that may influence rater reliability are experience with the test, the examiner's ability to clearly present the instructions, and errors in scoring.

There are many methods used to estimate reliability. Some of the more common methods are Pearson product-moment correlation coefficients, intraclass correlation coefficients, percent agreement, and Kappa values (Burton & Miller, 1998).

Validity

A test can have good reliability but still be totally meaningless if it does not have established *validity*. That is, the test needs to measure what it is supposed to test. Validity assesses whether an assessment tool can be used for the purpose stated (Burton & Miller, 1998). This may be the purpose stated by the test developers or, in many cases, the purpose the test has been used for. In other words, although validity measures are provided for many infant tests, the user must ensure that the test is appropriate for the purpose for which it is intended.

Validation procedures fall into three principal categories, *content, construct,* and *criterion-related validity*. All three categories have been used to test the validity of infant motor assessment tools.

Content Validity

It is important to determine whether the test content "covers a representative sample of the behavior domain to be measured" (Anastasi, 1968, p. 100). This is generally achieved by having the test reviewed by experts in the field. Take, for example, the BSID, which is one of the most widely used tests for infant assessment. A multistep process was utilized to determine its content validity. Initially, a panel of experts was used to determine the ability domains that needed to be included in the test. These same experts then examined the test items within each of these domains to ensure that there was adequate content coverage for each domain. The final stage involved adding items to the domains that were considered to have insufficient content.

Construct Validity

Construct validity "is the extent to which the test may be said to measure a theoretical construct or trait" (Anastasi, 1968, p. 114). It determines whether the test can differentiate groups known to differ on the construct being measured.

In order to assess construct validity, it is first important to define the construct that is to be measured. This involves a description of how this construct is related to, and distinguished from, other constructs (Burton & Miller, 1998). A frequently used method of examining construct validity in infant tests is to determine whether the test can differentiate between groups that differ on a variable known to affect the construct being measured. Often this is age, as motor ability is known to change with age. In neonatal measures, risk factors such as infants being born preterm, or infants with or without abnormal brain scans have been used to measure construct validity (Majnemer & Mazer, 1998). Factor analysis is often used to identify subsets of tasks within the construct that relate to specific performance factors.

Criterion-Related Validity

The prediction capabilities of a test are examined through criterion-related validity. The test results are compared with some external or "gold standard" criterion measure that should be predicted from the test being validated.

Two main types of criterion-related validity are utilized in infant tests, *concurrent* and *predictive validity.* Concurrent validity assesses the predictability of the measures at approximately the same time. That is, the tests for comparison are administered concurrently (for infant assessment this is often the same day or within a few days). Predictive validity is more concerned with the test's ability to predict later behavior. Therefore the earlier test results are compared with a suitable measure at a later time.

Again, take the example of the BSID. The scores obtained on the mental scale have been compared with later scores on intelligence measures. Bayley (1993) noted that performance of at-risk infants on the mental scale of the BSID at six months of age predicted their subsequent score on the Stanford-Binet IQ test at 24 and 48 months of age, provided the infants did not receive any intervention. This example demonstrates the complexity of predictive validity and the need to elucidate the conditions that lead to good prediction.

When a test is used for diagnosis, predictive validity can be presented in terms of the test's **sensitivity** and **specificity.** Sensitivity, termed the *true positive,* is the likelihood that an individual who demonstrates a problem at follow-up will have been accurately identified by the initial testing.

$$\text{Sensitivity} = \frac{\text{infants with impairment at initial testing}}{\text{infants/children diagnosed with impairment}}$$

■■■ It is important to examine the validity of an assessment tool before deciding whether it is suitable for the population to be tested with the instrument.

Specificity, the *true negative,* is the likelihood that an individual diagnosed without a problem initially will prove to be without that problem at the follow-up testing.

$$\text{Specificity} = \frac{\text{infants without impairment at initial testing}}{\text{infants/children diagnosed without impairment}}$$

Standardization Sample

██ When assessing the usefulness of a particular assessment tool, one should examine the standardization sample to determine whether it represents appropriately the population that is being assessed.

Touwen (1976) argued that "one of the main difficulties in the use of developmental tests is the application of norms, as these can vary depending on standardisation, operationalisation, and the type of study population used" (p. 4). For example, in the case of infants, a variety of factors increase the risk of disability. If the test is to be used on infants with any of these risk factors, then the standardization sample must include infants with these risk factors. Norms may be inappropriate due to racial or cultural differences, which can encompass such factors as child-rearing practices. They may also vary for urban and rural children, and depending on *when* the norms were developed. As shown in table 6.1, there is evidence that infants may achieve milestones earlier in the present day compared with 50 or 60 years ago. This demonstrates that norms need to be regularly updated. When using a test, check to see when and where the norms were developed.

In assessment of motor ability, who should be represented in the standardization sample? Do variables such as sex, culture or race, and socioeconomic status influence motor ability? Some of the variables that one needs to consider when choosing an appropriate standardization sample are described next.

Sex Differences

It is commonly assumed that there are no sex differences in motor ability in infancy. For example, in discussing the motor milestones developed by Shirley and Bayley (see table 6.1), Haywood (1993) states that "neither of the published motor milestone charts lists separate ages of skill acquisition for boys and girls, simply because no significant gender differences exist in the sequence of skill acquisition or in the average ages for skill onset" (p. 102). When developing the age norms for her BSID, Bayley (1965) found no significant differences between the sexes for both the mental and motor scales. She examined the overall scores for these at each month from 1 to 15 months of age. However, she did suggest that an analysis of separate items may yield sex differences.

A large variety of infant movements were examined by Touwen (1976), including walking, rolling over, vocalization, grasping, and eye movements. He found *appreciable* sex differences in 17 of these movements. In particular, gross motor milestones such as walking and sitting appeared to develop sooner in boys, whereas girls were faster to develop more functional skills such as grasping and vocalizing. As a result of these findings, Touwen argued for systematic differences in the motor development of boys and girls, with early gross motor development ment linked to boys, and speech and items dependent on vision (e.g., fine motor skills) linked to early development in girls.

There has been some support for Touwen's findings since these were reported in 1976. Capute and colleagues (1985) found support for the notion that boys may be more advanced in gross motor development. Although they were not statistically significant, Largo (1993) observed similar trends in his cohort of 97 full-term and 108 preterm infants. Thomas and French (1985) carried out an extensive meta-analysis of sex differences in motor ability. They examined 64 studies on children and adolescents aged 3 to 20 years. They suggested that sociological factors may be part of the explanation for differences identified between girls and boys on tasks such as running, jumping, and catching. However, this explanation could not account for a large difference in throwing tasks between boys and girls aged three years. There appeared to be a biological component to the better performance in boys—a view that had previously been suggested by Anastasi (1981), who also argued for a gross motor advantage of boys over girls in infancy and childhood.

Recently, gender differences have been identified in some kinematic variables relating to interlimb coordination in infants under six months of age (Piek et al., 2002). When the infants performed spontaneous arm and leg movements, it was found that the two arms were more strongly coordinated in girls, and there was a trend for the two legs to be more coordinated in the boys. These differences could not be attributed to differences in gestational age or physical characteristics such as birth weight, birth length, or head circumference.

Although many of the infant assessment tools have included equal numbers of boys and girls in their standardization sample, different norms for boys and girls at different ages have not been considered. The increasing evidence that different rates of development may be present for boys and girls suggests that this should be seriously considered in the assessment of motor ability. Until this issue is more fully investigated, failure to adjust for possible sex differences in development must be considered a limitation in the current tools used to examine infant motor development.

Culture, Race, and Society

The early maturational theorists argued that the early motor patterns found in infants were *invariant* to race, culture, and society. As a result, these factors were not seriously considered in the development of infant tests throughout the 20th century. It has now been established that different customs and child-rearing practices in different societies, cultures, and races can affect behavior, including motor behavior. Therefore, if infant tests are to be used in different countries or on different races, norms should be established for these different environments.

Even in countries where culture and race are quite similar, there has been evidence of differences in motor ability. Livesey (1997) noted that Australian children aged between four and five years performed better on the Movement Assessment Battery for Children (MABC) than did the children used in the United States norms (see table 7.1). What factors could produce this outcome? Australia is a very sport-minded country, but then so is the United States. The climate in most of the populated areas in Australia is ideal for outdoor activities. Other social factors such as standard of living, type of residence (e.g., apartments vs. houses with large yards/gardens), and use and standard of child care facilities may all have an influence. A further example, of differences between two European countries, was provided by Schoemaker at al. (2003), who noted that the English norms for the checklist that accompanies the MABC do not appear to be valid for the Dutch population.

But what of the early infant years? Are there cultural and social influences that affect the early infant milestones? Research suggests that this is the case. For example, research has examined sandbag rearing, which occurs in the valleys of the Yellow and Huaihe Rivers in northern China (Mei, 1994). Infants are placed in bags filled with fine sand (a cheap alternative to diapers/nappies), restricting leg and trunk movement. They lie on their backs, unable to turn around or locomote. This practice can occur for up to one year and has been identified in some cases as occurring for up to two years. Mei found that this practice retarded both motor and intellectual ability.

In contrast to the practice of rearing babies in sandbags, there has been evidence for an "African infant precocity" (Super, 1976) in motor skills for over half a century. In the United States, research has addressed the impact of race by comparing Caucasians and African Americans. The findings show that African American infants tend to achieve motor milestones earlier than Caucasian infants (Bayley, 1965; Capute et al., 1985). Bayley noted that these differences were significant in the first year of life and argued that the differences may be due to a genetic factor. Other researchers have suggested that environmental and social factors may play a greater role in producing these differences. In his investigation of infants' development in a Kipsigis farming community in Western Kenya, Super (1976) found that these infants achieved sitting, standing, and walking considerably earlier than the

Table 7.1 Total Impairment Score*

Percentile	US4/5	AUS4/5	AUS3
5th	17	9	17.5
15th	10.5	6.5	11
25th	7.5	5.5	9.5

*Total Impairment Score at the 5th, 15th, and 25th percentiles for the US four and five year old (US4/5), norms, Australian four and five year old (AUS4/5), and Australian three year-old (AUS3) norms on the Movement Assessment Battery for Children.

Adapted from Livesey, 1997

U.S. norms provided in the BSID (Bayley, 1969). Other milestones in the prone position such as lifting the head and crawling were not more advanced. These differences were attributed to the fact that around 80% of the mothers in this community had particular training methods to teach their infants to sit and walk, but not to teach them to crawl. For example, at around five or six months of age, the mothers would place their infants in a special hole in the ground made to support the back. This was carried out on a daily basis until the baby could sit unsupported. In contrast, Kenyan infants reared in urban societies did not demonstrate the more advanced motor development.

A similar finding was obtained in a study that compared early milestones in Australian Aboriginal infants with those in Caucasian infants (Kearins, 1984). Australian Aboriginals who live in outback communities were found to rear their children in a manner similar to that of the people of the Kalahari Desert. Hamilton (1981) noted that the awake infant was always held vertical. For example, when mothers are sitting on the ground, there are two predominant positions for the infants. Adults may support the infants under the arms so that they are in a standing position that puts their body weight onto their feet. Often they are in a sitting position facing away from the mother, with their back against the mother's abdomen. These practices are thought to facilitate postural development and as a result lead to earlier motor milestones.

Cognitive Differences/IQ

What is the impact of cognitive ability, or *intelligence,* on motor skills? This is another issue that has not been given careful consideration in the development of motor assessment tools in infants. Diamond (2000) argued for a close interrelationship between motor and cognitive development because brain structures such as the striatum and neocerebellum are involved in both motor and cognitive functions. The relationship between motor and mental ability has been demonstrated in children with intellectual disability (Sugden & Keogh, 1990), where the severity of mental retardation often reflects the level of delay in motor skills development. The more delayed a child is (usually measured by IQ), the later the achievement of milestones such as standing and walking. How does this compare with what happens in the general population?

Correlations between motor and mental scales in infant tests are quite high, but it is often argued that this is a result of the motor ability's affecting the mental ability. That is, because an infant cannot verbalize a solution to a problem, performance will be assessed through the infant's movements. Take as a simple example the item in the BSID, *attempts to bring hand to mouth,* which is part of the motor scale. Is this purely a measure of motor ability, or could it also be linked to the infant's adaptive ability to explore the environment? In other words, do we also need to control for cognitive ability when developing tests of motor ability? Recent research with a large sample of normally developing children indicates that abilities are related (Dyck et al., 2004), suggesting that factors such as adaptive ability or "intelligence" may need to be considered in the standardization of motor assessment instruments.

And what of the impact of motor ability on cognitive development? According to the early views of Piaget (1953), cognitive development occurs as a result of early motor activity (see chapter 2 for further details on this). An increasing number of studies have identified a relationship between early motor problems and later cognitive difficulties. As described in the previous section, the practice of sandbag rearing in northern China was found to affect both later motor and cognitive ability (Mei, 1994). However, this cognitive delay may not only be linked to delayed motor development, but may also be the result of reduced environmental exploration and limited stimulation and social contact in infancy. This issue has more recently been explored by Campos and colleagues (2000). They examined the influence of crawling on processes such as the use of parallax information, attention to distal events, and social interactions, suggesting that the "investigations of functional consequences of motor-skill acquisition have been seriously neglected" (p. 212).

According to Wijnroks and van Veldhoven (2003), "Cognitive development comes about as a result of the infant's spontaneous exploratory behaviour and the knowledge acquired from this exploration of the environment" (p. 15). These authors identified a relationship between early postural control in infancy and cognitive ability 6 to 18 months later. Recently, Gasson and colleagues (2005) have also noted a link between early gross motor ability in eight-month-old infants and later problem-solving skills using a parent-administered screening tool, the Ages and Stages test developed by Squires and colleagues (1995). This sample included both full-term and preterm infants. Using a sample of children who were born less than 1,000 g (2.2 lb), Burns and colleagues (2004) found an association between the performance of the infants on a motor development assessment at one year of age and their cognitive performance at both one year and four years of age. They argued that a detailed motor assessment of very preterm infants at one year of age may be important in the identification of later cognitive deficits.

███ The infant's sex, IQ, race, culture, and socioeconomic status are just some of the factors that may affect motor development and need to be considered in the assessment process.

Special Issues of Infant Testing

Motor skills do not develop in a stable or predictable manner in infants, and there may be dramatic changes in their skills over a very short period of time. For example, Darrah, Redfern, and colleagues (1998a) used the Alberta Infant Motor Scale to assess gross motor ability in 47 infants. Monthly assessments were carried out from age two weeks until the infants achieved independent walking. At 18 months the infants were assessed for any delayed or abnormal gross motor development. The authors observed that over 30% of the infants who were found to have normal development at 18 months scored below the 10th percentile on at least one testing session. This demonstrates that the rate of development is "extremely variable," and there is a need for serial assessments to identify infants with motor delay (Darrah, Redfern, et al.).

Infants are a unique population requiring unusual approaches for assessment. It has already been pointed out that because infants do not talk, it is through their actions that their abilities are interpreted. There are other difficulties with assessing an individual who cannot speak and who also cannot understand what is required in the assessment process. One of these is motivation. Testing must be enjoyable so that the infant will perform, as the examiner cannot ask the infant "to do his or her best" in the task.

Because the scores are based on the infant's motor actions rather than an oral or written answer, the examiner must be very observant, as there is no permanent record of performance unless it is recorded with a video or digital movie camera. Sometimes the result depends on the observation of a relatively fleeting behavior. As the outcome is based on observation, scoring may be difficult and relatively subjective at times. These difficulties in administration and scoring then affect the test reliability.

An infant may quite quickly become fatigued, inattentive, or even frightened by the unfamiliar environment and strange people. The behavioral state of the infant is an important aspect of testing, and the examiner must be specially trained to determine this state and, if possible, adjust it to maximize the infant's performance. Another important factor to consider when testing infants is whether they were born preterm. This is covered in more detail later.

Behavioral States

An infant's motor behavior and level of activity at any one time are dependent upon his or her state at that particular time. That is, different responses can be elicited to the same stimulus when the infant is in different states. Examples of these different states include sleeping, active, crying, and attending (Rosenblith, 1992). As Rosenblith points out, "All studies of infants demand that the state of the infant be taken into account" (p. 207). This also applies to the assessment of infants.

The first descriptive rating scale of state was designed by Peter Wolff (1959). On this basis, Prechtl and Beintema (1964) developed a behavioral scale consisting of five different states. This scale became an integral part of their neonatal assessment tool, which is described in the next chapter. The authors made a significant contribution in terms of understanding the importance of an infant's behavioral state in the assessment process, arguing that infants must be in the appropriate behavioral state when assessed in order for an accurate assessment to be carried out. According to Prechtl (1974), these states are "finite and discrete vectors representing distinct and qualitatively different conditions" (p. 185). He argued that these different states are not a result of a continuum of arousal but are produced by different modes of brain activity.

According to Prechtl (1974), behavioral states can be described through four aspects of the infant's behavior, namely regularity of breathing, whether the eyes are open or closed, head and limb movements, and vocalizations. These were formalized into vectors that could be categorized as either present (+1) or absent (–1), as shown in table 7.2. Furthermore, these vectors could be identified objectively through polygraphic recordings of respiration, electroencephalographs and heart rate (to monitor sleep states), electro-oculographs (eyes open or closed), electromyographs (for head and limb movements), and microphone for vocalizations. In the second edition of this tool (Prechtl, 1974), a sixth state was added, *other state*, which included such exceptions as coma. An infant was considered to be in a new state when the state remained for at least three minutes. The five states are outlined in table 7.2.

Throughout the 1960s and '70s, several other systems for classifying an infant's state were developed. These are summarized in table 7.3. Thoman (1990) developed a classification that included three sleep states, two transition states, and five awake states. However, recently this was reduced to a simpler classification of six states, as Thoman (2001) acknowledged that 10 was a substantial number to be able to identify and record. The combined states are noted in parentheses in table 7.3.

Behavioral states now form a major part of most neonatal infant assessments. The state required for optimal performance is usually given, and many tests describe how best to elicit the appropriate state in the infant. It is also now recognized that the infant's state is important in development. For example, states influence how well infants perceive the environment and are also an important behavioral indicator of caregiver–infant interaction (Thoman, 2001). As a result, many assessment tools include a measure of state as part of the overall assessment.

▮▮▮ Infants will perform differently depending on their behavioral state. Test administrators need to be aware of the infant's state throughout the testing and take this into account when determining the assessment outcome.

Table 7.2   Vectors of Behavioral States

	Eyes open	Respiration regular	Gross movements	Vocalization
State 1	−1	+1	−1	−1
State 2	−1	−1	−1	−1
State 3	+1	+1	−1	−1
State 4	+1	−1	+1	−1
State 5	0	−1	+1	+1

Reprinted with permission from Livesey, 1997

Table 7.3   Five Different Systems Developed for Classifying Infant Behavioral States

	Prechtl & Beintema (1964)	Brown (1964)	Wolff (1966)	Korner (1972)	Thoman (2001)
Asleep states	1. Eyes closed; regular respiration 2. Eyes closed	1. Deep sleep 2. Regular sleep 3. Disturbed sleep	1. Regular sleep 2. Periodic sleep 3. Irregular sleep	1. Regular sleep 2. Irregular sleep	1. Quiet sleep (including active-quiet) 2. Active sleep (including active-quiet)
Transition states	3. Eyes open; no gross movement	4. Drowsy	4. Drowsiness	3. Drowsiness	3. Sleep-wake (including drowse)
Awake states	4. Eyes open; gross movements; no crying 5. Crying; eyes open or closed	5. Alert activity 6. Alert and focused 7. Inflexibly focused	5. Waking activity 6. Alert inactivity 7. Crying	4. Waking activity 5. Alert inactivity 6. Crying 7. Indeterminate	4. Non-alert waking (including daze) 5. Alert 6. Crying (including fuss)

Reprinted from Rosenblith, 1995.

Risk Factors

When an infant is born, he or she already has a considerable *history*. This is essential in determining whether the infant is considered to be *at risk* of any developmental abnormalities. Many assessment tools, particularly those for the newborn, take into account and include this history.

Defining *at risk* is a further contentious issue. Thus researchers have developed indicators of risk, or measures of optimality. For example, Prechtl (1977, 1980) described the *optimality concept,* according to which a list of criteria is provided that indicates optimal performance for each measure. Such measures include the mother's age and blood pressure, fetal heart rate, and the length of apnea preceding the first breath. The infant receives a score of 0 or 1 depending on whether the performance is optimal (1) or not (0), with a possible score of 42 for the 42 different criteria.

Prematurity

One of the most common risk factors for developmental delay or disorders is prematurity. As a result, this topic is covered in a chapter of its own (see chapter 10). Preterm infants are infants who either are born too early or have a birth weight smaller than expected. With a much higher risk of disability, it is clear that this group of infants should be assessed as early as possible in order to diagnose any developmental disorders. However, this group presents its own unique problems when it comes to assessment.

The primary concern is whether the infant's development is considered in relation to normal development. That is, can full-term infants be used for the standardization sample in assessment tools for preterm infants, or is development affected by the prematurity of these infants? If infants are born early, should they be assessed according to their chronological age or their expected age if they were to have been born at term? This issue, like many others described so far in this volume, needs to be considered from both a maturational and an environmental perspective.

This problem is represented in figure 7.1. In this figure by Largo (1993), the possible impact of prematurity on motor development is represented in three separate graphs. In the first, a purely maturationist view is presented, which argues that even though the environment has changed (that is, from in utero to being born), development still progresses along the same path, as it is endogenously determined. In this case, there is the argument for correcting for gestational age (GA). That is, the infant's development can be compared with that of full-term infants only if the infant's age is considered in terms of the age it would be if it had been born full term. In the graph labeled c, the purely *nurture* rather than *nature* view is depicted. Development for the full-term and preterm groups is the same, as it is the environment that is responsible for appropriate motor development. When age is corrected in this case, it can be seen that the preterm infants develop earlier. In the middle graph (b), both maturational and environmental influences are considered important for development. Hence, preterm infants are considered behind in development in comparison to full-term infants (the maturational influence), but not as behind as would be expected if their age was corrected (the environmental influence).

These three models have been tested through comparison of the performance of full-term and preterm infants (with corrected and

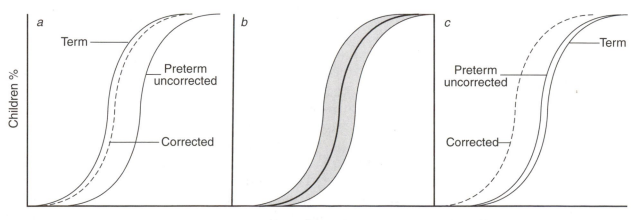

Figure 7.1 Does maturation or the environment have the greater impact on development in preterm infants? Here, *a* depicts development if maturation is important; *b* depicts an integrated model where both environment and maturation affect development; *c* depicts the environment as the primary factor determining development.
Reprinted from Largo, 1993.

uncorrected age) on motor assessment batteries. Most studies have shown that preterm infants develop at a slower rate than full-term infants when their age has not been corrected for prematurity. There appear to be delays in the first two years, after which time the preterm infants "catch up." Largo and colleagues (1993) described a cohort of 108 preterm children whose birth weights were appropriate for GA. Motor development was examined during the first two years using the Griffiths scales and a standardized neurological examination. The authors examined the onset of pivoting and walking in preterm children who were neurologically unimpaired and argued for a maturational approach to motor development as this depends primarily on conceptional rather than postnatal age.

Other studies have not produced such a clear distinction between actual and adjusted age. Barrera and colleagues (1987) compared the performance of 59 preterm infants (20 with a birth weight of less than 1,500 g [3.3 lb] and 39 with a birth weight between 1,500 and 2,000 g [4.4 lb]) with that of 24 full-term infants at 4, 8, 12, and 16 months uncorrected and corrected age. They argued that both should be considered in assessment of preterm infants as many factors influence the development of these infants, and a single score does not necessarily reveal the true picture. Lems and colleagues (1993), using the BSID, argued for only partial correction for motor development in the second half of the first year.

Cioni and colleagues (1993) compared the early stages of independent walking of a group of 25 normal full-term infants with 25 low-risk preterm infants. Once the age was corrected for prematurity, no differences were observed between the two groups for onset of walking. In addition, wide individual differences were observed in the early stages of walking. The authors argued that this supports the findings for other motor patterns that have also shown wide variations between subjects with normal development. Cioni and colleagues (1993) found that these differences were not related to such dynamic characteristics as anthropometric measures, muscle power, or resistance to passive movements, but explained them in terms of the "characteristics of the neural structures involved in goal-directed locomotion" (p. 204), such as the spinal networks in the spinal cord and subsystems in the brainstem, motor cortex, basal ganglia, and cerebellum.

Using several neurobehavioral tests (Movement Assessment of Infants; Wolanski Motor Scale of Infants), Piper and colleagues (1989) compared the motor performance of a preterm (32-36 weeks GA) group with a very preterm (less than 32 weeks GA) group of infants at both four months chronological and four months adjusted age. On the basis of their findings, they argued for the maturational model (part a in figure 7.1) when examining volitional movements. That is, the infant's age should be fully adjusted for prematurity to represent the expected age if born full term. In contrast, the development of primitive reflexes appeared to be influenced by both biological and environmental factors (part b in figure 7.1). The authors suggested that the reduced time spent in utero may have been responsible for the hypotonicity that

■■■ A dilemma faced in the assessment of preterm infants is whether to correct for gestational age or not. The effect of being born early appears to have different implications for different types of motor abilities. Like motor development in full-term infants, development in preterm infants appears to be affected by biological, environmental, and task factors.

often characterizes very preterm infants. From this one study it can be seen that no single model will account for motor development in general. Not only are there biological and environmental factors, but, as Newell (1986) argued, task factors also play a role in determining the developmental course for preterm as well as full-term infants.

It is also important to point out that an infant born too late (i.e., post-term—greater than 42 weeks GA) is also at risk. However, this event is now quite rare in most Western societies, as labor is often induced when infants are at risk due to late delivery.

How Does This Research Inform Therapeutic Practice?

Therapists must be aware of a multitude of factors that may influence motor development. Although maturation is still considered to play a major role in motor development, environmental factors are also important. The findings of studies on different cultural practices provide promising evidence that motor development can be fostered through suitable intervention programs. An investigation of these different cultural practices may provide clues to how infants with motor delay (and possibly disability) can be offered enrichment programs that may assist in developing appropriate milestones sooner.

Summary

Appropriate intervention is dependent on accurate identification of any problem. Developing suitable assessment instruments for infants is a challenge, as many factors must be considered in the development of an appropriate assessment tool. In particular, a test must have suitable validity and reliability; and if it is a norm-referenced test, an appropriate standardization sample must have been used to develop norms.

Infants are not easy to test. In order to ensure that tests are administered in an objective and reliable way, the administrator needs to be appropriately trained. Performance measures are often based on observation, which can lead to subjectivity. Also, testing infants is challenging, and the test administrator must be knowledgeable regarding the best way to get the best performance out of an infant. In particular, the behavioral state of the infant must be carefully monitored.

Despite these difficulties, there are many assessment tools available. The remainder of this part of the book describes some of the approaches taken to assess infant motor ability.

eight ■■■

Neurobehavioral Motor Assessment and Other Tests

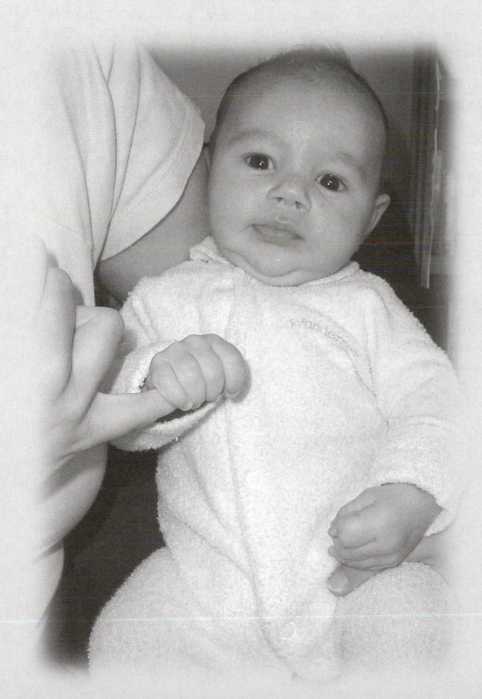

chapter objectives

This chapter will do the following:

- Discuss the importance of the Apgar score
- Describe the difference between neonatal neurological and neurobehavioral examinations
- Describe some of the more common neurobehavioral assessment tools available
- Examine a new neonatal test that addresses spontaneous movements

Early intervention is considered a key factor in achieving optimal outcomes for children with developmental disorders. The earlier these disorders can be identified, the earlier an intervention can be initiated. How soon can a problem in motor development be identified in infants? Although some limited assessments are available to test the fetus, the first opportunity for most health professionals to assess an infant is at birth or soon after. With this in mind, researchers and clinicians have, over the last 50 years, been developing assessment tools for this age range.

As described in chapter 1, newborn infants have very poor motor ability, with movements primarily reflexive or spontaneous. An evaluation of motor ability in the newborn infant would rely on the evaluation of these types of movements. However, these movement patterns have taken on an even greater significance than simply as a measure of motor ability. They are considered the best, and were at one time the only, means of assessing the neurological status of the newborn infant. Hence, the assessment of primitive and postural reflexes, as well as muscle tone, became the basis for what is generally termed the "neurological" examination (Burton & Miller, 1998).

This chapter describes assessment tools designed specifically for the neonate. Although these are designed to assess other aspects of development besides motor development (e.g., cognitive, emotional), all measure some aspect of motor control. They usually include muscle tone, reflexes, and postural control. A more recent test utilizing spontaneous motor activity is also described.

Apgar Assessment

Over 50 years ago, Virginia Apgar developed the **Apgar** screening technique as a fast and reliable method of assessing the newborn (Apgar, 1953). This test was quickly adopted in most modern hospitals and is still extensively used as the first test of an infant's physical condition as soon as he or she is born.

The Apgar test consists of five items that measure the integrity of the infant's heart rate, respiration, muscle tone, reflex irritability, and skin tone. These are rated either 0, 1, or 2 depending on the infant's status (see table 8.1). For example, in recording muscle tone, the infant may be limp (hence a score of 0), weak and inactive (a score of 1), or strong and active (a score of 2). Recordings are generally taken 1 min after birth, with additional measures usually taken at 3, 5, and 10 min after birth. The 5-min recording is considered the best indicator of the infant's condition (Drage et al., 1964). A score between 7 and 10 is considered good to excellent and usually indicates no immediate need for attention. If the neonate scores between 4 and 6, then there is a need for further observation and possible assistance with breathing. Any score under 4 indicates a need for resuscitation if the baby is to survive (Mercer, 1998).

Table 8.1   Summary of the Apgar Scoring Criteria

Score	PHYSIOLOGICAL SIGN				
	Appearance (Skin tone)	Pulse (Heart rate)	Grimace (Reflex irritability)	Activity (Muscle tone)	Respiration (Breathing effort)
0	Body pale or blue	Pulse absent	No response	Flaccid	Absent
1	Natural skin tone on body, extremities blue	Pulse rate slow (<100)	Grimace/facial expression evident	Flexion of extremities evident	Slow, shallow, and irregular
2	Natural skin tone over entire body	Pulse rate rapid (>100)	Sneezing, coughing, or crying	Good, active movement	Normal, crying

This test was standardized by Apgar and James (1962) using 27,715 infants. Standardization showed that infants with the lowest Apgar scores had the highest mortality rates. Also, Apgar scores were directly related to the type of delivery. Breech deliveries had the lowest average score, followed by cesarean section deliveries, with spinal (epidural) anesthesia and natural childbirth deliveries receiving the highest scores. Recently, a large case-control study in Denmark demonstrated that planned vaginal deliveries have a 15-fold higher risk of low Apgar scores than elective cesarean sections when infants are born in breech position (Krebs & Langhoff-Roos, 1999). Other risk factors have been identified in a study of over 1 million full-term infants from the Swedish Medical Birth Registry (Thorngren-Jerneck & Herbst, 2001). Increased maternal age, maternal smoking, birth weight (both too light and too heavy), parity (firstborn infants are more at risk), and multiple births were identified as factors that increase the risk of a lower Apgar score. Also, boys were more likely to have lower Apgar scores than girls, even when birth weight was taken into account. This study also confirmed the greater risk of low Apgar scores for infants born breech.

The Apgar test was designed to screen for infants in need of special immediate attention. Virginia Apgar (1953) argued that the survival of the infant in the first month is related to the infant's condition in the delivery room. Hence, the Apgar was designed specifically to measure this condition. Recent research has confirmed that the use of the Apgar in this respect is still as meaningful in the present day as it was in 1953. In a study of 151,891 live-born infants, Apgar scores taken at 5 min for both preterm and full-term infants were related to survival rates (Casey et al., 2001). Furthermore, the Apgar was a better indicator of survival than more objective tests such as the measurement of pH in umbilical-artery blood. The Apgar has also been identified as a powerful predictor of survival within different race or ethnic groups. Doyle and colleagues (2003) found that for Anglos and Mexican Americans, Apgar had a greater predictive value than low birth weight with regard to infant mortality.

■■■ The Apgar test is an important tool for the assessment of the state of the infant at birth. It is an essential tool for identifying whether a newborn is in immediate need of attention, but it has limited predictive value.

The Apgar is limited in its use in predicting later developmental outcome. Recent studies have provided evidence that a low Apgar score at 5 min is a risk factor for neurological disorders such as cerebral palsy, epilepsy, and mental retardation (e.g., Moster et al., 2001; Thorngren-Jerneck & Herbst, 2001). In the case of breech deliveries, a relationship has been found between low Apgar score and later disability. In one study, 323 infants who were delivered in breech presentation at term were followed up from ages 4 to 15 years (Krebs et al., 2001). Of these, 105 had Apgar scores less than 7 at 5 min, and the remaining 218 had Apgar scores of 7 or more. A small, but significant, increase in the risk of handicap or disability was identified in the infants with the lower Apgar score. Around 25% of the children with the low Apgar score, compared with 8% of the control children, were found to have a disability. Given that 75% of the children with a low Apgar score developed normally, the Apgar test should be considered only as a risk factor, not a tool for predicting disability.

Neonatal Neurological Examination

Infant neurological examinations were originally developed in the 1950s by three French physicians, André-Thomas, Chesni, and Saint-Anne Dargassies. They examined both passive and active muscle tone in addition to some reflexes and reactions (Harris & Brady, 1986). In 1960, Paine (cited in Harris & Brady, 1986) published a paper on the neurological examination of infants and children. In addition to assessing tone and reflexes, this examination included the assessment of vision, hearing, taste, and smell, as well as evaluations of speech, mental state, and autonomic function. Although many of these new tests were not suitable for infants, this tool formed the basis for many of the current neurological assessment instruments.

Infant neurological examinations generally require an evaluation of the "global" quality of a response rather than quantifying or measuring the particular performance (Touwen, 1976). They were not necessarily designed to determine future motor or cognitive ability, but, like the Apgar test, focus on the current needs of the infant (figure 8.1). If infants perform poorly on the examinations, this indicates a need for immediate treatment. In addition to determining whether an infant has a current neurological problem, these tests are used to evaluate any day-to-day changes, and to a limited degree, for long-term prognosis.

An initial neurological examination is generally performed by a pediatric neurologist and is designed to determine any neurological abnormalities. These examinations take around 5 to 10 min and are only one part of the examination of the neonate. Assessment also includes the infant's prenatal and perinatal history, laboratory tests of blood samples, and in some cases testing for brain abnormalities using tools such as brain ultrasound scans.

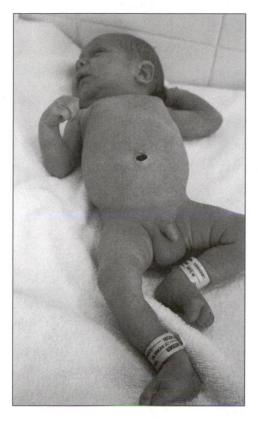

Figure 8.1 The neurological examination is important for investigating the current status of the newborn infant.

The Amiel-Tison Neurological Assessment at Term (ATNAAT: Amiel-Tison, 2002) is administered at term age and was developed to assess the risk of later neurological impairment. This test was based on an earlier version (Amiel-Tison, 1968) considered one of the more commonly used neurological assessment tools (Zafeiriou, 2004). In the recent version only about 5 min is needed to administer the 35 items. These are divided into eight categories measuring functions of alertness, behavior and spontaneous activity, active and passive tone, and primary reflexes. A recent study has verified that the ATNAAT has excellent interobserver reliability, with a Kappa coefficient of 0.76 (Deschênes et al., 2004). However, these authors suggest that more research is needed to determine its predictive validity.

Standardized neurological tests generally take considerably longer to administer than the brief 5- to 10-min examination performed by the pediatric neurologist. These longer tests are designed to provide a comprehensive neurological examination for infants whose earlier examinations or histories indicate that they may be at risk. Therefore, not all infants receive these longer examinations, which are generally administered by occupational or physical therapists, nurses, or psychologists (Majnemer & Mazer, 1998).

Prechtl designed the Neurological Examination of the Full Term Newborn Infant (Prechtl & Beintema, 1964) for infants from birth to four weeks of age. The second edition of this examination was published in 1977. The tool is based on the observation of the infant's posture, limb position, motility (whether hyperkinetic or hypokinetic), muscle tone (hypertonia or hypotonia), the presence of any tremor or pathological movements, and the threshold and intensity of reflexes. These are examined in two stages. The first is the observation stage, in which the infant is examined while lying undisturbed. The infant's state, resting posture, and spontaneous motor activity are examined in this stage. Reflexes are tested in the second examination stage, in which the infant is undressed and placed on an examination table. An example of the procedure used to test each of the reflexes is given in figure 8.2.

Prechtl (1977) argued that through a neurological examination at the neonatal stage, it is possible to document the current condition of the infant's nervous system. Prechtl points out, however, that "an abnormal or pathological finding in the newborn period cannot justify making any prediction about the individual's neurological condition several months or even years later" (p. 1). What it indicates is that the infant requires follow-up at regular intervals in order to make diagnosis of any persistent abnormalities as early as possible.

Palmar Grasp	
State	Optimal 3 and 4, exclude 1, 2, and 5.
Position	Put fingers (usually the index finger) from the ulnar side into the hands and gently press the palmar surface. Never touch the dorsal side of the hands. Ensure the head stays in the midline: supine, strictly symmetrical, the head in the midline, and the arms semiflexed.
Procedure	Put fingers (usually the index finger) from the ulnar side into the hands and gently press the palmar surface. Never touch the dorsal side of the hands. Ensure the head stays in the midline.
Response	Flexion of all fingers around the examiner's finger.
Recording	− absent + short, weak flexion **++ strong and sustained for several seconds** +++ sustained grasp with the tips of the infant's fingers going white
Significance	Watch for difference of intensity between the two sides. Sucking movements facilitate grasping. If grasping is absent or weak, try the facilitating influence of simultaneous sucking. If there is no effect, the reason for the absent palmar grasp is probably peripheral and not central. Asymmetries occur in Erb's and in Klumpke's paresis. The response is weak or absent in depressed babies.
Developmental course	It may be less intense during the first and second days.

Figure 8.2 A description of the process to assess the palmar grasp in infants using the Neurological Examination of the Full Term Newborn Infant.
Reprinted from Prechtl, 1977.

■■■ Neonatal neurological examinations are designed to examine the current neurological status of the newborn and are not considered useful tools for predicting later developmental outcome.

One of the main difficulties with Prechtl's neurological assessment technique is that a large amount of training is required in order to appropriately administer the test and interpret the findings (Harris & Brady, 1986), although others have argued that specialized training is not required to administer this test (Majnemer & Mazer, 1998). Although reliability and validity measures are not provided in the manual, others have attempted to determine these (Harris & Brady, 1986). These studies have determined that the test tends to generate a high rate of false positives (i.e., diagnosed abnormal but normal when tested at a later age), particularly when assessment is carried out during the newborn period. Another difficulty with the test is that it is very lengthy, usually lasting an hour or more.

A major criticism of neurological examinations is that because they are based primarily on the evaluation of reflexes, they are addressing only the neurological integrity of the subcortical neuroanatomic structures, not the higher centers (van Kranen-Mastenbroek et al., 1994). As Lester and Tronick (2001) point out, "Even asphyxiated infants and anencephalic infants generated variable reflexes" (p. 364). Around the middle of the 20th century, behaviorally oriented assessment became popular (Singer, 2001). These tests, referred to as "neurobehavioral," recognize that the newborn is capable of higher cortical functioning.

These newer tests were based on the neurological examination but also included items that addressed factors such as habituation and social interaction.

Neonatal Neurobehavioral Assessment

Neurobehavioral assessments have been designed to take into account factors that influence early development, such as whether the infant is full term or preterm, or whether the infant has any of the risk factors described in the previous chapter. A few of the more common tests are described in more detail in the following sections. These have been divided into two categories. The first category comprises tests that can only be administered once the infant is at term, or 40 weeks gestational age (GA). The second category includes tests that can be administered to neonates as soon as they are born (regardless of GA).

Neonatal Neurobehavioral Assessments Administered From Term Age

Table 8.2 details several standardized neonatal assessment tests. The main content of the test, reliability, validity, testing time, and the author details are provided. All of these tests require the infant to be term age before assessment, although some are suitable for preterm infants once they have reached term age.

One of the best known and most widely used is the Neonatal Behavioral Assessment Scale (NBAS) developed by Berry Brazelton (1973). This scale arose as a result of research demonstrating that "there was a brain in the baby" (Lester & Tronick, 2001, p. 364) and that infants were not just reflexive. The NBAS has been described as the "most popular and well studied neonatal assessment exam in both medical and psychological research" (Singer, 2001, p. 4). A second edition was published in 1984 (Brazelton, 1984), and a third edition has also been published (Brazelton & Nugent, 1995).

The underlying basis of Brazelton's scale is that the newborn is a complexly organized whole whose adaptations include fending for himself or herself against negative stimuli and interacting to varying degrees with social stimulation (Brazelton, 1973). The test examines the infant's ability to change his or her behavior depending on the context. This is achieved by including emotional-behavioral dimensions in the test through a complex series of observations. Understanding the parent–infant interaction is a key factor in the assessment. Brazelton's goal is to "assess the baby's contribution to the failures that resulted, when parents were presented with a difficult or deviant infant" (Brazelton & Nugent, 1995, p. 1). As with other neurological examinations, this test investigates motor capabilities such as reflexes and muscle tone.

Four dimensions of functioning in the neonate are identified with the scale (Als et al., 1982): physiologic, motor, state, and attentional/interactional. These are determined with 28 behavioral items that are

Table 8.2 Commonly Used Neonatal Neurobehavioral Examinations That Can Be Administered to Infants Once They Are at Term Age

Test and author	Test description	Reliability	Validity	Testing time
Einstein Neonatal Neurobehavioral Assessment Scale (Daum et al., 1977; cited in Majnemer & Mazer, 1998)	20 test items with 4 summary items: Passive and active movement Tone Reflexes Response to auditory and visual stimuli	Interrater: r = 0.97	Construct Predictive	30–45 min
Neonatal Behavioral Assessment Scale (Brazelton & Nugent, 1995)	28 behavioral items 18 reflex items	Internal consistency: r = −0.15 to 0.32 Test-retest: r = −0.11 to 0.52 Interrater: 65–100% agreement	Construct Concurrent Predictive Responsiveness	30 min
Neonatal Neurobehavioral Examination (Morgan et al., 1988)	Tone Motor patterns Primitive reflexes	Interrater: 88% agreement on items 95% agreement on sections Internal consistency: r = 0.5 to 0.63 between sections r = 0.8 to 0.86 section to total score	Construct	15 min
Neonatal Neurological Examination (Sheridan-Pereira et al., 1991)	32 items 7 factors of: Hypertonus Primitive reflexes Limb tone Neck support Reflexes and tremor Alertness Fussy	Test-retest: r = 0.73 Internal consistency: (short form) r = 0.80, 0.73	Construct	Not specified

Adapted from Majnemer and Mazer, 1998.

scored on a 9-point scale and 18 reflex items that are scored on a 4-point scale (see table 8.3). An addition to the second edition, published in 1984 (Brazelton, 1984), was the inclusion of seven supplementary items that examined the quality of the infant's responsiveness (Lester & Tronick, 2001). These were specifically designed for high-risk infants. Apart from some minor changes, these items were retained in the third edition, as shown in table 8.3 (Brazelton & Nugent, 1995).

There is a preferred order of administration, but this can be modified depending on the infant's state. Also, test items are grouped into five *packages* that are administered in a particular order. First is the *habituation* package, followed by the *motor-oral*, then the *truncal*, and

Table 8.3 Behavioral, Supplementary, and Reflex Items on the Revised NBAS

Behavioral items	Supplementary items
Response decrement to light	Quality of alertness
Response decrement to rattle	Cost of attention
Response decrement to bell	Examiner facilitation
Response decrement to tactile stimulation of the foot	General irritability
Orientation inanimate visual	Robustness and endurance
Orientation inanimate auditory	State regulation
Orientation inanimate visual and auditory	Examiner's emotional response
Orientation animate visual	
Orientation animate auditory	
Orientation animate visual and auditory	**Reflex items**
Alertness	Plantar grasp
General tonus	Babinski
Motor maturity	Ankle clonus
Pull-to-sit	Rooting
Defensive movements	Sucking
Activity level	Glabella
Peak of excitement	Passive movements—arms
Rapidity of build-up	Passive movements—legs
Irritability	Palmar grasp
Lability of states	Placing
Cuddliness	Standing
Consolability	Walking
Self-quieting	Crawling
Hand-to-mouth	Incurvation (gallant response)
Tremulousness	Tonic deviation of head and eyes
Startles	Nystagmus
Lability of skin color	Tonic neck reflex
Smiles	Moro

Reprinted from Brazelton & Nugent, 1995

lastly the *vestibular* package. Items in the *social/interactive* package are observed in between the other four packages when the child is in the appropriate state for these items. Items within each package are organized according to how intrusive or difficult they are. Less intrusive items are first and the most intrusive are at the end of the package.

Although this test includes some aspects of a neurological examination, it was designed to examine the adaptive and coping abilities of the infant from term to 48 weeks post-GA. The supplementary items included since the second edition allow the examination of healthy preterm infants once they reach term age. It is not recommended for infants who require neonatal intensive care, as the procedure may overstress the infant (Brazelton & Nugent, 1995).

Brazelton and Nugent (1995) note that the normative base for the NBAS is quite limited, recognizing, for example, that newborns from different cultures behave differently. They advise researchers to ensure that they control for ethnic and cultural variables in addition to identified risk factors. Test-retest reliability is considered poor, with only low to moderate correlations (Majnemer & Mazer, 1998). However, as Brazelton and Nugent point out, "Change not stability characterizes healthy development in this period" (p. 67), and they question how useful test-retest reliability measures are for neonates.

Examining patterns of change with repeated examinations is an important component of the NBAS, as this measures how the infant adapts to change with age. Like most other infant assessments, the NBAS is not considered a useful tool in predicting long-term development. However, repeated examinations over time using the NBAS have proven useful in predicting later developmental status. Recent research on a sample of 209 premature infants born in Japan suggests that the NBAS may have some predictive validity. Specific cluster scores from the NBAS were found to predict disability at age five years. In particular, lower motor and orientation cluster scores were associated with increased risk of mild and severe disability when assessed using multinomial logistic regression analysis (Ohgi et al., 2003).

The NBAS is lengthy to administer and score. It takes around 30 to 45 min to administer and another 20 to 30 min to score (Lester & Tronick, 2001). It is also difficult to learn and cannot be learned through a clinical manual. Intensive training is required, resulting in certification to administer and score the NBAS. Brazelton and Nugent (1995) recommend training to a level of interrater reliability of 90% and suggest that reliability should be checked every two to three years. Certification is valid for three years, and information on training is available from the Brazelton Center for Infants and Parents (address: The Children's Hospital, 1295 Boylston St., Boston, MA 02215, USA). There are limited places around the world where training can be obtained, which is problematic given the additional time and travel costs involved.

Touwen (1976) questioned the inclusion by Brazelton of some 20 neurological items in the original test, as the procedures explicitly state that the test is not a formal neurological evaluation. "To the naïve reader, the presence of these neurological items is confusing, as their number and quality is insufficient for neurological assessment, and their meaning with regard to the tested behaviour is not clear" (Touwen, 1976, p. 5). Consequently, Touwen warns against using this test in place of a neurological one.

■■■ The NBAS is designed to examine the adaptive and coping skills of the newborn and is considered the benchmark in neurobehavioral tests that examine the infant from term age.

Despite these criticisms, the Brazelton scale has been very popular as a device for identifying high-risk infants and for studying the effects of obstetric medication, cross-cultural infant behavior, and caregiver intervention. The NBAS has been described as the "benchmark neurobehavioral examination" (Lester & Tronick, 2001, p. 367) and has been the basis for many other tests, including several tests described later that have been developed primarily for preterm and high-risk infants.

Neonatal Neurological Assessment Administered From Birth Regardless of Gestational Age

The tests outlined in table 8.2 require infants to be at term age before they can be assessed. This is problematic for infants who are born very preterm, especially when one considers that these infants are in the *high-risk* category and therefore in need of early assessment. This has resulted in many neurological assessment tools that can assess the infant at birth regardless of GA. That is, many tests examining the neonate have taken into account the special needs of the preterm population. There are now a wide variety of tools for preterm infants. They are unique in that they have used normative samples including preterm infants and therefore can assess infants as soon as they are born. Other tests that have been standardized using full-term infants cannot be used with preterm infants until they reach term age, and even then it is contentious whether these infants should be assessed against the full-term sample. Table 8.4 lists some of the tools that can be administered regardless of GA, and several are described in more detail in the following subsections.

Assessment of the Preterm Infant's Behavior (APIB)

Based on the NBAS, the Assessment of the Preterm Infant's Behavior (APIB) (Als et al., 1982) was designed to specifically assess the level of functioning of preterm infants. It investigates five different behavioral systems: physiological (autonomic system), motor, state-regulatory, attentional-interactive, and self-regulatory. By introducing a graded sequence of increasingly more demanding stimuli, the APIB assesses the threshold at which an infant shifts from an organized to a disorganized response. Level of organization is determined through factors such as irregularities in respiration and muscle tone (Als & Duffy, 1989). There are 285 measures that are then reduced to 32 summary scores. This test takes around 30 to 45 min to administer, and like the NBAS requires extensive training.

Although reliability scores were not provided with the initial test description (Als et al., 1982), later findings have shown significant split-half reliability measures. Construct validity has been determined with the APIB being able to discriminate between infants who were born with different GAs, namely 26-32 weeks GA, 33-37 weeks GA, and 38-41

Table 8.4   Common Neonatal Examinations Administered at Birth, Regardless of GA

Test and author	Test description	Reliability	Validity	Testing time
Assessment of Preterm Infant's Behavior (Als et al., 1982)	Tests 5 systems: Physiological Motor State-regulatory Attentional-interactive Self-regulatory	None provided	Construct Responsiveness	30–45 min
Network Neurobehavioral Scale (Lester & Tronick, 2001)	Neurological items arranged in 8 packages Stress/abstinence scale arranged in 7 packages (see examples, table 8.5)	Test-retest	Construct	30 min
Neurobehavioral Assessment of the Preterm Infant (Korner et al., 2001)	27 items divided into 7 dimensions: Motor development and vigor Scarf sign Popliteal angle Alertness and orientation Irritability Cry quality Percent asleep ratings	Internal consistency Test-retest Interrater	Predictive Concurrent Responsiveness	30 min
Neurological Assessment of the Preterm and Full-term Newborn Infant (Dubowitz & Dubowitz, 1981)	33 items divided into 4 subsections: Habituation Movement and tone Reflexes Neurobehavioral responses	None provided	Construct Concurrent Predictive	15 min
Test of Infant Motor Performance (TIMP) (Campbell et al., 1995)	27 spontaneously observed behaviors 26 elicited items	Internal consistency Interrater Intrarater	Content Construct Predictive	25–40 min

Adapted from Majnemer and Mazer, 1998.

weeks GA. The APIB clearly identified differences in the three groups in the expected direction (Als & Duffy, 1989).

Neurobehavioral Assessment of the Preterm Infant (NAPI)

Anneliese Korner commenced a longitudinal study in 1977 that required an evaluation of the level of maturity of functioning in preterm infants. As a result, she realized there was a need for an assessment tool suitable for preterm infants (Korner & Constantinou, 2001). Consequently, this work resulted in the publication of the Neurobehavioral Assessment of the Preterm Infant (NAPI) in 1990 (Korner & Thom, 1990). A second edition of this test was released in 2001 (Korner et al., 2001).

The NAPI is suitable for infants from 32 weeks postconceptional age to term age (i.e., 34 to 40 weeks GA). These infants need to be breathing unaided and free of intravenous lines and gastric tubes when examined. Seven neurobehavioral dimensions are measured from 27 subitems. Scoring occurs following each test item to ensure that the examiner does not forget the infant's response.

Van Kranen-Mastenbroek and colleagues (1994) argued that general neurological examinations may not be suitable for preterm infants, as infants born small for GA appear more stressed when handled, and neurological examination involves frequent handling. The design of the NAPI takes this problem into account and is aimed at limiting the amount of interference with the infant.

The sequence of presentation of items is strictly invariant, an aspect that differentiates the NAPI from many other tests. This decision was based on evidence that the sequence resulted in the behavioral states most appropriate to elicit the responses required of the infant. That is, the authors designed "a standard sequence of rousing, soothing, and altering items that would maximize the chance of testing the various functions in appropriate states and would minimize the need to intervene with some infants more than with others" (Korner & Constantinou, 2001, p. 385).

When the NAPI was first developed, 179 preterm infants were involved, with a total of 354 examinations. The test was then validated with a sample of 290 preterm infants undergoing a total of 553 examinations (Korner et al., 1991). As a result of these quite rigorous procedures, the NAPI has sound reliability and validity. Test-retest reliability scores are between 0.6 and 0.85 (Korner & Constantinou, 2001), whereas interobserver reliability is between 0.64 and 0.98 (Korner & Thom, 1990). Validity was confirmed through examination of changes in the infants as a result of increasing conceptional age. For all seven dimensions, there was a significant improvement in performance with age (Korner et al., 1991). Concurrent and predictive validity have also been established in recent studies (Korner & Constantinou, 2001). These latter studies were surprising given that the predictive validity of most infant assessments is known to be quite poor.

Weekly normative data are available for preterm infants between 32 and 38 weeks postconceptional age. These can provide an indication of any delay in performance. As the authors state, there is considerable variability in the performance of preterm infants, and decisions should be made based on repeated examinations, not just one test outcome (Korner & Constantinou, 2001).

As with most of the neurological examinations, training to administer the NAPI is essential, as is experience with young preterm infants. Training consists of an instruction manual and a training video. It is recommended that a qualified teacher evaluate the quality of the administration and scoring at the completion of the training. A Web site is also provided to assist with training (www-med.stanford.edu/school/pediatrics/NAPI). Although rigorous training is required, the advantage of this test over others is that it does not require travel to a training venue.

■■■ Preterm infants are often more stressed with excessive handling. The NAPI takes this into account and has a strictly invariant sequence of item administration to ensure that interference on the infant is minimal.

NICU (Neonatal Intensive Care Unit) Network Neurobehavioral Scale (NNNS)

A recent test based on Brazelton's NBAS (Brazelton, 1973) has been designed specifically for drug-exposed and other high-risk infants. The NICU Network Neurobehavioral Scale (NNNS) (Lester & Tronick, 2001) considers the multiple risk factors associated with infants exposed to drugs prenatally, including prematurity, poor nutrition, and lack of prenatal care. Many of the tests outlined in this chapter were considered in the development of this test. The test is based on a "holistic view" that does not consider any specific functional domain more important than any other. Like most traditional neurological assessments, the test examines reflexes, tone, and posture. In addition, it investigates social and self-regulatory competencies and signs of stress (Lester & Tronick, 2001). The latter are particularly important for infants who are drug affected.

Like the NAPI, the test should be performed on a medically stable infant in an open crib. It is recommended for infants between 28 weeks GA and four weeks postterm age, and can be administered to both full-term infants and preterm infants with varying GAs. It comprises a set of neurological items and also a stress/abstinence scale (see table 8.5). Both the neurological and stress items are arranged in packages.

Packages for the neurological items (table 8.5) represent changes in position or focus. They include a range of reflexes arranged in packages such as lower extremity reflexes (e.g., plantar grasp and Babinski) and upright responses (e.g., placing and stepping responses). Muscle tone is examined under both active and passive conditions. The distribution

Table 8.5 The Two Components of the NICU Network Neurobehavioral Scale (NNNS)

Neurobehavioral packages (examples)	Stress/abstinence organ systems (examples)
Preexamination observation (initial state observation)	Physiological (labored breathing)
Response decrement (response decrement to rattle)	Autonomic nervous system (sneezing)
Unwrap and supine (skin color)	Central nervous system (hypertonia)
Lower extremity reflexes (leg recoil)	Skin (pallor)
Upper extremity and facial reflexes (sucking)	Visual (roving eye movements)
Upright responses (stepping)	Gastrointestinal (gagging and choking)
Infant prone (head raise in prone position)	State (extreme irritability)
Pick up infant (cuddle on shoulder)	
Infant supine on examiner's lap (orientation)	
Infant spin (nystagmus)	
Infant supine in crib (Moro reflex)	
Postexamination observation (postexamination state observation)	

Adapted from Lester & Tronick, 2001.

of tone (proximal or distal) is also considered, as flexor tone in preterm infants is not uniform. For example, tone in the lower extremities may develop first (Lester & Tronick, 2001). Whereas the NAPI is strictly invariant in the presentation of items, the NNNS states a "preferred" order of presentation of the neurobehavioral items, with the order of presentation being relatively invariant. In contrast to what happens with the NAPI, administration of some of the packages requires the infant to be in particular behavioral states based on Prechtl's (1974) traditional 1-6 criteria (see previous chapter). State-dependent performance is an essential component of the NNNS.

The stress/abstinence items are organized into packages that represent different biological systems of the body, such as the autonomic nervous system, skin, and visual system (see table 8.5). These items are recorded as either present or absent and are observed throughout the neurobehavioral examination. For example, with the gastrointestinal system, is gagging or choking present, or in the central nervous system, are startles present or absent (Lester & Tronick, 2001)?

The test was originally developed using a sample of 1,388 infants from the Maternal Lifestyle study (Lester, 1998). The authors comment that this "is not a standardization sample in the traditional sense" (Lester & Tronick, 2001, p. 375), but they argue that it is quite a large sample considering the standardization samples of other comparable infant tests. Although the test is relatively new, ongoing studies in the United States and India have estimated the test-retest reliability at between 0.30 and 0.44 (Lester & Tronick). Validity is primarily based on the findings of the Maternal Lifestyle study, where the NNNS summary scores were influenced independently by different drugs (cocaine, opiates, alcohol, and tobacco) and birth weight.

Certification is required for the administration and scoring of the NNNS, and a training kit is available. There are training programs in the United States, Europe, South America, and Southeast Asia, but training may be achieved elsewhere through the use of telemedicine and videoconferencing (Lester & Tronick, 2001).

■■■ The NNNS has been designed specifically for drug-exposed and other high-risk infants and includes both a neurological and a stress/abstinence scale.

Test of Infant Motor Performance (TIMP)

The Test of Infant Motor Performance (TIMP) (Campbell et al., 1995) is suitable for preterm infants from 32 weeks GA and up to four months following term age. It was developed for physical and occupational therapists to administer in order to examine movement and postural control. Spontaneously emitted movements, such as "head in midline," "pelvic lifting," and "oscillation of arm or leg during movement," are measured by 27 dichotomous "Observed items of posture and active movement." Many of these items are based on the spontaneous movements described by Prechtl and colleagues (e.g., Hadders-Algra & Prechtl, 1992). There are also 26 "Elicited items" such as "head rotation side to side," "pull to sit," and "crawling movements in prone," which are scored on either 5-, 6-, or 7-point ordinal scales. Several of these items are taken from previous tests such as the NBAS (Brazelton, 1973).

Intrarater and interrater reliability have been assessed at between 0.95 and 0.99 for the TIMP. Concurrent validity was assessed through comparison of scores on the TIMP at three months of age with those obtained for the Alberta Infant Motor Scale (AIMS), a test of gross motor functioning (Campbell & Kolobe, 2000). Predictive validity has recently been assessed through comparison of scores on the TIMP at 7, 30, 60, and 90 days with those on the AIMS at 6, 9, and 12 months of age (Campbell et al., 2002). The greatest predictive ability was obtained when the TIMP at three months was compared with the AIMS at 12 months.

Qualitative Assessment of General Movements in Infants

In a different approach to the early identification of disability, Heinz Prechtl and colleagues examined spontaneous movements rather than reflexes or muscle tone. The work of Prechtl and colleagues (e.g., Cioni & Prechtl, 1990; Ferrari et al., 1990; Prechtl, 1990; Prechtl et al., 1997) on spontaneous motility of the neonate was outlined in chapter 1. They described several types of spontaneous activity in the young infant (e.g., Prechtl, 1984) but found that the types of movements they termed *general movements* were the most appropriate to observe when identifying abnormal behavior. Prechtl and Nolte (1984) noticed that these movements appeared qualitatively different in high-risk infants compared to normal infants, leading to further investigation of these movements as a potential tool for early identification of motor disability.

According to Prechtl (1997), general movements are the most frequent and most complex of the early movement patterns. Normal general movements are described as gross movements that involve the whole body, lasting from a few seconds to several minutes or even longer. Of particular interest are the complexity and variability of these movements in terms of intensity, force and speed, and the sequence of leg, arm, neck, and trunk movements that are produced (Prechtl, 1990). One can assess the quality of these general movements by viewing video recordings of the infant in the supine position and in a state of active wakefulness (Einspieler et al., 1997). Weekly recordings of the infant are recommended during the preterm period. A recording is then taken at term age, another between the ages of 3 and 6 weeks, and several between 9 and 15 weeks. These latter recordings coincide with the emergence of the *fidgety stage,* when there appears to be a significant change in the characteristics of the general movements. They become small, rounded, elegant movements involving primarily the limbs and head. These movements can last from four to six weeks. Prechtl suggested that these types of movements indicate the emergence of the first transitional stage in postnatal neurological development (Prechtl, 1993).

Analysis of the movements is based on a global judgment, initially of *normal* versus *abnormal* quality, based on principles of Gestalt perception. Using this approach, Ferrari and colleagues (1990) noted that the movements of brain-damaged infants were less variable and at times monotonous in comparison with the movements of low-risk infants. Movements of brain-damaged infants often lacked the fluency and complexity found for the normal group. Hadders-Algra (1996) also noted that abnormal movements frequently have an abrupt onset with all parts of the body moving synchronously, suggesting a loss of supra-spinal control in these infants.

A crucial stage in the assessment appears to be around three months, when *sensitivity* (the accuracy of identifying infants with disability) has been assessed at between 94% and 100%, and *specificity* (the accuracy of identifying infants without disability) between 82% and 100% (Einspieler et al., 1997). At this stage, the absence of fidgety general movements appears to be the primary marker for cerebral palsy and mental retardation. Although sensitivity was reasonably high at all ages, specificity was considerably lower at ages less than three months, with a large proportion of infants diagnosed as abnormal producing a normal outcome. Overall, however, qualitative assessment of spontaneous movements in young infants has proven to be a reliable tool for the early identification of cerebral palsy (Einspieler et al., 1997; Touwen, 1990; van Kranen-Mastenbroek et al., 1992, 1994).

As with most of the early assessment tools, this process requires intensive training, and training is available in only a few countries in the world. This test has limited psychometric properties and does not appear to be very reliable for the neonate, with the best results obtained for infants around three months of age. It is also very time-consuming, given that multiple testing is recommended.

Evaluation of Neonatal Examinations

Majnemer and Mazer (1998) point out that normative data are lacking for most of the neurological and neurobehavioral examinations that are currently available. They examined the reliability and validity of eight of the nine tests outlined in tables 8.2 and 8.4 (the NNNC was not included in their paper) and Prechtl's neurological assessment tool outlined at the beginning of this chapter. Whereas most tests had good validity measures, reliability information was scarce. The authors pointed out the negative impact on reliability if infants who are at risk are evaluated based on the reliability estimates from a normal population. Testing conditions must also be strictly adhered to in order to prevent excessive variability. These include the lighting, temperature, and noise level. Infants must also be tested in the appropriate behavioral state.

> ### ■■■■ How Does This Research Inform Therapeutic Practice?
>
> Ideally, given the immature nature of the infant's brain at birth, intervention should commence as early as possible. However, it is clear from this chapter that predicting a newborn infant's later outcome is very difficult. What insight can be gained from this early assessment? The shift from purely neurological to neurobehavioral assessment was a positive step, as it recognized that the neonate is an interacting individual from the time of birth (and probably prior to this). The new assessment tools, based on this relatively new approach, will aid in understanding this interactive process and hopefully provide clues on how to approach intervention in these very young infants.

Summary

It is now acknowledged that early identification of disorders is a key aspect of successful intervention. It is no wonder, then, that interest in developing assessment tools for the newborn has been considerable. These tools have proven very effective in identifying immediate risk for the newborn but less successful in predicting the infant's later developmental outcome.

Some tests are generating some hopeful results in relation to prediction. The NAPI and NNNS have recently been shown to have reasonable predictive validity. Also, the assessment of general spontaneous movements by Prechtl and colleagues appears to be useful for predicting some disorders, although this does not appear to be an effective tool until the infant is around three months of age.

As described in the previous chapter, there are too many factors that affect the newborn infant to allow true assessment of how well that infant will fare in the future. In chapter 3, the issue of neural plasticity was discussed, and it is clear that the infant's brain is still developing well into the childhood years. At what age, then, can assessment tools accurately predict later developmental outcome? The next chapter reviews assessment tools for the older infant.

nine ■■■

Diagnostic Motor Assessment and Screening Tests

chapter objectives

This chapter will do the following:

- Discuss several popular stage-dependent tests for infant motor development used for diagnostic purposes

- Examine recently developed criterion-referenced assessment tools used for diagnosis

- Examine common screening tools used to evaluate large populations of infants

- Review other approaches to diagnosis such as brain scanning and kinematic and kinetic analysis

Chapter 2 covered the influence of Gesell, McGraw, and others on our understanding of how motor control develops. These researchers argued for a primarily maturational approach to understanding the development of motor control. One of the most significant outcomes from this period of research was the influence of this stage- or sequence-oriented approach on the assessment of infant development, both motor and cognitive. These researchers mapped out what is commonly termed the motor milestones and utilized these to produce assessment tools based on the infant's achievements at a particular age (called stage-dependent tests). That is, these tests are based on the notion that there is an invariant developmental sequence followed by infants as they become more proficient in motor skill. This chapter describes some of the more common assessment tools that developed from this traditional maturational approach.

Despite the criticisms of norm-referenced tests outlined in chapter 7, this approach continues to be popular in the 21st century. These tests are regularly used for both research and clinical purposes. The next section provides a description of the diagnostic tools developed to assess motor ability in infancy. Diagnostic instruments are comprehensive assessments that are generally administered when infants are thought to be at risk of developmental delay or disability. Recently, other theoretical approaches such as the ecological or dynamic systems approach have influenced test development. This has resulted in many criterion-referenced tools used to examine movement ability in infants. Several of these tests are reviewed here.

Several diagnostic instruments have been adapted to produce screening instruments designed to provide a quick assessment of the infant. They are capable of examining a large population to determine whether further assessment should be carried out. Some of these instruments are also examined in this chapter. Finally, other approaches to diagnosis are discussed, in particular, brain scanning techniques and kinetic and kinematic analysis of movements.

Norm-Referenced Developmental Diagnostic Tests

The traditional maturational approach to infant testing relies on standardized instruments whereby the infant is compared to normative scores based on a large sample of infants. That is, the tests are norm referenced. Several of these tests are listed in table 9.1. Some of these tools have been designed to assess only motor development, such as the Peabody Developmental Motor Scales (Folio & Fewell, 1983). Most, however, have been designed to investigate additional aspects of development such as cognition, speech, and social skills. These include the popular Bayley Scales of Infant Development (Bayley, 1993). Also, some examine a very narrow age range, such as the Evaluation of Motor Development in Infants (Wolanski & Zdanska-Brincken, 1973), which is suitable for infants from one month to when they start walking. Others investigate a much broader age range, such as the Battelle Develop-

Table 9.1   Norm-Referenced Diagnostic Tools for Infants

Test and author	Test description	Age range	Reliability	Validity	Testing time
Battelle Developmental Inventory (Newborg et al., 1984)	5 domains: personal-social, adaptive, motor, communication, cognition	Birth–8 years	Internal consistency Interrater Test-retest	Content Criterion related Construct	1–2 hr
Bayley Scales of Infant Development (Bayley, 1993)	Motor scale Mental scale	1–42 months	Internal consistency Interrater Test-retest	Content Criterion related Construct	25–35 min for infants 1–15 months; up to 60 min for older children
Evaluation of Motor Development in Infants (EMDI) (Wolanski & Zdanska-Brincken, 1973)	Measures 4 aspects of movement: head and trunk, sitting, standing, and locomotion	1 month to onset of walking	Not reported	Construct	Not reported
Gesell's Developmental Schedules (Gesell, 1925)	5 domains: personal-social, adaptive, motor, language, cognition	4 weeks–5 years	Interrater	Predictive	Not reported
Griffiths Mental Developmental Scales (Griffiths, 1970, 1984)	5 domains: locomotor, personal-social, hearing and speech, hand-and-eye coordination, performance	0–8 years	Test-retest	Construct	Not reported
Peabody Developmental Motor Scales (Folio & Fewell, 1983)	Fine motor: manual dexterity, hand use, eye–hand coordination, grasping Gross motor: reflexes, locomotor skills, nonlocomotor skills, balance	Birth–6 years 11 months	Interrater Test-retest	Content Criterion related Construct	45–60 min (20–30 min per scale)

Adapted from Burton & Miller, 1998.

mental Inventory (Newborg et al., 1984), which can assess children from birth to eight years of age.

Gesell's Developmental Schedules

Arnold Gesell has been considered the *grandfather of infant testing* (Goodman, 1990). His research was primarily designed to describe, through close observations, structural changes (or morphogenesis) in development. Gesell argued that behavior, growth, and the mind are not conceptually separated. He wrote, "Attained growth is an indicator

Arnold Gesell is often considered the grandfather of infant testing, as most of the norm-referenced infant tools developed in the 20th century were based on his original Developmental Schedules.

of past growth processes and a foreteller of growth yet to be achieved (Gesell & Amatruda, 1945)." That is, there is a *lawfulness* of growth, a constancy of the sequence of development.

Using observational analysis, Gesell described a set of invariant sequences of development that were published in the 1920s (Gesell, 1925). These were incorporated into Developmental Schedules, which were historically the first developmental scales used in the United States (Gesell & Amatruda, 1941, 1947). Gesell's manuals included administration and scoring instructions as well as detailed normative data for ages 1 to 42 months. These tests have had a profound influence on the testing and structuring of developmental tests to the present day. Many of the infant tests that are still popular today were developed on the basis of Gesell's original research (Goodman, 1990).

Gesell's schedules examine motor ability under headings such as gross and fine motor control, postural control, locomotion, prehension, drawing, and hand control. They also examine three other broad categories of behavior. Cognitive functions come under the scope of adaptive behaviors and involve items that require problem solving. As described in chapter 7, a difficulty with this, particularly for infants who cannot verbalize an answer, is that the solution involves considerable manual dexterity or hand–eye coordination. That is, there is a confound between the infant's motor ability and cognitive ability. This is also an issue for the other two domains that Gesell's schedules examine. Language ability is assessed through prelinguistic vocalizations, gestures, facial expressions, postural movements, and speech, all of which are influenced by the infant's or child's movement ability. Likewise, personal-social behaviors are determined through assessment of behaviors such as feeding ability, play activities, and toilet training. Although this highlights the problems associated with assessing other domains such as cognition, speech, and social abilities, particularly in infancy, it also highlights the importance of identifying infants with motor delay or disability in order to make an accurate assessment of the infant's abilities in other developmental domains.

Gesell's schedules were revised and updated by Knobloch and Pasamanick in 1974, but they remain fundamentally the same as those initially developed by Gesell. They are suitable for children aged from four weeks to three years, although there are additional tests that assess children up to five years of age. Interrater reliability was tested using 18 different pediatric residents who carried out 100 clinical examinations during a five- to six-week training period. The correlation between their scores and those of their instructor was 0.98 (Knobloch & Pasamanick). The schedules have been criticized for their complex testing procedures, which require quite extensive training (Brenneman, 1994).

Griffiths Mental Developmental Scales

One of the popular tests based on Gesell's schedules that is currently used to assess infant development is the Griffiths Mental Developmental Scales, developed by Ruth Griffiths in 1951 (Griffiths, 1970, 1984). She was concerned with developing an assessment tool that would assist in the diagnosis of the mental status in various conditions found among young children. However, as Goodman (1990) points out, Griffiths did not define *mental status* but instead defined five scales of assessment that she claimed would cover virtually the whole range of abilities of children from zero to two years. These were locomotor, personal-social, hearing and speech, hand-and-eye coordination, and performance. These scales were developed for children up to eight years of age, although there was an additional scale assessing practical reasoning for children two to eight years of age. One difficulty is that there is an overlap between items for the different scales. For example, there are throwing items in both the locomotor and the hand–eye coordination sections. This makes it difficult to assess the differential abilities of children despite the fact that the test was designed to do this.

Despite these difficulties, the Griffiths Mental Developmental Scales remains a popular tool, particularly for use with infants. These scales are often used because they cover the range from birth to eight years, allowing follow-up to be continued past infancy with the same test. It is reported to have favorable reliability and validity (Luiz, Foxcroft, & Stewart, 2001).

The Bayley Scales of Infant Development (BSID)

When first developed, the Bayley Scales of Infant Development (BSID; Bayley, 1969) was considered the most popular and psychometrically sophisticated set of infant scales of the time. More recently, the second edition of the BSID (Bayley, 1993) was published and is still considered by some as "the best measure for the assessment of infants" (Sattler, 2001, p. 548) with excellent norms and sound technical properties.

In 1933, Bayley published scales originally intended to evaluate the mental development of the infant, originating from the California First Year Mental Scale (Bayley, 1933). A motor scale modeled on the items developed by Gesell was published in 1936 (Bayley, 1936). In 1969, the mental and motor scales were included in one assessment tool, the BSID (Bayley, 1969). Also included was an Infant Behavior Record that allows for the systematic assessment and recording of the infant's behavior throughout the testing session. This edition covered the age range of 2 to 30 months. A further revision in 1993 (Bayley, 1993) increased the age range from 1 month to 42 months (figure 9.1).

The scales were originally standardized on 1,262 infants and children in 14 age groups. The number of infants used to norm the scale has inspired more confidence from researchers than in other tests designed around the same time. The stratification variables included geographic area, urban–rural residence, sex, race, and education of head of household. Observer agreement of trained observers for the mental scale was rated at 89.4% and for the motor scale at 93.4%. Werner and Bayley (1966) also achieved test-retest reliability ratings of 0.76 for the mental scale and 0.75 for the motor scale. As a result of this comprehensive standardization process, the Bayley scales have been used extensively

Figure 9.1 The Bayley Scales of Infant Development is one of the most popular assessment instruments for infants and young children. It assesses both mental and motor ability in infants.

as a research instrument. Bayley conceded that development in the first two years of life is unstable, and therefore suggested that her scales were designed more to evaluate the current status of the infant than for prediction of later mental or motor disability.

One of the major criticisms of the Bayley scales is the distinction between the motor and mental scales. As with the Griffiths scales, there appears to be some overlap of items between the two sets of scales in the Bayley tests. For example, items in the mental scale include tasks requiring considerable manual dexterity for infants of that age, such as building a tower of blocks or placing blocks into a cup, leading to the question of whether this is measuring cognitive or motor competence. A serious consequence is the underestimation of the intelligence of a child with poor motor coordination.

Bayley attempted to address this issue in the most recent version of the scales (Bayley, 1993). In this version, the correlations between the motor and mental scales were substantially reduced, although there is still considerable overlap at the younger ages. However, as described in chapter 7, a relationship between motor and cognitive ability appears to be present throughout childhood. Our own research has identified correlations in children aged three to four years to be significant between verbal IQ and fine motor ability (r = 0.35) and verbal IQ and gross motor ability (r = 0.32), although these correlations diminish with increasing age (Dyck et al., submitted for publication).

■■■ Despite its criticisms, the Bayley Scales of Infant Development is considered one of the best measures of mental and motor development in infancy.

The Bayley scales require considerable training, as the tester must have extensive knowledge of all tests at and around the age being examined. Palisano (1986) criticized the original Bayley motor scales for containing only a small number of items at each level of development. Some stages that are usually acknowledged as part of the motor development sequence have also been omitted, including running and kicking. Palisano argued that motor skills are not adequately covered and that there is no delineation of gross and fine motor development. The motor scales have also been criticized for not including the assessment of primitive reflexes, muscle tone, and equilibrium responses, considered necessary in evaluating infants with disabilities (Cowden et al., 1998).

One of the difficulties with early motor assessment relates to the rapid rate of development during the first year of life. This can lead to substantial changes over a relatively short period. If there are too few items in the test, as argued by Palisano (1986), then there can be large discrepancies in performance depending on the age of testing. This demonstrates one of the difficulties with utilizing standardized norms for infants of this age.

Battelle Developmental Inventory

The Battelle Developmental Inventory (Newborg et al., 1984) examines five domains; personal-social, adaptive, motor, communication, and cognition; consistent with other earlier tests (e.g., Gesell's Developmental Schedules and Griffiths Mental Developmental Scales). Again, this test is "based on the concept that a child normally attains critical skills (developmental milestones) in a specific developmental sequence" (Case-Smith, 1998, p. 54). The motor domain consists of 82 items in five distinct motor areas covering motor control, body coordination, locomotion, fine muscle control, and perceptual motor control.

Peabody Developmental Motor Scales

The Peabody Developmental Motor Scales (PDMS; Folio & Fewell, 1983) was one of the top motor scales used by occupational therapists in the United States in the late 1980s (Lawlor & Henderson, 1989). The original version was published in 1973, and there have been many subsequent revisions of the test, with the most recent produced in 1983 (Folio & Fewell, 1983). This is a standardized, norm-referenced test of both fine and gross motor ability in children from birth to 83 months of age. The 112 fine motor items assess manual dexterity, hand use, eye–hand coordination, and grasping, whereas the 170 gross motor items examine reflexes, locomotor skills, nonlocomotor skills, and balance. Each scale takes around 20 to 30 min to administer, giving a total administration time of around 45 to 60 min.

Each item is scored either as 0 (no evidence of the skill), 1 (evidence of the skill but not to the criterion level), or 2 (the skill achieved at criterion level). For example, the criterion for walking in the 10- to 11-month-old range is "takes four alternating steps forward." This system has the potential to be more sensitive than a yes/no scoring system. However it has been criticized because there are limited definitions of criteria for the score of 1. "The test manual does not provide clear criteria for each item for assigning a score of 1, thereby leaving the raters to decide whether there is a resemblance to the criteria needed for a successful performance" (Brenneman, 1994, p. 38). This results in greater subjectivity in deciding the score.

Reliability has been comprehensively assessed for this test. The manual provides results for test-retest, interrater, and standard error of measure reliability. Although interrater and test-retest reliability coefficients are high, Burton and Miller (1998) recommend that actual scores be interpreted with caution as "some confidence intervals of true scores as calculated by standard errors of measure were quite large" (p. 202). Burton and Miller also have concerns with the validity of the test, arguing that this has not been clearly established. The manual provides information on content, criterion-related, and construct validity. However, as with other tests based on a maturational approach, the assumption that there is an invariant sequence of motor events means that its predictive power is restricted, as this assumption is known to be inappropriate. Recently, Darrah, Piper, and Watt (1998) found that the gross motor scale of the PDMS has poor predictive ability in infants tested at four and eight months of age and assessed for abnormal development at 18 months of age. A comprehensive review of the test, listing strengths and weaknesses, can be found in Burton and Miller (1998), although most of the criticisms outlined are related to testing of older children rather than infants.

Usefulness of Norm-Referenced Tests

It is not within the scope of this book to critically evaluate all available tests, and therefore only a small number of tests have been detailed. Some tests have proven more popular than others. In 1989, Lawlor and Henderson published the findings of a survey of 118 occupational therapists who were asked to identify the standardized tests that they had used on children aged from birth to four years over the previous three months. Popular diagnostic tools were the Peabody Developmental Motor Scales (Folio & Fewell, 1983), the Hawaii Early Intervention Profile (Furuno et al., 1985), the BSID (Bayley, 1969), and the Gesell Developmental Scales (Knobloch & Pasamanick, 1974). Other tests have been developed since this study, although most are based on these and earlier tests. Despite their popularity, these tests are still criticized by theorists who disagree with their theoretical basis.

Tests of infant ability based on the achievement of motor milestones were used extensively during the 20th century to assess and investigate infant development. However, as pointed out by many of the researchers who developed these tests (e.g., Bayley, 1993), they were not designed to predict later developmental status but rather to determine the infant's current abilities in relation to other infants of the same age. There are two major arguments associated with the poor predictive ability (Goodman, 1990). One argument is that there are too many factors affecting young developing infants that could influence their later outcome, such as the evolving neural structure that results in considerable plasticity (described in chapter 3). Hence, no tests will be able to predict later developmental status. The other argument is that tests have not yet been developed that can adequately assess the infant's ability, a line taken by Goodman (1990) in her excellent review of these positions. She argues that stage-related tests do serve a purpose, and that this is in identifying those children at greatest risk of abnormal development. In a meta-analysis, she found that for studies examining infants with low scores (indicating developmental delay), correlations between infant performance and later childhood scores were much higher than for studies that included infants whose scores covered the full range. This argument related primarily to cognitive development but is also relevant to motor development.

In terms of motor development, the tests appear to be better predictors of later motor performance than tests examining cognitive or overall development. This is promising in terms of current research efforts to find early predictors of motor disability. However, recent tools that focus on qualitative or functional characteristics rather than the reflexes and motor milestones show promise. Some of these new tools are reviewed next.

Criterion-Referenced Developmental Diagnostic Tests

Infants' development proceeds rapidly, and many of the norm-referenced tests have difficulty in providing adequate test items to address these rapid changes. To deal with this problem, several assessment tools have recently been developed to evaluate qualitative or functional aspects of movement and posture (Case-Smith, 1998). Functional movement skills are movements that are self-directed and have a meaningful context for the individual (Burton & Miller, 1998). For infants, these involve movements important for their daily living, such as feeding skills, and also activities involved in play. Some tests of this type are listed in table 9.2, and several of these are briefly reviewed next.

Harris Infant Neuromotor Test (HINT)

The Harris Infant Neuromotor Test (HINT), developed by Harris and Daniels (1996), was designed specifically for infants aged from 3 to 12 months. It is a tool for early identification of both movement disorders, such as cerebral palsy, and cognitive delay. The test has three parts.

Table 9.2 Criterion-Referenced Diagnostic Tools for Infants

Test and author	Test description	Age range	Reliability	Validity	Testing time
Alberta Infant Motor Scale (AIMS) (Piper & Darrah, 1994)	58 items examining early motor milestones and motor abilities	Birth–18 months	Test-retest Interrater	Content Criterion related	20 min
Assessment, Evaluation and Programming System (AEPS) (Bricker, 1993)	164 objectives in 6 domains: fine motor, gross motor, adaptive, cognitive, social-communication, social; 23 common behavior categories; 64 goals	1 month–3 years	Test-retest Interrater	Content Criterion related Construct	Initial assessment is 1–2 hr; subsequent assessments are 15–30 min
Brigance Diagnostic Inventory of Early Development (BDI) (Brigance, 1991)	122 items test specific skills in 11 motor areas	Birth–7 years	Not reported	Content	60 min
Harris Infant Neuromotor Test (HINT) (Harris & Daniels, 1996)	Includes (a) infant demographics and risk factors, (b) caregiver questionnaire on development, and (c) 22 items on posture, locomotion, and behavior	3–12 months	Interrater Test-retest Intrarater	Concurrent Predictive	Less than 30 min
Infant Neurological International Battery (INFANIB) (Ellison, 1994)	Battery of 20 items including muscle range and resistance, reflexes, and motor milestones	Birth–18 months	Interrater	Construct	Not reported
Pediatric Evaluation of Disability Inventory (PEDI) (Haley et al., 1992)	Includes 3 parts: (a) 197 functional skills, (b) 20 items on caregiver assistance, and (c) a measurement of modification frequency for items in b	6 months–7.5 years	Intraclass Intrarater	Content Concurrent validity Construct	Up to 60 min
Posture and Fine Motor Assessment of Infants (PFMAI) (Case-Smith, 1991, 1992)	Two sections, one measuring posture, the other fine motor	2–6 months	Test-retest Interrater Internal consistency	Criterion related Construct	45 min
Toddler and Infant Motor Evaluation (TIME) (Miller & Roid, 1994)	5 subscales of mobility, stability, motor organization, social-emotional, and functional performance 3 additional subtests for atypical movements	4–42 months	Interrater Internal consistency	Construct	Not reported
Vulpe Assessment Battery (VAB) (Vulpe, 1982)	1,300 items in 8 subtests: basic senses and functions, gross motor, fine motor, language, cognitive processes, organization of behavior, activities of daily living, the environment, plus 5 supplementary tests	Birth–6 years	Intrarater	Not reported for infants	60 min

Adapted from Burton & Miller, 1998.

The first records demographic information such as the infant's age, sex, and birth weight; prenatal and neonatal risk factors; and caregiver information such as age, occupation, and highest level of education. In the second part of the test, the parent or primary caregiver is asked a series of five questions related to the infant's development. The first three (Harris & Daniels, 1996, p. 730) are as follows:

When I pick up, carry, or play with my baby, she or he feels...

Overall, my baby moves and plays...

Compared to other babies the same age, my baby's movement and play is...

These questions are followed by lists of descriptors to assist the caregiver in identifying any possible concerns. The final two questions in this part of the test, which are open-ended, allow either the primary caregiver (question 4) or others (question 5) to identify any areas of concern. The third part of the test includes 22 items that assess the motor domain: 19 items involving different postures, one item on the behavioral domain (the behavioral state of the infant throughout the testing period), and one item of physical measurement, namely head circumference. Item 22 is a two-part developmental and qualitative judgment item that summarizes the examiner's overall impressions of the infant's neurological state.

The reliability and validity of the HINT have recently been evaluated by Harris and colleagues (2003). The intraclass correlation coefficient for interrater reliability was 0.99 for the total score on the HINT. When 20 infants were tested twice within nine days, the test-retest reliability was found to be 0.98. Harris and Daniels (2001) had previously tested intrarater reliability for each of five therapists and found this to range from 0.98 to 0.99.

Both concurrent and predictive validity have been assessed by comparison with the BSID-II mental and motor scores (Harris et al., 2003). Concurrent validity was assessed for infants aged 3 to 12 months, with r = –0.73 for comparison with the mental score and –0.89 with the motor score. Predictive validity, based on the BSID-II scores taken when the infants were aged from 17 to 22 months, was modest for the motor score (r = –0.49) but poor for the mental score (r = –0.11). This suggests that one needs to treat the test results with caution when considering any possible cognitive deficits.

Pediatric Evaluation of Disability Inventory (PEDI)

Another test that was designed to assess functional capabilities is the Pediatric Evaluation of Disability Inventory (PEDI; Haley et al., 1992). Its focus is on three particular domains of functional ability, with 73 items on self-care, 59 on mobility, and 65 assessing social functions. This produces the Functional Skills Scale. In addition there is a Caregiver Assistance Scale based on the amount of assistance required for 20 complex functional activities (Burton & Miller, 1998). A third scale, the Modifications Scale, determines the degree of modification required for the child to carry out the 20 complex activities assessed for the Caregiver Assistance Scale. Scores are based on structured parental interviews, observation, and judgments made by professionals such as therapists and teachers.

The PEDI is a criterion-referenced test that covers the ages of six months to 7.5 years. Older children whose functional abilities have not reached the level of 7.5 years can also be assessed using this tool, as the scaled scores, ranging from 0 to 100, are not based on age. Limited information is available on reliability. Intraclass and intrarater reliabilities have been assessed and generally vary between 0.74 and 0.99. Although the PEDI manual contains information on content, construct, and concurrent validity, Burton and Miller (1998) suggest that these do not cover the areas that the test was designed for and therefore represent a weakness that needs to be addressed. Further strengths and weaknesses of this test are covered by Burton and Miller (1998) and Reid and colleagues (1993).

Toddler and Infant Motor Evaluation (TIME)

The Toddler and Infant Motor Evaluation (TIME; Miller & Roid, 1994) was designed for children aged 4 to 42 months of age. It has a battery of eight subtests. Five scales cover *typical* movement patterns, namely mobility, stability, motor organization, social-emotional abilities, and functional performance. These are standardized subtests whose scores can be converted to standardized scores. The additional three subtests cover *atypical* movement, namely atypical positions, quality rating, and component analysis. These subtests are not standardized.

The TIME is designed both to diagnose motor delays and to identify motor problems. It has also been used to assist in the planning of appropriate intervention and to evaluate these interventions over time (Case-Smith, 1998).

Alberta Infant Motor Scale (AIMS)

The Alberta Infant Motor Scale (AIMS; Piper & Darrah, 1994) is a recently developed test of delayed gross motor performance. It measures gross motor ability and posture in the infant's natural environment, therefore minimizing the amount of interference or disruption to the infant required during test administration. Designed for infants from birth to 18 months of age, it has 58 items that are performed in four different positions—supine, prone, sitting, and standing. These items were designed to identify immature or atypical movements and to determine how the movements change over time (Case-Smith & Bigsby, 2001). Assessment is observational, and each item is scored in terms of the infant's capabilities of weight bearing, posture, and antigravity movement.

The test was standardized on 2,202 infants in Alberta, Canada, and provides a total score that can be converted to a percentile. It is considered to have excellent interrater and test-retest reliability when retesting occurs within three to seven days (Darrah, Redfern, et al., 1998). Reliability coefficients have ranged from 0.82 to 0.98. Piper and Darrah (1994) determined concurrent validity by comparing scores on the AIMS with the gross motor scales of the PDMS (r = 0.97) and the BSID (r = 0.98). The AIMS is considered to have predictive validity for identifying infants at four and eight months of age who will have a poor neuromotor outcome at 18 months of age (Darrah, Redfern et al.). Given its potential for predicting poor motor outcome, it is used in neonatal follow-up clinics in the United States, Canada (Darrah, Redfern et al.), and Australia (see chapter 10 for an example).

Screening Instruments

An assessment of motor ability involves many facets of the infant's performance. It includes the examination of gross and fine motor skills as well as neurological functioning such as muscle tone. Most assessments require individual administration and can be quite lengthy. Thus these lengthy diagnostic tools are usually used only in cases in which some developmental problems are suspected. Large samples of infants, however, can be assessed using "screening" instruments that are typically quick to administer and do not necessarily involve individual administration. Screening is designed to "identify the presence of any significant deviations from normal growth and development" (Case-Smith, 1998, p. 49). It identifies children in need of further, more comprehensive testing.

Screening tools have been criticized for a lack of usefulness in predicting later outcome and therefore should not be used for this purpose. However, another useful approach for screening tools has been termed *developmental surveillance* (Dworkin, 1989), which involves ongoing monitoring of the infant. Many of the recent screening tools recommend multiple testing of the infant.

Table 9.3 provides a list of popular screening tests that measure movement ability in infancy. Lawlor and Henderson (1989) identified the Denver Developmental Screening Test (Frankenburg et al., 1975) and the Movement Assessment of Infants (Chandler et al., 1980) as popular screening tools for occupational therapists in the 1980s.

Movement Assessment of Infants (MAI)

The Movement Assessment of Infants (MAI), developed by Chandler and colleagues (1980), is a screening tool developed to follow up high-risk infants (Case-Smith & Bigsby, 2001). It investigates muscle tone, reflexes, automatic ractions, and volitional control in infants aged from

Table 9.3   Screening Tools Suitable for Assessing Motor Ability in Infants

Test and author	Test description	Age range	Reliability	Validity	Testing time
Ages and Stages Questionnaires (ASQ) (Squires et al., 1995)	30 items divided into 5 areas: communication, gross motor, fine motor, problem solving, personal-social	4–48 months	Interobserver Test-retest Internal consistency	Concurrent	10–30 minutes
Battelle Developmental Inventory Screening Test (Newborg et al., 1984)	96 items including 20 in the motor domain	Birth–8 years	Not reported	Concurrent	10–30 min
Bayley Infant Neurodevelopmental Screener (BINS) (Aylward, 1995)	Includes 4 areas of ability: basic neurological functions/intactness, expressive functions, receptive functions, cognitive processes	3–24 months	Internal consistency	Concurrent Predictive	Not reported
Denver Developmental Screening Test (Denver II) (Frankenburg et al., 1992)	125 tasks in examining 4 areas: personal-social, fine motor-adaptive, language, gross motor	Birth–6 years	Interrater Test-retest	Content	15–30 min
Milani-Comparetti Developmental Screening Test (Milani-Comparetti, 1967)	27 items scored as present or absent test primitive reflexes, tilting, righting, protective reactions, spontaneous posture, movement through attainment of independent ambulation	1–16 months	Interrater	Not tested	10–15 min
Movement Assessment of Infants (MAI) (Chandler et al., 1980)	65 items evaluate muscle tone, primitive reflexes, automatic reactions, and volitional movements	Birth–12 months	Interrater Test-retest	Criterion related	90 min
Movement General Outcome Measurement (Movement GOM) (Greenwood et al., 2002)	Determines a general outcome based on the following indicators: transition in position (for postural control), grounded or vertical (for locomotion), and throw/roll or catch/trap (for object control)	Birth–3 years	Odd–even Alternate forms	Criterion	A play session lasting 6 min

birth to 12 months. The 65 items are divided into four subtests, with 6 items on muscle tone, 11 on primitive reflexes, 14 on automatic reactions such as the equilibrium and righting responses, and 23 on volitional movements including motor milestones and responses to visual and auditory stimuli.

The test was designed to address the following needs:

- To identify motor dysfunction in infants up to 12 months of age
- To establish the basis for an early intervention program
- To monitor the effects of physical therapy
- To serve as a research tool that provides a standard system of assessment
- To serve as a teaching tool for the observation of normal and abnormal motor development

The ability of the MAI to quantify movement quality is seen as one of its strengths (Einarsson-Backes & Stewart, 1992). However, as it does not provide normative data, it cannot be used as a diagnostic tool. Given that it takes up to 90 min to test and score, this is a very lengthy screening instrument. The MAI has also been criticized for its poorly organized scoring criteria and scoring protocol, making administration time-consuming and difficult (Cowden et al., 1998). Questionable reliability in several items has also been reported (Brenneman, 1994), and predictive validity is low when one compares scores with outcome at 4.5 years (Case-Smith & Bigsby, 2001).

Battelle Developmental Inventory Screening Test

The Battelle Developmental Inventory Screening Test forms part of the longer Battelle Developmental Inventory (Newborg et al., 1984) described earlier in the chapter. The screening tool consists of a total of 96 items, although there are only 20 in the motor domain, examining body coordination, perceptual-motor, locomotion, and fine muscle control. The other domains examined are personal/social, adaptive, communication, and cognition. The test is designed for an age range of birth to 8 years.

This screening tool is relatively quick and easy to administer, taking between 10 and 30 min. However, the small number of motor items (20) has been criticized as a problem with the test. For example, gross and fine movement are assessed with only one item at each age increment (Cowden et al., 1998). Furthermore, the age increments are quite large, with five- to six-month intervals up to two years and one-year increments after that. Cowden and colleagues point out that each subdomain is not assessed at every age level, and also that no reliability data are presented for the screening instrument.

Denver Developmental Screening Test II (Denver II)

One of the most widely used standardized screening instruments is the Denver II (Frankenburg & Dodds, 1967; Frankenburg et al., 1992). This test was standardized on 2,096 children in urban, semirural, and rural Colorado and is suitable for children aged from birth to six years (Case-Smith, 1998). This norm-referenced instrument measures the areas of personal-social, fine motor-adaptive, language, and gross motor. Specific criteria are provided for screening children with normal, suspect, and untestable results and those that indicate a need for referral.

Bayley Infant Neurodevelopmental Screener (BINS)

A more recent screening instrument is the Bayley Infant Neurodevelopmental Screener (BINS; Aylward, 1995), which was developed from the more extensive BSID described earlier. However, it is not considered to be a shortened version of the BSID-II, as it includes items that examine neurological function, and there are differences in the scoring and measurement of performance. Four areas of ability are assessed. Basic neurological functions/intactness, examines muscle tone, posture, movement, asymmetries, and abnormal indicators. Expressive functions are examined through gross and fine motor tasks and oral motor/verbal tasks. Visual, auditory, and verbal tasks cover receptive functions, and cognitive processes are assessed through problem solving, object permanence, and goal-directedness (Aylward & Verhulst, 2000). The BINS is suitable for infants aged between 3 and 24 months.

Little information is available on reliability. Concurrent validity was established in a normal population using the BSID-II (Aylward, 1995). Predictive validity was also examined in a high-risk sample of infants through comparison of the BINS scores at 6, 12, and 24 months with classification of neurodevelopmental function at 36 months (Aylward & Verhulst, 2000). The authors concluded that the BINS has good concurrent and predictive validity.

Ages and Stages Questionnaires (ASQ)

Recent research suggests that parent report measures may be useful as possible screening instruments for motor development (Bodnarchuk & Eaton, 2004; Johnson et al., 2004). For example, Bodnarchuk and Eaton (2004) found that parents can reliably report on the emergence of motor milestones such as sitting, crawling, and walking. The Ages and Stages Questionnaires: A Parent Completed Child Monitoring System (ASQ; Squires et al., 1995) is a series of 11 questionnaires designed to identify infants and young children who show potential developmental problems. The questionnaires were designed to be completed by the parents when the child is 4, 8, 12, 16, 20, 24, 30, 36, and 48 months of age, with optional questionnaires available at 6 and 18 months. Each questionnaire is composed of 30 items that cover five areas: communication, gross motor, fine motor, problem solving, and personal-social.

Although the authors of the questionnaire present extensive information on its reliability and validity, no independent studies have addressed the usefulness of this questionnaire in distinguishing among infants of differing risk status. Further, no studies have investigated the consistency of problem identification over various ages in typically developing infants and preterm infants.

Recent Technological Advances in Diagnostic Assessment

Over the last few decades there have been considerable advances in medical and scientific technology. This has resulted in the application of such technology to aid in the diagnosis of motor disability. Basically, the technology falls into two main categories. The first is the use of brain imaging techniques to identify any brain abnormalities. The other is the use of objective measures of movement, such as force plates, video analysis, and motion analysis, to quantify normal and abnormal movement in terms of **kinetics** and **kinematics**. These two categories are briefly reviewed next.

Brain Imaging Techniques

Noninvasive brain imaging techniques have developed rapidly over the last decade. They can provide information on structure, metabolism, and function of the developing brain (Singer, 2001). These techniques may also be able to demonstrate compensatory mechanisms, in particular neural plasticity, in infants with neural injury (Black et al., 2004). Some techniques are useful for young infants, whereas others may not be appropriate for use with developing brains. Some of the available brain imaging techniques include neonatal cerebral ultrasound, computerized tomography (CT), electroencephalogram (EEG), evoked potentials (EP), positron emission tomography (PET), magnetic resonance imaging (MRI), and functional MRI (fMRI).

Cranial ultrasound is a noninvasive technique used to detect brain lesions that often occur in preterm infants. Introduced in the 1970s, it is still a popular tool for detecting brain abnormalities in newborn infants, particularly those born preterm. Other techniques are more invasive and the effect on the infant's developing brain is unknown. For example, PET scanning is dependent on the injection of radiopharmaceuticals that allow the cerebral blood flow to be measured directly.

Magnetic resonance imaging and fMRI have the advantage that they are noninvasive. Magnetic resonance imaging has been used to investigate the severity of brain injury such as **periventricular leukomalacia** (PVL), as MRI is considered more accurate than techniques such as cranial ultrasonography (Hashimoto et al., 2001; Murgo et al., 1999). Results from a relatively large study on 89 infants and children aged between 1 and 14 years showed that the classification of PVL using MRI "provided significant prognostic value for neurodevelopmental outcome and specific outcomes including motor, visual, developmental and epilepsy" (Serdaroglu et al., 2004, p. 736).

Functional MRI, which is an indirect measure of blood flow, assesses metabolic changes by changes in regional brain activity. However, up until recently it has been limited to older children, as the child needs to cooperate and be in an alert state while keeping the head very still. Such instructions cannot be given to an infant. Recent studies have used fMRI on sedated infants (e.g., Erberich et al., 2003; Seghier et al., 2004), although there is debate over how the sedation affects the functional responses obtained.

Another noninvasive technique is the event-related potential (ERP). These are scalp recordings of populations of neurons activated during an event or task and therefore can be used when a reliable behavioral measure cannot be obtained. This makes ERP an ideal tool for use with infants (Black et al., 2004).

Kinematic and Kinetic Analysis of Movement

Heriza (1988a) pointed out that earlier techniques for the analysis of movements "including narrative descriptions, stick figures, frequency counts, or duration of movement, are global, static, often subjective, and capture none of the complexities of the dynamic process" (p. 1340). She further argued that the study of reflexes and motor milestones provides little information on the organization of movements.

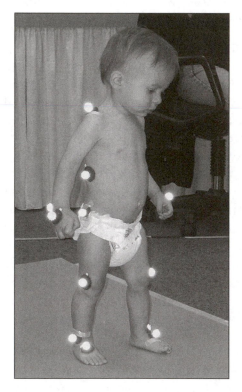

A technique that takes into account the dynamic nature of movement control is *kinematic* motion analysis. "Kinematics is that branch of biomechanics that is concerned with the detailed descriptive analysis of a movement pattern" (Heriza, 1993, p. 257). Kinematic analysis has been used extensively over the last few decades to examine infant movements. It produces real-time data by sampling the position of different body parts throughout a movement many times a second. Hence a continuous movement is transformed into a series of discrete quantifiable measurements that can then be used to determine how the different body segments are interrelated throughout the movements investigated (Heriza). For example, joint angles can be analyzed to provide information on joint angle displacement, velocity and acceleration curves, and other dynamic characteristics of the movements observed. Using correlation techniques, the relationship between joints or body segments can be determined.

These techniques have primarily been used for research purposes, but they are now gradually being introduced for possible diagnostic purposes. For example, motion analysis has been used to examine normal and abnormal gait (see figure 9.2). An advantage of this method is that it not only demonstrates whether a movement pattern is normal or abnormal but also provides information on the location and possible causes of the abnormal pattern.

Figure 9.2 Motion analysis can be used to determine gait patterns in normal and at-risk infants. Three-dimensional time series can be determined from the x, y, z coordinates obtained from the markers attached to the infant's body.

A variety of tools can describe motor patterns through kinematics. Three-dimensional motion analysis describes both the spatial location and the orientation of the body at any given time. It is one of the most popular techniques used to examine motor patterns. Electromyography, which records the electrical activity of the muscles, is also a popular tool for examining motor patterns. This involves placing electrodes on the skin over the muscle in order to monitor the excitation or electrical input of the muscle. It has been successfully used in infants in the investigation of areas such as postural control (e.g., Sveistrup & Woollacott, 1997) and infant kicking (e.g., Thelen & Fisher, 1983b). Goniometers are instruments that are used on specific joints to determine the relative rotation at that joint, but they have rarely been used in infant research.

Whereas kinematic variables provide a description of the movement, kinetic variables relate to the forces that produce these movements. Both are necessary to provide a comprehensive understanding of movement production (Kamm et al., 1990; Winter, 1989). In the study of infants, the technique of inverse dynamics (using kinematics to determine the underlying forces) in relation to Newton's laws of motion is often used to examine **torque** (e.g., Kamm et al., 1990; Schneider et al., 1990). For example, Roncesvalles and colleagues (2001) examined the development of balance in infants and children aged nine months to 10 years. They identified a shift from multimodal torque patterns to unimodal patterns in the progression from standing in infancy to more complex bipedal movements such as galloping and skipping. Often in the study of balance, ground reaction force, or the "reaction force provided by the supporting horizontal surface" (Enoka, 1994, pp. 46-47), is measured using a force plate or force platform. Center of pressure can also be derived from force platform information.

How Does This Research Inform Therapeutic Practice?

How useful are these assessment tools for the practitioner? This question can be answered only through continuing research on the reliability and validity of the various tools. Such research is lengthy and costly, as questions related to the prediction of any tool can be resolved only through longitudinal research extending well into childhood.

In choosing the most appropriate tool for a particular individual, the therapist or practitioner needs to be familiar with the research that has examined reliability and validity issues. One important issue to note with infant assessment is that development in infants is very erratic, and it is always important to carry out serial assessments. The use of different types of assessment tools will also aid in providing a better picture of the infant's abilities and disabilities. Many of the newer assessment tools are incorporating information from different sources, such as the therapist, pediatrician, parents, and even other nonprimary caregivers. These are valuable resources that the test developers have identified.

Summary

The researcher and practitioner have a huge selection of assessment tools that measure infant motor development. These include the traditional norm-referenced assessments that generally include other abilities such as cognition and speech. However, predictive validity for these tools has proven quite poor in the past, particularly for infants younger than 12 months of age.

Recently a variety of criterion-referenced assessments have been developed. These have focused on functional outcomes and largely rely on observation to determine the infant's motor capabilities. These tools appear more promising in terms of predictive validity, although quite a bit more research is required to ensure that they are capable of accurately determining major and minor motor disability in the early months of life.

An area that requires considerably more attention is that of screening tools. Very few assessments are carried out on all infants. Perhaps one of the few is the Apgar test described in the previous chapter. Until a fast, reliable screening tool is developed that can be used on every infant born, many infants who may be in need of early intervention will slip through the assessment process.

With the advance of technology, many new approaches to assessment are being developed. Brain scanning has proven effective in identifying infants who are at greater risk than others for later delay and disability. However, these techniques are very costly and cannot be performed on every child. They are generally carried out only on infants already considered to be "at risk."

Understanding the kinematics and kinetics of movement will also aid in the detection of abnormal development. The use of these techniques in understanding infant motor development is still quite new, and more investigation is needed before they can be used as assessment tools.

part IV ■■■

Motor Control and Developmental Disorders

Kalverboer (1993) stated, "As yet, theory on motor development has had little impact on the diagnosis and treatment of movement disorders" (p. 12). Has this situation changed in the last decade? Although this book has addressed development only throughout infancy, can we now see theory-driven interventions, or are interventions still guided by observation and intuition?

One group of infants known to be at greater risk for motor disability is preterm infants. These infants are born earlier than the normal 38 weeks following conception. These infants have received a great deal of attention over the last few decades. Not only are they a group of infants at greater risk of disability, but they are also an increasing population given the improvement in neonatal intensive care facilities. Chapter 10 reviews this special group of infants. Research in this area has flourished in the last decade, although most of the studies have been primarily concerned with long-term outcomes of prematurity rather than investigating the developmental differences present in this population in the early years. Prematurity has been associated with a large proportion of children who have developed motor disabilities such as cerebral palsy and developmental coordination disorder.

The next two chapters deal with two particular disorders, cerebral palsy (chapter 11) and Down syndrome (chapter 12). These chapters provide descriptions of these disorders, including the types of movement problems associated with them. Past, present, and potential future interventions are then discussed.

ten

Motor Development in Preterm Infants

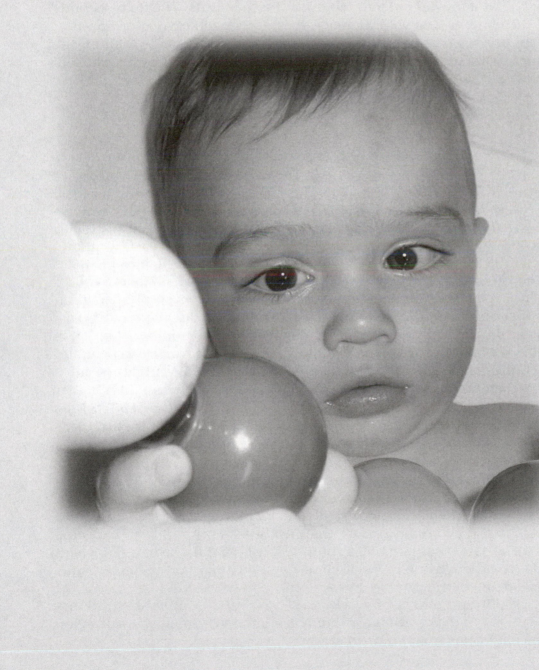

■■■ **M**any figures who have contributed substantially to history in some way were born as preterm infants. Examples include Isaac Newton, Albert Einstein, Daniel Webster, Napoleon Bonaparte, Mark Twain, Winston Churchill, Charles Darwin, and John Keats (Sammons & Lewis, 1985).

Infants born before their due date or born with a low birth weight are at much greater risk than others of developmental delay and disability, particularly motor disability. Hence a separate chapter is devoted to discussion of these infants. This chapter covers the potential problems associated with preterm infants and the short-term and long-term consequences of being born too early. Firstly, it is important to define "preterm," as this is dependent on many factors and has implications for the assessment of motor ability in these infants. The final sections of the chapter deal with the most recent research carried out on preterm infants that examines their motor development, as well as the types of interventions that are appropriate for this special group of individuals.

Preterm Birth

In 1985, the incidence of preterm births was stated to be anywhere between 5% and 15% (Sammons & Lewis, 1985). Over the last few decades, interest in preterm birth has increased because of the increase in the number of such infants born. The U.S. Department of Health records for 1993 showed a 15% increase in low-birth-weight infants from 1981 (Als, 1995), and Moore reported a 20-year high of 11.9% in preterm births recorded in the United States for 2001 (Moore, 2003).

In the last few years, hundreds of papers have been published on this population of infants, primarily examining later outcome. This interest has been fueled by a large increase in the number of preterm infants who now survive at birth due to the major advances in neonatal technology over recent years. The implementation of ventilators, infusion techniques, and microtechnology has resulted in a much higher survival rate for infants born early (Sammons & Lewis, 1985). This has also resulted in a shift in the number of weeks required in utero for the infant to survive, and there have been instances of survival of infants born as early as 22 weeks gestational age.

How do we determine whether an infant is preterm? The number of weeks spent in utero, the *gestational age* (GA), is a major parameter used to describe prematurity in infants. Infants are generally considered *preterm* if they are born more than two weeks prior to their expected or term date, that is, at less than 38 weeks GA (Lukeman & Melvin, 1993), although there is not consensus on this. For example, some have defined preterm birth as less than 37 weeks GA (e.g., Korner et al., 1993) and others 36 weeks GA (e.g., Piper et al., 1989). Infants born less than 33 weeks GA are considered very preterm, but again this age varies from study to study.

In order to know how early an infant is born, the GA needs to be accurately determined. In the past the method was to calculate the expected date of delivery from the date of the mother's last menstrual cycle. Other techniques used the infant's head circumference (Usher & McLean, 1969) and gestational assessment (Ballard et al., 1979). Although the mother's and obstetrician's estimations of the expected date of delivery based on the mother's cycle are still the primary determinant of GA, these are generally confirmed through ultrasound examination and other obstetrical measures.

Many infants are born full term but are at risk because they are too light. The normal birth weight of a full-term infant is usually between 3 and 4 kg (6 and 8 lb), and average birth length is 49 to 52 cm or 19 to 21 in. (Gallahue & Ozmun, 1998). According to Lukeman and Melvin (1993), birth weight can be categorized as low when the infant is born at less than 2,500 g (5.5 lb), very low when birth weight is less than 1,500 g (3.3 lb), or extremely low when birth weight is less than 1,000 g (2.2 lb). In the United States around 53,000 infants are born with very low birth weight annually (Singer et al., 1997). Of concern is that as many as 50% of these infants will have developmental delay or disability that requires supportive services once they reach school age.

> ■■■ Prematurity in infants can be defined by the number of weeks spent in utero (gestational age), the weight of the infant at birth, or a combination of the two (small for gestational age).

Recent research suggests that both birth weight and GA need to be considered when one is examining the risk of an infant. That is, there is a need to examine the influence on development of infants born **small for gestational age** (SGA), also termed *small for date, intrauterine growth retarded,* or *intrauterine growth restricted.* An infant is SGA when his or her weight is less than the 10th percentile for that particular GA; severe growth restriction refers to those with less than the 3rd percentile weight for their GA (Henderson-Smart, 1995). Although intrauterine growth retardation has been associated with the occurrence of a higher incidence of developmental delay, Topp and colleagues (1996) found that SGA was associated with cerebral palsy only for preterm infants born more than 33 weeks GA and was not a significant factor for infants born less than 33 weeks GA. A recent study (Gortner et al., 2003), however, failed to show any differences in outcome between a group of SGA infants (birth weight <10th percentile) and AGA (appropriate for GA) infants when outcome was assessed at 22 months of age. Also, Dammann and colleagues (2001) argued against the use of SGA but recommended that study cohorts be identified in GA rather than birth weight. It seems that determining whether preterm infants should be defined by GA, birth weight, or both, remains a contentious issue.

Causes of Preterm Birth and Low Birth Weight

The causes of preterm birth are poorly understood. Suggestions include maternal factors such as changes in hormone levels, problems associated with infection of the upper genital tract, stress, or genetic factors. Others include poor nutrition, hypoxia, or fetal stress (Moore, 2003).

Preterm delivery is also associated with women of lower socioeconomic status, but this may be related to several of the other factors such as poor nutrition, infections, and greater stress overall. If a mother has a history of miscarriages, particularly after the first trimester, this also increases the risk of a preterm birth (Sammons & Lewis, 1985).

Moore (2003) investigated which risk factors for preterm birth could be amenable to change or treatment. It is clear that some factors cannot be changed, such as previous preterm births, vaginal bleeding, and race or ethnic origin. Intervention is appropriate for other factors, either prior to pregnancy or in the prenatal period. Table 10.1 lists the risk

Table 10.1   Risk Factors for Preterm Birth That Can Be Influenced by Appropriate Treatment, As Outlined Below

Factor	Activities to bring about change
Unplanned pregnancy	Family planning education Provision of appropriate contraception
Number of embryos implanted in assisted reproduction	Discussion with physician and families seeking assisted reproduction
Young age at pregnancy	Comprehensive education about family planning and contraception at community, state, and national levels

Weight at time of pregnancy:
  Low prepregnancy weight
  Obesity
	Encourage appropriate weight for height at every health visit

General health status:
  Hypertension
  Diabetes mellitus
  Clotting disorders
  Anemia
  Other chronic health problems
	Identification of problems
	Treatment to assure best health status prior to pregnancy
	In certain instances, consideration of pregnancy avoidance

Uterine fibroids	Treatment prior to pregnancy
Low income, life stress, unsafe neighborhood	Individual support Advocacy for education, employment, community improvements
Genitourinary infections	Assess and treat
Periodontal disease	Assess at dental visits Provide referral if needed
Intimate partner violence	Assess at every health care visit Provide appropriate counseling and/or referral Provide educational material at all health care settings

Employment:
  Long hours
  Long periods of standing
	Education (general and prenatal) at work sites
	Promote policies for work safety for pregnant women

Cigarette smoking	Assess at every health visit Provide referral for smoking cessation
Other substance abuse	Refer for specific substance abuse assistance

Data from Moore, 2003.

factors that were identified as ones that could be changed given the appropriate information, and provides a description of the appropriate intervention for these.

Immediate Problems

If an infant is born preterm, one of the immediate problems faced is fetal lung immaturity. This may result in *respiratory distress syndrome* (RDS), also called *hyaline membrane disease* (HMD), which is a major cause of death in preterm infants. It occurs because of a decreased production of surfactant that is required to prevent the lungs from collapsing while breathing. Because of reduced alveoli surface tension, the alveoli collapse during expiration and require a great deal of effort by the infant to reinflate (Soltesz-Sheahan & Farmer-Brockway, 1994). Respiratory distress syndrome may lead to chronic lung disease such as *bronchopulmonary dysplasia* (BPD), which requires mechanical ventilation and supplementary oxygen. This can also result from infection, **asphyxia,** and meconium aspiration.

Asphyxia, or lack of oxygen, is a major problem for the preterm infant. Lung problems at birth may result in problems with the exchange of oxygen and carbon dioxide that may lead to asphyxia. Asphyxia can also result from interference with umbilical blood flow, which can occur throughout the pregnancy or at the time of delivery. When asphyxia causes damage to the neonate's brain immediately following birth, this is called *hypoxic-ischemic encephalopathy* (HIE). This is the most common cause of severe nonprogressive neurologic defects such as mental retardation and cerebral palsy (CP) (Soltesz-Sheahan & Farmer-Brockway, 1994).

Brain damage is identified in the newborn infant using brain scanning techniques described in the previous chapter, such as ultrasound, computerized tomography (CT), or magnetic resonance imaging (MRI) (cf. Accardo et al., 2004; de Vries et al., 2004). The most common type of lesion in preterm infants is *periventricular leukomalacia* (PVL), which is necrosis, or cell death, of the white matter surrounding the lateral ventricles. It is often accompanied by **intraventricular hemorrhage** (IVH), that is, bleeding into the ventricles. Infants with low birth weight and more complicated medical histories are at greatest risk of IVH (Soltesz-Sheahan & Farmer-Brockway, 1994), which tends to occur within the first three or four days following birth (Lenke, 2003). The severity of IVH has been graded according to the degree of bleeding and areas of the brain that have been affected. Infants who are graded I or II IVH are at minimal risk of long-term developmental disability. However, grades III and IV have been linked to disabilities such as cerebral palsy and mental retardation (Soltesz-Sheahan & Farmer-Brockway, 1994).

Recent medical advances have improved the outcome for preterm infants with respiratory difficulties and hence reduced the likelihood of brain damage. The National Institutes of Health Consensus Development Conference (1995) recommended that antenatal corticosteroids,

■■■ Compared to other infants, preterm infants are at much greater risk of asphyxia, which can lead to brain damage, in particular, periventricular leukomalacia or intraventricular hemorrhage.

such as betamethasone or dexamethasone, be given to all women who go into labor between 24 and 34 weeks GA. This has proven effective in minimizing RDS, caused by immature lungs, and is also effective in reducing the incidence and severity of IVH. However, the long-term outcomes of repeated antenatal courses of corticosteroids to women at risk of preterm birth (an increasing practice) have not fully been investigated. Effects such as reduced body weight and head circumference at birth have been identified (French et al., 1999). In a follow-up of the same cohort, French and colleagues (2004) found that this treatment appeared effective in reducing the risk of cerebral palsy. However, there was a higher incidence of behavioral problems later in childhood, particularly hyperactivity and distractibility.

Another study addressed factors that influence developmental outcome at 18 and 24 months in a sample of very preterm infants (GA <32 weeks). Although antenatal steroids did not appear to have an impact at this age, a major risk factor for delayed motor development was the postnatal treatment of dexamethasone in infants who continued to have severe respiratory problems following birth (Stoelhorst et al., 2003). The authors recommended that dexamethasone be used with caution. In an earlier study, Hack and colleagues (1996) also noted that postnatal dexamethasone therapy did not appear to have an appreciable affect on survival rates.

Another common treatment for RDS is the administration of natural or synthetic surfactants. When these are administered to infants born either less than 30 weeks GA or weighing less than 1,500 g (3.3 lb), mortality rate is decreased (Hack et al., 1996; Vaucher et al., 1993). As with corticosteroids, there is limited information on whether this has an effect on the later developmental status of the infant. According to D'Angio and colleagues (2002), "Premature infants born in the surfactant era remain at high risk of neurodevelopmental compromise" (p. 1094). They found little evidence to suggest that the outcome for these children is any better than for children born in the presurfactant era. In another study, infants born less than 30 weeks GA who were treated with human surfactant immediately after birth were found to have lower scores on the Bayley Scales of Infant Development (BSID) at 12 months adjusted age (Vaucher et al., 1993). It was suggested that the destabilizing effect of administering the drug immediately after birth may have had an impact on physiological factors such as brain blood flow.

■■■ Although the use of treatments such as corticosteroids and surfactants has been found to improve survival rate of preterm infants, the long-term consequences of these therapies are still unknown.

Long-Term Outcome

Although infants with PVL or IVH are known to be at higher risk of motor disorders, the degree of disorder is not necessarily linked to the level of brain damage. A recent study using structural MRI to examine adults who were born with a birth weight below 1,500 g (3.3 lb) showed diffuse abnormalities of both the gray and white matter (Allin et al., 2004). The diverse nature of these abnormalities may be a result of the interaction between the perinatal brain lesions that occur in preterm infants and the normal developmental processes that occur throughout life. Not only would the severity of damage be a factor, but other factors would also come into play such as the timing of the damage in relation to the developmental processes that are occurring at the time. Therefore, one cannot predict the child's developmental outcome based on the degree of brain damage. Even when there is no diagnosis of IVH or PVL, infants can still have motor disorders (Lenke, 2003). It appears, then, that many factors contribute to the final outcome for children born at risk. Given the plentiful amount of research that has been carried out on this issue over the last decade, the following sections outline just some of the more recent studies that have attempted to identify these risk factors.

Outcome Throughout Infancy

Many studies have used norm-referenced tests such as the BSID to examine the differences in development in preterm compared with full-term infants in the first two years of life. A list of some of the more recent ones is given in table 10.2. For example, in a Dutch sample of very preterm infants (<32 weeks GA), follow-up at ages 18 and 24 months identified 40% of the children as having delayed mental or psychomotor development, or both, as measured by the BSID (Stoel-horst et al., 2003). A Finnish sample of extremely low-birth-weight (ELBW) infants (birth weight <1,000 g [2.2 lb]) identified 24% with motor impairments, 23% with ophthalmic abnormalities, and 42% with speech delay by age two years. A total of 58% of infants overall had some type of impairment (Tommiska et al., 2003).

Several problems are associated with examining the development of infants in their first two years. Firstly, accurate identification of motor disability is difficult in the early years of life. Disorders such as developmental coordination disorder (American Psychiatric Association, 2000) are often not identified until school age. Also, diagnosis of cerebral palsy can be inaccurate prior to two years of age (Doyle & Casalaz, 2001).

A further problem was described in chapter 7. That is, assessment of preterm infants can be problematic, particularly in the first two years, as there is the issue of whether to correct for the early GA of birth. Since the effects of the early extrauterine environment on development have not been established, how can we compare the performance of preterm infants with those born full term? Do we assume that neural maturation is the key issue and compare the infants according to their conceptional age, or are there environmental issues that may advantage or disadvantage preterm infants and need to be taken into account when we are comparing the two groups? Also, norm-referenced tests for infants have been criticized for their lack of predictive validity (Goodman, 1990). Hence, many studies have examined preterm outcome once these children have reached school age.

Table 10.2 Studies Carried Out on Preterm Infants—Follow-Up Within Two Years

Author	Country	Cohort birth years and description	Sample size and description	Age of follow-up	Results
Gortner et al. (2003)	Germany	1995–1997 All infants with GA <36 weeks	74 SGA 74 AGA	22 months	No differences between groups for neurodevelopmental outcome at 22 months.
Harding & McCowan (2003)	New Zealand	1993–1997 Infants SGA—below the 10th percentile	283 children with mean birth weight = 2,100 g and mean GA = 36.4 weeks	6 and 18 months	Around 75% had rapid growth following birth that led to weights exceeded 10th percentile by 6 months.
Ruiz-Extremera et al. (2001)	Spain	1994–1997 492 infants treated in the NICU	275 preterm 217 full term	6, 12, 18 and 24 months	At 2 years, total CP prevalence was 6.8%, 14.6% in those weighing ≤1,500 g.
Stoelhorst et al. (2003)	Netherlands	1996–1997 266 infants born <32 weeks GA	168 infants at 18 months 151 infants at 24 months	18 and 24 months	40% of the children had delayed mental and/or psychomotor development.
Sweet et al. (2003)	USA	1994–1998 104 infants with birth weight <600 g	21 infants at follow-up	2 years	All but one had abnormal placental history. Extremely poor neurodevelopmental outcome at 2 years.
Tommiska et al. (2003)	Finland	1997 211 surviving ELBW infants (<1,000 g)	National cohort: 211 ELBW infants Regional cohort: 78 ELBW infants and 75 full-term infants	National cohort at 18 months Regional cohort at 24 months	Prevalence of CP = 11%, motor impairments = 24%, ophthalmic abnormalities = 23%, speech delay = 42%. No impairment in 42% of children and severe impairment in 18%.

Outcome at School Age

Perhaps the most widely researched aspect of preterm birth has been long-term outcome. A multitude of papers have been published over the last decade that describe the impact of preterm birth on later development. In the 21st century, the findings of longitudinal studies have been published on large preterm cohorts from the United States (e.g., D'Angio et al., 2002), Australia (e.g., Doyle & Casalaz, 2001), the United Kingdom (e.g., Foulder-Hughes & Cooke, 2003), France (e.g., Monset-Couchard et al., 2002), Germany (e.g., Weindrich et al., 2003), and many others. Some of these are listed in table 10.3.

Several of these cohort studies have followed infants through to adolescence. For example, in the United States, D'Angio and colleagues (2002) examined the outcome for infants who were born less than 29 weeks GA. At primary school age (4 to 10 years), 69% had some form of impairment, whereas by adolescence (ages 12 to 15 years), 59% were identified with some type of impairment. Likewise, in an Australian sample of infants with ELBW (<1,000 g [2.2 lb]), 54% had some disability at age 14 years (Doyle & Casalaz, 2001). In both of these studies, over 50% of preterm infants had a disability in adolescence.

Despite considerable cohort differences, the findings of the studies in table 10.3 are surprisingly similar. One of the major differences between studies is the way in which the preterm infants are defined, that is, in terms of GA or birth weight or the relationship between the two (i.e., SGA). Many of the earlier studies on prematurity defined the population of preterm infants in terms of one of these variables, although in more recent studies there has been an attempt to describe the populations in terms of all three factors.

How do the recent studies compare with earlier studies? That is, how has more advanced perinatal care affected outcome over recent years? Kitchen and colleagues (1980) followed up a cohort of 159 infants with birth weights between 1,000 and 1,500 g (2.2 and 3.3 lb) at two, six, and eight years of age. Level of handicap was based on several criteria including IQ and level of sensorimotor dysfunction. The authors found that 5.1% were profoundly handicapped, 10.8% were severely handicapped, and 40.5% had significant handicap, while only 43.6% had minimal or no handicap. These infants were born between 1966 and 1970, a time when neonatal intensive care techniques were relatively unsophisticated, yet there appears to be little change in the outcomes compared with recent studies presented in table 10.3. Blaymore-Bier and colleagues (1994) compared the survival rate of 302 ELBW infants (500-750 g [1.1-1.6 lb]) born between 1980 and 1990 at the Women and Infants' Hospital of Rhode Island. There was a significant improvement in survival rate over the decade examined, but an incidence of approximately 20% remained for serious neurodevelopmental deficits. Stanley (1994) noted that the number of very low-birth-weight infants born with cerebral palsy increased from 15 per 1,000 live births in 1967 to 1970 to over 60 for infants born in 1983 to 1985, which coincided with a fall in mortality rate for very low-birth-weight infants. It

Table 10.3 Cohort Studies Published in This Century in Which Children Are Followed Up Postinfancy

Author	Country	Cohort birth years and description	Sample size and description	Age at follow-up	Results
Böhm et al. (2002)	Sweden	1988–1993 291 VLBW infants with birth weight ≤1000 g and GA <37wks	182 ELBW group 125 term group	5.5 years	Although the ELBW children had normal cognitive development, full-scale verbal and performance LQS were significantly poorer than for the term group
Dammann et al. (2001)	Germany	1983–1986 591 live-born infants ≤1,500 g	324 followed up	6 years	20% had CP (16% were AGA and 4% SGA).
D'Angio et al. (2002)	USA	1985–1987 213 infants born <29 weeks GA	127 in 4–10 year follow-up 126 in 12–15 year follow-up	7–10 years (primary school) 12–15 years (secondary school)	Primary school: 15% had CP, 21% had at least one severe disability; 31% had no impairment Secondary school: 15% had CP, 19% had at least one severe disability; 41% had no impairment
Doyle & Casalaz (2001)	Australia	1979–1980 351 infants with birth weight of 500–999 g	79 surviving ELBW infants 42 normal birth weight of >2,499 g	14 years	ELBW infants: 14% severely disabled; 15% moderately disabled; 25% with mild disability; 46% had no disability; 10% had CP NBW infants: 2% had severe disability; 14% mild disability; 83% no disability
Foulder-Hughes & Cooke (2003)	UK	1991–1992 380 preterm infants born <32 weeks GA	280 preterm infants 210 term infants	7–8 years	Preterm group: 30.7% with motor impairment Term group: 6.7% with motor impairment

Study	Country			Age	Findings
Goyen et al. (2003)	Australia	1987–1994 infants with bw <1,500 g	21 pairs of twins born 27–34 weeks GA with discordant birth weight 26 pairs of nondiscordant twins	3 years	1 larger twin had CP in the discordant group. 5 children had CP in the nondiscordant twins.
Goyen & Lui (2002)	Australia	1992–1993 85 infants born at <29 weeks GA or <1,000 g	58 infants	18 months, 3 years, and 5 years	Fine motor deficits in 54% at 18 months; 47% at 3 years; 64% at 5 years Gross motor deficits in 14% at 18 months; 33% at 3 years; 81% at 5 years
Ong et al. (2001)	Malaysia	1989–1992 419 VLBW infants born at Maternity Hospital Kuala Lumpur	116 VLBW survivors	4 years	10.3% had CP with 75% of these having multiple disabilities; 27.5% had poor motor function; 17.6% had IQ of <70.
Sullivan & McGrath (2003)	USA	1985–1989 184 infants	34 term infants (HT) 41 healthy preterm (HPT) infants (GA ≤ 37 weeks) 59 preterm with medical complications (SPT) 34 preterms with neurological illness (NPT)	4 years and 8 years	At 4 years: poorer performance on total, fine and gross motor, and visual-motor integration scores in all preterm groups compared with HT with scores decreasing for increasing morbidity. These results were linked to poorer school performance at 8 years.

appears that the improved neonatal care has dramatically increased the incidence of cerebral palsy in this population of infants. However, an important factor is survival rate, as well as level of prematurity. More recent cohorts would include many infants who would not have survived in previous decades because of the less sophisticated neonatal intensive care (Piek, 1998).

The primary objective of research investigating the long-term outcome of prematurity is to identify the factors that can predict abnormal outcomes. As pointed out by Lukeman and Melvin (1993), there are a multitude of factors, biological and environmental, that influence the development of preterm infants. These include such factors as neonatal IVH (D'Angio et al., 2002), social factors such as ethnicity and socioeconomic status (D'Angio et al.; Stoelhorst et al., 2003), maternal age at birth (Stoelhorst et al., 2003), and birth weight (Foulder-Hughes & Cooke, 2003; Stoelhorst et al.), to name but a few. It is clear that preterm birth is complex in terms of both the developmental problems that can result and the factors that influence developmental problems.

Motor Development in the First Few Months

Can an understanding of the early development of motor ability in infants assist in understanding some of the later problems that result? This has become an important issue for researchers investigating early motor development.

Preterm infants are often born with low muscle tone, or hypotonicity. The earlier the infant is born, the greater the hypotonicity (Soltesz-Sheahan & Farmer-Brockway, 1994). It is generally believed that this results from the lack of exercise within the uterus as the infant is not compressed against the uterine walls as he or she grows in size in the later stages of pregnancy. This results in less muscle strength and poorer flexion of limbs, trunk, and pelvis than in infants who spend longer in utero. As a result of these changes, the preterm infant has a greater range of motion and flexibility around the limb joints.

Once the infant is born, gravitational forces continue to affect the infant's extended posture (Soltesz-Sheahan & Farmer-Brockway, 1994), resulting in differences in his or her reflexes and spontaneous movements compared with infants who were born full term. For example, the asymmetric tonic neck reflex (ATNR) is more "frequent, intense and pure" in preterm infants (Bigsby, 1983), with a lower prevalence of the ATNR in full-term neonates than in newborn preterm infants (Clopton et al., 2000). It was noted by Saint-Anne Dargassies in 1977 that the ATNR can be stronger in preterm infants once they reach 40 weeks GA compared with the newborn born full term (Bigsby, 1983). The leg response also appears to be stronger than the arm response.

Extended posture could also explain the differences found in a study by Davis and colleagues (Davis et al., 1994). They examined treadmill walking in 12 preterm infants at one, six, and nine months corrected age. The preterm infants could perform alternating steps on a treadmill at one month of age, with the number of steps increasing by six months of age. At nine months of age, some infants reached a plateau whereas the number of steps for other infants decreased. The same patterns and individual variability have also been found in full-term infants (Thelen & Ulrich, 1991). Davis and colleagues found evidence that the preterm infants at corrected age of one and six months produced more steps than full-term infants, which implies a developmental advantage in having less restricted movements in the first few months of life (compared with full terms encased within the uterus wall) and more energy-intensive movements after birth (as they shift from a liquid to a gas environment). Davis and colleagues explained the differences in terms of more extended posture, stronger active flexor muscle activation in the preterm infants, and the fact that preterm infants had less fat on their legs, making the legs easier to lift. Despite this, however, there is evidence that preterm infants born with very low birth weight are at greater risk of delayed walking even when they have no evidence of brain damage (Jeng et al., 2004).

The techniques developed by Thelen in the 1980s for examining infant movement using motion analysis (see chapter 6) have led to similar research on preterm infants. Heriza (1988a, b) compared spontaneous leg kicks in low-risk preterm infants and full-term infants at 40 weeks post-GA. The relationships between the hip, knee, and ankle joints were examined using pair-wise correlations and phase lags in the key kinematic events, in addition to the timing of flexion and extension. It was argued that extrauterine environmental events did not influence the highly organized synergies found for the spontaneous leg kicks.

In contrast, other studies have found differences between full-term and low-risk preterm infants. Als (1995) provided evidence for neurobehavioral differences in these two groups even when the preterm infants were medically healthy, that is, not considered to be at risk. Full-term infants were better in their autonomic, motoric, state, attentional, and self-regulatory processes, implying that environment can influence development. Others have found differences when comparing joint coupling during kicking (e.g., Geerdink et al., 1996; Jeng et al., 2004; Piek, 2001; Piek & Gasson, 1999). In a longitudinal study, Geerdink and colleagues examined intralimb coordination in six full-term and eight low-risk preterm infants using pair-wise cross-correlations. Although no significant differences were found between the two groups when the hip and knee joints were compared, there were differences between the hip and ankle and between the knee and ankle, with lower values found for the preterm infants, particularly at ages 6 and 12 weeks. Overall there appeared to be a decrease in cross-correlations for all joint comparisons over age. Factors that did not appear to influence the results were leg volume and postural control.

Low-risk preterm infants were also found to have different limb dynamics from full-term infants in a longitudinal study by Piek and Gasson (1999). Results similar to those of Geerdink and colleagues

(1996) were obtained, with the ankle–knee and ankle–hip joints behaving differently for the preterm compared with the full-term group. In addition, there was an indication of a tightening of the synchrony between these joints for the preterm infants as the infants became older. Jeng and colleagues (2004) also examined preterm infants who had no evidence of brain damage. They found a relationship between a high hip–knee correlation at two months corrected age and a delay in the ability to walk. Other factors that appeared to predict delayed walking were high kick frequencies at four months of age and a short intrakick pause in combination with low variability in interlimb coupling at two and four months of age.

The tendency for increased synchrony of joints in preterm infants has also been investigated in high-risk populations. Heriza (1991) compared the performance of 24 high-risk preterm infants with that of low-risk preterm and full-term infants. As found previously for the low-risk infants, there was evidence of strong coupling between the hip, knee, and ankle joints in the high-risk infants, although for several individual infants the joints appeared to be out of phase. One high-risk infant with severe IVH was followed longitudinally to 12 months of age. In this infant, although the pattern of kicking was the same as for the low-risk infants at 40 weeks conceptional age, at 8 and 12 months of age the hip and knee coupling became stronger.

Studies on full-term infants have demonstrated that around five months of age there is a loosening of these tight synergies in the leg joints (e.g., Thelen, 1985; Vaal, 2001). This appears necessary for the infant to develop more complex, coordinated skills such as creeping and walking. Tight coupling between joints would greatly hinder the ability of the infant to produce coordinated movements at this age. This tight coupling may also be related to the lack of fluency and complexity of movement found by Ferrari and colleagues (1990) for brain-damaged infants using the qualitative assessment of spontaneous movements.

These research findings suggest that there may be a link between this inability to uncouple the early joint synergies and abnormal motor development. Vaal and colleagues (2000) also found tighter intralimb couplings during spontaneous kicking at ages 18 and 26 weeks in infants with PVL compared with infants who had no evidence of brain damage. Fetters and colleagues (2004) have identified differences in kicking patterns between infants with and without white matter damage who are only four weeks old (corrected age). Again, tighter couplings were found for the infants with brain damage. There was also little coordination between amplitude and velocity of movement in the infants with white matter damage. These parameters were found to be coordinated in the full-term and preterm infants without brain damage. Coordination of such parameters would be expected in normal development as these are the conditions usually found in skilled movements.

Vaal (2001) suggested that one neurophysiological mechanism affected in infants with increased synchrony may be the inability to distinguish reciprocal excitation of the agonist muscles in addition

Research employing kinematic analysis of early motor patterns of preterm infants has provided information on what processes are different in the early development of full-term infants compared with preterm infants with and without brain damage.

to poor reciprocal inhibition. This suggestion was supported by some earlier work by Hadders-Algra and colleagues. Hadders-Algra and Prechtl (1993) carried out a longitudinal study on two preterm infants with GAs between 28 and 33 weeks, comparing the EMG activity of the biceps and triceps brachii during general movements at ages 33 to 34 weeks GA, then at term age, and finally at three months postterm. They found characteristic differences in the spontaneous movements of preterm infants compared with those of the normal full-term infants. Whereas coactivation of the antagonists was found to be present in the full-term neonates for more than 70% of the time, the two preterm infants demonstrated an increase in coactivation with increasing age. In another study, EMG was used to examine spontaneous arm movements in two brain-damaged infants (Hadders-Algra et al., 1997). Strong co-contraction of the muscles with uncharacteristically longer burst duration was found in the brain-damaged infants compared with the control infants.

These research techniques are promising as they aid in understanding the mechanisms that may be associated with poor motor ability in preterm infants (Piek, 2001, 2002). With such knowledge, more effective intervention strategies could be developed.

Intervention Approaches for the High-Risk Preterm Infant

When the infant is born, it is very difficult to accurately predict later developmental outcome, although clues are present in terms of the many risk factors already outlined in this and previous chapters of the book. However, there are huge individual differences, and there are also many factors, biological and environmental, that influence later outcome. This leads to the question of how one can be sure that *any* intervention is useful or may not even be harmful to the high-risk infant. Control groups are difficult to incorporate into evaluation, partly for ethical reasons, but also because outcome is often unknown at this early age. However, it would also be inappropriate to decide against any intervention just because it has not been evaluated for its effectiveness. What is required is research to determine the most theoretically viable intervention programs. That is, intervention must be based on sound research and theoretically justified models. The next step is to develop appropriate research designs to investigate the interventions carried out. With the increasing sophistication of statistical testing, this is now becoming more likely.

Intervention for the Neonate

The preceding sections have emphasized the profound effect that prematurity can have on later developmental outcome. It was initially assumed that outcome was due to neurological impairment associated with such conditions as PVL and IVH. However, it is now clear that even when preterm infants do not have such brain insults, their neurodevelopmental outcome can still be challenged. Therefore, it appears that appropriate brain development is influenced by the environmental changes that occur for the preterm infant (Als, 1995). This approach to brain development is highlighted in such theories as Edelman's neuronal selection theory outlined in chapter 3 (Sporns & Edelman, 1993).

An infant born very preterm is placed in an environment necessary for his or her survival but very different from what is regarded as the "norm." The neonatal intensive care unit (NICU) provides the required medical technology to keep the infant alive but, as can be seen in figure 10.1, it is very different from the mother's uterus, where the infant would complete development if born full term.

What are the implications of this new environment? With the rise in preterm births over the last two decades, this has been a key issue for researchers and therapists. The NICU is essential for the infant's survival, but what are the implications for this child's later development? In chapter 1, the importance of fetal motility was discussed. Yet in the case of the preterm infant, motor activity is both minimal and very different from the types of movements that would be found in utero. Other factors that have been investigated include the social implications, that is, the impact of this start to life on factors such as maternal attachment and infant temperament.

In the 1980s, considerable research was carried out to determine the best types of environment and intervention for infants within the NICU. However, one of the difficulties in this area was the different approaches of the different disciplines (Fetters, 1986). Up to the mid-1980s, the

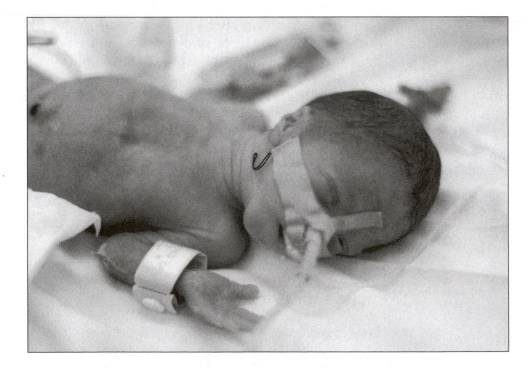

Figure 10.1   This young infant was born 16 weeks early (i.e., 24 weeks GA) and was dependent on the neonatal intensive care unit for survival.

literature was written primarily by psychologists and medical personnel, with terminology not familiar to other professionals such as physical and occupational therapists. One of the main concerns of these professions was the motor ability of the infants, and this was generally not a specific outcome for much of the earlier research that was concerned with general physical, cognitive, and psychosocial outcomes.

Campbell (1986) described *neonatology* as "a specialized area of pediatric practice for physical or occupational therapists" (p. 191), with its own distinct issues to consider in the provision of the appropriate environment for the neonate. The approach to developmental care of preterm infants was influenced considerably by the work of Als (1986), who developed the model of synactive organization (see figure 10.2). This proposes four subsystems of development: the autonomic, motor, state, and attentional/interactive. These systems interact with each other, "influencing and supporting one another or infringing on one another's relative stability" (Als, 1989, p. 71). The organism–environment interaction is emphasized in this model. Particularly important is the parent–child interaction. As a result of this model, Als (1995) proposed individualized developmental care plans for preterm infants. This would be considered a *transactional* rather than a *medical* model of intervention as it takes into account environmental factors such as family interaction and societal influences as well as medical and support services (Campbell, 1993). Some of the important considerations in Als' plan are outlined in the following paragraphs.

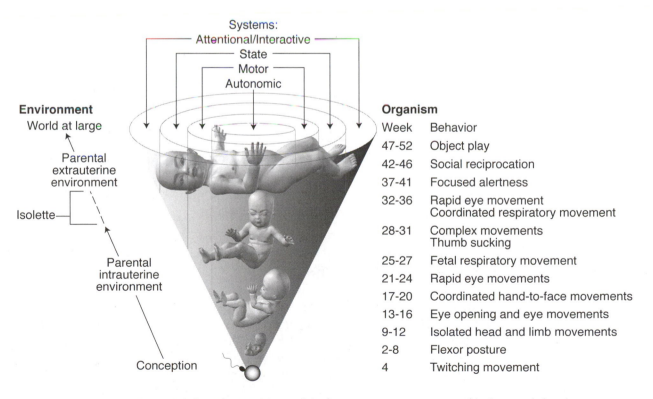

Figure 10.2 Als' (1982) model of synactive organization of behavioral development.
Reprinted from Als, 1982.

Given the importance of the environment on development, it is essential to consider the external environment, or "ecology," of the intensive care nursery. In the 1980s these nurseries were very noisy as a result of the equipment being used, background conversation, and radios playing in these environments. Also, the infants were handled a great deal because of the medical procedures involved. However, there was very little social contact such as rocking or talking to the baby (Campbell, 1986). Research in the 1970s and '80s identified these and other factors, such as disrupted sleep patterns and continual supine positioning, as having detrimental effects on the developmental outcome (Als, 1995). As a result, many changes have been implemented in the NICUs. One that has received considerable attention is the appropriate positioning of the infant.

Adaptive positioning has been investigated since the early 1980s. It is defined as "a therapeutic means of placing the infant in his or her world, in order to satisfy principles of normal neuromotor development" (Bellefeuille-Reid & Jakubek, 1989, p. 93). Some positions are considered better than others. It has been argued that the supine position results in complications such as excessive shoulder elevation, reduced muscle tone, asymmetrical posturing, and trunk hypertension. Placing the infant in a flexion position, on the other hand, encourages the development of postural control and antigravity movements (Bottos & Stefani, 1982). Many approaches have been adopted to promote flexion in the NICU. For example, comfort pads similar to beanbags have been used. The supine support pillow was foam with a hole cut in the middle. This formed a nest for the infant's head and trunk (Updike et al., 1986). The use of waterbed flotation has also been investigated and found to improve approach and avoidance behaviors (Pelletier et al., 1985).

Frequently changing the positioning of the infant is recommended by Soltesz-Sheahan and Farmer-Brockway (1994), as is the side-lying position. This position reduces the effect of gravity and promotes midline and flexor responses. Using alternate right and left side-lying positions enhances symmetrical development. Infant stability can be provided with sandbags, blanket rolls, and bags of intravenous fluid.

Prone positioning has been found to improve sleep patterns and self-calming skills. Hip and knee flexion can be promoted in the prone position through placement of a small diaper roll or washcloth under the infant's pelvis and below the abdomen. Symmetry can be reinforced by placement of rolls along the infant's sides (Soltesz-Sheahan & Farmer-Brockway, 1994).

Infants often need to be in the supine position for medical procedures. Blanket rolls can again be used to improve flexor patterns. For the upper extremities, these can be placed along the infant's sides and under the shoulder girdle. Placing them under the knees promotes hip and knee flexion (Soltesz-Sheahan & Farmer-Brockway, 1994).

A total developmental therapy program is recommended that includes the direct treatment services within the NICU, the modification of the infant's environment, and involvement and education of the parents. Regular visits by the parents are an essential component of the infant's development, especially when one considers the important contribution of factors such as maternal attachment to the infant's later mental and physical health. Parents need to be educated on the appropriate cues to look for in their infant, such as signs of stress. Also, showing parents appropriate positioning and handling techniques is essential (Soltesz-Sheahan & Farmer-Brockway, 1994). Attachment is also promoted by encouraging parents to spend time carrying and holding their infants (see figure 10.3).

Assessment of programs that adopt a total developmental therapy approach has provided mixed results, although results are generally positive. A recent study in Sweden tested the Newborn Individualized Developmental Care and Assessment Program (NIDCAP) using a randomized control trial (Kleberg et al., 2002). Although the sample size was small, the infants in the NIDCAP group (n = 11) showed significantly better cognitive development than the control group (n = 9) at age one year. However, no difference in psychomotor development was observed. Both cognitive and motor development were assessed using the BSID (see previous chapter for a description of this test). However, as described earlier, assessment of infant development can be unreliable and often not predictive of later outcome, and assessing preterm infants is especially problematic. Longitudinal studies that follow these infants up in childhood are needed to appropriately assess the benefits of these types of programs.

■■■ A total developmental therapy program is recommended for infants in the NICU. This includes direct treatment of the infants within the NICU, changing the infants' environment to most suit their needs, and education and involvement of parents.

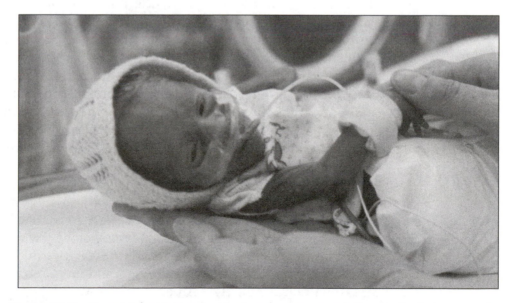

Figure 10.3 Parent–infant interaction is strongly recommended, even for the young infant born very preterm.

Intervention Approaches Throughout Infancy

Follow-up programs are generally recommended for high-risk preterm infants once they leave the hospital. Although they are medically stable, their development is still influenced by their early birth. This is particularly true for motor development.

The NICU Developmental Follow-Up Clinic at the Lutheran General Children's Medical Center in Illinois has the primary goal of early identification of disability (Lenke, 2003). The team involved in this program includes a physician specializing in rehabilitation or a neonatologist, an occupational therapist, a nurse, an audiologist, a speech therapist, and a social worker. Parents are encouraged to return with their infants at 4, 8, and 18 months corrected age for follow-up, and then at two, three, and four years of age.

Hospitals also provide regular therapy programs for these infants once they leave the hospital. Western Australia is unique in that all very preterm births are directed through King Edward Memorial Hospital for Women (KEMH). Because of this, all parents in Western Australia whose infants are born less than 1,500 g (3.3 lb) and were less than 32 weeks GA are invited to join the Preterm Follow-Up Play Group, which is run through KEMH with assistance from the State Child Development Centre. Infants who as a result of some other medical condition spent a long period of time in the Special Care Nursery are also invited. The term "Play Group" has been deliberately used to place less emphasis on the medical model and to make the mothers feel more at ease with the program.

Infants are seen once a month from corrected age 2 months to 12 months. One aim of this program is to provide an appropriate environment for the parents and their infants, allowing them to develop their own support structures. Also, parents learn the appropriate ways to handle and play with their infants in order to promote suitable muscle activity and motor control. Individualized programs are determined for each infant and include massage, movement play, and sensory and speech evaluation. The program is run by physical therapists, with the assistance of speech therapists at 4, 8, and 11 months corrected age. An occupational therapist becomes involved when the infant is 11 months old. Parents are encouraged to work with their infants at home between these visits and are provided with appropriate exercises for their infants.

As stated by the senior physiotherapist in this program, "One of the most important aspects is that we provide an informal assessment and follow-up of infants 'at risk' and liaise very closely with the pediatricians. This results in very early individual intervention if needed and referral to more appropriate services" (Arlette Coenen, personal communication, 22 December, 2003). The Alberta Infant Motor Scale (Piper & Darrah,

1994) is used to evaluate the infant's progress. A detailed description of this scale is provided in the preceding chapter.

Determining how effective these follow-up programs are is very difficult. As diagnosis of many developmental disorders and disabilities such as cerebral palsy, intellectual disability, and developmental coordination disorder is often not possible until later, it is unclear whether the infant has a disability or not.

Only a small number of studies have presented research on physical therapy programs starting prior to 12 months of age. For example, Butler and Darrah (2001) found no studies on neurodevelopmental treatment (arguably the most common intervention used by physiotherapists) that started prior to 5 months of age, and only four on treatment started before 12 months of age. A recent study by Kanda and colleagues (2004) examined a group of high-risk preterm infants who started intensive physiotherapy within the first three months of life for the purpose of determining whether early-onset intensive physiotherapy was effective for these children. The physiotherapy used was based on the Vojta method (see chapter 11 for a description of this approach), which is an intensive physiotherapy program. Parents who adhered to the program provided their infants with three or four 30 min sessions of therapy per day. Intensive therapy started within the first three months of age and continued until follow-up at around five years of age. The investigators found that children in this group achieved motor milestones at an earlier age than the group of children who had "insufficient" training.

■■■ How Does This Research Inform Therapeutic Practice?

One of the key concepts to therapy is the need for "active" therapy. This was noted as early as 1926 by Crothers (cited in Scherzer & Tscharnuter, 1990), who stressed the need for active movement and avoidance of overprotection of the child, even in the most severely disabled children. For example, in order to learn how to make the appropriate postural adjustments for a new movement, the infant or child must be actively involved (Bly, 1991). For an infant, this is not necessarily an easy job. However, recent research outlined throughout this volume has demonstrated that the young infant is capable not only of reflexive or spontaneous movements but also of movements through intent. Research outlined in chapter 1 showed that infants as young as three and four months of age can adjust their movements (e.g., kicking) to match the environment (Angulo-Kinzler, 2001; Angulo-Kinzler & Horn, 2001; Angulo-Kinzler et al., 2002; Chen et al., 2002; Thelen, 1994). This research provides clues to possible early intervention practices that could increase motor activity in high-risk infants.

(continued)

Toy manufacturers have also made use of these principles. For example, some toys react when the infant claps his or her hands, which leads to the infant's repeating that behavior (see secondary circular reactions outlined in chapter 2). Other toys encourage the infant to kick. For example, as shown in figure 10.4, the toys move or make noises when the infant kicks them. This again encourages the infant to repeat the movements. Future therapy may include the development of interactive "toys" that will generate appropriate motor responses. This would be an active, pleasurable approach for infants in need of additional sensorimotor interaction.

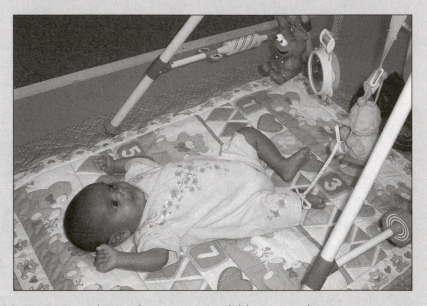

Figure 10.4   Toys can be used to encourage children to produce more spontaneous kicking. The infant's right leg is attached to the mobile, making it move as she kicks.

Summary

As medical technology improves, more infants who are born preterm survive. As a result, this is currently a very active research area. However, it is also one with many problems. From this chapter it can be seen that even the definition of preterm birth is controversial. What is clear, however, is that this is a population that has significant developmental problems. In particular, there is a high incidence of developmental delay and disability in motor skills.

Recent research has been promising in suggesting possible motor mechanisms that may be affected by preterm birth. However, this research is very new, and a great deal more investigation is required before these findings can be incorporated into appropriate intervention programs aimed at preventing motor delay and disability in the future.

eleven ■■■
Cerebral Palsy

chapter objectives

This chapter will do the following:

- Define and describe cerebral palsy
- Discuss the motor consequences of cerebral palsy
- Discuss traditional and current intervention approaches

The group of disabilities called *cerebral palsy* have been described as the "most common and severe childhood motor disorders" (Stanley, 1997, p. 92). Consequently, a complete chapter has been dedicated to addressing this often debilitating disorder. The chapter defines and describes the many types of cerebral palsies and then discusses recent research on cerebral palsy in infants. How has this research influenced the treatment and intervention practices for infants with cerebral palsy? This issue will be taken up at the end of the chapter.

Definition of Cerebral Palsy

Cerebral palsy (CP) literally means *brain paralysis.* Stanley and Blair (1994) define the cerebral palsies as "non-progressive disorders of movement or posture" (p. 473) that originate in early childhood. They occur as a result of interference with or a defect of the developing brain. These characteristics of CP were recognized by John Little, an English orthopedist, as early as 1861. He found a link between complications during pregnancy or birth and the subsequent development of CP. He suggested that these difficulties resulted in cerebral hemorrhage as a consequence of anoxia that occurred at some stage during the birth process. John Little's insight resulted in the foundations of our current understanding and treatment of CP (Scherzer & Tscharnuter, 1990).

Cerebral palsy is distinguished from other motor disorders caused by brain damage in that it relates to the developing, immature brain rather than the mature brain (Sugden & Keogh, 1990). Although it is clear that causation during the prenatal and neonatal period falls under the category of "early life," the definition is somewhat vague in terms of what it includes if the infant develops the problem following the neonatal period. This is not a problem clinically, or in relation to management of the disorder, but the definition needs to be clear in order to allow understanding of causation and interpretation of epidemiological findings (Cogher et al., 1992).

Although CP is a *nonprogressive* disorder in that neurological impairment does not progress, the problems associated with the disorder frequently become more complex with age. At birth, it is often not possible to identify infants with mild to moderate CP. As they become older, the motor problems become more obvious. If the arms are affected, this will result in considerable difficulties with manual dexterity. This will affect the child's ability to use a knife and fork, draw, and eventually write. If the lower limbs are affected, the first signs may become evident when the infant is delayed in walking or develops an unusual gait. Hence, although early cerebral damage may be the cause, the problems associated with the disability tend to be progressive. If early development is delayed or abnormal, this will affect later development, so it is imperative that research determine normal developmental pathways, as well as ways of correcting abnormal development as early as possible. Appropriate early intervention is therefore essential to ensure the best possible outcome for these individuals.

Occurrence of Cerebral Palsy

Studies investigating the occurrence of CP have examined both the **prevalence,** "the total number of cases . . . in existence in a given population at a certain time" (O'Toole, 1992, p. 1214), and **incidence,** which is the rate of occurrence described as "the number of new cases of a specific disease occurring during a certain period" (O'Toole, 1992, p. 759). Most studies describe the occurrence of CP in terms of the number per 1,000 live births, which implies a rate or incidence. However, Stanley and Blair (1994) suggest that this is more appropriately considered prevalence as "the usual method of data collection for cerebral palsy is to ascertain the number of cases prevalent in a population of a certain age and to relate this number to the population of births" (p. 475).

In the 1980s, Stanley and Alberman (1984) found that most studies gave an estimate of 2 per 1,000 births despite any differences in methodology. This is comparable with the incidence quoted by Aicardi and Bax (1992) of between 1.5 and 2.5 per 1,000. Recent estimates in industrialized countries such as Australia and Sweden are 1 to 2.4 per 1,000 live-born infants (Blair, 2001; Hagberg et al., 2001). No recent figures appear to be available for North America (Nelson, 2002), but it appears that these prevalence rates are consistent across industrialized countries and, surprisingly, across decades.

Given the improved medical practices over the last 30 years, a drop in incidence would be expected. However, it is these advances in technology that have improved the survival rate of high-risk infants, the infants most at risk of CP. For example, in Japan, the rate of occurrence of CP for infants with birth weights over 2,499 g (~5.5 lb) was 2.2% in 1991. This figure was based on infants in 12 neonatal intensive care units in Japan, hence the higher proportion. For infants between 1,000 and 2,499 g (2.2 and ~5.5 lb), the incidence was 4.6%, and for infants less than 1,000 g it increased to 11.8% (cited in Ohgi et al., 2003).

The changes in rate and severity of CP in the United Kingdom over the period 1984 to 1995 were examined by Surman and colleagues (2003) using the Oxford Register of Early Childhood Impairments (ORECI). The relationship between birth weight and rate of CP already described is clearly seen in figure 11.1. This figure also indicates reduced rates of CP over time for each category. Overall, there was a decline in CP rate from 2.5 out of every 1,000 in the 1984 to 1986 period to 1.7 in the 1993 to 1995 period. Improvement in perinatal care practices may be one reason for the reduction in rates of CP, although the authors warned that factors such as population differences over the years may also contribute to the changing rates.

The figures just presented relate to industrialized countries. Few studies have addressed prevalence rates in developing countries. It would be very difficult to trace all births and follow up on the developmental progress of these infants in such countries, but as Aicardi and Bax (1992) point out, one would expect a much higher incidence of CP in these countries due to the limited perinatal and neonatal care available.

■■■ Infants born very preterm or with a very low birth weight are at a much greater risk than others of developing CP.

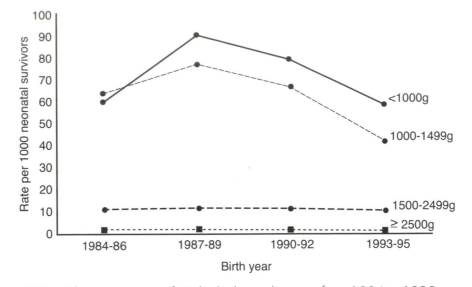

Figure 11.1 Changes in rates of CP by birth weight group from 1984 to 1995
Reprinted from Surman et al., 2003.

Categories of Cerebral Palsy

The poor movement control found in children with CP cannot easily be categorized. This is the case because the severity and type of disorder are affected by many factors. For example, the stage of development at which the lesion occurs influences the pathways affected, as "different neural circuitry appears to control motor behavior at different stages of development" (Leonard, 1992, p. 51).

Severity varies considerably and is generally classified as mild, moderate, or severe. The lesions that produce CP influence many different motor pathways, so the resulting movement difficulties are quite complex. Not only is movement affected in different ways, but the degree of involvement of body and limbs also differs. This has led to problems in classifying the types of CP. Other issues also lead to difficulties in categorization. For example, clinical signs change over time, and clinicians also tend to interpret definitions and terms quite differently (Cogher et al., 1992).

Categorization by Movement Type

Evans and Alberman (1985) developed a system of recording motor deficits based on four main types of motor involvement: spasticity, ataxia, dyskinesia, and hypotonia.

Spasticity

Spasticity is perhaps the best known of the motor problems associated with CP. It is characterized by a *rigidity like that of lead pipe* (Cogher et al., 1992), which occurs as a result of **hypertonia,** that is, increased tone in some muscle groups. There is an abnormal resistance to passive movement. As this resistance builds up, there is a rapid release of tension with exaggerated stretch reflexes and increased deep tendon reflexes (Sugden & Keogh, 1990). In severe cases, the child may be fixed in a few specific patterns as a result of the strong co-contraction of muscles (Bobath, 1980). This rigidity can be present even when the child is at rest. Spasticity has been associated with damage involving the motor portion of the cerebral cortex and pyramidal tracts (Scherzer & Tscharnuter, 1990).

Ataxia

Ataxia is described as excessive incoordination and difficulty with balance. It has been linked with cerebellar damage (Evans & Alberman, 1985). The arms are particularly affected, with evidence of overreaching or underreaching. Intention tremors are also sometimes evident (Sugden & Keogh, 1990). These children may also have difficulties with producing eye movements that are independent of head movements, and as a result they may have difficulty visually tracking objects (Bobath, 1980). Motor milestones are frequently delayed, with infants often being unable to sit until 15 to 18 months, and they may not stand or walk until two or three years of age or older.

Dyskinesia

Dyskinesia has been associated with damage to the extrapyramidal pathways (Scherzer & Tscharnuter, 1990). Evans and Alberman (1985) divide dyskinesia into two types. **Athetoid** movements are unnecessary, purposeless movements that occur during volitional movements. These extraneous involuntary movements have been described as swiping, jerky, and rotary patterns (Sugden & Keogh, 1990), often slow and writhing in character, that result from the recruitment of inappropriate muscle groups (Cogher et al., 1992). **Dystonia** refers to movement disrupted by changing tone. Generally, these fluctuations occur from normal to increased tone, although occasionally hypotonicity is involved.

Given that both athetosis and dystonia may be evident in the same individual, these are often described under the one category of athetosis (e.g., Sugden & Keogh, 1990). Indeed, Bobath (1980) stated that "all athetoid children show an unsteady and fluctuating type of postural tone" (p. 59). He categorized the athetoid group into three different subgroups. The first he called dystonia dyskinesia; the second group was a mixed group involving spasticity and ataxia or athetosis; and the third group he described as athetosis, floppy infant, ataxia. It is clear from this classification scheme that even when it comes to describing the loss of muscle control in CP children, there is considerable disagreement.

Hypotonia

Hypotonia, or decreased muscle tone, is categorized separately by Evans and Alberman (1985). It is characterized by soft and floppy muscles that usually result in increased joint range. Deep tendon reflexes may also be affected, sometimes with diminished and sometimes with exaggerated responses (Cogher et al., 1992).

Categorization by Affected Body Part

Not only is there difficulty in describing the different types of abnormal movement control found in children with CP; there is also confusion in the identification of which parts of the body are affected by the disability. Terminology used to describe the areas affected by CP has been defined by Scherzer and Tscharnuter (1990) as follows:

- Monoplegia—only one limb is affected
- Hemiplegia—both the arm and leg of one side are affected
- Paraplegia—both legs are affected
- Quadriplegia—all four limbs are equally involved
- Diplegia—the four limbs are unequally involved, with the arms having only mild difficulties

Classification by Type of Deficit, Location, or Both

Cerebral palsy is generally classified according to the type of motor difficulty and its location. Aicardi and Bax (1992) distinguish five broad categories of CP: hemiplegia, spastic and ataxic diplegia, tetraplegia, athetoid CP, and ataxic CP. These are described in the following subsections. Cogher and colleagues (1992) include a sixth category, called *mixed types,* which covers children in whom the motor disorder is difficult to classify in the categories just listed.

Hemiplegia

Often referred to as spastic hemiplegia because it is mostly spastic in type of motor disorder, hemiplegia is also termed *hemiparesis,* or *unilateral spastic paresis.* It is found in 20% to 40% of CP cases (Nelson, 1991). It appears to be attributable to lesions of the sensorimotor cortex and corticospinal tract in the hemisphere contralateral to the affected side. Learning difficulties are also associated with this type of CP, and seizures occur in around 25% of cases (Cogher et al., 1992). There is also evidence to suggest that the right side of the body is more often affected than the left (Nelson, 1991), although there appear to be similar clinical patterns for right and left hemiparetic CP (Kulak & Sobaniec, 2004). The infant shown in figure 11.2 was diagnosed at eight months with mild right spastic hemiplegia.

Asymmetrical gait is one of the most common features of a child with spastic hemiplegia. During walking, most of the body weight is carried by the unaffected leg, and arm swing occurs only on the unaffected side, as the shoulder of the affected arm is generally hyperextended and the elbow flexed (Styer-Acevedo, 1994). A fisted hand held close to the body is often evidence of hemiplegia in the infant. Another indication is the use of the mouth to explore an object held in the unaffected hand rather than exploration with the other (affected) hand. Although lifting of the head may not be a problem for these infants, rolling over may be delayed as the infant has difficulty coordinating the affected limbs (Cogher et al., 1992).

Spastic and Ataxic Diplegia

Although spastic and ataxic diplegia are clinically and etiologically quite distinct (Cogher et al., 1992), both syndromes involve mainly the hips and legs, with only minor involvement of the arms. They are among the most common forms of CP, accounting for around 41% of cases (Aicardi & Bax, 1992). Spastic diplegia is often related to low-birth-weight infants with periventricular leukomalacia that occurs between 24 and 36 weeks gestation. The motor fibers to the lower limbs appear to be mainly affected, as the lesions are generally located along the outer angle of the lateral ventricles (Aicardi & Bax, 1998). The stretching of these fibers as a result of **hydrocephalus** results in ataxic diplegia.

Figure 11.2 This young girl aged 19 months was diagnosed with mild right spastic hemiplegia at age 8 months. She began walking at an age typical of normally developing children, aided with a splint on her right foot.

A major problem for infants with diplegia is the ability to sit, as they have difficulty opening their legs wide enough to provide a stable base of support. As a result, they need to support themselves with their arms, which then restricts their ability to use their hands to play with toys. Hence these infants often prefer to play while in supine position (Cogher et al., 1992). Gait is characterized by excessive mobility through the head, neck, upper trunk, and upper extremities in order to compensate for the poor mobility in the lower body. Hips cannot achieve full extension and are flexed in the stance position, while knees may be either hyperextended or flexed (Styer-Acevedo, 1994).

Tetraplegia

Tetraplegia, also termed *spastic quadriplegia* or *bilateral hemiplegia*, is the most severe form of CP. Its **etiology** is more heterogeneous, and in many cases the cause is not known (Nelson & Ellenberg, 1986). This disorder involves the whole body, including the spasticity of the four limbs although predominantly in the upper limbs. Occurring in only 5% of cases, it is associated with significant problems including feeding and absence of speech due to oral difficulties (Aicardi & Bax, 1992). Asymmetries are found in most children with this disorder, and accompanying problems such as epilepsy and severe mental retardation are often also present.

Athetoid Cerebral Palsy

The diagnosis of athetoid CP covers the dyskinetic movement problems already described and includes a variety of terminology such as *athetosis, chorea, dystonia,* and *dyskinesia.* Athetoid CP covers between 10% and 15% of the CP cases. Its pathology is well defined, with selective involvement of the central gray nuclei (Aicardi & Bax, 1992). The abnormal movement and muscle tone do not appear until the infant is around 5 to 10 months old and are never present in the first few months (Aicardi & Bax), making early identification virtually impossible. Added to the difficulty of early diagnosis is the finding that apparently normal infants can have transient dystonia in their first year of life (Willemse, 1986).

Ataxic Cerebral Palsy

Although both disorders are primarily congenital in origin, ataxic CP is distinct from ataxic diplegia in that the former refers only to individuals who demonstrate cerebellar symptoms and signs most prominently (Aicardi & Bax, 1992). Ataxic CP occurs in around 10% to 15% of cases and is generally not diagnosed until infants are between one and two years old when they are expected to initiate independent walking. Infants with ataxic CP are generally hypotonic.

■■■ The classification of CP is complex. It generally includes a combination of the following: the degree of disability (i.e., mild, moderate, or severe), the location of the primary motor disability (e.g., monoplegia or hemiplegia), and the type of motor disability (e.g., spasticity, dyskinesia).

Etiology of Cerebral Palsy

If we are to prevent or at least reduce the incidence of CP, then we need to know the *etiological pathway,* that is, "the sequence of interdependent events culminating in disease" (Blair & Stanley, 1993a, p. 302). How do we determine what causes CP? Stanley (1997) suggests two primary ways. The first is to "identify and measure the prenatal exposures and then to observe the occurrence and types of motor disorders in the different exposure cohorts. . . . The second approach is to select a group of similar cases of motor disorders (e.g., a cerebral palsy subtype such as spastic quadriplegia) and a group of controls without cerebral palsy and delve backwards to identify common prenatal exposures that may have been causes" (p. 92). Both approaches are challenging for the researcher.

There is no one etiological pathway for CP; rather, and for most cases of CP, the cause cannot be identified (Aicardi, 1992). For most of the last century, asphyxia and birth trauma were cited as the primary causes of CP. It appears now that only a small proportion of cases can be attributed to **intrapartum** insult, that is, insult during delivery. Blair and Stanley (1993b) suggested that the proportion was around 10% of cases in their Western Australian sample, whereas Hagberg and colleagues (2001) argued that it may be more like 28% of cases based on their Swedish sample. Recently it has been argued that in the majority of cases, the pathway may begin prenatally (e.g., Aicardi & Bax, 1992; Stanley, 1997). Findings from the European Cerebral Palsy

Study suggest that around 75% of all CP cases may be a result of injury during the late second or third trimester of pregnancy (Jacobsson & Hagberg, 2004). When the etiology can be traced back to intrauterine, natal, or perinatal factors, this is referred to as congenital CP (Scherzer & Tscharnuter, 1990).

Preterm birth is a major etiological factor, especially when linked with intrauterine growth retardation (see chapter 10), with 28% of CP cases being born preterm (Jacobsson & Hagberg, 2004). Other factors found to increase the risk of CP include maternal factors such as maternal diabetes mellitus, threatened abortion, preeclampsia, and multiple pregnancy. Factors that are considered *high risk* include intraventricular hemorrhage, ventricular dilation, chronic lung disease, polycythemia, and clinically manifest hypoxic-ischemic encephalopathy (Aicardi & Bax, 1992). Unreliable predictors include "Apgar score, intrapartum and neonatal pH, and late fetal heart deceleration during labour" (Aicardi & Bax, 1992, p. 333).

Nelson and Ellenberg (1986) carried out a multivariate analysis of risk factors associated with CP on a sample of 45,449 children, 189 of whom had been diagnosed with CP by age seven years. The authors divided the factors into stages of pregnancy and birth and carried out separate analyses for each stage. Their findings are detailed in table 11.1. Many factors that had been identified previously as antecedents of CP were not included as they did not demonstrate significant associations in the univariate analyses. These included factors such as maternal age, parity, socioeconomic status, history of smoking, and diabetes.

When all characteristics were examined over all stages using stepwise multiple logistic regression, the overall R^2 was very small (0.0745), with the main predictors being neonatal seizures, birth weight less than 2,000 g (4.4 lb), crying not occurring within the first 5 min after birth,

Table 11.1 Antecedents of Cerebral Palsy According to Various Stages of Pregnancy and Birth, As Determined by Stepwise Multiple Logistic Regression

State of pregnancy	Prevalence of antecedent in NCPP (%)	Predicted risk (%)	95% confidence limits	% of CP cases with antecedent
Before pregnancy $R^2 = 0.0121)$				
Maternal mental retardation	0.4	2.3	0.9/5.5	2.7
Motor deficit in older sibling	1.2	1.4	0.7/2.9	4.4
Hyperthyroidism	0.6	1.8	0.8/4.4	2.7
Maternal seizures	0.4	1.6	0.6/4.4	2.7
Prior fetal deaths >2	0.6	1.2	0.4/3.2	2.2

(continued)

Table 11.1   *Continued*

State of pregnancy	Prevalence of antecedent in NCPP (%)	Predicted risk (%)	95% confidence limits	% of CP cases with antecedent
Pregnancy R² = 0.0102)				
Severe proteinuria	1.1	1.3	0.6/2.6	4.3
Third-trimester bleeding	13.7	0.6	0.4/0.9	22.3
Thyroid and estrogen use	0.14	1.9	0.4/8.0	1.1
Asymptomatic heart disease	0.9	1.2	0.5/2.8	2.7
Incompetent cervix	0.3	1.5	0.5/5.0	1.6
(Rubella)				
Labor and delivery R² = 0.0635)				
Gestational age ≤32 weeks	3.3	1.4	0.9/2.0	21.0
Lowest fetal rate ≤60 beats/min	1.0	1.4	0.7/2.7	5.7
Breech presentation	2.6	0.8	0.5/1.3	11.1
Chorionitis	2.3	0.7	0.4/1.2	10.1
Placental weight ≤325 g	8.7	0.5	0.4/0.8	25.6
Placental complications	3.2	0.6	0.4/1.0	11.2
Immediately postpartum R² = 0.0610)				
Birth weight ≤2,000 g	1.7	1.6	1.0/2.6	22.2
Time to cry ≥5 min	1.1	1.0	0.6/1.9	12.0
Moro's reflex asymmetric	4.5	0.4	0.3/0.7	18.8
White race	45.8	0.3	0.2/0.5	55.0
Microcephaly	2.0	0.6	0.3/1.2	4.9
(Male sex)				
Nursery period R² = 0.0876)				
Neonatal seizures	0.3	9.6	6.0/15.2	12.2
Major non-CNS malformation	6.8	0.8	0.6/1.2	21.7
Antibiotics, no infection	9.2	0.7	0.5/1.0	20.8
Infection	1.2	1.2	0.7/2.3	7.5

Adapted from Nelson & Ellenberg, 1986

and major malformations not related to the central nervous system (CNS). These malformations were quite heterogeneous but included vertebral anomalies, inguinal hernias, and micrognathia (abnormal smallness of the jaws). Note that "no factor in labor or delivery was a major predictor" (Nelson & Ellenberg, 1986, p. 85). It is interesting to note that when the authors considered the subtypes of CP separately (i.e., spastic diplegia, quadriplegia, hemiparesis, and mixed), they found that the same factors in general emerged, with very few factors predicting only one type of CP.

Genetic factors are not thought to play a major part in the etiological pathway to CP, although ataxia has been found to have a genetic link (Aicardi & Bax, 1992). Postnatal factors are thought to be responsible for around 5% to 10% of cases (Blair & Stanley, 1982).

Cerebral Palsy Registers

Over the last few years, our knowledge and understanding of CP have increased due to the development of several CP registers throughout the world. Given that CP occurs in only 2 to 3 of 1,000 live births, such registers are needed to amass large enough numbers to address important issues such as etiology. These registers are designed to provide a better understanding of the risk factors in the birth cohorts examined. "In addition, registers can be used to identify occurrence in cohorts exposed to various factors or to select cases for case-control studies" (Stanley, 1997, p. 92).

One of the first of these registers was instigated by the Hagbergs in Sweden (Hagberg et al., 1993). Another with a high profile was initiated by Fiona Stanley and colleagues in Western Australia (Bax, 2003). Both of these registers are ideally located as they have access to large numbers of infants. Five active registers within the United Kingdom have recently collaborated to form the United Kingdom Cerebral Palsy network (UKCP). Recently, a large number of CP surveys and registers throughout Europe formed a network, the Surveillance of Cerebral Palsy in Europe (SCPE, 2000), in order to promote collaboration and provide the large numbers needed to monitor trends in CP rates. The network consists of 14 centers in eight countries (United Kingdom [the UKCP], Denmark, Sweden, Ireland, Germany, Netherlands, France, and Italy), and the hope is to establish "a database of children with CP who were born between 1980 and 1990 from a total live-born population of over 300,000 per year" (SCPE, 2000, p. 823).

Identifying Cerebral Palsy in the Early Years

Research on CP in infancy has been hindered by the fact that in mild and moderate cases, CP may not be identified until the child is older (Aicardi & Bax, 1992). Some children may not be diagnosed until three or four years of age (Nelson & Ellenberg, 1982). If an infant is diagnosed in the first year, this often means that the case is a severe one with major motor disability and often with accompanying problems such as mental retardation and sensory deficits (Cogher et al., 1992).

Another issue regarding diagnosis relates to the earlier description of brain plasticity and the accuracy of early diagnosis. Because of the large degree of individual differences in brain development, maturation, and repair, as well as the many other intervening factors, early diagnosis of CP may need to be revised as the child matures (Cogher et al., 1992). One large prospective study by Nelson and Ellenberg (1982) showed that infants diagnosed at birth with CP can indeed "grow out of it." The authors examined 37,282 children at one and seven years of age and found that 118 of the 229 children (i.e., 51%) originally diagnosed with CP at age one year demonstrated remission of the clinical signs at seven years of age. Why is this? Are the intervention strategies used a factor? Has the brain adapted to utilize undamaged parts to compensate for the damaged neural tissue? Has there been some repair of this young developing brain? These are issues that are yet to be resolved. With rapidly expanding medical technology, these issues are challenges for the future.

Cogher and colleagues (1992) argued that with less severe cases, it is often necessary to observe children into their second year and occasionally into their third before a diagnosis of CP can be confidently made. In a recent study in Australia (Doyle & Casalaz, 2001), 10 children (14% of the sample) born with extremely low birth weight (<1,000 g [2.2 lb]) were diagnosed with CP at age two years. However, 5 of these children with mild CP were no longer diagnosed when followed up at ages 5, 8, and 14 years. An additional child with CP not identified at age two years was identified at a later age. The severity of the diagnosis also varied across ages, highlighting the "subjective nature" of these classifications (Doyle & Casalaz).

Researchers in the field of developmental medicine have been searching for a means of early identification of CP for over half a century (Harris, 1987). However, there has been little progress in the identification of CP, particularly in the first month (Palmer, 2004). Although "at-risk" infants can be identified with reasonable sensitivity, the specificity is generally low. For example, the qualitative assessment of general movements (see chapter 8) developed by Prechtl and colleagues (e.g., Ferrari et al., 1990; Prechtl et al., 1997) has proven to be a reliable tool in predicting CP in infants three months or older (corrected age). However, although the sensitivity is still reasonably high for younger infants (60-100%), the specificity is considerably poorer for these younger infants (46%-86%) (Einspieler et al., 1997). That is, many younger infants identified with abnormal motor patterns will not develop major disabilities such as CP or mental retardation.

Burns and colleagues (1989) also noted that at one month of age, an examination of neurological signs, motor milestones, primitive reflexes, and postural control was not very effective in identifying infants with CP. They examined two groups of 26 infants: one group where the infants were later diagnosed as having hypertonic CP at age two years and a control group of infants who did not develop CP, matched on birth date, sex, birth weight, and gestation. Identification was more successful at four months compared with one month of age, although there was a tendency for overidentification at four months. Assessment at eight months of age was highly predictive of CP, although a few mild cases were not detected. Burns and colleagues concluded that "identification depends, not on the presence of isolated specific abnormal signs, but on a combination of suspicious and abnormal signs revealed during comprehensive assessment of motor attainments, neurological signs, primitive reflexes and postural reactions" (p. 218). Boehme (1990) lists potential markers for CP for three different age ranges in the first year. These are depicted in table 11.2.

Table 11.2 Potential Problem Signs at Different Stages of Development in the First 12 Months

Signs to watch for from birth to 3 months	Signs to watch for from 4 to 8 months	Signs to watch for from 9 to 12 months
1. Limited random movements	1. Hypotonia	1. Limited variety of movement
2. Easy and frequent startle responses	2. Mass patterns of movement	2. Poor trunk control
3. Poor head control	3. Limited variety of movements	3. Poor protective responses
4. Increased stiffness that may not feel like true spasticity	4. Asymmetry	4. Poor balance responses
5. Reliance on head and neck hyperextension during movement	5. Limited spinal extension/limited control in prone position	5. Poor manual skills
6. Feeding problems	6. Limited visual control	6. Hypotonicity
7. Respiratory problems	7. Limited reach and grasp/fisted hands	7. Hypertonicity
8. Irritability		

Reprinted from Boehme, 1990, page 4.

Orthopedic Approaches to Intervention

Bobath (1980) highlighted the problems faced by children with CP when he stated, "A child, whether normal or abnormal, can only use what he has experienced before. The normal child will use and modify his normal motor patterns by practice, repetition and adaptation. The child with cerebral palsy will continue to use and, by repetition, to reinforce abnormal patterns" (p. 26).

As a result, later motor patterns will be built from the earlier abnormal movements. This was depicted by Alexander and colleagues (1993) with the following progression:

Original problem → Compensations → Habit → Contractures → Deformities

Contractures are a major problem for children with CP. Contractures occur where there is an abnormal shortening of the muscle tissue, resulting in muscles that are highly resistant to stretch (O'Toole, 1992). This results from maintained abnormal postures, as muscle growth is dependent to some extent on the stretch of the muscle (Aicardi & Bax, 1992). Spasticity produces shortened muscles, and if shortening is maintained, it will lead to contractures affecting joint function. The ankle is particularly vulnerable, leading to foot deformities. Also, abnormalities of the hip joint may occur as a result of internal rotation and adduction at the hips.

Over the last 100 years, treatment of CP has changed dramatically. Initially, it was considered an orthopedic problem that could be improved by surgery or through the use of orthoses to correct the secondary musculoskeletal problems that resulted primarily from contractures (Forssberg & Hirschfeld, 1992). A more recent approach has been the use of serial casting on the young child; progressive casting is considered to increase muscle length as would occur with normal development. There is also evidence to suggest that the benefits of serial casting can be improved with use of the drug botulinum toxin type A—BTX-A (Bottos et al., 2003). This produces partial denervation of the muscle, causing a period of muscle weakness that can last around four months. This can result in reduced spasticity and improved functional performance. The use of BTX-A is a relatively new procedure, with research demonstrating mixed results. For example, Glanzman and colleagues' (2004) findings suggested that casting was a better procedure than BTX-A and found no benefit in combining the two procedures. Such procedures are currently in a stage of infancy but have considerable potential.

Early Intervention Approaches

A major aim of early intervention is to ensure that the compensatory movement patterns do not become habit, therefore reducing the likelihood of contractures and the need for orthopedic intervention. It is therefore important to develop appropriate interventions for infants and young children.

Around the middle of 20th century, neurophysiological theories were proposed to account for CP. These theories were based on reflex theory, and physical therapists developed programs that assisted in manipulating reflexes. Some of the more popular approaches developed around this time were those of Karel and Berta Bobath, who targeted the inhibition of postures and patterns, and of Vaclav Vojta, who aimed at provoking or eliciting reflex locomotor patterns (Cratty, 1994). Theories stressing the importance of sensory integration were highlighted by Ayres in the 1970s (Ayres, 1972). This approach became popular with occupational therapists. An alternative approach was conductive education, which was developed in eastern Europe and is designed to improve the child's overall functioning.

Several excellent books and book chapters have reviewed earlier intervention techniques and introduced more recent management approaches to CP (e.g., Aicardi & Bax, 1992; Cogher et al., 1992; Forssberg & Hirschfeld, 1992; Scrutton, 1984). Several of these early approaches remain popular today and are briefly outlined next.

Neurodevelopmental Therapy

The neurodevelopmental therapy (NDT) developed by Bobath (1980) was considered by many to be the most common therapy approach at the end of the 20th century for children with neurological disorders (Bly, 1991; DeGangi & Royeen, 1994; Law et al., 1997; Mayo, 1991), and it remains popular in the 21st century. This approach originally focused on improving motor control by inhibiting abnormal automatic reactions and reflexes. That is, in order for new patterns to emerge, abnormal motor patterns needed to be inhibited. This view was based on the early hierarchical reflex theories arguing that reflexes were the basis of later movement. One particularly influential theory was the reflex inhibition theory of McGraw (Bobath, 1980), outlined in chapter 2.

Another important component of this therapy was the acknowledgment of the importance of posture in motor development. The Bobaths noticed that children with CP produced more stereotyped, or less fluid, postural adjustments, which were often associated with differences in muscle tone (Bly, 1991). The term *postural tone* was preferred to *muscle tone* as the Bobaths believed that muscle tone had the purpose of maintaining posture (Bly, 1991). Specific handling techniques were developed to improve postural tone that would then facilitate new movement patterns. These techniques necessitate a good knowledge of the appropriate muscle tone required. "Adequate postural tone exists when the body has high enough muscle activation to maintain a posture against gravity and yet low enough activation to allow the body to move through gravity" (Boehme, 1990, p. 1).

Neurodevelopmental therapy has been criticized for its basic reflexive approach, although recently the method takes into account the importance of the practice of functional skills throughout the treatment

(Fetters & Kluzik, 1996). Therefore, although based on an outdated theory, NDT continues to be popular because its procedures appear to "fit" more recent motor control approaches. However, it is very intensive, requiring both regular therapy attendance and a program for parents to follow at home, which has been described as stressful and time-consuming (Mayo, 1991). Despite the popularity of this program, "Many health professionals doubt that the benefits derived from therapy warrant the time and effort expended by parent and child" (Mayo, 1991, p. 258).

Vojta

The Vojta treatment is based on the notion that movements that can be observed and provoked in children with CP are found in the newborn and have a subcortical origin. Vojta argues that "the persistence in cerebral-palsied patients of the movement patterns of a disturbed newborn is the outcome of nothing other than the blocking of postural ontogenesis during the earliest period of human motor development" (Vojta, 1984, p. 76). This approach is based on a maturational perspective, as it aims to activate "postural ontogenesis," that is, to activate normal muscle responses that will then provide the child with proprioceptive information that can be utilized by the CNS.

The Vojta method uses isometric strengthening techniques. Normal movement patterns are encouraged through application of tactile stimulation. The program involves multiple daily therapy sessions by parents who receive extensive training. A recent study by Kanda and colleagues (2004) demonstrated that it appears to be an effective program when initiated in early infancy on high-risk preterm infants. However, research on its effectiveness in older children with CP has received little attention.

Sensory-Integration Approach

The ability to organize and integrate different sensory inputs is recognized as an important component of motor control. Poor visual-spatial organization and cross-modal integration have been identified as key problems in children with movement problems such as developmental coordination disorder (Piek & Pitcher, 2004; Wilson & McKenzie, 1998). Ayres (1972) defined the integrative process as "the interaction and coordination of two or more functions or processes in a manner which enhances the adaptiveness of the brain's response" (p. 25-26). This process produces a whole picture from the fragmented information provided from different sources.

Sensory-integrative abilities in children with CP are thought to be disrupted as a result of neurological dysfunction within the brainstem, or because poor motor ability limits the sensory experiences of the infants and children (White, 1984). The therapy involves the stimulation of vestibular, kinesthetic, and tactile senses through equipment such as swings and balls to lie on and materials of different textures such as sand and water. The therapist utilizes these to train the child to be able to appropriately input, interpret, and integrate different sensory stimuli. Unlike the other therapies already described that involve the appropriate execution of movement, the sensory-integration approach emphasizes sensory processing and movement planning (Fisher & Bundy, 1992). Critical to this approach is the notion of active participation, with the individual requiring an inner drive to develop the appropriate sensory-integration skills. For infants, this would require pleasurable, playful activities.

The sensory-integration approach has remained popular, especially within the discipline of occupational therapy. However, it has been subject to considerable criticism. Shaw (2002) conducted a meta-analysis on 41 studies that evaluated the outcome of sensory-integration therapy in children with a number of different diagnoses including motor problems, learning disabilities, mental retardation, autism, and multiple developmental problems. Although small significant effect sizes were found for improvement in motor skills and psychoeducational performance, these effects disappeared when maturational factors were taken into account. Shaw concluded, as have others, that "there is simply no evidence of the efficacy of [sensory-integration] therapy" (p. 10).

How Effective Are These Approaches?

Perhaps one of the most difficult questions posed by interventions is "How do we know that they work?" Research testing the efficacy of different intervention programs is limited, and much of it has been based on poor design and methodology. Perhaps this is the area that requires the greatest amount of research, but the task is not easy. Several issues, such as the heterogeneity of CP, the frequency and intensity of the intervention, and the types of assessment tools used to measure outcome, mean that it is very difficult to compare studies. These issues are discussed more fully next.

Issue of Heterogeneity of Disorder

One of the difficulties in describing and researching CP is its heterogeneity in terms of etiology, pathology, and level and type of disability. Consequently, there have been many descriptions of CP, but not a great deal of behavioral research has been done to illuminate the underlying processes that have been disrupted in this disorder. There have, of course, been many speculations on these processes based on observation, such as the inability to inhibit reflexes or poor sensory integration. Indeed, many of the past and current therapies have been based on the principles that have emerged from these earlier observational analyses.

As Williams (1989) stated, it is impossible to find a *generic* patient. The outcome for a brain-damaged infant can range from normal to severely handicapped, with huge heterogeneity in terms of the sensory, motor, mental, and behavioral problems. Is it possible for one type of intervention approach to address all of these affected infants?

Issue of Appropriate Measures of Improved Performance

A concern highlighted by Fetters (1991) is the type of assessment used to evaluate movement outcome. Many assessments are based on the norm-referenced tests outlined in chapter 9. The problems associated with these tests for infants were also outlined previously. As Fetters states, "A major problem with these types of scales is their failure to measure functional movement or to capture the qualitative aspects of movement" (p. 245). Tests that measure movement quality such as range of movement, strength, and kinematic factors like movement time may provide more information on the changes that occur with intervention.

This approach to measurement has become more popular over the last decade (e.g., Fetters & Kluzik, 1996; Fonseca et al., 2001; van der Weel et al., 1991, 1996). For example, Fetters and Kluzik examined the effectiveness of NDT compared with practice by measuring the improvement in speed and control in a reaching task. They examined variables such as changes in movement time and the number of movement units to determine smoothness of reach (see chapter 5 for more detailed discussion of these types of variables). Using these kinematic measures, they were able to determine that time in treatment, rather than the type of treatment, appeared to be the key to improved performance.

Issue of Intensity and Frequency

The findings by Fetters and Kluzik (1996) highlight the importance of high-frequency programs that include time in treatment, but also time off treatment. Trahan and Malouin (2002) also noted that an intermittent program with intensive therapy that also included periods without therapy was the most effective. This study emphasizes the importance of practice in any intervention program.

Duration and intensity/frequency of therapy were also noted by Kanda and colleagues (2004) as key factors for an effective intervention program. In this respect, home therapy by parents and caregivers was a crucial factor. Case-Smith (1998) pointed out that in the area of occupational therapy, family involvement has been an integral part of early intervention strategies since the 1980s. She argued that in order to "understand developmental and maturational processes, infants must be viewed in the context of their environment and in the context of their relationships with caregivers" (p. 3).

The cognitive approach focuses on skill acquisition and motor learning theories. Gentile (1992) suggests that this model "emphasizes the active role of the learner and makes the therapist a partner in the problem-solving process" (p. 39). Active participation in therapy was highlighted in the previous chapter in relation to preterm infants. Another important component of this model is practice. Practice appears to be important to consolidate the learning achieved through the skill practice. With practice defined as "the repetition of movement," Fetters and Kluzik argued that "practice is a fundamental component of any physical therapy approach" (p. 348). How-

■■■ Research on the efficacy of intervention programs is very limited as a result of many factors. These include the difficulty in finding *generic* participants with CP, finding suitable measures for determining improvement in performance, and controlling and measuring the frequency and intensity of therapy sessions.

ever, they suggest that many interventions designed for children with CP have not seen this component as a critical feature of the program.

■■■■ How Does This Research Inform Therapeutic Practice?

According to Thelen (1992), the dynamic systems approach has enormous potential in terms of intervention because it is based on the notion of a "soft" assembly of motor patterns rather than hard-wiring by the CNS. This approach argues that once dysfunctional movement patterns are established they become stable and more difficult to disrupt. According to a dynamic systems view, "Therapy must first disrupt the abnormal patterns to establish more functional ones" (p. 172). Although this sounds very similar to the principles outlined by the neurophysiological approaches, the underlying theory is quite distinct. For example, Bly (1991) has used a dynamic systems approach to explain NDT handling techniques that are designed to control abnormal and fixing patterns. Bly argues that when the therapist uses these handling techniques, the degrees of freedom are reduced in the child's movements, therefore promoting particular movement patterns. This comes from Bernstein's notion of freezing degrees of freedom to assist in learning new skills (Vereijken et al., 1992), discussed in detail in chapter 2. Provided the handling techniques are not too restrictive, they will allow the child to develop new movement patterns without the interference of other inappropriate and excessive movements.

Fonseca and colleagues (2001) describe a model of locomotion in children with CP that is based on a dynamic systems approach. They argue that "gait patterns adopted by individuals with cerebral palsy are not limitations but adaptations to the changed dynamics" (p. 794). That is, as a result of changes in the musculoskeletal system, such as increased co-contraction and reflex activity and reduced muscle power, the gait pattern changes to accommodate these differences. One such change is the increased stiffness and less active force in the affected side of children with spastic hemiplegia. These are considered "optimal solutions" to the problem of locomotion given the constraints imposed on the child with CP. Fonseca and colleagues suggested that interventions focusing on "changes in specific parameters, such as functional muscle strength, may lead to a dynamic reorganization of the system, and provide altered functional behaviours" (p. 804). Dynamic models such as this provide exciting potential for unique approaches to intervention in children with movement disorders.

Summary

Although new theories and methodologies are providing greater insight into the motor control of children with CP, there remains a dearth of literature on infants with CP. Part of the difficulty is the problem of early diagnosis. Many children with CP are not diagnosed until around two years of age. Given the importance of early intervention, both early identification and appropriate interventions for young infants remain critical areas of research for those exploring CP.

The reflex/hierarchical model has been used for neurodevelopmental approaches such as Bobath's and Vojta's and the sensory-integration approach of Ayres. These assume that motor output is determined by sensory input and that development emerges hierarchically from low to high levels of CNS control (Horak, 1992). Although still one of the most popular approaches, it is now recognized that a neurophysiological approach to intervention may not be as effective as initially thought. Part of the difficulty with this approach is that it is based on assumptions that have been shown to be unfounded. For example, the development of the nervous system is no longer considered hierarchical, as higher centers do not necessarily depend on the development of the lower centers (Leonard, 1992). Also, the notion that reflexes need to be inhibited before functional movements emerge is another idea that needs to be reconsidered. Another, based on the early maturational theory of Gesell, is the notion that limb control develops in a proximal to distal direction. Evidence now suggests that these muscles develop simultaneously (Fetters et al., 1989).

The interventions described in the previous chapter for preterm infants may be useful as guidelines for research on CP. Also, potential new interventions for infants with other disabilities may be useful. One such disability is Down syndrome, on which some exciting research is emerging for interventions in infancy. These will be discussed in the next chapter.

twelve ▪▪▪

Down Syndrome

chapter objectives

This chapter will do the following:

- Describe motor development in infants with Down syndrome

- Identify possible causes of poor motor control in Down syndrome

- Describe recent intervention techniques to improve motor ability

 Another population that demonstrates marked delays in motor ability is the intellectually disabled. As with cerebral palsy (CP), there is considerable heterogeneity in this population. The level of motor disability is dependent on the type and degree of intellectual disability, although most who have some intellectual disability tend to have poorer motor skills. Sugden and Keogh (1990) suggest that the reason may be that "they are less capable of interacting with their environment, which restricts their opportunity to participate in a wide range of experiences and constrains their potential to profit from the limited experiences they do have" (p. 68).

Although research on the motor ability of children with intellectual disability has been extensive (cf. Sugden & Keogh, 1990), there has been very little research on development in this group in infancy. As with CP, only those severely affected are diagnosed at birth, and those with moderate intellectual disability are often not detected until after infancy when they are expected to begin talking. There is one notable exception, however, and this is the child with Down syndrome (DS). As this disorder can be detected at birth, and can even be identified in utero, the motor difficulties in these infants can be investigated at a very early age. The current chapter examines motor development in infants with DS as well as recent intervention strategies to improve their motor performance. Given that there have been extensive publications on motor development in DS, and also that around one-third to one-quarter of the children identified with severe intellectual disability have DS (Sugden & Keogh, 1990), the chapter is devoted to this particular population.

Definition of Down Syndrome

Down syndrome was named after John Langdon Haydon Down, who in 1866 wrote the first publication that described the clinical characteristics of t his disorder (Down, 1866). With an incidence in North America of around 1.25 (Torfs & Christianson, 1998) to 1.3 per 1,000 live births (Palisano et al., 2001), it is considered the "most common organic form of mental retardation" (Weeks et al., 2000, p. viii). There is an increase in incidence with increasing maternal age.

Unlike many other childhood disorders such as CP, developmental coordination disorder (DCD), or attention deficit hyperactivity disorder (ADHD), DS has a known etiology. It occurs as a result of an extra chromosome at position number 21, called trisomy 21. That is, individuals with DS have 47 chromosomes rather than 46. The full DS phenotype is revealed in trisomy 21q22 individuals, found in the majority (94%) of persons with DS (Benezra-Obeiter, 1991). This abnormality was identified in the 1950s with the development of the electron microscope.

■■■ Down syndrome, also termed trisomy 21, is caused by an extra chromosome at position 21 resulting in 47 rather than 46 chromosomes.

Characteristics of Individuals With Down Syndrome

Infants with DS are easily identified at birth, as they have characteristic facial and body features. They are often identified by their almond-shaped eyes, and in 90% of cases there is a flatness or depression of the bridge of the nose. These infants may also have inner epicanthic folds (a fold that covers the inner edge of the eye), midfacial hypoplasia, a smaller and round skull, reduced stature, excess skin on the back of the neck, a short second bone in the little finger, a single transverse palmar crease, and a protruding tongue (Benezra-Obeiter, 1991; Cratty, 1994; Sugden & Keogh, 1990). Increased joint flexibility is also often obvious. Notice the hyperextended elbow joints in the infant pictured in figure 12.1. With over 100 possible differences noted in their physical features (Cunningham, 1979; cited in Sugden and Keogh, 1990), there is considerable variation between individuals with DS.

Life-threatening cardiovascular abnormalities such as congenital heart disease occur in a large proportion of individuals with DS, with heart defects found in around 30% to 50% of cases (Benezra-Obeiter, 1991; Block, 1991). These problems resulted in a very short life expectancy prior to recent advances in medical technology. For example, in

Figure 12.1   This young infant with Down syndrome has the characteristic joint flexibility that is particularly noticeable in the elbow joints as she raises herself from prone position.

1944 to 1945, only 37% of persons with DS survived beyond 10 years of age. The life expectancy has now increased to 55 to 60 years (Cratty, 1994).

Other common problems include gastrointestinal abnormalities such as duodenal obstruction, clubfoot, dislocation of the hips, and spinal malformations. Vision and hearing problems are also common. Ophthalmic abnormalities include cataracts, strabismus, myopia, astigmatism, and nystagmus (Benezra-Obeiter, 1991). Ear infections are common in children with DS and may be associated with a narrower ear canal. Of particular relevance to later physical ability is the tendency for children with DS to be overweight.

The most prominent feature of children with DS is their mental retardation. All have some degree of mental retardation, although this can vary from mild to profound (Lauteslager, 1995). Although infants are born with a brain of normal weight, the weight diminishes by up to 24% with age. This has been implicated as the cause for diminished IQ scores after the first two years. However, the accuracy of the early infant tests, particularly for cognitive development, has been questioned (see chapter 9), and therefore it is unclear to what degree development deteriorates from infancy to childhood (Sugden & Keogh, 1990).

The areas of the brain that are particularly affected are the cerebellum and brainstem, but there are also fewer neural connections in the basal ganglia and motor cortex (Cratty, 1994). These are the primary centers of the brain for motor control (see chapter 3). Therefore, it is no wonder that individuals with DS have considerable motor disability.

Motor Development in Down Syndrome

It was originally assumed that the motor dysfunction found in DS was inextricably linked with the mental delay. Although the degree of motor delay is linked to IQ (Cratty, 1994), research has shown that children have distinct problems with their motor development that are not a result of their mental retardation (Lauteslager, 1995). As a result, extensive research has been carried out on the types of motor problems experienced by individuals with DS and the associated causes.

There have been several reviews of the literature on motor development in infants and children with DS over the last few decades (e.g., Block, 1991; Henderson, 1985), and a recently published volume by Weeks and colleagues (2000) provides a comprehensive description of newer research in this area. It includes chapters on performance measures such as reaction time (Anson & Mawston, 2000), the development of reaching and grasping (Charlton et al., 2000), and locomotor patterns (Mauerberg-deCastro & Angulo-Kinzler, 2000).

De Graaf (1995) lists five key features of motor dysfunction in DS. The first two, hypotonia and laxity of the ligaments, produce a general floppiness often termed the "rag doll" effect. Other features include slower reaction times, weaker voluntary muscular contraction, and delayed motor development. One of the major characteristics of infants with DS is their delay in achieving the motor milestones. Differences in the early spontaneous activity of infants with DS have also been identified.

General Movements

Recently, general movements in infants with DS have been investigated. Mazzone and colleagues (in press) compared the general movements of 23 infants with DS to those of 30 full-term infants using the Qualitative Assessment of General Movement technique developed by Prechtl and colleagues (see chapter 8 for a description of this technique). Infants were assessed from birth to six months corrected age.

Both a qualitative and a quantitative assessment were carried out each month. Qualitative differences were observed between the two groups of infants. Whereas Prechtl (1997) identified a distinct transition in general movements from writhing to fidgety at around three months, the infants with DS did not display this transition to fidgety movements. Rather, their writhing movements became progressively faster, more variable, and more complex with age. There was no evidence of a later transition to the fidgety movements.

For the quantitative assessment, five different aspects of the movements (amplitude, speed, sequence of movements, fluency and smoothness, onset and offset) were rated on a 2-point scale, with 2 points for optimal and 1 point for nonoptimal performance. Significant differences in the total optimality score were identified between DS and control infants at each month. The scores for the DS group also indicated considerable variability between individuals, although there appeared to be an improvement in the scores with age. It was also noted that there was a delay in the disappearance of spontaneous motor activity for the DS infants compared with the controls. This was linked to a delay in the development of voluntary movements, which can be associated with the finding of delays in motor milestones in infants with DS.

Delays in Motor Milestones

The mean age of onset and range of the major milestones for infants and children with and without DS are presented in table 12.1. In nearly all of these, there is an overlap, suggesting that some infants and children with DS can achieve their motor milestones within the age range specified for children with no disability. This is consistent with the large variability in performance found in most studies of motor development in DS. However, on average, milestones are delayed for the DS infant.

There has been some disagreement in the literature regarding the degree to which movements are affected in infants with DS, particularly in the first six months. These differences may be a result of different

Table 12.1 Comparison of Motor Milestones Achieved by Infants and Children With DS Compared With Nondisabled Infants

Milestone	DS CHILDREN		DISABLED CHILDREN	
	Mean age (months)	Range (months)	Mean age (months)	Range (months)
Gross motor activities				
Good head balance	5	3–9	3	1–4
Rolls over	8	4–12	5	2–10
Sits erect without support more than 1 minute	9	6–16	7	5–9
Pulls to stand	15	8–26	8	7–12
Pulls to stand with help	16	6–30	10	7–12
Stands alone	18	12–38	11	9–16
Walks without support	19	13–48	12	9–17
Climbs stairs with help	30	20–48	17	12–24
Comes down stairs with help	36	24–60	17	13–24
Runs	about 48			
Jumps up and down in one place	48–60			
Fine motor activities				
Follows objects with eyes, in circle	3	1.5–6	1.5	1.3
Grasps dangling ring	6	4–11	4	2–6
Passes objects from hand to hand	8	6–12	5.5	4–8
Pulls string to attain toy	11.5	7–17	7	5–10
Finds object hidden under cloth	13	9–21	8	6–12
Puts 3 or more objects into cup or box	19	12–34	12	9–18
Builds a tower of 2-inch cubes	20	14–32	14	10–19
Completes a simple 3-shape jigsaw	33	20–48	22	16–30+
Copies a circle	48	30–60+	30	24–40
Matches shapes and colors	48-60	—	—	—
Plays games with simple rules	48-60	—	—	—

Reprinted from Henderson, 1985

types of assessment tools used to investigate early infant movements (Block, 1991). The recent findings of Mazzone and colleagues (in press) described in the previous section provide evidence that there appears to be quite a different developmental course for infants with DS in the first six months. There is agreement, however, that infants with DS are delayed in motor development, and also that this delay increases as the infant gets older.

Hypotonia

Poor muscle tone, or hypotonia, is considered one of the key problems for individuals with DS. It has been implicated in the delay of the motor milestones. Hypotonia produces an increased range of motion, called hyperextensibility, of the joints. There is less joint resistance to passive movement, and unusual postures are seen as shown in figure 12.2. Notice in figure 12.2a the abnormally wide stance of the feet while squatting, and in 12.2b that the young girl can extend her arms behind

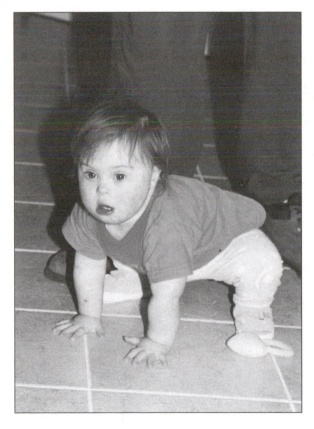

a   b

Figure 12.2 Hyperextensibility of the proximal joints. *(a)* Increased hip flexibility is noted in the squatting position and *(b)* increased shoulder flexibility when arms are raised behind the head.

her head. Hypotonia is thought to be responsible for the lack of variability and increased symmetry found in movement in DS, due to the need to stabilize the contractions around these hyperextended joints (Lauteslager, 1995). There is some evidence suggesting that hypotonia diminishes with age (Cratty, 1994). Some studies also report that the flexor muscles have a greater degree of hypotonia than the extensor muscles (de Graaf, 1995).

Davis and Kelso (1982) investigated hypotonia in DS, suggesting that it may be related to muscle stiffness or damping. Seven males with DS aged from 14 to 21 years were required to do an index finger positioning task involving flexion and extension of the finger when resistance or load was varied. The damping, or internal frictional force, was measured by the degree of overshoot or oscillation around the equilibrium point. This study was based on a dynamic systems approach suggesting that a simple mass-spring model would account for the results obtained, according to the following equation outlined by Davis and Kelso:

$$F = -K (l - l_0)$$

where

F = external force

$-K$ = stiffness

l = current length of the spring

l_0 = length of the spring when no forces are acting on it

In their first study, Davis and Kelso (1982) found that individuals with DS, like the controls, were able to specify the system parameters of stiffness and equilibrium length, which are important for joint movement. However, they found that the DS individuals were slower to respond to any changes in the resistance against the finger. When the individuals with DS responded to this resistance, they made more oscillations than the control group. Davis and Kelso's interpretation of these findings was that they resulted from difficulties in the damping of the muscle tone required for the resistance changes.

Intervention Approaches

Because DS is usually diagnosed at birth, this provides the opportunity for early intervention. However, the advantages of early intervention for infants with DS were not recognized until the later part of the 20th century. Prior to the 1960s, it was common for parents to place their infant with DS into an institution from birth. Research in the 1960s provided evidence that children who were reared at home in their first few years had less developmental delay than those who were institutionalized (de Graaf, 1995). Since then, there has been considerable interest in appropriate approaches to intervention for DS children. De Graaf suggests that research on DS "plays a pioneering role in the development and evaluation of intervention programmes" (p. 131).

Traditional approaches such as neurodevelopmental therapy (NDT), developmental skills training, and Ayres' sensory integration have provided mixed results in terms of improvement of motor development for infants with DS (e.g., Edwards & Yuen, 1989; Harris, 1981; Mahoney et al., 2001). One concern with the use of these approaches relates to how adaptable the programs are to different types of disorders (Mahoney et al.). For example, NDT has largely been developed for neurological disorders such as CP, in which motor disability is related to atypical motor patterns. Infants with DS generally achieve motor milestones, but development is delayed rather than disrupted. Can the same approach to therapy be applied to such distinctly different disorders? The outcome for NDT in infants with DS has been disappointing (Harris, 1981; Mahoney et al., 2001), suggesting that different approaches are needed for this special population.

Other researchers and therapists have recently adopted the view that for infants with DS, addressing the developmental delay is a primary goal of therapy. In particular, the motor milestone of walking has been considered an important aspect of the infant's development, with decreasing the delay of walking as a priority in early intervention. Walking is considered by parents of infants with DS to be one of the most valued goals they hope for concerning their child (Ulrich et al., 2001). It is an important achievement in terms of both independence and locomotion. With walking come increased explorative behavior and the ability to socialize more readily. Therefore, walking is important for all aspects of the child's development, including motor, cognitive, social, and emotional elements. As infants with DS take, on average, a year longer to accomplish independent walking than other infants (Henderson, 1986), there is a clear need to improve this aspect of motor development.

Early research by Ulrich, Thelen, and colleagues on treadmill walking in infants (e.g., Thelen et al., 1987; Ulrich et al., 1995) has recently been used as a basis for training in infants with DS (Ulrich et al., 2001). The aim of this training was to reduce the delay in development of motor milestones such as walking.

Ulrich and colleagues (2001) argued that training of particular limb movement patterns may be a suitable approach to promoting earlier walking in infants with DS. They cited evidence such as the training of the stepping response that was done by Zelazo and colleagues (Zelazo et al., 1972). That study was described more fully in chapter 6 (see figure 6.8). However, training the stepping response in infants would prove tedious for parents, as it would require a commitment to initiate training in the first few months of life and continue until the infant had achieved walking (which could be two years in some infants). Earlier studies using treadmill training have provided an approach that is an alternative to training the stepping reflex. These treadmill studies, described in chapter 6, demonstrated that young infants could produce the appropriate stepping response for walking at a young age. By the age of three to five months, they could "walk" supported on a treadmill with an alternating stepping pattern that was spontaneous and stable (Thelen et al., 1987; Thelen & Ulrich, 1991).

Research by Ulrich and colleagues on infants with DS (Ulrich et al., 1992, 1995) demonstrated that these infants had the same pattern of performance on the treadmill as normally developing infants. However, they were delayed and did not produce the stable stepping pattern until they were 14 months old. This was associated with the infants' ability to pull themselves to a stand position. Also, infants did not initiate steps spontaneously until they could sit independently.

An important component of the treadmill intervention used by Ulrich and colleagues (2001) is the involvement of the parents. The importance of parental involvement in therapy programs has been emphasized throughout this section of the book. Such involvement allows for more intensive therapy than would be possible by trained health professionals. Also, as stated by Ulrich and colleagues, "One of the most important elements in helping parents of infants with disabilities come to grips with their situation is to enable them to take ownership of the progress their children make" (p. 43). Therefore, parents were taught how to administer the treadmill training to their infants. Treadmills were provided to each family, and training was carried out in the home for 8 min every day, five days a week, until the infant achieved independent walking.

The treadmill intervention was assessed using a randomized clinical trial involving 30 infants with DS, 15 assigned randomly to the experimental group (treadmill training) and another 15 to a control group with no treadmill training (Ulrich et al., 2001). There was a significant improvement in the age at which the experimental group could both walk with help and walk independently. The mean age at which the treadmill group walked independently was 19.9 months compared with 23.9 months for the control group. This was an average difference of 101 days. These differences could not be attributed to changes in body weight or other anthropometric measures, which were not significantly different at age of onset of walking for the experimental group. Rather, the investigators argued that the training offered "repeated opportunities to improve balance, build strength in the lower extremities, and stimulate the neuronal connections that are involved in the generation of independent walking" (p. 46). These promising findings suggest that this approach may be useful for investigating other movement patterns that could be trained to improve other motor skills.

■■■■ How Does This Research Inform Therapeutic Practice?

Many infants with DS are "good" babies, in that they lie peacefully and do not require a great deal of stimulation to be content. However, this may be problematic for their later development. Chapter 1 emphasized the importance of the early spontaneous activity of the infant. These early motor activities appear important for the intrinsic exploration of the infant's movement capabilities. Furthermore, research has shown that heightened arousal increases spontaneous activity. In their book written for parents, Kelso and Price (1988) recommend that parents provide greater stimulation for infants with DS by handling and playing with them more often, that is, to stimulate the infants' interest or curiosity in their surroundings. The authors also recommend specific activities to help the infant experience what would be considered "normal movement." The use of active stimulation as described in chapter 10 for preterm infants may also be a suitable form of intervention for infants with DS.

Summary

Research on infants with motor delay or disabilities has often been impeded by the fact that disorders affecting motor control, such as CP, DCD, and ADHD, are not diagnosed until late infancy or in childhood. Infants with DS can be diagnosed at birth, and this provides a unique opportunity to carry out such research, as these infants are known to have significant motor problems. Even so, there has been little research on the motor abilities of infants with DS. The research carried out has primarily addressed issues such as identifying the types of motor disorders found in this population and determining the delay of motor milestones. Few studies have involved efforts to investigate the underlying processes that may be responsible for the movement problems.

One exception is the research on treadmill walking in infants with DS by Beverley Ulrich and colleagues. This research has utilized a dynamic systems approach to investigating the possible causes of the problems. Within a decade, the research not only provided some answers to the issues of why infants with DS take longer to walk, but also resulted in an intervention program that so far has produced quite favorable results. This highlights the importance of the process-oriented period that motor development is currently in. Theory-driven research that examines why movement problems exist is the key to intervention.

glossary

abduction—Movement outward away from the body.

adduction—Movement inward toward the body.

afferent—Progressing from the periphery to the central nervous system.

akinesia—Difficulty in movement initiation.

allele—One gene of a pair of alternative characteristics.

amnion—The sac surrounding the embryo and fetus containing clear fluid that supports the developing organism.

Apgar—A screening tool developed by Virginia Apgar for newborn infants.

apoptosis—Programmed cell death.

asphyxia—Lack of oxygen.

ataxia—Excessive incoordination and difficulty with balance.

athetoid—Referring to unnecessary, purposeless movements that occur during volitional movements.

bifurcation—A shift in a collective variable between stable modes of behavior resulting in a phase transition.

bradykinesia (also **hypokinesia**)—Slowing of movements.

center of gravity (also **center of body mass**)—The point of concentration of the earth's gravitational pull on an object or individual.

cephalocaudal—From head to foot.

chromosomes—Long, threadlike structures within cell nuclei that contain the genes.

cognition—The act of knowing; perception; awareness.

conceptional age—Prenatal age from fertilization of the egg.

congenital malformations—Anomalies or defects that are present at birth. These can be a result of genetic or environmental factors.

contracture—A permanent shortening of the muscle.

contralateral—Of opposite sides of the body.

coronal—Plane that is parallel to the ground and perpendicular to the spine during standing.

criterion-referenced test—Test that determines whether an infant has achieved some preestablished standard of performance.

digitigrade gait—Gait pattern found in quadrupeds, bipedal monkeys, and apes, in which the toes and not the heels are used during gait.

distal—Away from the trunk toward body's extremities (opposite of **proximal**).

dorsal—Referring to orientation toward the back of the body (opposite of **ventral**).

dystonia—Movement disrupted by changing tone, with fluctuations generally occurring from normal to increased tone.

efferent—Projecting from the central nervous system to the periphery.

empiricist—Believes that all knowledge is based on experience (opposite of **nativist**).

endogenous—Of internal origin (opposite of **exogenous**).

etiology—The cause or causes of disease.

extension—Stretching limbs out from the body (opposite of **flexion**).

flexion—Bending of limbs toward the body (opposite of **extension**).

gestational age (also **postmenstrual age**)—The prenatal period of development, measured from the first day of the mother's last period, generally lasting 40 weeks.

gustation—The sense of taste.

hydrocephalus—An accumulation of cerebrospinal fluid within the cranium, often resulting in enlargement of the head.

hyperkinesia—Excessive movements.

hypertonia—Excessive muscle tone.

hypokinesia (also **bradykinesia**)—Slowing of movements.

hypotonia—Diminished muscle tone.

incidence—The rate at which a certain event occurs.

interlimb—Between two limbs.

intralimb—Within a limb.

intrapartum—Occurring during childbirth or delivery.

intraventricular hemorrhage (IVH)—Bleeding into the ventricles of the brain cerebrum.

ipsilateral—Pertaining to the same side of the body.

kinematics—A description of movement in terms of space and time, including variables such as displacement, velocity, and acceleration.

kinesthesis—The sense of movement providing information on where the body parts are and how they are moving.

kinetics—A description of movement that takes into consideration the importance of force in the production of movement.

lateral—Referring to the side of the body (i.e., the left and right side of the body).

linear system—System in which if x is proportional to y, then x is a linear function of y.

locomotor reflexes—Reflexes named after the voluntary motor responses that they resemble.

maturational approach—View that development is determined through biological maturation.

medial—Close to the midline or center of the body.

morphogenesis—The growth and differentiation of cells and tissues during development.

myelin—A protective lamella or coating around some nerve fibers that is made of nonneuronal glial cells.

myogenic movements—Movements produced by local stimulation of individual muscles without nervous or other external stimulation.

nativist—Believes that all knowledge is innate (opposite of **empiricist**).

neonate—A newborn, usually described as less than one month old.

neurogenesis—The growth and differentiation of nervous tissue during development.

neurogenic movements—Movements generated by the central nervous system through the appropriate motoneuron pool.

norm-referenced test—A test that compares the performance of the individual to that of a normative group.

olfaction—The sense of smell.

ontogenetic—Not general to the species as a whole (see **phylogenetic**) but emerging as part of learning and the environment, for example, handwriting and piano playing.

operant conditioning—Increasing the probability of a particular behavior or response if it has been followed by a reward or reinforcer.

organogenesis—Process in the embryonic period in which body organs and systems are defined.

orienting response—A reduction in motor activity elicited as a result of the infant's attending to a novel stimulus.

periventricular leukomalacia (PVL)—Necrosis of the white matter surrounding the lateral cerebral ventricles.

perturbation—Disturbance of the system.

phase shift—An abrupt shift from one stable behavior to another without stable intermediate states.

phenylketonuria (PKU)—A genetic disorder resulting in the inability to manufacture an enzyme produced in the liver that is necessary for the metabolism of the amino acid phenylalanine. If not diagnosed and properly treated at birth, it can result in severe mental retardation with accompanying behavioral problems.

phylogenetic—Referring to fundamental behavioral activities that occur with the development of the species; biological and resistant to environmental influences (e.g., reaching and walking).

plantigrade gait—The standard heel-to-toe pattern characteristic of the human gait.

plasticity—The ability of the central nervous system to modify its neural connections through training or in response to neural damage.

postmenstrual age (also **gestational age**)—The prenatal period of development, measured from the first day of the mother's last period, generally lasting 40 weeks.

postural reflexes—Reflexes important for maintaining **posture** as the environment changes.

posture—Positions adopted by the body or parts of the body.

prehension—The manual skill of reaching and grasping.

prenatal—Prior to birth.

prereaching—Arm movement toward an object, usually occurring prior to four months of age, that does not usually result in contact with that object.

preterm—Before term age.

prevalence—The total number of cases in existence in a given population at any one time.

primitive reflexes—**Reflexes** that are prenatal in origin.

prone—Lying facedown (opposite of **supine**).

proprioception—The sense that includes tactile, vestibular, and kinesthetic information.

proximal—Close to the trunk of the body (opposite of **distal**).

reflexes—Involuntary actions that are triggered by some kind of external stimulus (also see **primitive, postural,** and **locomotor reflexes**).

schema—An internal representation that organizes and interprets information.

sensitivity—The likelihood that an individual demonstrating a problem at follow-up will be accurately identified by the initial testing (a true positive).

small for gestational age (SGA)—Describes an infant whose birth weight is less than the 10th percentile for that particular gestational age.

somatosensory—Referring to the tactile and kinesthetic senses.

spasticity—**Hypertonia** characterized by increased resistance to passive movement.

specificity—The likelihood that an individual diagnosed without a problem initially will prove to be without that problem at the follow-up testing (a true negative).

spontaneous movements—Movements, not elicited by any apparent stimulus, that are often rhythmical in nature and are prevalent in the fetus and early infancy.

standardization sample—A large representative sample of infants containing individuals who are similar to those being tested by the assessment tool.

supine—Lying flat on the back (opposite of **prone**).

synaptogenesis—The development of the connections, or synapses, between neurons.

teratogens—Substances that produce congenital malformations in utero.

torque—The tendency of force to produce rotation, as in body segments around their joint axes (Enoka, 1994).

ventral—Referring to orientation toward the front of the body (opposite of **dorsal**).

vestibular—Referring to the sensory system responsible for balance and motion perception.

zygote—The name given to the fertilized egg from initial fertilization to implantation in the uterus wall.

references ■■■

Abernethy, B., Burgess-Limerick, R., Engstrom, C., & Neal, R.J. (1995). Temporal coordination of human gait. In D.J. Glencross & J.P. Piek (Eds.), *Motor control and sensory motor integration: Issues and directions* (pp. 171-196). Amsterdam: Elsevier Science.

Abernethy, B., Kippers, V., Mackinnon, L.T., Neal, R.J., & Hanrahan, S. (Eds.). (1996). *The biophysical foundations of human movement.* Melbourne: Macmillan Education Australia.

Accardo, J., Kammann, H., & Hoon, A.H. (2004). Neuroimaging in cerebral palsy. *Journal of Pediatrics, 145,* S19-S27.

Adolph, K.E., Vereijken, B., & Denny, M.A. (1998). Learning to crawl. *Child Development, 69*(5), 1299-1312.

Adolph, K.E., Vereijken, B., & Shrout, P.E. (2003). What changes in infant walking and why. *Child Development, 74,* 475-497.

Aicardi, J. (1992). Neurological diseases in the perinatal period. In J. Aicardi (Ed.), *Diseases of the nervous system in childhood* (pp. 47-105). London: MacKeith Press.

Aicardi, J., & Bax, M. (1992). Cerebral palsy. In J. Aicardi (Ed.), *Diseases of the nervous system in childhood* (pp. 330-374). London: MacKeith Press.

Aicardi, J., & Bax, M. (1998). Cerebral palsy. In J. Aicardi (Ed.), *Diseases of the nervous system in childhood* (2nd Ed.)(pp. 210-239). London: MacKeith Press.

Alexander, R., Boehem, R., & Cupps, B. (1993). *Normal development of functional motor skills: The first year of life.* Tucson, AZ: Therapy Skill Builders.

Allin, M., Henderson, M., Suckling, J., Cosarti, C., Rushe, T., Fearon, P., Stewart, A.L., Bullmore, E.T., Rifkin, L., & Murray, R. (2004). Effects of very low birthweight on brain structure in adulthood. *Developmental Medicine and Child Neurology, 46,* 46-53.

Als, H. (1982). Toward a synactive theory of development: Promise for the assessment and support of infant individuality. *Infant Mental Health Journal, 3,* 229-243.

Als, H. (1986). A synactive model of neonatal behavioral organisation: Framework for the assessment of neurobehavioral development in the premature infant and support of infants and parents in the neonatal intensive care environment. *Physical and Occupational Therapy in Pediatrics, 6,* 3-53.

Als, H. (1989). Self-regulation and motor development in preterm infants. In J.J. Lockman & N.L. Hazen (Eds.), *Action in social context: Perspectives on early development* (pp. 65-97). New York: Plenum Press.

Als, H. (1995). The preterm infant: A model for the study of fetal brain expectation. In J. Lecanuet, W.P. Fifer, N.A. Krasnegor, & W.P. Smotherman (Eds.), *Fetal development: A psychobiological perspective* (pp. 439-471). Hillsdale, NJ: Erlbaum.

Als, H., & Duffy, F.H. (1989). Neurobehavioral assessment in the newborn period: Opportunity for early detection of later learning disabilities and for early intervention. In N.W. Paul (Ed.), *Research in infant assessment.* New York: March of Dimes Birth Defects Foundation.

Als, H., Lester, B., Tronick, E., & Brazelton, T.B. (1982). Manual for the assessment of preterm infants' behavior (APIB). In H. Fitzgerald, B. Lester, & M. Yogman (Eds.), *Theory and research in behavioral pediatrics* (pp. 65-132). New York: Plenum Press.

American Academy of Pediatrics. (1982). Policy statement: The Doman-Delacato treatment of neurologically handicapped children. *Pediatrics, 70,* 810-812.

American Academy of Pediatrics. (1999). Policy statement: The treatment of neurologically impaired children using patterning. *Pediatrics, 104,* 1149-1151.

American Psychiatric Association. (2000). *Diagnostic and statistical manual of mental disorders* (4th ed.). Washington, DC: Author.

Amiel-Tison, C. (1968). Neurological evaluation of the maturity of newborn infants. *Archives of Disability in Children, 43,* 89-93.

Amiel-Tison, C. (2002). Update of the Amiel-Tison Neurological Assessment for the Term Neonate or at 40 weeks corrected age. *Pediatric Neurology, 27,* 196-212.

Anastasi, A. (1968). *Psychological testing.* New York: Macmillan.

Anastasi, A. (1981). Sex differences: Historical perspectives and methodological implications. *Developmental Review, 1,* 187-206.

Angulo-Kinzler, R.M. (2001). Exploration and selection of intralimb coordination patterns in 3-month-old infants. *Journal of Motor Behavior, 33*(4), 363-376.

Angulo-Kinzler, R., & Horn, C.L. (2001). Selection and memory of a lower limb motor-perceptual task in 3-month-old infants. *Infant Behavior and Development, 24,* 239-257.

Angulo-Kinzler, R., Ulrich, B.D., & Thelen, E. (2002). Three-month-old infants can select specific motor solutions. *Motor Control, 6,* 52-68.

Annett, M. (1981). The genetics of handedness. *Trends in Neuroscience, 4,* 256-258.

Annett, M. (1998). Handedness and cerebral dominance: The right shift theory. *Journal of Neuropsychiatry and Clinical Neurosciences, 10*(4), 459-469.

Anson, J.G., & Mawston, G.A. (2000). Patterns of muscle activation in simple reaction-time tasks. In D.J. Weeks, R. Chua, & D. Elliott (Eds.), *Perceptual-motor behavior in Down syndrome* (pp. 3-24). Champaign, IL: Human Kinetics.

Apgar, V. (1953). A proposal for a new method of evaluation of the newborn infant. *Anesthesia and Analgesia, 32,* 260-267.

Apgar, V., & James, L.S. (1962). Further observations on the newborn scoring system. *American Journal of Disabled Children, 104,* 419-428.

Aslin, R.N. (1987). Motor aspects of visual development in infancy. In P. Salapatek & L. Cohen (Eds.), *Handbook of infant perception* (Vol. 1, pp. 43-113). New York: Academic Press.

Assaiante, C. (1998). Development of locomotor balance control in healthy children. *Neuroscience and Biobehavioral Reviews, 22*(4), 527-532.

Assaiante, C., & Amblard, B. (1995). An ontogenetic model for the sensorimotor organization of balance control in humans. *Human Movement Science, 14,* 13-43.

Aylward, G.P. (1995). *The Bayley Infant Neurodevelopmental Screener.* San Antonio: Psychological Corporation.

Aylward, G.P., & Verhulst, S.J. (2000). Predictive utility of the Bayley Infant Neurodevelopmental Screener (BINS) risk status classifications: Clinical interpretation and application. *Developmental Medicine and Child Neurology, 42,* 25-31.

Ayres, A.J. (1972). *Sensory integration and learning disorders.* Los Angeles: Western Psychological Services.

Ballard, J.L., Novak, K.K., & Driver, M. (1979). A simplified score for assessment of fetal maturation of newly born infants. *Journal of Pediatrics, 95,* 769-774.

Banich, M.T. (1997). *Neuropsychology: The neural bases of mental function.* Boston: Houghton Mifflin.

Barela, J.A., Godoi, D., Freitas, J., & Polastri, P.F. (2000). Visual information and body sway coupling in infants during sitting acquisition. *Infant Behavior and Development, 23,* 285-297.

Barela, J.A., Jeka, J.J., & Clarke, J.E. (1999). The use of somatosensory information during the acquisition of independent upright stance. *Infant Behavior and Development, 22*(1), 87-102.

Barnhart, C. L. & Barnhart, R.K. (1982). *The World Book Dictionary.* Chicago: Doubleday & Company Inc.

Barrera, M. E., Rosenbaum, P. L., & Cunningham, C. E. (1987). Corrected and uncorrected Bayley scores: Longitudinal developmental patterns in low and high birth weight preterm infants. *Infant Behavior and Development, 10*(36), 337-346.

Bax, M.C.O. (2003). Editorial: Prevention requires identification—can we do it? *Developmental Medicine and Child Neurology, 45,* 507.

Bayley, N. (1933). *The California First-Year Mental Scale.* Berkeley, CA: University of California Press.

Bayley, N. (1936). *The California Infant Scale of Motor Development.* Berkeley, CA: University of California Press.

Bayley, N. (1965). Comparisons of mental and motor test scores for ages 1-15 months by sex, birth order, race, geographical location, and education of parents. *Child Development, 36,* 379-411.

Bayley, N. (1969). *Manual for the Bayley Scales of Infant Development.* San Antonio: Psychological Corporation.

Bayley, N. (1993). *Manual for the Bayley Scales of Infant Development.* San Antonio: Psychological Corporation.

Bekoff, A. (1981). Embryonic development of the neural circuitry underlying motor coordination. In W.M. Cowan (Ed.), *Studies in developmental neurobiology: Essays in honor of Viktor Hamburger* (pp. 135-170). New York: Oxford University Press.

Bekoff, A. (1995). Development of motor behavior in chick embryos. In J. Lecanuet, W.P. Fifer, N.A. Krasnegor, & W.P. Smotherman (Eds.), *Fetal development: A psychobiological perspective* (pp. 191-204). Hillsdale, NJ: Erlbaum.

Bellefeuille-Reid, D., & Jakubek, S. (1989). Adaptive positioning intervention for premature infants: Issue for paediatric occupational therapy practice. *British Journal of Occupational Therapy, 52*(3), 93-97.

Benezra-Obeiter, R. (1991). Down's syndrome. In M. Gottlieb & J. Williams (Eds.), *Developmental behavioral disorders: Selected topics* (pp. 199-208). New York: Plenum Press.

Bernstein, N.A. (1967). *The coordination and regulation of movements.* London: Pergamon Press.

Bernstein, N. (1984). Some emergent problems of the regulation of motor acts. In H.T.A. Whiting (Ed.), *Human motor actions: Bernstein reassessed* (pp. 343-371). Amsterdam: North-Holland.

Bertenthal, B.I. (2001). Developmental changes in postural control during infancy. In J. van der Kamp, A. Ledebt, G. Savelsbergh, & E. Thelen (Eds.), *Advances in motor development and learning in infancy* (pp. 19-22). Amsterdam: Print Partners Ipskamp.

Bertenthal, B.I., Boker, S.M., & Minquan, X. (2000). Analysis of the perception-action cycle for visually inducted postural sway in 9-month-old sitting infants. *Infant Behavior and Development, 23,* 299-315.

Bertenthal, B., & von Hofsten, C. (1998). Eye, head and trunk control: The foundation for manual development. *Neuroscience and Biobehavioral Reviews, 22*(4), 515-520.

Best, C. (1988). The emergence of cerebral asymmetries in early human development: A literature review and a neuroembryological model. In D.L. Molfese & S.J. Segalowitz (Eds.), *Brain lateralisation in children: Developmental implications* (pp. 5-34). New York: Guilford Press.

Bigsby, R. (1983). Reaching and asymmetrical tonic neck reflex in pre-term and full-term infants. *Physical and Occupational Therapy in Pediatrics, 3*(4), 25-42.

Birnholz, J.C. (1988). On observing the human fetus. In W.P. Smotherman & S.R. Robinson (Eds.), *Behavior of the fetus* (pp. 47-60). Caldwell, NJ: Telford.

Birnholz, J.C., & Benaceraff, B.R. (1983). The development of human fetal hearing. *Science, 222,* 516-518.

Bishop, D.V.M. (1990). *Handedness and developmental disorder.* Hillsdale, NJ: Erlbaum.

Black, L.S., deRegnier, R.-A., Long, J., Georgieff, M.K., & Nelson, C.A. (2004). Electrographic imaging of recognition memory in 34-38 week gestation intrauterine growth restricted newborns. *Experimental Neurology, 190* Suppl 1, S72-83.

Blair, E. (2001). Trends in cerebral palsy. *Indian Journal of Pediatrics, 68,* 433-437.

Blair, E., & Stanley, F.J. (1982) An epidemiological study of cerebral palsy in WA, 1956-1975 - III Postnatal aetiology. *Developmental Medicine & Child Neurology, 24,* 575-585.

Blair, E., & Stanley, F. (1993a). Aetiological pathways to spastic cerebral palsy. *Paediatric and Perinatal Epidemiology, 7,* 302-317.

Blair, E., & Stanley, F. (1993b). When can cerebral palsy be prevented? The generation of causal hypothesis by multivariate analysis of a case-control study. *Paediatric and Perinatal Epidemiology, 7,* 272-301.

Blaymore-Bier, J., Pezzulo, J., Kim, E., Oh, W., Garcia-Coll, C., & Vohr, B.R. (1994). Outcome of extremely low birth weight infants: 1980-1990. *Acta Paediatric, 83,* 1244-1248.

Bloch, H., & Carchon, I. (1992). On the onset of eye-hand co-ordination in infants. *Behavioral Brain Research, 49,* 85-90.

Block, M.E. (1991). Motor development in children with Down syndrome: A review of the literature. *Adapted Physical Activity Quarterly, 8,* 179-209.

Bly, L. (1991). A historical and current view of the basis of NDT. *Pediatric Physical Therapy,* 131-135.

Bly, L. (1994). *Motor skills acquisition in the first year: An illustrated guide to normal development.* Tucson, AZ: Therapy Skill Builders.

Bobath, K. (1980). *A neurophysiological basis for the treatment of cerebral palsy.* London: William Heinemann Medical Books.

Bodnarchuk, J.L., & Eaton, W.O. (2004). Can parent reports be trusted? Validity of daily checklists of gross motor milestone attainment. *Applied Developmental Psychology, 25,* 481-490.

Boehme, R. (1990). *Approach to treatment of the baby.* Tucson, AZ: Therapy Skill Builders.

Böhm, B., Katz-Salamon, M., Smedler, A-C., Lagercrantz, H., & Forssberg, H. (2002). Developmental risks and protective factors for influencing cognitive outcome at 5.5 years of age in very-low-birthweight children. *Developmental Medicine and Child Neurology, 44,* 508-516.

Bottos, M., Benedetti, M., Salucci, P., Gasparroni, V., & Giannini, S. (2003). Botulinum toxin with and without casting in ambulant children with spastic diplegia: A clinical and functional assessment. *Developmental Medicine and Child Neurology, 45,* 758-762.

Bottos, M., Dalla Barba, B., Stefani, D., Pettena, G., Tonin, C., & D'Este, A. (1989). Locomotor strategies preceding independent walking: Prospective study of neurological and language development in 424 cases. *Developmental Medicine and Child Neurology, 31,* 25-34.

Bottos, M., & Stefani, D. (1982). Postural and motor care of the premature baby. *Developmental Medicine and Child Neurology, 24,* 706-707.

Bower, T.G.R. (1977). *A primer of infant development.* San Francisco: Freeman.

Bower, T.G.R., Broughton, J.M., & Moore, M.K. (1970). Demonstration of intention in the reaching behavior of neonate humans. *Nature, 228,* 679-681.

Bradshaw, J.L. (2003). Developmental disorders of the frontostriatal system: Neuropsychological, neuropsychiatric and evolutionary perspectives. *Archives of Clinical Neuropsychology, 18,* 215-217.

Brazelton, T.B. (1973). *Neonatal Behavioral Assessment Scale.* Philadelphia: Lippincott.

Brazelton, T.B. (1984). *Neonatal Behavioral Assessment Scale.* Philadelphia: Lippincott.

Brazelton, T.B., & Nugent, J. (1995). *Neonatal Behavioral Assessment Scale. Clinics in Developmental Medicine* (No. 50). London: MacKeith Press.

Brenière, Y. (1996). Why we walk the way we do. *Journal of Motor Behavior, 2,* 291-298.

Brenière, Y. (1999). How locomotor parameters adapt to gravity and body structure changes during gait development in children. *Motor Control, 3,* 186-204.

Brenneman, S.K. (1994). Tests of infant and child development. In J.S. Tecklin (Ed.), *Pediatric physical therapy* (pp. 24-55). Philadelphia: Lippincott.

Bricker, D. (1993). *Assessment, evaluation, and programming system for infants and children: Vol. 1: AEPS measurement for birth to 3 years.* Baltimore: Brookes.

Brigance, A.H. (1991). *Revised Brigance Diagnostic Inventory of Early Development.* North Billerica, MA: Curriculum Associates.

Bril, B., & Brenière, Y. (1989). Steady-state velocity and temporal structure of gait during the first six months of autonomous walking. *Human Movement Science, 8,* 99-122.

Brown, J.L. (1964). States in newborn infants. *Merrill-Palmer Quarterly, 10,* 313-327.

Bruner, J.S. (1970). The growth and structure of skill. In K.J. Connolly (Ed.), *Mechanisms of motor skill development* (pp. 63-92). London: Academic Press.

Burns, Y., O'Callaghan, M., McDonell, B., & Rogers, Y. (2004). Movement and motor development in ELBW infants at 1 year is related to cognitive and motor abilities at 4 years. *Early Human Development, 80,* 19-29.

Burns, Y.R., O'Callaghan, M., & Tudehope, D.I. (1989). Early identification of cerebral palsy in high risk infants. *Australian Paediatric Journal, 25,* 214-219.

Burton, A.W., & Miller, D.E. (1998). *Movement skill assessment.* Champaign, IL: Human Kinetics.

Butler, C., & Darrah, J. (2001). Effects of neurodevelopmental treatment (NDT) for cerebral palsy: An AACPDM evidence report. *Developmental Medicine and Child Neurology, 43,* 778-790.

Butterworth, G., & Hopkins, B. (1988). Hand-mouth coordination in the new-born baby. *British Journal of Developmental Psychology, 6,* 303-314.

Campbell, S.B., & Kolobe, T.H.A. (2000). Concurrent validity of the Test of Infant Motor Performance with the Alberta Infant Motor Scale. *Pediatric Physical Therapy, 12,* 1-8.

Campbell, S.K. (1986). Organisational and educational considerations in creating an environment to promote optimal development of high-risk neonates. *Physical and Occupational Therapy in Pediatrics, 6,* 191-204.

Campbell, S.K. (1993). Future Directions for physical therapy in early infancy. In I.J. Wilhelm (Ed.), *Physical therapy assessment in early infancy* (pp. 293-308). New York: Churchill Livingston.

Campbell, S.K., Kolobe, T., Osten, E.T., Lenke, M., & Girolami, G.L. (1995). Construct validity of the test of infant motor performance. *Physical Therapy, 75,* 585-597.

Campbell, S.K., Kolobe, T.H.A., Wright, B.D., & Linacre, J.M. (2002). Validity of the test of infant motor performance for prediction of 6-, 9- and 12-month scores on the Alberta Infant Motor Scale. *Developmental Medicine and Child Neurology, 44,* 263-272.

Campos, J.J., Anderson, D.I., Barbu-Roth, M., Hubbard, E.M., Hertenstein, M.J., & Witherington, D.C. (2000). Travel broadens the mind. *Infancy, 1*(2), 149-219.

Campos, J., Hiatt, S., Ramsay, D., Henderson, C., & Svejda, M. (1978). The emergence of fear on the visual cliff. In M.L.L. Rosenblum (Ed.), *The development of affect.* New York: Plenum.

Capute, A.J., Palmer, F.B., Shapiro, B.K., Ross, A., & Accardo, P.J. (1984). Primitive reflex profile: A quantitation of primitive reflexes in infancy. *Developmental Medicine and Child Neurology, 26,* 375-383.

Capute, A.J., Shapiro, B.K., Palmer, F.B., Ross, A., & Wachtel, R.C. (1985). Normal gross motor development: The influences of race, sex and socio-economic status. *Developmental Medicine and Child Neurology, 27,* 635-643.

Carmichael, L. (1946). The onset and early development of behavior. In L. Carmichael (Ed.), *Manual of child psychology* (pp. 43-166). New York: Wiley.

Case-Smith, J. (1991). *Posture and fine motor assessment of infants.* Rockville, MD: American Occupational Therapy Foundation.

Case-Smith, J. (1992). A validity study of the posture and fine motor assessment of infants. *American Journal of Occupational Therapy, 46,* 597-605.

Case-Smith, J., & Bigsby, R. (2001). Motor assessment. In L.T. Singer & P.S. Zeskind (Eds.), *Biobehavioral assessment of the infant* (pp. 423-442). New York: Guilford Press.

Casey, B.M., McIntire, D.D., & Leveno, K.J. (2001). The continuing value of the apgar score for the assessment of newborn infants. *New England Journal of Medicine, 344*(7), 467-471.

Cesari, P., & Newell, K.M. (2000). Body-scaled transitions in human grip configurations. *Journal of Experimental Psychology: Human Perception and Performance, 26*(5), 1657-1668.

Chandler, L.S., Andrews, M.S., & Swanson, M.W. (1980). *Movement assessment of infants.* Rolling Bay, WA: Authors.

Changeux, J-P. (1997). Letters to the editor: Variation and selection in neural function. *Trends in Neuroscience, 20,* 291-293.

Changeux, J., & Danchin, A. (1976). Selective stabilisation of the developing synapses as a mechanism for the specification of neural networks. *Nature, 264,* 705-713.

Changeux, J.-P., & Dehaene, S. (1989). Neuronal models of cognitive functions. *Cognition, 33,* 63-109.

Charlton, J.L., Ihsen, E., & Lavelle, B.M. (2000). Control of manual skills in children with Down syndrome. In D.J. Weeks, R. Chua, & D. Elliott (Eds.), *Perceptual-motor behavior in Down syndrome* (pp. 25-48). Champaign, IL: Human Kinetics.

Chen, Y.-P., Fetters, L., Holt, K.G., & Saltzman, E. (2002). Making the mobile move: Constraining task and environment. *Infant Behavior and Development, 25,* 195-220.

Cioni, G., Duchini, F., Milianti, B., Paolicelli, P.B., Sicola, E., Boldrini, A., et al. (1993). Differences and variations in the patterns of early independent walking. *Early Human Development, 35,* 193-201.

Cioni, G., & Prechtl, H.F.R. (1988). Development of posture and motility in preterm infants. In C. von Euler, H. Forssberg, & H. Lagercrantz (Eds.), *Neurobiology of early infant behaviour* (pp. 69-78). Stockholm: Stockton Press.

Cioni, G., & Prechtl, H.F.R. (1990). Preterm and early posterm motor behaviour in low-risk premature infants. *Early Human Development, 2,* 159-191.

Clark, J., & Phillips, S.J. (1993). A longitudinal study of intralimb coordination in the first year of independent walking: A dynamical systems analysis. *Child Development, 64,* 1143-1157.

Clark, J.E., Truly, T.L., & Phillips, S.J. (1993). On the development of walking as a limit-cycle system. In L.B. Smith & E. Thelen (Eds.), *A dynamical systems approach to development: Applications* (pp. 71-93). Cambridge, MA: MIT Press.

Clark, J.E. & Whitall, J. (1989). What is motor development? The lessons of history. *Quest, 41,* 183-202.

Clark, J.E., Whitall, J., & Phillips, S.J. (1988). Human interlimb coordination: The first 6 months of independent walking. *Developmental Psychobiology, 21*(5), 445-456.

Clifton, R.K., Rochat, P., Robin, D.J., & Bertheir, N.E. (1994). Multimodal perception in the control of infant reaching. *Journal of Experimental Psychology: Human Perception & Performance, 20,* 876-886

Clopton, N.A., Duvall, T., Ellis, B., Musser, M., & Varghese, S. (2000). Investigation of trunk and extremity movement associated with passive head turning in newborns. *Physical Therapy, 80*(2), 152-159.

Cogher, L., Savage, E., & Smith, M.F. (1992). *Cerebral palsy: The child and young person.* Cambridge: Cambridge University Press.

Cohen, L.B. (1998). An information-processing approach to infant perception and cognition. In F. Simion & G. Butterworth (Eds.), *The development of sensory, motor, and cognitive capacities in early infancy* (pp. 277-301). Hove, Sussex: Psychological Press.

Connolly, K.J. (Ed.). (1970). *Mechanisms of motor skill development.* London: Academic Press.

Connolly, K., & Dalgleish, M. (1989). The emergence of a tool-using skill in infancy. *Developmental Psychology, 25,* 894-912.

Connolly, K., & Dalgleish, M. (1993). Individual patterns of tool use by infants. In A.F. Kalverboer, B. Hopkins, & R. Geuze (Eds.), *Motor development in early and later childhood: Longitudinal approaches* (pp. 174-204). Cambridge: Cambridge University Press.

Corbetta, D., & Bojczyk, K.E. (2002). Infants return to two-handed reaching when they are learning to walk. *Journal of Motor Behavior, 34*(1), 83-95.

Corbetta, D., & Thelen, E. (1994). Interlimb coordination in the development of reaching. In J.H.A. van Rossum & J.I. Laszlo (Eds.), *Motor development: Aspects of normal and delayed development.* Amsterdam: Free University Press.

Corbetta, D., & Thelen, E. (1999). Lateral biases and fluctuations in infants' spontaneous arm movements and reaching. *Developmental Psychobiology, 34,* 237-255.

Corbetta, D., & Thelen, E. (2002). Behavioral fluctuations and the development of manual asymmetries in infancy: Contributions of the dynamic systems approach. In S.J. Segalowitz & I. Rapin (Eds.), *Handbook of neuropsychology* (2nd ed., pp. 311-330). Philadelphia, PA: Elsevier Science.

Corbetta, D., Thelen, E., & Johnson, K. (2000). Motor constraints on the development of perception-action matching in infant reaching. *Infant Behavior and Development, 23,* 351-374.

Coryell, J., Henderson, A., & Liederman, J. (1982). Factors influencing the asymmetrical tonic neck reflex in normal infants. *Comparative*

Performance Levels of Female and Male Infants With Down Syndrome, 2(3), 51-65.

Cowden, J.E., Sayers, K.L., & Torrey, C.C. (1998). *Pediatric adapted motor development and exercise: An innovative, multisystem approach for professionals and families.* Springfield, IL: Charles C Thomas.

Cratty, B.J. (1994). *Clumsy child syndromes: Descriptions, evaluations and remediation.* Langhorne, PA: Harwood Academic Press.

Crook, C. (1987). Taste and olfaction. In P. Salapatek & L. Cohen (Eds.), *Handbook of infant perception: Vol. 1. From sensation to perception.* New York: Academic Press.

Dammann, O., Dammann, C.E.L., Allred, E.N., & Veelken, N. (2001). Fetal growth restriction is not associated with a reduced risk for bilateral spastic cerebral palsy in very-low-birthweight infants. *Early Human Development, 64,* 79-89.

D'Angio, C.T., Sinkin, R.A., Stevens, T.P., Landfish, N.K., Merzbach, J.L., Ryan, R.M., et al. (2002). Longitudinal, 15-year follow-up of children born at less than 29 weeks gestation after introduction of surfactant therapy into a region: Neurologic, cognitive, and educational outcomes. *Pediatrics, 110,* 1094-1102.

Darrah, J., Piper, M., & Watt, M.J. (1998a). Assessment of gross motor skills of at risk infants: Predictive validity of the Alberta Infant Motor Scale. *Developmental Medicine and Child Neurology, 40,* 485-491.

Darrah, J., Redfern, L., Maguire, T.O., Beaulne, A.P., & Watt, J. (1998b). Intra-individual stability of rate of gross motor development in full-term infants. *Early Human Development, 52,* 169-179.

Davis, D.W., Thelen, E., & Keck, J. (1994). Treadmill stepping in infants born prematurely. *Early Human Development, 39,* 211-223.

Davis, W.E., & Kelso, J.A.S. (1982). Analysis of "invariant characteristics" in the motor control of Down syndrome and normal subjects. *Journal of Motor Behavior, 14,* 194-212.

DeGangi, G.A., & Royeen, C.B. (1994). Current practice among neurodevelopmental treatment association members. *American Journal of Occupational Therapy, 48*(9), 803-809.

de Graaf, E.A.B. (1995). Early intervention for children with Down syndrome. In A. Vermeer & W.E. Davis (Eds.), *Physical and motor development in mental retardation* (Vol. 40, pp. 120-143). Basel: Karger.

Delacato, C.H. (1963). *The diagnosis and treatment of speech and reading problems.* Springfield, IL: Charles C Thomas.

Delacato, C.H. (1966) *Neurological organization and reading.* Springfield, IL: Charles C Thomas.

Deschênes, G., Gosselin, J., Couture, M., & Lachance, C. (2004). Interobserver reliability of the Amiel-Tison Neurological Assessment at term. *Pediatric Neurology, 30,* 190-194.

de Vries, J.I.P., Visser, G.H.A., & Prechtl, H.F.R. (1982). The emergence of fetal behaviour. I. Qualitative aspects. *Early Human Development, 7,* 301-322.

de Vries, J.I.P., Visser, G.H.A., & Prechtl, H.F.R. (1985). The emergence of fetal behaviour. II. Quantitative aspects. *Early Human Development, 12,* 99-120.

de Vries, J.I.P., Visser, G.H.A., & Prechtl, H.F.R. (1988). The emergence of fetal behaviour. III. Individual differences and consistencies. *Early Human Development, 16,* 85-103.

de Vries, J.I.P., Wimmers, R.H., Ververs, I.A.P., Hopkins, B., Savelsbergh, G.J.P., & van Geijn, H.P. (2001). Fetal handedness and head preference: A developmental study. *Developmental Psychobiology, 39,* 171-178.

de Vries, L.S., Van Haastert, I.L., Rademaker, K.J., Koopman, C., & Groenendaal, F. (2004). Ultrasound abnormalities preceding cerebral palsy in high-risk preterm infants. *Journal of Pediatrics, 144,* 815-820.

Diamond, A. (2000). Close interrelation of motor development and cognitive development and of the cerebellum and prefrontal cortex. *Child Development, 71*(1), 44-56.

Donker, S.F., Wagenaar, R.C., Beek, P.J., & Mulder, T. (2001). Coordination between arm and leg movements during locomotion. *Journal of Motor Behavior, 33*(1), 86-102.

Down, J.L. (1866). Observations on an ethnic classification of idiots. *London Hospital Clinical Lectures and Reports, 3,* 259-262.

Doyle, J.M., Echevarria, S., & Parker, W. (2003). Race/ethnicity, Apgar and infant mortality. *Population Research and Policy Review, 22,* 41-64.

Doyle, L.W., & Casalaz, D. (2001). Outcome at 14 years of extremely low birthweight infants: A regional study. *Archives of Disease in Childhood. Fetal and Neonatal Edition, 85*(3), F159-F164.

Drachman, D. B., & Sokoloff, L. (1966). The role of movement in embryonic joint development. *Developmental Biology, 14,* 401-420.

Drage, J.S., Kennedy, C., & Schwarz, B.K. (1964). The Apgar scores as an index of neonatal mortality: A report from the collaborative study of cerebral palsy. *Obstetrics and Gynecology, 1964,* 222-230.

Droit, S., Boldrini, A., & Cioni, G. (1996). Rhythmical leg movements in low-risk and brain-damaged preterm infants. *Early Human Development, 44,* 210-213.

Dubowitz, L. & Dubowitz, V. (1981). *The neurological assessment of the preterm and full-term newborn infant. Clinics in Developmental Medicine No. 79.* London: Spastics International Medical Publications.

Dworkin, P.H. (1989). British and American recommendations for developmental monitoring: The role of surveillance. *Pediatrics, 84,* 1000-1010.

Dyck, M.J., Hay, D.A., Anderson, M., Smith, L.M., Piek, J.P., & Hallmayer, J. (2004). Is the discrepancy criterion for defining developmental disorders valid? *Journal of Child Psychology and Psychiatry, 45,* 979-995.

Dyck, M.J., Piek, J.P., Kane, R. , Hay, D.A., Smith, L.M., & Hallmayer, J. How does the structure of ability vary across childhood? Submitted for publication.

Edelman, G. (2001). Building a picture of the brain. In G.M. Edelman & J.-P. Changeux (Eds.), *The brain* (pp. 37-69). Somerset, NJ: Transaction.

Edelman, G.M. (1987). *Neural Darwinism.* New York: Basic Books.

Edelman, G., & Mountcastle, V. (1978). *The mindful brain.* Cambridge, MA: MIT Press.

Edwards, S., & Yuen, H.K. (1989). An intervention program for a fraternal twin with Down syndrome. *American Journal of Occupational Therapy, 44*(3), 454-458.

Einarsson-Backes, L.M., & Stewart, K.B. (1992). Infant neuromotor assessments: A review and preview of selected instruments. *American Journal of Occupational Therapy, 46*(3), 224-232.

Einspieler, C., Prechtl, H.F.R., Ferrari, F., Cioni, G., & Bos, A.F. (1997). The qualitative assessment of general movements in preterm, term and young infants—review of the methodology. *Early Human Development, 50,* 47-60.

Ellison, P. (1994). *The INFANIB: A reliable method for the neuromotor assessment of infants.* Tucson, AZ: Therapy Skill Builders.

Enoka, R.M. (Ed.). (1994). *Neuromechanical basis of kinesiology.* (2nd Ed.). Champaign, IL: Human Kinetics.

Erberich, S.G., Friedlich, P., Seri, I., Nelson, M.D., & Bluml, S. (2003). Functional MRI in neonates using neonatal head coil and MR compatible incubator. *NeuroImage, 20,* 683-692.

Eswaran, H., Lowery, C.L., Wilson, J.D., Murphy, P., & Preissl, H. (in press). Functional development of the visual system in human fetus using magnetoencephalography. *Experimental Neurology.*

Evans, P.M., & Alberman, E. (1985). Recording motor defects of children with cerebral palsy. *Developmental Medicine and Child Neurology, 27,* 401-406.

Fagard, J. (2000). Linked proximal and distal changes in the reaching behaviour of 5 to 12-month-old human infants grasping objects of different sizes. *Infant Behavior and Development, 23,* 317-329.

Ferrari, F., Cioni, G., & Prechtl, H.F.R. (1990). Qualitative changes of general movements in preterm infants with brain lesions. *Early Human Development, 23*, 193-231.

Fetters, L. (1986). Sensorimotor management of the high risk neonate. *Physical and Occupational Therapy in Pediatrics, 6*, 217-229.

Fetters, L. (1991). Measurement and treatment in cerebral palsy: An argument for a new approach. *Physical Therapy, 71*(3), 244-247.

Fetters, L., Chen, Y.-P., Jonsdottir, J., & Tronick, E. (2004). Kicking coordination captures differences between full-term and premature infants with white matter disorder. *Human Movement Science, 22*, 729-748.

Fetters, L., Fernandez, B., & Cermak, S.A. (1989). The relationship of proximal and distal components in the development of reaching. *Journal of Human Movement Studies, 12*, 832.

Fetters, L., & Kluzik, J. (1996). The effects of neurodevelopmental treatment versus practice on the reaching of children with spastic cerebral palsy. *Physical Therapy, 76*(4), 346-358.

Fetters, L., & Todd, J. (1987). Quantitative assessment of infant reaching movements. *Journal of Motor Behavior, 19*, 147-166.

Fisher, A.G., & Bundy, A.C. (1992). Sensory integration theory. In H. Forssberg & H. Hirschfeld (Eds.), *Movement disorders in children* (pp. 16-20). Basel: Karger.

Folio, M.R., & Fewell, R.R. (1983). *Peabody Developmental Motor Scales and Activity Cards.* Austin, TX: PRO-ED.

Fonseca, S.T., Holt, K.G., Saltzman, E., & Fetters, L. (2001). A dynamical model of locomotion in spastic hemiplegic cerebral palsy: Influence of walking speed. *Clinical Biomechanics, 16*, 793-805.

Forssberg, H. (1985). Ontogeny of human motor locomotor control I. Infant stepping supported locomotion and transition to independent locomotion. *Experimental Brain Research, 57*, 480-493.

Forssberg, H., & Hirschfeld, H. (1992). *Movement disorders in children* (Vol. 36). Basel: Karger.

Forssberg, H., & Hirschfeld, H. (1994). Postural adjustments in sitting humans following external perturbations: Muscle activity and kinematics. *Experimental Brain Research, 97*, 515-527.

Foulder-Hughes, L.A., & Cooke, R.W.I. (2003). Motor, cognitive, and behavioural disorders in children born very preterm. *Developmental Medicine and Child Neurology, 45*, 97-103.

Frankenburg, W.K., & Dodds, J.B. (1967). The Denver Developmental Screening Test. *Journal of Pediatrics, 71*, 181-191.

Frankenburg, W. K., Dodds, J. B., Fandal, A.W., Kazuk, E., & Cohrs, M. (1975). *The Denver Developmental Screening Test.* (Rev. ed.). Denver: University of Colorado Medical Centre.

Frankenburg, W.K., Dodds, J.B., Fandal, A.W., Kazuk, E., & Cohrs, M. (1992). The Denver II: A major revision and restandardization of the Denver Developmental Screening Test. *Pediatrics, 89,* 91-97.

Freedland, R.L., & Bertenthal, B.I. (1994). Developmental changes in interlimb coordination: Transition to hands-and-knees crawling. *Psychological Science, 5*(1), 26-31.

French, N.P., Hagan, R., Evans, S.F., Godfrey, M., & Newnham, J.P. (1999). Repeated antenatal corticosteroids: Size at birth and subsequent development. *American Journal of Obstetrics and Gynecology, 180,* 114-121.

French, N.P., Hagan, R., Evans, S.F., Mullan, A., & Newnham, J.P. (2004). Repeated antenatal corticosteroids: Effects on cerebral palsy and childhood behavior. *American Journal of Obstetrics and Gynecology, 190,* 588-595.

Furuno, S., O'Reilly, K.A., Hosaka, C.M., Inatsuka, T.T., Allman, T.L., & Zeisloft, B., (1985). *Hawaii Early Learning Profile - activity guide.* Palo Alto, CA: VORT.

Gallahue, D.L., & Ozmun, J.C. (1998). *Understanding motor development: Infants, children, adolescents, adults.* Boston: McGraw Hill.

Galloway, J.C., & Thelen, E. (2004). Feet first: Object exploration in young infants. *Infant Behavior and Development, 27,* 107-112.

Garrett, B. (2003). *Brain and behavior.* Belmont, CA: Wadsworth/Thomson Learning.

Gasson, N., Piek, J.P., Barrett, N.C., & Dewey, D. (2005). *Predicting developmental outcomes at 3 and 4 years from infant performance.* Paper presented at the 2nd International Congress on Motor Development and Learning in Infancy. Murcia, Spain, May.

Geerdink, J., Hopkins, B., Beek, W., & Heriza, C. (1996). The organisation of leg movements in preterm and full-term infants after term age. *Developmental Psychobiology, 29*(4), 335-351.

Gentile, A.M. (1992). The nature of skill acquisition: Therapeutic implications for children with movement disorders. In H. Forssberg & H. Hirschfeld (Eds.), *Movement disorders in children* (Vol. 36, pp. 31-40). Basel: Karger.

Gesell, A. (1925). *The mental growth of the preschool child: Infancy through adolescence.* New York: Macmillan.

Gesell, A. (1946). The ontogenesis of infant behavior. In L. Carmichael (Ed.), *Manual of child psychology* (pp. 295-331). New York: Wiley.

Gesell, A. (1952). *Infant development: The embryology of early human behavior.* London: Hamish Hamilton.

Gesell, A., & Amatruda, C.S. (1941). *Developmental diagnosis.* New York: Hoeber.

Gesell, A., & Amatruda, C. (1945). *The embryology of behavior.* Westport, CT: Greenwood Press.

Gesell, A., & Amatruda, C.S. (1947). *Developmental diagnosis: Normal and abnormal child development: Clinical methods and pediatric applications.* New York: Hoeber.

Gesell, A., & Ames, L.B. (1940). The ontogenetic organisation of prone behavior in human infancy. *Journal of Genetic Psychology, 56,* 247-263.

Gesell, A., & Ames, L.B. (1947). The development of handedness. *Journal of Genetic Psychology, 70,* 155-175.

Gibson, E.J. (1982). The concept of affordances in development: The renascence of functionalism. In W.A. Collins (Ed.), *The concept of development: The Minnesota symposium on child psychology* (Vol. 15, pp. 55-81). Hillsdale, NJ: Erlbaum.

Gibson, E.J., & Walk, R.D. (1960). The "visual cliff." *Scientific American, 202,* 64-71.

Gibson, E.. & Gibson, J.J. (1991). The senses as information-seeking systems. In E. J. Gibson (Ed.) *An odyssey in learning and perception* (pp. 503-510). Cambridge, MA: MIT Press.

Gibson, J.J. (1977). The theory of affordances. In R. Shaw & J. Bransford (Eds.), *Perceiving, acting and knowing: Toward an ecological psychology* (pp. 67-82). Hillsdale, NJ: Wiley.

Gibson, J.J. (1979). *The ecological approach to visual perception.* Boston: Houghton Mifflin.

Glanzman, A.M., Kim, H., Swaminathan, K., & Beck, T. (2004). Efficacy of botulinum toxin A, serial casting, and combined treatment for spastic equinus: A retrospective analysis. *Developmental Medicine and Child Neurology, 46,* 807-811.

Glencross, D.J. (1977). Control of skilled movements. *Psychological Bulletin, 84,* 14-29.

Goldfield, E. (1989). Transition from rocking to crawling: Postural constraints on infant movement. *Experimental Psychology, 25*(6), 913-919.

Goodman, J.F. (1990). Infant intelligence: Do we, can we, should we assess it? In C.R. Reynolds & K.W. Kamphaus (Eds.), *Handbook of psychological and educational assessment of children: Intelligence and achievement.* New York: Guilford Press.

Gortner, L., van Husen, M., Thyen, U., Gembruch, U., Friedrich, H., & Landmann, E. (2003). Outcome in preterm small for gestational age infants compared to appropriate for gestational age preterms at the age of 2 years: A prospective study. *European Journal of Obstetrics, Gynecology, and Reproductive Biology, 110,* S93-S97.

Gould, E., Reeves, A.J., Graziano, M.S.A., & Gross, C.G. (1999). Neurogenesis in the neocortex of adult primates. *Science, 286,* 548-552.

Goyen, T.-A., & Lui, K. (2002). Longitudinal motor development of "apparently normal" high-risk infants at 18 months, 3 and 5 years. *Early Human Development, 70,* 103-115.

Goyen, T.-A., Veddovi, M., & Lui, K. (2003). Developmental outcome of discordant premature twins at 3 years. *Early Human Development, 73,* 27-37.

Greenough, W.T., Black, J., & Wallace, C.S. (1987). Experience and brain development. *Child Development, 58,* 539-559.

Greenwood, C.R., Luze, G.J., Cline, G., Kuntz, S., & Leitschuh, C. (2002). Developing a general outcome measure of growth in movement for infants and toddlers. *Topics in Early Childhood Special Education, 22,* 143-157.

Griffiths, R. (1970) *The abilities of young children.* London: Child Development Research Centre.

Griffiths, R. (1984) *The abilities of young children.* Amersham: ARICD.

Grillner, S. (1975). Locomotion in vertebrates: Central mechanisms and reflex interaction. *Physiological Review, 55,* 247-304.

Haas, G., & Diener, H.C. (1988). Development of stance control in children. In B. Amblard, A. Berthoz, & F. Clarac (Eds.), *Posture and gait: Development, adaptation, and modulation* (pp. 49-58). Amsterdam: Elsevier.

Hack, M., Friedman, H., & Fanaroff, A.A. (1996). Outcomes of extremely low birth weight infants. *Pediatrics, 98*(5), 931-936.

Hadders-Algra, M. (1996). The assessment of general movements is a valuable technique for the detection of brain dysfunction in young infants. *Acta Paediatrica, 416,* 39-43.

Hadders-Algra, M. (2002). Variability in infant motor behaviour: A hallmark of a healthy nervous system. *Infant Behavior and Development, 25,* 433-451.

Hadders-Algra, M., Brogren, E., & Forssberg, H. (1996). Ontogeny of postural adjustments during sitting in infancy: Variation, selection and modulation. *Journal of Physiology, 493,* 273-288.

Hadders-Algra, M., Klip-Van den Nieuwendijk, A., Martijn, A., & van Eykern, L. (1997). Assessment of general movements: Towards a better understanding of a sensitive method to evaluate brain function in young infants. *Developmental Medicine and Child Neurology, 39,* 89-99.

Hadders-Algra, M., & Prechtl, H.F.R. (1992). Developmental course of general movements in early infancy: Descriptive analysis of change in form. *Early Human Development, 28,* 201-213.

Hadders-Algra, M., & Prechtl, H.F.R. (1993). EMG correlates of general movements in healthy preterm infants. *Journal of Physiology, 49,* 330.

Hadders-Algra, M., Van Eykern, A.W.J., den Nieuwendijk, K.-V., & Prechtl, H.F.R. (1992). Developmental course of general movements in early infancy. II. EMG correlates. *Early Human Development, 28,* 231-251.

Haehl, V., Vardaxis, V., & Ulrich, B. (2000). Learning to cruise: Bernstein's theory applied to skill acquisition during infancy. *Human Movement Science, 19,* 685-715.

Hagberg, B., Hagberg, G., Beckung, E., & Uverant, P. (2001). Changing panorama of cerebral palsy in Sweden. VIII. Prevalence and origin in the birth year period 1991-1994. *Acta Paediatrica, 90,* 271-277.

Hagberg, B., Hagberg, G., & Olow, I. (1993). The changing panorama of cerebral palsy in Sweden. IV. Prevalence and origin during the birth year period 1983-1986. *Acta Paediatrica, 82,* 387-393.

Haley, S.M., Coster, W.J., Ludlow, L.H., Haltiwanger, J., & Andrellos, P.J. (1992). *Pediatric evaluation of disability inventory.* Boston: New England Medical Center Hospitals.

Halverson, H.M. (1931). An experimental study of prehension in infants by means of systematic cinema records. *Genetic Psychology Monographs, 10,* 107-286.

Halverson, H.M. (1937a). Studies of the grasping responses of early infancy: I. *Journal of Genetic Psychology, 12,* 371-392.

Halverson, H.M. (1937b). Studies of the grasping responses of early infancy: II. *Journal of Genetic Psychology, 12,* 393-424.

Halverson, H.M. (1937c). Studies of the grasping responses of early infancy: III. *Journal of Genetic Psychology, 12,* 425-449.

Hamburger, V., & Oppenheim, R. (1967). Prehatching motility and hatching behavior in the chick. *Journal of Experimental Zoology, 166,* 171-204.

Hamburger, V., & Oppenheim, R. (1982). Naturally occurring cell death in vertebrates. *Neuroscience Comment, 1,* 39-55.

Hamilton, A. (1981). *Nature and nurture: Aboriginal child-rearing in north-central Arnhem land.* Canberra: Australian Institute of Aboriginal Studies.

Harbourne, R., & Stergiou, N. (2003). Nonlinear analysis of the development of sitting postural control. *Developmental Psychobiology, 42,* 368-377.

Harding, J.E., & McCowan, L.M.E. (2003). Perinatal predictors of growth patterns to 18 months in children born small for gestational age. *Early Human Development, 74,* 13-26.

Harris, S.R. (1981). Effects of neurodevelopmental therapy on motor performance of infants with Down's syndrome. *Developmental Medicine and Child Neurology, 23,* 477-483.

Harris, S.R. (1987). Early neuromotor predictors of cerebral palsy in low-birthweight infants. *Developmental Medicine and Child Neurology, 29,* 508-519.

Harris, S.R., & Brady, D. (1986). Infant neuromotor assessment instruments: A review. *Physical and Occupational Therapy in Pediatrics, 6,* 121-153.

Harris, S.R., & Daniels, L.E. (1996). Content validity of the Harris Infant Neuromotor Test. *Physical Therapy, 76,* 727-737.

Harris, S.R., & Daniels, L.E. (2001). Reliability and validity of the Harris Infant Neuromotor Test. *Journal of Pediatrics, 139,* 249-253.

Harris, S.R., Megens, A.M., Backman, C.L., & Hayes, V. (2003). Development and standardization of the Harris Infant Neuromotor Test. *Infants and Young Children, 16,* 143-151.

Hashimoto, K., Hasegawa, H., Kida, Y., & Takeuchi, Y. (2001). Correlation between neuroimaging and neurological outcome in periventricular leukomalacia: Diagnostic criteria. *Pediatrics International, 43,* 240-245.

Hayes, M., Kumar, S., & Delivoria-Papadopoulos, M. (1994). Functional analysis of spontaneous movements in preterm infants. *Developmental Psychobiology, 27,* 271-287.

Haywood, K.M. (1993). *Life span motor development.* Champaign, IL: Human Kinetics.

Haywood, K.M., & Getchell, N. (2001). *Life span motor development* (2nd ed.). Champaign, IL: Human Kinetics.

Henderson, S.E. (1985). Motor skill development. In D. Lane & B. Stratford (Eds.), *Current approaches to Down syndrome* (pp. 187-218). London: Holt, Rinehart & Winston.

Henderson, S.E. (1986). Some aspects of the development of motor control in Down's syndrome. In H.T.A. Whiting & M.G. Wade (Eds.), *Themes in motor development* (pp. 69-92). Boston: Martinus Nijhoff.

Henderson-Smart, D.J. (1995). Postnatal consequences of chronic intrauterine compromise. *Reproduction Fertility Development, 7,* 559-565.

Heriza, C.B. (1988a). Organization of leg movements in preterm infants. *Physical Therapy, 68,* 1340-1346.

Heriza, C.B. (1988b). Comparison of leg movements in preterm infants at term with healthy full-term infants. *Physical Therapy, 68*(11), 1687-1693.

Heriza, C.B. (1991). Implications of dynamical systems approach to understanding infant kicking behaviour. *Physical Therapy, 71*(3), 222-235.

Heriza, C.B. (1993). Kinematic motion analysis. In I.J. Wilhelm (Ed.), *Physical therapy assessment in early infancy* (pp. 257-292). New York: Churchill Livingstone.

Herschkowitz, N. (1988). Brain development in the fetus, neonate and infant. *Biology of the Neonate, 54,* 1-19.

Hinojosa, T., Sheu, C-F., & Michel, G.F. (2003). Infant hand-use preferences for grasping objects contributes to the development of a hand-use preference for manipulating objects. *Developmental Psychobiology, 43,* 328-334.

Hooker, D. (1969). *The prenatal origin of behavior.* New York: Hafner.

Hooley, M., & Crassini, B. (2003). Are individual differences in temperament of relevance to Gibson's theory of affordances? Proceedings of the 12th International Conference on Perception and Action (ICPA). Surfers Paradise, Gold Coast, Australia, 13-18 July.

Hopkins, B., Beek, P.J., & Kalverboer, A.F. (1993). Theoretical issues in the longitudinal study of motor development. In A.F. Kalverboer, B. Hopkins, & R. Geuze (Eds.), *Motor development in early and later childhood: Longitudinal approaches* (pp. 343-371). Cambridge: Cambridge University Press.

Hopkins, B., & Rönnqvist, L. (1998). Human handedness: Developmental and evolutionary perspectives. In F. Simion & G. Butterworth (Eds.), *The development of sensory, motor, and cognitive capacities in early infancy: From perceptions to cognition* (pp. 191-239). Hove, Sussex: Psychology Press.

Horak, F.B. (1992). Motor control models underlying neurologic rehabilitation of posture in children. In H. Forssberg & H. Hirschfeld (Eds.), *Movement disorders in children* (Vol. 36, pp. 21-30). Basel: Karger.

Hoyt, D.F., & Taylor, R. (1981). Gait and the energetics of locomotion in horses. *Nature, 292,* 239-240.

Iaccino, J.F. (1993). Are there handedness differences in brain lateralisation? In J.F. Iaccino (Ed.), *Left-brain–right-brain differences: Inquiries, evidence and new approaches* (pp. 157-203). Hillsdale, NJ: LEA.

Inman, V.T., Ralston, H.J., & Todd, F. (1981). *Human walking.* Baltimore, MD: Williams & Wilkins.

Ivry, R.B. (2003). Cerebellar involvement in clumsiness and other developmental disorders. *Neural Plasticity, 10,* 143-155.

Ivry, R.B., & Spencer, M.C. (2004). The neural representation of time. *Current Opinion in Neurobiology, 14,* 225-232.

Jacobsson, B., & Hagberg, G. (2004). Antenatal risk factors for cerebral palsy. *Best Practice and Research Clinical Obstetrics and Gynaecology, 18,* 425-436.

Jeannerod, M. (1981). Intersegmental coordination during reaching at natural visual objects. In J. Long & A. Baddeley (Eds.), *Attention and performance IX* (pp. 153-168). Hillsdale, NJ: Erlbaum.

Jeannerod, M. (1984). The timing of natural prehension movements. *Journal of Motor Behavior, 16,* 235-254.

Jeannerod, M. (1988). The neural and behavioural organisation of goal-directed movements. Oxford, England: Oxford University Press.

Jeannerod, M. (1996). Reaching and grasping. Parallel specification of visuomotor channels. In H. Heuer & S.W. Keele (Eds.), *Handbook of perception and action: Vol. 2. Motor skills* (pp. 405-460). London: Academic Press.

Jeng, S.-F., Chen, L.-C., Tsou, K.-I., Chen, W.J., & Lou, H.-J. (2004). Relationship between spontaneous kicking and age of walking attainment in preterm infants with very low birth weight and full-term infants. *Physical Therapy, 84,* 159-172.

Jenkins, W.M., Merzenich, M.M., & Recanzone, G. (1990). Neocortical representational dynamics in adult primates: Implications for neuropsychology. *Neuropsychologica, 28,* 573-584.

Jensen, J., Schneider, K., Ulrich, B.D., Zernicke, R.F., & Thelen, E. (1994). Adaptive dynamics of the leg movement patterns of human infants: I. The effect of posture on spontaneous kicking. *Journal of Motor Behavior, 26*(4), 303-312.

Jensen, J.L., Thelen, E., Ulrich, B.D., Schneider, K., & Zernicke, R.F. (1995). Adaptive dynamics of the leg movement patterns of human infants: III. Age related differences in limb control. *Journal of Motor Behavior, 27,* 366-374.

Jensen, R.K., Sun, H., Treitz, T., & Parker, H.E. (1997). Gravity constraints in infant development. *Journal of Motor Behavior, 29,* 64-71.

Johnson, S., Marlow, N., Wolke, D., Davidson, L., Marston, L., O'Hare, A., Peacock, J., & Schulte, J. (2004). Validation of a parent measure of cognitive development in very preterm infants. *Developmental Medicine and Child Neurology, 46,* 389-397.

Jouen, F. (1988). Visual-proprioceptive control of posture in newborn infants. In B. Amblard, A. Berthoz, & F. Clarac (Eds.), *Posture and gait: Development, adaptation and modulation* (pp. 13-22). Amsterdam: Elsevier.

Jouen, F., & Lepecq, J. (1990). Early perceptuo-motor development: Posture and locomotion. In C.-A. Hauert (Ed.), *Developmental psychology: Cognitive, perceptuo-motor, and neuropsychological perspectives* (pp. 61-83). Amsterdam: Elsevier.

Kalverboer, A.F. (1993). Motor development in children at risk: Two decades of research in experimental clinical psychology. In A.F. Kalverboer, B. Hopkins, & R. Geuze (Eds.), *Motor development in early and later childhood: Longitudinal approaches* (pp. 1-15). Cambridge: Cambridge University Press.

Kalverboer, A.F., Hopkins, B., & Geuze, R. (Eds.). (1993). *Motor development in early and later childhood: Longitudinal approaches.* Cambridge: Cambridge University Press.

Kamm, K., Thelen, E., & Jensen, J. (1990). A dynamical systems approach to motor development. *Physical Therapy, 70,* 763-775.

Kamptner, N.L., Cornwell, K.S., Fitzgerald, H.E., & Harris, L.J. (1985). Motor asymmetries in the human infant: Stepping movements. *Infant Mental Journal, 6,* 145-157.

Kanda, T., Pidcock, F.S., Hayakawa, K., Yamori, Y., & Shikata, Y. (2004). Motor outcome differences between two groups of children with spastic diplegia who received different intensities of early onset physiotherapy followed for 5 years. *Brain and Development, 26,* 118-126.

Kawai, M., Savelsbergh, G.J.P., & Wimmers, R.H. (1999). Newborns spontaneous arm movements are influenced by the environment. *Early Human Development, 54,* 15-27.

Kearins, J. (1984). *Child-rearing practices in Australia: Variation with life-style.* Perth: Education Department of Western Australia.

Keele, S.W. (1968). Movement control in skilled motor performance. *Psychological Bulletin, 70,* 387-403.

Kelso, J.A.S. (1984) Phase transitions and critical behavior in human bimanual coordination. *American Journal of Physiology, 15,* R1000-R1004.

Kelso, J.A.S. (1995). *Dynamic patterns: The self-organization of brain and behavior.* Cambridge, MA: MIT Press.

Kelso, R., & Price, S. (1988). *Activities for babies and toddlers with Down syndrome: A physiotherapy approach.* St Lucia, QLD: University of Queensland.

Kisilevsky, B.S., & Low, J.A. (1998). Human fetal behavior: 100 years of study. *DevelopmentalReview, 18,* 1-29.

Kitchen, W.H., Ryan, M.M.R., Mcdougall, A.B., Billson, F.A., Keir, E.H., & Naylor, F.D. (1980). A longitiudinal study of very low-birthweight infants. IV: An overview of performance at eight years of age. *Developmental Medicine and Child Neurology, 22,* 172-188.

Kleberg, A., Westrup, B., Stjernqvist, K., & Lagercrantz, H. (2002). Indications of improved cognitive development at one year of age among infants born very prematurely who received care based on the newborn individualized developmental care and assessment program (NIDCAP). *Early Human Development, 68,* 83-91.

Knobloch, H., & Pasamanick, B. (1974). *Gesell and Amatruda's Developmental Diagnosis: The evaluation and management of normal and abnormal neuropsychologic development in infancy and early childhood* (3rd ed.). Hagerstown, MD: Harper & Row.

Korner, A. (1972). State as a variable, as obstacle, and as mediator of stimulation in infant research. *Merrill-Palmer Quarterly, 18,* 77-94.

Korner, A.F., Brown, J.V., Thom, V.A., & Constantinou, J.C. (2001). *The neurobehavioral assessment of the preterm infant.* Van Nuys, CA: Child Development Media.

Korner, A.F., & Constantinou, J.C. (2001). The neurobehavioral assessment of the preterm infant. In L.T. Singer & P.S. Zeskind (Eds.), *Biobehavioral assessment of the infant* (pp. 381-397). New York: Guilford Press.

Korner, A., Constantinou, J., Dimiceli, S., & Brown, B. (1991). Establishing the reliability and developmental validity of a neurobehavioural assessment for preterm infants: A methodological process. *Child Development, 62,* 1200-1208.

Korner, A.F., Stevenson, D.K., Kraemer, H.C., Spiker, D., Scott, D., & Constantinou, J. (1993). Prediction of the development of low birth weight preterm infants by a new neonatal medical index. *Developmental and Behavioural Pediatrics, 14*(2), 106-111.

Korner, A.F., & Thom, V.A. (1990). *Neurobehavioral assessment of the preterm infant.* San Antonio: Psychological Corporation.

Kravitz, H., & Boehm, J. (1971). Rhythmic habit patterns in infancy: Their sequences, age of onset and frequency. *Child Development, 42,* 399-413.

Krebs, L., & Langhoff-Roos, J. (1999). Breech delivery in Denmark, 1982-92: A population-based case-control study. *Pediatric Perinatal Epidemiology, 13,* 431-441.

Krebs, L., Langhoff-Roos, J., & Thorngren-Jerneck, K. (2001). Long-term outcome in term breech infants with low Apgar score: A population-based follow-up. *European Journal of Obstetrics, Gynecology, and Reproductive Biology, 100,* 5-8.

Kulak, W., & Sobaniec, W. (2004). Comparisons of right and left hemiparetic cerebral palsy. *Pediatric Neurology, 31*(2), 101-108.

Kuypers, H.G.J.M. (1962). Corticospinal connections: Postnatal development in the rhesus monkey. *Science, 138,* 678-680.

Largo, R.H. (1993). Early motor development in preterm children. In G.J.P. Savelsbergh (Ed.), *The development of coordination in infancy* (pp. 425-443). Amsterdam: Elsevier.

Largo, R.H., Kunda, S., & Thun-Hohenstein, L. (1993). Early motor development in term and preterm children. In A.F. Kalverboer, B. Hopkins, & R. Geuze (Eds.), *Motor development in early and later childhood: Longitudinal approaches* (pp. 247-265). Cambridge: Cambridge University Press.

Laszlo, J.I., & Bairstow, P.J. (1985). Assessment of perceptual-motor behaviour. In J.I. Laszlo & P.J. Bairstow (Eds.), *Perceptual-motor behaviour: Developmental assessment and therapy.* London: Holt, Rinehart & Winston.

Latash, M.L. (1998a). *Neurophysiological basis of movement.* Champaign, IL: Human Kinetics.

Latash, M.L. (1998b). *Progress in motor control: Vol. 1. Bernstein's traditions in movement studies.* Champaign, IL: Human Kinetics.

Lauteslager, P.E.M. (1995). Motor development in young children with Down syndrome. In A. Vermeer & W.E. Davis (Eds.), *Physical development in mental retardation* (Vol. 40, pp. 75-98). Basel: Karger.

Law, M., Russell, D., Pollock, N., Rosenbaum, P., Walter, S., & King, G. (1997). A comparison of intensive neurodevelopmental therapy plus casting and a regular occupational therapy program for children with cerebral palsy. *Developmental Medicine and Child Neurology, 39,* 664-670.

Lawlor, M.C., & Henderson, A. (1989). A descriptive study of the clinical practice patterns of occupational therapists working with infants and young children. *American Journal of Occupational Therapy, 43*(11), 755-764.

Lecanuet, J-P., & Schaal, B. (1996). Fetal sensory competencies. *European Journal of Obstetrics and Gynecology, 68,* 1-23.

Ledebt, A. (2000). Changes in arm posture during the early acquisition of walking. *Infant Behavior and Development, 23,* 79-89.

Lee, D.N., & Thomson, J.A. (1982). Vision in action: The control of locomotion. In D.J. Ingle, M.A. Goodale, & R.J.W. Mansfield (Eds.), *Analysis of visual behavior* (pp. 411-433). Cambridge, MA: MIT Press.

Lems, W., Hopkins, B., & Samson, J. (1993). Mental and motor development in preterm infants: The issue of corrected age. *Early Human Development, 34,* 113-123.

Lenke, M.C. (2003). Motor outcomes in premature infants. *Newborn and Infant Nursing Reviews, 3,* 104-109.

Lenneberg, E. (1967). *Biological foundations of language.* New York: Wiley.

Leonard, C. (1992). Neural and neurobehavioral changes associated with perinatal damage. In H. Forssberg & H. Hirschfeld (Eds.), *Movement disorders in children* (Vol. 36, pp. 50-56). Basel: Karger.

Lester, B.M. (1998). The Maternal Lifestyles study. *Annals of the New York Academy of Science, 846,* 296-306.

Lester, B., & Tronick, E. (2001). Behavioral assessment scales: The NICU Network Neurobehavioral Scale, the Neonatal Behavioral Assessment Scale, and the Assessment of the Preterm Infant's Behavior. In L.T. Singer & P.S. Zeskind (Eds.), *Biobehavioral assessment of the infant* (pp. 363-380). New York: Guilford Press.

Livesey, D. (1997). Use of the Movement Assessment Battery for Children with young Australian children: Identifying 3- and 4-year old children at risk of motor impairment. Paper presented at the 4th Biennial Motor Control and Human Skill Research Workshop, Perth, Western Australia, December

Lobo, M.A., Galloway, J.C., & Savelsbergh, G. (2004). General and task-related experiences affect early object interaction. *Child Development, 75*(4), 1268-1281.

Lockman, J.J. (1990). Perceptuo-motor coordination in infancy. In C.-A. Hauert (Ed.), *Developmental psychology: Cognitive, perceptuo-motor, and neuropsychological perspectives* (pp. 85-109). Amsterdam: Elsevier.

Lourie, R.S. (1949). The role of rhythmic patterns in childhood. *American Journal of Psychiatry, 103,* 653-660.

Luiz, D.M., Foxcroft, C. D., & Stewart, R. (2001) The construct validity of the Griffiths Scales of Mental Development. *Child: Care, Health and Development, 27,* 73-83.

Lukeman, D., & Melvin, D. (1993). The preterm infant: Psychological issues in childhood. *Journal of Child Psychology and Psychiatry, 34*(6), 837-849.

Lundy-Ekman, L., Ivry, R., Keele, S., & Woollacott, M. (1991). Timing and force control deficits in clumsy children. *Journal of Cognitive Neuroscience, 3,* 367-376.

Mahoney, G., Robinson, C., & Fewell, R. (2001). The effects of early motor intervention on children with Down syndrome or cerebral palsy: A field-based study. *Journal of Development and Behavioural Pediatrics, 22*(3), 153-162.

Majnemer, A., & Mazer, B. (1998). Neurologic evaluation of the new-born infant: Definition and psychometric properties. *Developmental Medicine and Child Neurology, 40,* 708-715.

Mathew, A., & Cook, M. (1990). The control of reaching movements by young infants. *Child Development, 61,* 1238-1257.

Mauerberg-deCastro, E., & Angulo-Kinzler, R. (2000). Locomotor patterns of individuals with Down syndrome: Effects of environmental and task constraints. In D.J. Weeks, R. Chua, & D. Elliott (Eds.), *Perceptual-motor behavior in Down syndrome* (pp. 71-98). Champaign, IL: Human Kinetics.

Mayo, N.E. (1991). The effect of physical therapy for children with motor delay and cerebral palsy. *American Journal of Physical Medicine and Rehabilitation, 70,* 258-267.

Mazzone, L., Mugno, D., & Mazzone, D. (in press). The general movements in children with Down syndrome. *Early Human Development.*

McDonnell, P.M., Anderson, V., & Abraham, W. (1983). Asymmetry and orientation of arm movements in three- to eight-week-old infants. *Infant Behavior and Development, 6,* 287-298.

McDonnell, P.M., & Corkum, V.L. (1991). The role of reflexes in the patterning of limb movements in the first six months of life. In J. Fagard & P.H. Wolff (Eds.), *The development of timing control and temporal organistion in coordinated action* (pp. 151-173). Amsterdam: Elsevier.

McDonnell, P.M., Corkum, V.L., & Wilson, D.L. (1989). Patterns of movement in the first 6 months of life: New directions. *Canadian Journal of Psychology, 43*(2), 320-339.

McGraw, M.B. (1940). Neuromuscular development of the human infant as exemplified in the achievement of erect locomotion. *Journal of Pediatrics, 17,* 747-771.

McManus, I.C., Sik, G., Cole, D.R., Mellon, A.F., Wong, J., & Kloss, J. (1988). The development of handedness in children. *British Journal of Developmental Psychology, 6,* 257-273.

Mei, J. (1994). The northern Chinese custom of rearing babies in sandbags: Implications for motor and intellectual development. In J.H.A. van Rossum & J.I. Laszlo (Eds.), *Motor development: Aspects of normal and delayed development* (pp. 41-48). Amsterdam: VU University Press.

Melekian, B. (1981). Lateralization in the newborn at birth: Asymmetry of the stepping reflex. *Neuropsychologia, 20,* 707-711.

Meltzoff, A., & Borton, R.W. (1979). Intermodal matching by human neonates. *Nature, 282,* 403-404.

Mercer, J. (1998). *Infant development: A multidisciplinary introduction.* Pacific Grove, CA: Brooks/Cole.

Merzenich, M.M., Allard, T.T., & Jenkins, W.M. (1990). Neural ontogeny of higher brain function: Implications of some recent neurophysiological findings. In O. Franzn & P. Westman (Eds.), *Information processing in the somatosensory system* (pp. 293-311). London: Macmillan.

Merzenich, M.M., Nelson, R.J., Stryker, M.P., Cynader, M.S., Schoppmann, A., & Zook, J. M. (1984). Somatosensory cortical map changes following digit amputation in adult monkeys. *The Journal of Comparative Neurology, 224,* 591-605.

Metcalfe, J.S., & Clark, J.E. (2000). Sensory information affords exploration of posture in newly walking infants and toddlers. *Infant Behavior and Development, 23,* 391-405.

Michel, G.F. (1983). Development of hand-use preference during infancy. In G. Young, S.J. Segalowitz, C.M. Corter, & S.E. Trehub (Eds.), *Manual specialisation and the developing brain* (pp. 33-70). New York: Academic Press.

Michel, G.F. (1998). A lateral bias in the neuropsychological functioning of human infants. *Developmental Neuropsychology, 14*(4), 445-469.

Michel, G.F., & Harkins, D.A. (1986). Postural and lateral asymmetries in the ontogeny of handedness during infancy. *Developmental Psychobiology, 19,* 247-258.

Michel, G.F., Sheu, C.-F., & Brumley, M.R. (2002). Evidence of a right-shift factor affecting infant hand-use preferences from 7 to 11 months of age as revealed by latent class analysis. *Developmental Psychobiology, 40,* 1-13.

Milani-Comparetti, A.M., & Gidoni, E.A. (1967). Routine developmental examination in normal and retarded infants. *Developmental Medecine and Child Neurology, 9,* 631-638.

Miller, L.J., & Roid, R.G. (1994). *The T.I.M.E.: Toddler and Infant Motor Evaluation—a standardized assessment.* Tucson, AZ: Therapy Skill Builders.

Miyahara, M., Jongmans, M.J., Mercuri, E., de Vries, L., Henderson, L., & Henderson, S.E. (in press). Multiple birth versus neonatal brain lesions in children born prematurely as predictors of perceptuo-motor impairment at age six. *Developmental Neuropsychology.*

Mondschein, E.R., Adolph, K.E., & Tamis-LeMonda, C.S. (2000). Gender bias in mother's expectation about infant crawling. *Journal of Experimental Child Psychology, 77,* 304-316.

Monset-Couchard, M., de Bethmann, O., & Kastler, B. (2002). Mid and long-term outcome of 166 premature infants weighing less than

1000g at birth, all small for gestational age. *Biology of the Neonate, 81,* 244-254.

Moore, K.L. & Persaud, T.V.N. (1993) *Before we are born: Essentials of embryology and birth defects* (4th Ed.). Philadelphia, PA: W.B. Saunders.

Moore, M.L. (2003). Preterm labor and birth: What have we learned in the past two decades. *Journal of Obstetric, Gynecologic, and Neonatal Nursing, 32,* 638-649.

Morgan, A., Koch, V., Lee, V., & Aldag, J. (1988). Neonatal neurobehavioral examination: A new instrument for quantitative analysis of neonatal neurological status. *Physical Therapy, 68,* 1352-1358.

Moster, D., Lie, R.T., Irgens, L.M., Bjerkedal, T., & Markestad, T. (2001). The association of Apgar score with subsequent death and cerebral palsy: A population-based study in term infants. *Journal of Pediatrics, 138*(6), 798-803.

Murgo, S., Avni, E.F., Muller, D.P., Golzarian, J., Balleriaux, D., & Struyven, J. (1999). Periventricular leukomalacia in premature infants: Prognostic role of ultrasonography and MRI. *Journal of Radiology, 80,* 715-720.

Myers, D.G. (2001). *Psychology.* New York: Worth.

National Institutes of Health Consensus Development Conference. (1995). Effect of corticosteroids for fetal maturation on perinatal outcomes, February 25-March 2, 1994. *American Journal of Obstetrics and Gynecology, 173,* 246-252.

Nelson, K.B. (1991). Prenatal origin of hemiparetic cerebral palsy: How often & why? *Pediatrics, 88*(5), 1059-1062.

Nelson, K.B. (2002). The epidemiology of cerebral palsy in term infants. *Mental Retardation and Developmental Disabilities Research Reviews, 8,* 146-150.

Nelson, K.B., & Ellenberg, J.H. (1982). Children who "outgrew" cerebral palsy. *Pediatrics, 69*(5), 529-536.

Nelson, K.B., & Ellenberg, J.H. (1986). Antecedents of cerebral palsy. Multivariate analysis of risk. *New England Journal of Medicine, 315,* 81-86.

Newborg, J., Stock, J.R., Wnek, L., Guidubaldi, J., & Svinicki, J. (1984). *Battelle Developmental Inventory.* Allen, TX: DLM Teaching Resources.

Newell, K.M. (1986). Constraints of the development of coordination. In M.G. Wade & H.T.A. Whiting (Eds.), *Motor development in children: Aspects of coordination and control* (pp. 341-360). Dordrecht: Martinus Nijhoff.

Newell, K.M. (1989). On task and theory specificity. *Journal of Motor Behavior, 21*(1), 92-96.

Newell, K.M. (1997). Degrees of freedom and the development of center of pressure profiles. In K.M. Newell & P.M.C. Molenaar (Eds.), *Applications of nonlinear dynamics to developmental process modeling* (pp. 63-84). Hillsdale, NJ: Erlbaum.

Newell, K.M., Liu, Y-T., & Mayer-Kress, G. (2003). A dynamical systems interpretation of epigenetic landscapes for infant motor development. *Infant Behavior and Development, 26*, 449-472.

Newell, K.M., Scully, D.M., McDonald, P.V., & Baillargeon, R. (1989). Task constraints and infant grip configurations. *Developmental Psychobiology, 22*(8), 817-832.

Newell, K.M., Scully, D., Tenenbaum, F., & Hardiman, S. (1989). Body scale and the development of prehension. *Developmental Psychobiology, 22*(8), 1-13.

Newell, K.M., & Slifkin, A.B. (1998). The nature of movement variability. In J.P. Piek (Ed.), *Motor behavior and human skill: A multidisciplinary approach* (pp. 143-160). Champaign, IL: Human Kinetics.

Newell, K.M., & van Emmerik, R.E.A. (1990). Are Gesell's developmental principles general principles for the acquisition of coordination. In C. Humphreys (Ed.), *Advances in motor development research* (Vol. 3, pp. 143-165). New York: AMS Press.

Newell, K., van Emmerik, R.E.A., & McDonald, P.V. (1989). Biomechanical constraints and action theory. *Human Movement Science, 8*, 403-409.

Ohgi, S., Arisawa, K., Takahashi, T., Kusumoto, T., Goto, Y., Akiyama, T., et al. (2003). Neonatal behavioral assessment scale as a predictor of later developmental disabilities of low birth-weight and/or premature infants. *Brain and Development, 25*, 313-321.

Ong, L.C., Boo, N.Y., & Chandran, V. (2001). Predictors of neurodevelopmental outcome if Malaysian very low birthweight children at 4 years of age. *Journal of Paediatric Child Health, 37*, 363-368.

O'Toole, M. (Ed.). (1992). *Miller-Keane encyclopedia and dictionary of medicine, nursing and allied health.* Philadelphia: Saunders.

Palisano, R.J. (1986). Use of chronological and adjusted ages to compare motor development of healthy preterm and fullterm infants. *Developmental Medicine and Child Neurology, 28*, 180-187.

Palisano, R.J., Walter, S.D., Russell, D.J., Rosenbaum, P.L., Gemus, M., Galuppi, B.E., et al. (2001). Gross motor function of children with Down syndrome: Creation of motor growth curves. *Archives of Physical Medicine and Rehabilitation, 82*, 494-500.

Palmer, F.B. (2004). Strategies for the early diagnosis of cerebral palsy. *Journal of Pediatrics, 145,* S8-S11.

Parker, H. (1992). Children's motor rhythm and timing: A dynamical approach. In J.J. Summers (Ed.), *Approaches to the study of motor control and learning* (pp. 163-195). Amsterdam: Elsevier.

Payne, V.G., & Isaacs, L.D. (1995). *Human motor development: A life-span approach* (3rd Ed.). Mountain View, CA: Mayfield.

Pelletier, J.M., Short, M.A. & Nelson, D.L. (1985). Immediate effects of waterbed flotation on approach and avoidance behaviors of premature infants. *Physical and Occupational Therapy in Pediatrics, 5,* 81-92.

Penfield, W., & Rasmussen, T. (1952). *The cerebral cortex of man.* New York: Macmillan.

Peters, M. (1988). Footedness: Asymmetries in foot preference and skill and neuropsychological assessment of foot movement. *Psychological Bulletin, 103,* 179-192.

Peters, M., & Petrie, B.F. (1979). Functional asymmetries in the stepping reflex of human neonates. *Canadian Journal of Psychology, 33,* 198-200.

Piaget, J. (1953). *The origin of the intelligence in the child.* London: Routledge & Kegan Paul.

Piaget, J., & Inhelder, B. (1969). *The psychology of the child.* London: Routledge & Kegan Paul.

Piek, J.P. (1995). The contribution of spontaneous movements in the acquisition of motor coordination in infants. In D.J. Glencross & J.P. Piek (Eds.), *Motor control and sensory motor integration: Issues and directions* (pp. 199-230). Amsterdam: Elsevier.

Piek, J. (1998). The influence of preterm birth on early motor development. In J. Piek (Ed.), *Motor behavior and human skill: A multidisciplinary approach* (pp. 233-253). Champaign, IL: Human Kinetics.

Piek, J.P. (2001). Is a quantitative approach useful in the comparison of spontaneous movements in fullterm and preterm infants? *Human Movement Science, 20,* 717-736.

Piek, J.P. (2002). The role of variability in early motor development. *Infant Behavior and Development, 25,* 452-465.

Piek, J.P., Barrett, N.C., & Martin, N. (2005). *Limb asymmetries in early infancy and their impact on the development of crawling and handedness in preterm and fullterm infants.* Paper presented at the 2nd International Congress on Motor Development and Learning in Infancy. Murcia, Spain, May.

Piek, J.P., & Carman, R. (1994). Developmental profiles of spontaneous movements in infants. *Early Human Development, 39,* 109-126.

Piek, J.P., & Gasson, N. (1999). Spontaneous kicking in fullterm and preterm infants: Are there leg asymmetries? *Human Movement Science, 18,* 377-395.

Piek, J., Gasson, N., Barrett, N., & Case, I. (2002). Limb and gender differences in the development of coordination in early infancy. *Human Movement Science, 21,* 621-639.

Piek, J.P., & Pitcher, T.A. (2004). Processing deficits in children with movement and attention deficits. In D. Dewey & D.E. Tupper (Eds.), *Developmental motor disorders* (chapter 14, pp. 313-327). New York: Guilford Press.

Piek, J., & Skinner, R. (1999). Timing and force during a sequential tapping task in children with and without motor coordination problems. *Journal of the International Neuropsychological Society, 5,* 320-329.

Piper, M.C., & Darrah, J. (1994). *Motor assessment of the developing infant.* Philadelphia: Saunders.

Piper, M., Darrah, J., & Byrne, P. (1989). Impact of gestational age on preterm motor development at 4 months chronological and adjusted age. *Child: Care, Health and Development, 15,* 105-115.

Pitcher, T.M., Piek, J.P., & Barrett, N. (2002). Timing and force control in boys with attention deficit hyperactivity disorder: Subtype differences and the effect of comorbid developmental coordination disorder. *Human Movement Science, 21,* 919-945.

Ponsonby, A., Dwyer, T., Gibbons, L.E., Cochrane, J.A., & Wang, Y-G. (1993). Factors potentiating the risk of sudden infant death syndrome associated with the prone position. *The New England Journal of Medicine, 329,* 377-382.

Porter, R., & Lemon, R. (Eds.). (1993). *Corticospinal function and voluntary movement.* Oxford: Clarendon Press.

Prechtl, H.F.R. (1974). The behavioural states of the newborn infant: A review. *Brain Research, 76,* 185-212.

Prechtl, H.F.R. (1977). *The neurological examination of the full term newborn infant.* London: William Heinemann Medical Books.

Prechtl, H.F.R. (1980). The optimality concept. *Early Human Development, 4,* 201-205.

Prechtl, H.F.R. (1981). The study of neural development as a perspective of clinical problems. In K.J. Connolly & H.R. Prechtl (Eds.), *Clinics in developmental medicine no. 77/78. Maturation & development: Biological and psychological perspectives* (pp. 198-211). London: William Heinemann Medical Books.

Prechtl, H.F.R. (1984). Continuity and change in early neural development. In H.R. Prechtl (Ed.), *Continuity of neural function from prenatal to postnatal life* (pp. 1-15). Philadelphia: Leffcott.

Prechtl, H.F.R. (1990). Qualitative changes of spontaneous movements in fetus and preterm infant are a marker of neurological dysfunction. *Early Human Development, 23,* 151-158.

Prechtl, H.F.R. (1993). Principles of early motor development in the human. In A.F. Kalverboer, B. Hopkins, & R. Geuze (Eds.), *Motor development in early and later childhood: Longitudinal approaches* (pp. 35-50). Cambridge: Cambridge University Press.

Prechtl, H.F.R. (1997). State of the art of a new functional assessment of the young nervous system. An early predictor of cerebral palsy. *Early Human Development, 50,* 1-11.

Prechtl, H.F.R., & Beintema, D.J. (1964). *The neurological examination of the full term newborn infant.* London: Heinemann.

Prechtl, H.F.R., Einspieler, C., Cioni, G., Bos, A.E., Ferrari, F., & Sontheimer, D. (1997). An early marker for neurological deficits after perinatal brain lesions. *Lancet, 349*(9062), 1361-1363.

Prechtl, H.F.R., Fargel, J.W., Weinmann, H.M., & Bakker, H.H. (1979). Postures, motility and respiration of low risk preterm infants. *Developmental Medicine and Child Neurology, 21,* 3-27.

Prechtl, H.F.R., & Hopkins, B. (1986). Developmental transformations of spontaneous movements in early infancy. *Early Human Development, 14,* 233-238.

Prechtl, H.F.R., & Nolte, R. (1984). Motor behaviour of preterm infants. In H.R. Prechtl (Ed.), *Continuity of neural function from prenatal to postnatal life. Clinics in Developmental Medicine, 94.* (pp. 79-90). Oxford: Blackwell Scientific.

Provine, R.R. (1993). Natural priorities for developmental study: Neuro-embryological perspectives of motor development. In A.F. Kalverboer, B. Hopkins, & R. Geuze (Eds.), *Motor development in early and later childhood: Longitudinal approaches* (pp. 1-73). Cambridge: Cambridge University Press.

Purves, D. (1994). *Neural activity and the growth of the brain.* Cambridge: Cambridge University Press.

Purves, D., White, L.E., & Riddle, D.R. (1996). Is neural development darwinian? *Trends in Neuroscience, 19,* 460-464.

Purves, D., White, L.E., & Riddle, D.R. (1997). Reply—Letters to the editor. *Trends in Neuroscience, 20,* 293.

Rakic, P. (1985). Limits of neurogenesis in primates. *Science, 227,* 1054-1055.

Ramsay, D.S. (1984). Onset of duplicated syllable babbling and unimanual handedness in infancy: Evidence for developmental change in hemisphere specialization? *Developmental Psychology, 20,* 64-71.

Reed, E.S. (1989). Changing theories of postural development. In H.G. Williams (Ed.), *Development of posture and gait across the life span* (pp. 3-24). Columbia, SC: University of South Carolina Press.

Reid, D.T., Boschen, K., & Wright, V. (1993). Critique of the Pediatric Evaluation of Disability Inventory. *Physical and Occupational Therapy in Pediatrics, 13,* 57-87.

Robertson, S. (1990). Temporal organisation in fetal and newborn movement. In H. Bloch & B. I. Bertenthal (Eds.), *Sensory-motor organisations and development in infancy and early childhood* (pp. 105-122). Dordrecht, The Netherlands: Kluwer Academic.

Robertson, S.S., Bacher, L.F., & Huntington, N.L. (2001). Structure and irregularity in the spontaneous behavior of young infants. *Behavioral Neuroscience, 115,* 758-763.

Rochat, P. (1992). Self-sitting and reaching in 5- to 8-month-old infants: The impact of posture and its development on early eye-hand coordination. *Journal of Motor Behavior, 24,* 210-220.

Rochat, P. (1993). Hand-mouth coordination in the newborn: Morphology, determinants and early development of a basic act. In G. Savelsbergh (Ed.), *The development of coordination in infancy* (pp. 265-288). Amsterdam: Elsevier Science.

Rochat, P., Blass, E.M., & Hoffmeyer, L.B. (1988). Oropharyngeal control of hand-mouth coordination in newborn infants. *Developmental Psychology, 24,* 459-463.

Roncesvalles, M.N.C., Woollacott, M.H., & Jensen, J.L. (2001). Development of lower extremity kinetics for balance control in infants and young children. *Journal of Motor Behavior, 33*(2), 180-192.

Rosenblith, J.F. (1992). *In the beginning: Development from conception to age two.* Thousand Oaks, CA: Sage.

Rovee, C.K., & Rovee, D.T. (1969). Conjugate reinforcement of infant exploratory behavior. *Journal of Experimental Child Psychology, 8,* 33-39.

Ruiz-Extremera, A., Robles-Vizcaino, C., Salvatierra-Cuenca, M.-T., Ocete, E., Lainez, C., Benitez, A., et al. (2001). Neurodevelopment of neonates in neonatal intensive care units and growth of surviving infants at age 2 years. *Early Human Development, 65,* S119-S132.

Saigal, S., Rosenbaum, P., Szatmari, P., & Hoult, L. (1992). Non-right-handedness among ELBW and term children at eight years in relation to cognitive function and school performance. *Developmental Medicine and Child Neurology, 34,* 425-433.

Sammons, W.A.H., & Lewis, J.M. (1985). *Premature babies: A different beginning.* St. Louis: Mosby.

Samsom, J.F., Sie, L.T.L., & de Groot, L. (2002). Muscle power development in preterm infants with periventricular flaring or leukomalacia in relation to outcome at 18 months. *Developmental Medicine and Child Neurology, 44,* 735-740.

Sattler, J.M. (1990). *Assessment of children.* San Diego: Jerome M Sattler.

Sattler, J.M. (2001). *Assessment of children: Cognitive applications.* San Diego: Jerome M Sattler.

Savelsbergh, G.J.P. (Ed.). (1993). *The development of coordination in infancy. Advances in psychology.* Amsterdam: Elsevier Science.

Savelsbergh, G.J.P., & van der Kamp, J. (1994). The effect of body orientation to gravity on early infant reaching. *Journal of Experimental Child Psychology, 58,* 510-528.

Scherzer, A.L., & Tscharnuter, I. (1990). *Early diagnosis and therapy in cerebral palsy.* New York: Marcel Dekker.

Schmidt, R.A. (1975). A schema theory of discrete motor skills learning. *Psychological Review, 82,* 225-260.

Schmidt, R.A. (1988). *Motor control and learning.* Champaign, IL: Human Kinetics.

Schmidt, R.C., & O'Brien, B. (1998). Modeling interpersonal coordination dynamics: Implications for a dynamical theory of developing systems. In K.M. Newell & P.C.M. Molenaar (Eds.), *Applications of nonlinear dynamics to developmental process modeling* (pp. 221-240). Mahwah, NJ: Erlbaum.

Schneider, K., Zernicke, R.F., Ulrich, B.D., Jensen, J.L., & Thelen, E. (1990). Understanding movement control in infants through the analysis of limb intersegmental dynamics. *Journal of Motor Behavior, 22,* 493-520.

Schoemaker, M.M., Smits-Engelsman, B.C.M., Bouwien, C.M., & Jongmans, M.J. (2003). Psychometric properties of the Movement Assessment Battery for Children—Checklist as a screening instrument for children with a developmental coordination disorder. *British Journal of Educational Psychology, 73,* 425-441.

Schucard, J.L., & Schucard, D.W. (1990). Auditory evoked potentials and hand preference in 6-month-old infants: Possible gender-related differences in cerebral organization. *Developmental Psychology, 26*(6), 923-930.

Scrutton, D. (1984). *Management of the motor disorders of children with cerebral palsy.* Philadelphia: Lippincott.

Seghier, M.L., Lazeyras, F., Zimine, S., Maier, S.E., Hanquinet, S., Delavelle, J., Volpe, J., & Huppi, P. (2004). Combination of event-related fMRI and diffusion tensor imaging in an infant with perinatal stroke. *NeuroImage, 21,* 463-472.

Serdaroglu, G., Tekgul, H., Kitis, O., Serdaroglu, E., & Gokben, S. (2004). Correlative value of magnetic resonance imaging for neurodevelopmental outcome in periventricular leukomalacia. *Developmental Medicine and Child Neurology, 46*(11), 733-739.

Sergeant, J. (2000). The cognitive-energetic model: An empirical approach to attention-deficit hyperactivity disorder. *Neuroscience and Biobehavioral Reviews, 24,* 7-12.

Seth, G. (1973). Eye-hand coordination and "handedness": A developmental study of visuo-motor behaviour in infancy. *British Journal of Educational Psychology, 43,* 35-49.

Shankle, W.R., Landing, B.H., Rafii, M.S., Schiano, A., Chen, J.M., & Hara, J. (1998). Evidence for postnatal doubling of neuron number in the developing human cerebral cortex between 15 months and 6 years. *Journal of Theoretical Biology, 191,* 115-140.

Shankle, W.R., Rafii, M.S., Landing, B.H., & Fallon, J.H. (1999). Approximate doubling of numbers of neurons in postnatal human cerebral cortex and in 35 specific cytoarchitectural areas from birth to 72 months. *Pediatric and Developmental Pathology, 2,* 244-259.

Shaw, S.R. (2002). A school psychologist investigates sensory integration therapies: Promise, possibility, and the art of placebo. *National Association of School Psychologists Communique, 31*(2), 9-13.

Sheridan-Pereira, M., Ellison, P., & Helgeson, V. (1991). The construction of a scored neonatal neurological examination for assessment of neurological integrity in full-term neonates. *Journal of Developmental and Behavioral Pediatrics, 12,* 25-30.

Sherrington, C. (1906). *The integrative action of the nervous system.* Ann Arbor, MI: University Microfilms International.

Shirley, M.M. (1931). *The first two years: A study of twenty-five babies.* Minneapolis: University of Minnesota Press.

Shirley, M.M. (1963). The motor sequence. In W. Dennis (Ed.), *Readings in child psychology* (2nd Ed.) (pp. 72-82). Englewood Cliffs, NJ: Prentice-Hall.

Shumway-Cook, A., & Woollacott, M. (1993). Theoretical issues in assessing postural control. In I.J. Wilhelm (Ed.), *Physical therapy assessment in early infancy* (pp. 161-171). New York: Churchill Livingstone.

Singer, L.T. (2001). General issues in infant assessment and development. In L.T. Singer & P.S. Zeskind (Eds.), *Biobehavioral assessment of the infant* (pp. 3-17). New York: Guilford Press.

Singer, L.T., Yamashita, T., Lilien, L., Collin, M., & Baley, J. (1997). A longitudinal study of developmental outcome of infants with bronchopulmonary dysplasia and very low birthweight. *Pediatrics, 100,* 987-993.

Smith, L.B., & Thelen, E. (Eds.). (1993). *A dynamic systems approach to development: Applications.* Cambridge, MA: MIT Press.

Soltesz-Sheahan, M., & Farmer-Brockway, N. (1994). The high risk infant. In J.S. Tecklin (Ed.), *Pediatric physical therapy* (pp. 56-88). Philadelphia: Lippincott.

Spencer, J., & Thelen, E. (2000). Spatially specific changes in infants' muscle coactivity as they learn to reach. *Infancy, 1*(3), 275-302.

Sporns, O. (1997). Letters to the editor: Variation and selection in neural function. *Trends in Neuroscience, 20,* 291.

Sporns, O., & Edelman, G. (1993). Solving Bernstein's problem: A proposal for the development of coordinated movement by selection. *Child Development, 64,* 960-981.

Sprague, R.L., & Newell, K.M. (Eds.). (1996). *Stereotyped movements: Brain and behaviour relationships.* Washington, DC: American Psychiatric Association.

Squires, J., Potter, L., & Bricker, D. (1995). *The Ages and Stages Questionnaire users guide.* Baltimore: Brookes.

Stanley, F. (1994). Cerebral palsy trends. *Acta Obstetrics and Gynecology Scandinavia, 73,* 5-9.

Stanley, F.J. (1997). Prenatal determinants of motor disorders. *Acta Paediatrica Supplement, 442,* 92-102.

Stanley, F.J., & Alberman, E. (1984). *The epidemiology of the cerebral palsies.* Spastics International Medical Publications. Clinics in Developmental Medicine, No. 87. Oxford: Blackwell Scientific.

Stanley, F.J., & Blair, E. (1994). Cerebral palsy. In I.B. Pless (Ed.), *The epidemiology of childhood disorders* (pp. 473-497). New York: Oxford University Press.

Stelmach, G. (1982). Information-processing framework for understanding human motor behavior. In J.A.S. Kelso (Ed.), *Human motor behavior: An introduction* (pp. 63-91). Hillsdale, NJ: Erlbaum.

Stoelhorst, G.M.S.J., Rijken, M., Martens, S.E., van Zwieten, P.H.T., Feenstra, J., Zwinderman, A.H., et al. (2003). Developmental outcome at 18 and 24 months of age in very preterm children: A cohort study from 1996 to 1997. *Early Human Development, 72,* 83-95.

Styer-Acevedo, J. (1994). Physical therapy for the child with cerebral palsy. In J.S. Teckiln (Ed.), *Pediatric physical therapy* (pp. 89-134). Philadelphia: Lippincott.

Sugden, D.A., & Keogh, J. (1990). *Problems in movement skill development.* Columbia, SC: University of South Carolina.

Sullivan, M.C., & McGrath, M.M. (2003). Perinatal morbidity, mild motor delay, and later school outcomes. *Developmental Medicine and Child Neurology, 45,* 104-112.

Summers, J.J. (1998). Has ecological psychology delivered what it promised? In J.P. Piek (Ed.), *Motor behavior and human skill: A multidisciplinary approach* (pp. 385-402). Champaign, IL: Human Kinetics.

Super, C.M. (1976). Environmental effects on motor development: The case of "African infant precocity." *Developmental Medicine and Child Neurology, 18,* 561-567.

Surman, G., Newdick, H., & Johnson, A. (2003). Cerebral palsy rates among low-birthweight infants fell in the 1990s. *Developmental Medicine and Child Neurology, 45,* 456-462.

Surveillance of Cerebral Palsy in Europe. (2000). Surveillance of Cerebral Palsy in Europe: A collaboration of cerebral palsy registers. *Developmental Medicine and Child Neurology, 42,* 816-824.

Sveistrup, H., & Woollacott, M. (1996). Longitudinal development of the automatic response in infants. *Journal of Motor Behavior, 28,* 58-70.

Sveistrup, H., & Woollacott, M.H. (1997). Practice modifies the developing automatic postural response. *Experimental Brain Research, 114,* 33-43.

Swanson, J., Posner, M.I., Cantwell, D., Wigal, S., Crinella, F., Filipek, P., et al. (1998). Attention-deficit/hyperactivity disorder: Symptom domains, cognitive processes, and neural networks. In R. Parasuraman (Ed.), *The attentive brain* (pp. 445-460). Cambridge, MA: MIT Press.

Sweet, M.P., Hodgman, J.E., Pena, I., Barton, L., Pavlova, Z., & Ramanathan, R. (2003). Two-year outcome in infants weighing 600 grams or less at birth and born 1994 through 1998. *Obstetrics and Gynecology, 101,* 18-23.

Swinnen, S., Heuer, H., Massion, J., & Casaer, P. (Eds.). (1994). *Interlimb coordination: Neural, dynamical, and cognitive constraints.* San Diego, CA: Academic Press.

Takaya, R., Yukuo, K., Bos, A., & Einspieler, C. (2003). Preterm to early postterm changes in the development of hand-mouth contact and other motor patterns. *Early Human Development,* Suppl., S193-S202.

Teitelbaum, P., Teitelbaum, O., Nye, J., Fryman, J., & Maurer, R.G. (1998). Movement analysis in infancy may be useful for early diagnosis of autism. *Proceedings of the National Academy of Sciences,95,* 13982-13987.

Thelen, E. (1979). Rhythmical stereotypes in normal human infants. *Animal Behavior, 27,* 699-715.

Thelen, E. (1981). Kicking, rocking and waving: Contextual analysis of rhythmical stereotypes in normal human infants. *Animal Behavior, 29,* 3-11.

Thelen, E. (1983). Learning to walk is still an old problem: A reply to Zelazo (1983). *Journal of Motor Behavior, 15*(2), 139-161.

Thelen, E. (1985). Developmental origins of motor coordination: Leg movements in human infants. *Developmental Psychobiology, 18*(1), 1-22.

Thelen, E. (1986). Development of coordinated movement: Implications for early human development. In M.G. Wade & H.T.A. Whiting (Eds.), *Motor development in children: Aspects of coordination and control* (pp. 107-124). Dordrecht: Martinus Nijhoff.

Thelen, E. (1992). Development of locomotion from a dynamic systems approach. In H. Forssberg & H. Hirschfeld (Eds.), *Movement disorders in children* (Vol. 36, pp. 169-173). Basel: Karger.

Thelen, E. (1994). Three-month-old infants can learn task-specific patterns of interlimb coordination. *Psychological Science, 5*, 280-285.

Thelen, E. (1995). Motor development: A new synthesis. *American Psychologist, 50*(2), 79-95.

Thelen, E. (1998). Bernstein's legacy for motor development: How infants learn to reach. In M.L. Latash (Ed.), *Progress in motor control: Bernstein's traditions in movement studies* (pp. 267-288). Champaign, IL: Human Kinetics.

Thelen, E., Bradshaw, G., & Ward, J.A. (1981). Spontaneous kicking in month-old infants: Manifestation of a human central locomotor program. *Behavioral and Neural Biology, 32*, 45-53.

Thelen, E., Corbetta, D., Kamm, K., Spencer, J.P, Schneider, K., & Zernicke, R. (1993). The transition to reaching: Mapping intention and intrinsic dynamics. *Child Development, 64*, 1058-1098.

Thelen, E., Corbetta, D., & Spencer, J.P. (1996). Development of reaching during the first year: Role of movement speed. *Journal of Experimental Psychology: Human Perception and Performance, 25*(5), 1059-1076.

Thelen, E., & Fisher, D.M. (1982). Newborn stepping: An explanation for a "disappearing" reflex. *Developmental Psychology, 18*(5), 760-775.

Thelen, E., & Fisher, D. (1983a). From spontaneous to instrumental behavior: Kinematic analysis of movement changes during very early learning. *Child Development, 54*, 129-140.

Thelen, E., & Fisher, D. (1983b). The organization of spontaneous leg movements in newborn infants. *Journal of Motor Behavior, 15*(4), 353-377.

Thelen, E., Fisher, D.M., & Ridley-Scott, R. (1984). The relationship between physical growth and a newborn reflex. *Infant Behaviour and Development, 7*, 479-493.

Thelen, E., Jensen, J.L., Kamm, K., Corbetta, D., Schneider, K., & Zernicke, R.F. (1991). Infant motor development: Implications for neuroscience. In J.R.G.E. Stelmach (Ed.), *Tutorials in motor neuroscience* (pp. 43-57). Amsterdam: Kluwer Academic.

Thelen, E., Ridley-Johnson, R., & Fisher, D. (1983). Shifting patterns of bilateral coordination and lateral dominance in the leg movements of young infants. *Developmental Psychobiology, 16*(1), 29-46.

Thelen, E., & Smith, L.B. (1994). *A dynamic systems approach to the development of cognition and action.* Cambridge, MA: MIT Press.

Thelen, E., & Spencer, J.P. (1998). Postural control during reaching in young infants: A dynamic systems approach. *Neuroscience and Biobehavioral Reviews, 22*(4), 507-514.

Thelen, E., & Ulrich, B.D. (1991). Hidden skills: A dynamical systems analysis of treadmill stepping during the first year. *Monographs of the Society for Research in Child Development, 56*(1), 1-97.

Thelen, E., Ulrich, B.D., & Jensen, J.L. (1989). The developmental origins of locomotion. In H.G. Williams, M.H. Woollacott., & W.A. Shumway-Cook (Eds.), *Development of posture and gait across the life span* (pp. 25-47). Columbia, SC: University of South Carolina Press.

Thelen, E., Ulrich, B.D., & Niles, D. (1987). Bilateral coordination in human infants: Stepping on a split-belt treadmill. *Journal of Experimental Psychology, 13*(3), 405-410.

Thoman, E.B. (1990). Sleeping and waking states in infants: A functional perspective. *Neuroscience and Biobehavioral Reviews, 14*, 93-107.

Thoman, E.B. (2001). Sleep-wake states as context for assessment, as components of assessment, and as assessment. In L.T. Singer & P.S. Zeskind (Eds.), *Biobehavioral assessment of the infant* (pp. 125-148). New York: Guilford Press.

Thomas, J.R., & French, K.E. (1985). Gender differences across age in motor performance: A meta-analysis. *Psychological Bulletin, 98*, 260-282.

Thomas, R.M. (1996). *Comparing theories of child development.* Pacific Grove, CA: Brooks/Cole.

Thorngren-Jerneck, K., & Herbst, A. (2001). Low 5-minute apgar score: A population-based register study of one million term births. *Obstetrics and Gynecology, 98*(1), 65-70.

Tommiska, V., Heinonen, K., Kero, M.-L., Tammela, O., Jarvenpaa, A.-L., Salokorpi, T., et al. (2003). A national two year follow up study of extremely low birthweight infants born in 1996-1997. *Archives of Disease in Childhood. Fetal and Neonatal Edition, 88,* F29-F35.

Topp, M., Langhoff-Roos, J., Uldall, P., & Kristensen, J. (1996). Intrauterine growth and gestational age in preterm infants with cerebral palsy. *Early Human Development, 44,* 27-36.

Torfs, C.P., & Christianson, R.E. (1998). Anomalies in Down syndrome individuals in a large population-based registry. *American Journal of Medical Genetics, 77,* 431-438.

Touwen, B. (1976). *Neurological development in infancy.* London: William Heinemann Medical Books.

Touwen, B. (1978). Variability and stereotypy in normal and deviant development. *Clinical Developmental Medicine, 67,* 99-110.

Touwen, B.C. (1984). Primitive reflexes—conceptual or semantic problem. In H. Prechtl (Ed.), *Continuity of neural functions from prenatal to postnatal life* (pp. 115-125). Oxford, England: Blackwell.

Touwen, B.C.L. (1990). Variability and stereotypy of spontaneous motility as a predictor of neurological development of preterm infants. *Developmental Medicine and Child Neurology, 32,* 501-508.

Trahan, J., & Malouin, F. (2002). Intermittent intensive physiotherapy in children with cerebral palsy: A pilot study. *Developmental Medicine and Child Neurology, 44,* 233-239.

Trevarthen, C. (1982). Basic patterns of psychogenetic change in infancy. In T. Bever (Ed.), *Regressions in mental development* (pp. 7-46). Hillsdale, NJ: Erlbaum.

Tuller, B., Turvey, M., & Fitch, H. (1982). The Bernstein perspective: II. The concept of muscle linkage or coordinative structure. In J.A.S. Kelso (Ed.), *Human motor behavior: An introduction* (pp. 253-270). Hillsdale, NJ: Erlbaum.

Turvey, M.T. (1990). Coordination. *American Psychologist, 45*(8), 938-953.

Turvey, M.T., Fitch, H.L., & Tuller, B. (1982). The Bernstein perspective: I. The problems of degrees of freedom and context-conditioned variability. In J.A.S. Kelso (Ed.), *Human motor behavior: An introduction* (pp. 239-252). Hillsdale, NJ: Erlbaum.

Turvey, M.T., & Fitzpatrick, P. (1993). Commentary: Development of perception-action systems and general principles of pattern formation. *Child Development, 64,* 1175-1190.

Ulrich, B.D., & Ulrich, D.A. (1993). Dynamic systems approach to understanding motor delay in infants with Down syndrome. In G.J.P. Savelsburgh (Ed.), *The development of coordination in infancy* (pp. 445-459). Amsterdam: Elsevier.

Ulrich, B.D., Ulrich, D.A., & Collier, D.H. (1992). Alternating stepping patterns: Hidden abilities of 11-month-old infants with Down syndrome. *Developmental Medicine and Child Neurology, 34,* 233-239.

Ulrich, B.D., Ulrich, D.A., Collier, D.H., & Cole, E.L. (1995). Developmental shifts in the ability of infants with Down syndrome to produce treadmill steps. *Physical Therapy, 75*(1), 20-28.

Ulrich, D.A., Ulrich, B.D., Angulo-Kinzler, R.M., & Yun, J. (2001). Treadmill training of infants with Down syndrome: Evidence-based developmental outcomes. *Pediatrics, 108*(5), 42-48.

Updike, C., Schmidt, R.E., Cahoon, J., & Miller, M. (1986). Positional support for premature infants. *American Journal of Occupational Therapy, 40,* 712-715.

Usher, R., & McLean, F. (1969). Intrauterine growth of live-born caucasian infants at sea level: Standards obtained from measurements in 7 dimensions of infants born between 25 and 44 weeks of gestation. *Journal of Pediatrics, 74,* 900-910.

Usherwood, J.R., & Bertram, J.E.A. (2001). Per-step energetic cost of changing gait. http://asbbiomech.org/onlineabs/abstracts2001/pdf/113.pdf.

Vaal, J. (2001). Spontaneous kicking: On the organization of spontaneous leg movements in early human development. *Faculty of Human Movement Studies* (Vol. 127). Amsterdam: Vrije University.

Vaal, J., van Soest, A.J.K., Hopkins, B., Sie, L.T.L., & van der Knaap, M.S. (2000). Development of spontaneous leg movements in infants with and without periventricular leukomalacia. *Experimental Brain Research, 135,* 94-105.

van der Maas, H.L.J., & Hopkins, B. (1998). Developmental transitions: So what's new? *British Journal of Developmental Psychology, 16,* 1-13.

van der Weel, F.R., van der Meer, A.L., & Lee, D.N. (1991). Effect of task on movement control in cerebral palsy: Implications for assessment and therapy. *Developmental Medicine and Child Neurology, 33,* 419-426.

van der Weel, F.R., van der Meer, A.L., & Lee, D.N. (1996). Measuring dysfunction of basic movement control in cerebral palsy. *Human Movement Science, 15,* 253-283.

van Geert, P. (1994). *Dynamic systems of development: Change between complexity and chaos.* London: T J Press (Padstow) Ltd.

van Heijst, J.J., Touwen, B., & Vos, J.E. (1999). Implications of a neural network model of early sensori-motor development for the field of developmental neurology. *Early Human Development, 55,* 77-95.

van Hof, P., van der Kamp, J., & Savelsbergh, G. (2002). The relation of unimanual and bimanual reaching to crossing the midline. *Child Development, 73*(5), 1353-1362.

van Kranen-Mastenbroek, V.H., Kingma, H., Caberg, H.B., Ghys, A., Hasaart, T.H.M., & Vles, J.S.H. (1994). Quality of spontaneous general movements in full-term small for gestational age and appropriate for gestational age newborn infants. *Neuropediatrics, 25,* 145-153.

van Kranen-Mastenbroek, V.H., van Oostenbrugge, R., Palmans, L., Stevens, A., Kingma, H., Blanco, C., Hasaart, T., & Vles, J. (1992). Inter- and intra-observer agreement in the assessment of the quality of spontaneous movements in the newborn. *Brain and Development, 14,* 289-293.

Van Sant, A.F. (1994). Motor development. In J.S. Tecklin (Ed.), *Pediatric physical therapy* (pp. 1-23). Philadelphia: Lippincott.

Vaucher, Y.E., Harker, L., Merritt, T.A., Halman, M., Gist, K., Bejar, R., et al. (1993). Outcome at twelve months of adjusted age in very low birth weight infants with lung immaturity: A randomised, placebo-controlled trial of human surfactant. *Journal of Pediatrics, 122,* 126-132.

Vereijken, B., van Emmerik, R.E.A., Whiting, H.T.A., & Newell, K.M. (1992). Free(z)ing degrees of freedom in skill acquisition. *Journal of Motor Behavior, 24,* 133-142.

Vilensky, J.A., & O'Connor, B.L. (1997). Stepping in humans with complete spinal transection: A phylogenetic evaluation. *Motor Control, 1,* 284-292.

Vojta, V. (1984). The basic elements of treatment according to Vojta. In D. Scrutton (Ed.), *Management of the motor disorders of children with cerebral palsy* (pp. 75-85). Philadelphia: Lippincott.

von Hofsten, C. (1982). Eye-hand coordination in the newborn. *Developmental Psychology, 18*(3), 450-461.

von Hofsten, C. (1986). The emergence of manual skills. In M.G. Wade & H.T.A. Whiting (Eds.), *Motor development in children: Aspects of coordination and control* (pp. 167-185). Dordrecht: Martinus Nijhoff.

von Hofsten, C. (1989). Mastering reaching and grasping: The development of manual skills in infancy. In S.A. Wallace (Ed.), *Perspectives on the coordination of movement* (pp. 223-258). Amsterdam: Elsevier.

von Hofsten, C. (1990). Development of manipulation action in infancy. In H. Bloch & B.I. Bertenthal (Eds.), *Sensory-motor organisation and development in infancy and early childhood* (pp. 273-283). Dordrecht: Kluwer Academic.

von Hofsten, C. (1993). Studying the development of goal-directed behaviour. In A.F. Kalverboer, B. Hopkins, & R. Geuze (Eds.), *Motor development in early and later childhood: Longitudinal approaches* (pp. 109-124). Cambridge: Cambridge University Press.

von Hofsten, C., & Lindhagen, K. (1979). Observation on the development of reaching for moving objects. *Journal of Experimental Child Psychology, 28,* 158-173.

von Hofsten, C., & Rönnqvist, L. (1988). Preparation for grasping objects: A developmental study. *Journal of Experimental Psychology: Human Perception and Performance, 14,* 610-621.

von Hofsten, C., & Rönnqvist, L. (1993). The structuring of neonatal arm movements. *Child Development, 64,* 1047-1057.

Vulpe, S.G. (1982). *Vulpe Assessment Battery.* Downsview, ON, Canada: National Institute on Mental Retardation.

Wallace, P., & Whishaw, I.Q. (2003). Independent digit movements and precision grip patterns in 1-5-month-old human infants: Hand-babbling, including vacuous then self-directed hand and digit movements, precedes targeted reaching. *Neuropsychologia, 41,* 1912-1918.

Watson, S., & Bekoff, A. (1990). A kinematic analysis of hindlimb motility in 9- and 10-day-old chick embryos. *Journal of Neurobiology, 21,* 651-661.

Weeks, D.J., Chua, R., & Elliott, D. (2000). *Perceptual-motor behavior in Down syndrome.* Champaign, IL: Human Kinetics.

Weindrich, D., Jennen-Steinmetz, C., Laucht, M., & Schmidt, M. (2003). Late sequelae of low birthweight: Mediators of poor school performance at 11 years. *Developmental Medicine and Child Neurology, 45,* 463-469.

Werner, E.E. & Bayley, N. (1966). The reliability of Bayley's revised scale of mental and motor development during the first year of life. *Child Development, 37,* 39-50.

Whitall, J., & Clark, J.E. (1994). The development of bipedal interlimb coordination. In J.M.P. Casaer (Ed.), *Interlimb coordination: Neural, dynamical, and cognitive constraints.* San Diego: Academic Press.

White, R. (1984). Sensory integrative therapy for the cerebral-palsied child. In D. Scrutton (Ed.), *Management of the motor disorders of children with cerebral palsy* (pp. 86-95). Philadelphia: Lippincott.

Whiting, H.T.A. (1984). *Human motor actions: Bernstein reassessed.* Amsterdam: North-Holland.

Willemse, J. (1986). Benign idiopathic dystonia with onset in the first year of life. *Developmental Medicine and Child Neurology, 28,* 355-363.

Williams, H.G., Woollacott, M.H., & Ivry, R. (1992). Timing and motor control in clumsy children. *Journal of Motor Behavior, 24*(2), 165-172.

Williams, J.E. (1989). The efficacy of early intervention. In S.H.J.H. French & P. Casaer (Eds.), *Child neurology and developmental disabilities* (pp. 265-269). Baltimore: Brookes.

Wilson, P.H., & McKenzie, B.E. (1998). Information processing deficits associated with developmental coordination disorder: A meta-analysis of research findings. *Journal of Child Psychology and Psychiatry, 39,* 829-840.

Wimmers, R.H., Beek, P.J., & Savelsbergh, G.J.P. (1998). Developmental changes in action: Theoretical and methodological issues. *British Journal of Developmental Psychology, 16,* 45-63.

Wijnroks, L., & van Veldhoven, N. (2003). Individual differences in postural control and cognitive development in preterm infants. *Infant Behavior and Development, 26,* 14-26.

Winter, D. (1989). Coordination of motor tasks in human gait. In S.A. Wallace (Ed.), *Perspectives on the coordination of movement* (pp. 329-363). Amsterdam: Elsevier.

Winter, D.A. (1987). *Biomechanics and motor control of human gait.* Waterloo, Canada: University of Waterloo Press.

Wolanski, N., & Zdanska-Brincken, M. (1973). A new method for the evaluation of motor development in infants. *Polish Psychological Bulletin, 4,* 43-53.

Wolff, P.H. (1959). Observations on newborn infants. *Psychosomatic Medicine, 221,* 110-118.

Wolff, P.H. (1966). The causes, controls and organization of behavior in the neonate. *Psychological Issues, 5,* 1-106.

Wolff, P.H. (1967). The role of biological rhythms in early psychological development. *Bulletin of the Menninger Clinic, 31,* 197-218.

Wolff, P.H. (1968). Stereotypic behavior and development. *Canadian Psychologist, 9,* 474-483.

Woollacott, M.H. (1993). Early postnatal development of posture control: Normal and abnormal aspects. In A.F. Kalverboer, B. Hopkins, & R. Geuze (Eds.), *Motor development in early and later childhood: Longitudinal approaches* (pp. 89-108). Cambridge: Cambridge University Press.

Woollacott, M., & Jensen, J.L. (1996). Posture and locomotion. In H. Heuer & S.W. Keele (Eds.), *Handbook of perception and action: Vol. 2. Motor skills* (pp. 333-403). San Diego: Academic Press.

Wyke, B. (1975). The neurological basis of movement—a developmental review. In K.S. Holt (Ed.), *Movement and child development: Clinics in developmental medicine* (pp. 19-33). Philadelphia: Lippincott.

Young, G., Segalowitz, S., Misek, P., Alp, I.E., & Boulet, R. (1983). Is early reaching left-handed? Review of manual specialisation research. In G. Young, S.J. Segalowitz, C.M. Corter, & S.E. Trehub (Eds.), *Manual specialisation and the developing brain* (pp. 13-32). New York: Academic Press.

Zafeiriou, D.I. (2004). Primitive reflexes and postural reactions in neurodevelopmental examination. *Pediatric Neurology, 31*(1), 1-8.

Zelazo, P.R. (1983). The development of walking: New findings and old assumptions. *Journal of Motor Development, 15*(3), 99-137.

Zelazo, P.R., Zelazo, N.A., & Kolb, S. (1972). Walking in the newborn. *Science, 175*, 314-315.

index ▪▪▪

Note: The italicized *t* and *f* following page numbers refer to tables and figures, respectively.

about the author

Jan P. Piek, PhD, is an associate professor at the Curtin University of Technology in Perth, Western Australia. Her major areas of research are motor control and motor development. Since 1992, she has received three research fellowships to conduct work in motor control. Her most recent fellowship was the Curtin University postdoctoral research fellowship, from 1997 to 2000.

Piek has published extensively in journals in Australia and internationally. She contributed a chapter to D.J. Glencross and J.P. Piek's Motor Control and Sensory-Motor Integration: Issues and Directions (Amsterdam: Elsevier Science, 1995). She is also the editor of Motor Behavior and Human Skill (Champaign: Human Kinetics, 1998).

Piek has coordinated the Motor Control & Human Skill Research Conferences since the program's inception in 1991. She is a member of the School of Psychology at Curtin University of Technology, where she also manages the Research Centre for Applied Psychology. She received the Vice-Chancellor's Award for Excellence from Curtin University of Technology in 1996.

She is a member of the Australian Psychological Society and the International Society for Infant Studies and an editorial board member of Infant Behavior and Development. She earned her PhD from the University of Western Australia.

DATE DUE

GAYLORD   PRINTED IN U.S.A.